Mind Readings

MIND READINGS

Writers' Journeys Through Mental States

EDITED BY

Sara Dunn,
Blake Morrison
and Michèle Roberts

Minerva

A Minerva Paperback
MIND READINGS

3 5 7 9 10 8 6 4 2

First published in Great Britain 1996
as a Minerva original

Minerva
Random House UK Limited
20 Vauxhall Bridge Road, London SW1V 2SA

Random House Australia (Pty) Limited
20 Alfred Street, Milsons Point, Sydney,
New South Wales 2061, Australia

Random House New Zealand Limited
18 Poland Road, Glenfield, Auckland 10, New Zealand

Random House South Africa (Pty) Limited
Endulini, 5a Jubilee Road, Parktown 2193, South Africa

Anthology copyright © 1996 by Mind
The authors have asserted their moral rights

Random House UK Limited Reg. No. 954009

A CIP catalogue record for this book
is available from the British Library

ISBN 0 7493 8618 5

Papers used by Random House UK Limited
are natural, recyclable products made from wood grown in
sustainable forests. The manufacturing processes conform to
the environmental regulations of the country of origin

Typeset in 10 on 12 point Sabon
by Falcon Oast Graphic Art
Printed and bound in Great Britain by
Cox & Wyman Ltd, Reading, Berkshire

Contents

Introduction

This book grew out of the annual Mind Book of the Year/Allen Lane Award. Anny Brackx, Director of Corporate Promotion at Mind, suggested an anthology might raise the organization's profile in its fiftieth anniversary year, as well as focus attention on mental health issues in general. Blake Morrison and Michèle Roberts, currently two of the Mind Book of the Year judges, together with freelance editor Sara Dunn, set about putting the book together.

We invited all the writers who we thought might want to get involved, or who we knew to be interested in the field, to send us a piece in whatever genre or form they chose. We wanted previously unpublished work where possible, but where it seemed apposite we have included some writings first published elsewhere. In particular we wanted to include some of the excellent and varied material which has been shortlisted for the Mind Book of the Year in the past decade.

The brief was to write, autobiographically or not as the author chose, about some aspect of mental or emotional life that was felt to be commonly shared or not, more or less problematic or difficult, negotiable or not, and so on. In one sense we were asking for pieces about simply being human, about the suffering that interrupts or suppresses human happiness and the myriad ways in which we deal with it. Different kinds of authorities over the centuries, religious or medical, for example, have classified, labelled and attempted to control varieties of human experience and suffering. We hoped to produce a book that, within its necessarily limited constraints, might take a fresh look at aspects of our mental and emotional life, whether or not it accepted traditional terminologies. The book does not pretend to be an authority; it expresses both the individuality of its authors, and our shared humanity. We asked writers to contribute, not so much because we assumed that linguistic creativity is linked in some crucial way to trauma or neurosis (a subject of much current debate), as because we thought that writers, whose job is to worry and burrow away at language, might have something to say about how difficult it is to find words in times of crisis, how hard it can be to translate experience, the reality of the psyche, into language.

As the responses from contributors began to come in and we sifted and read them, we found that the material could be distinguished by the recurrence of certain themes and subjects, and could therefore be grouped into certain categories. We adopted this way of shaping the book in the hope of aiding the reader by providing signposts. These are arbitrary rather than based in theory. The book is as varied as it is partial.

All proceeds from sales of this book go to Mind. Many people have worked hard to bring it into being. All the writers have donated their pieces. We are extremely grateful to them for their great generosity. We wish to thank all those publishers who have granted permissions to reprint, and also everyone at Secker.

Sara Dunn
Blake Morrison
Michèle Roberts

I

Fears

A. L. KENNEDY
Avoid the Spinning Plates

I think it would be useful for me to point out one thing straight away. I write with my mind. This is very obvious, of course, but its implications are, perhaps, not.

For instance, I have, on numberless occasions, been asked how unhappy my childhood was, how wicked my parents were, how close to suicide I am currently, how lousy a lay I am historically, how plainly sociopathic my every move betrays me to be, and so on and so forth. The assumption at the heart of all these questions? That creativity stems directly and almost solely from present mental anguish, or — if nothing else is available — from the vivid recreation of hideous torments past.

But what do I write with? My mind.

When do I feel like making the huge emotional commitment, the massive leap of faith that writing involves? When my mind is at its fittest. When I am happy and well.

People in torment don't write fiction. They may attempt to communicate their pains, they may suffer in silence, they may turn to compulsive/addictive behaviours, they may be drawn into the mental health system, they may be given prescribed drugs, they may struggle to keep a journal, they may become terribly isolated and suffer the gradual erosion of all that made them who they were, they may perform a whole range of activities, but they very, very rarely write novels. They have problems enough. They might produce something inspired by their experiences later, but I would be willing to take a number of bets that, during their illness, the crafting of fiction was not their top priority. Have you ever been depressed? You don't feel like breathing, never mind typing.

What I'm trying to battle here is the Romantic notion of genius (inspired by pain), which has replaced what I might call the Classical idea of genius (inspired by God). I often tend to favour the latter. I certainly find myself increasingly frustrated by the former.

I will return to the stock journalistic barrage of Questions To Ask A Writer later, but I want first to deal with the aspects of creative writing which *are* to do with healing, or passage from illness, the creation of self and even (that dreaded word) therapy.

For many years I have worked with people in a therapeutic context, assisting them to write creatively in whatever way they wished. These were writers who had 'special needs', sometimes related to their mental health. I have since worked with 'normal' writers and, throughout the last ten or twelve years, I have pursued my own writing. Perhaps because I am not a therapist and I have never done anything other than work with groups, individuals and myself on perfecting the art or craft of writing, I feel I can say that all of us have been doing exactly the same things and moving through exactly the same processes; year in, year out; irrespective of aspirations and circumstance.

As writers we bring together elements supplied by chance, by our characters, by our (particularly emotional) lives, by our subconsciouses and by what I will term Wearenotentirely-surewhatelse. We discover that these disparate fragments gradually coagulate and generate something which is greater than the sum of available parts. We allow this sum to develop its own life, follow this as best we can and then seek to put it into a form comprehensible to others. Hidden within the limits of each piece we can find an almost unlimited personal freedom. That, in my opinion, is one journey that most of us make.

We also move along a course from something we are doing for ourselves to something we do for other people. I don't mean for a market, I mean for other *people*. We usually also progress from a position of low confidence, low self-esteem and destructive criticism to one of more relaxation, assurance and joy. The dark beginnings of our journeys may be supplied by illness, or by pain; they may equally be supplied by the simple frailties of any human being embarking upon a new course of action, by the simple, natural doubt of our untried abilities. What drives us to set out at all could well be the desire for that particular brand of communication, that odd mix of self-obsession and spiritual generosity which a writer seems to incubate and then thrive on, quite naturally.

Each of these writing journeys will – to a certain extent – be repeated for every piece of work, although they will be mirrored in a larger progression from the private to the public, the fearful to the more familiar. Any writer, in whatever context, can benefit from the almost organic effects of writing. Creation is inherently therapeutic and the best creation, the most painstaking effort is, I believe, also the most healing. A writer has a daily opportunity to unveil worlds, to explore them as no one else has and then to give them to others. In a very fundamental way, she or he is not alone. For writers, a leap of faith can be made daily and with a degree of success. The spirit can be nourished, emotional and intellectual tensions experienced and then released. A life becomes full.

That I earn my living by writing has always seemed to me a source of immense surprise, insufficient gratitude and recurring joy. I did not look for this, it looked for me. The Quakers have suggested that the gates of the soul can be opened by great pain and also by great joy. Unsurprisingly, much the same can be said for any act of creation, including the writing of fiction. For some people, writing will begin in a process which is very clearly one of recovery from a state which is not their ideal. They begin with pain. A great many writers – because they are human beings and live lives – will encounter pain from time to time. My life is not unusual, it has had its ups and downs. It would not be unlikely for one of a writer's *eventual* responses to pain (or fear, hunger, sexual repression, anger, ennui or anything else you care to imagine) to be written.

Any excess of feeling, or depth of feeling, will eventually demand a response in words. Writers may equally be inspired by an excess of love, happiness, exhilaration, excitement. These people begin with joy.

Because, even in the worst of cases, writing can bring a positive result out of a negative situation, because it allows me to articulate the quiddity of my life, because it can spring simply from a delight in existence, ability and the sensation of language, I feel I can say that for me writing is generally very much more about joy than pain.

In short, I would warmly endorse the mental benefits of writing, rather than the myth which demands any author should not only write, but also find the energy to sustain a life of brooding and consumption, like a self-mutilating plate-spinning act in a dingy Freudian sideshow.

But if writing is such a rose-tinted activity, why do writers not skip merrily about their ways, dispensing largesse, or at the very least benevolent wisdom at every step? Why is the world of literature not peopled by saints with unshakeable mental stability and domestic situations simply asking for the opportunity to endorse household cleaners and gravy browning? Why does the Byronic myth persist? Why is the Booker Prize not given to the novelist with the nicest smile?

I won't lead you to believe that I can provide a definitive response to these questions. In fact, I rest easy in my bed at night considering that very few people on the planet have anything like an interest in finding their solution. If I didn't earn my living as a writer, I hope I would be much the same. I will try to set out on a tiny exploration of the world of book-making, only because this will allow me to deal with what I have found to be the mental effects of *being a writer*.

And there we have a major component in all my literary confusions. Although it is not in any way unusual for a person both *to write* and *to be a writer*, these two activities can often seem singularly unrelated. *Writing* is, in my opinion, very largely the positive process I have outlined in the paragraphs above. In the case of prose and poetry, it is also most often a sedentary, individual, quiet and private occupation. I have on many occasions described *writing* as being one of the more socially acceptable kinds of solitary vice. If we extend the simile, this would make *being a writer* something very close to unwitting participation in the nastiest possible al fresco pornographic film-making, involving strange people, strange substances, strange penetrations, frightening costumes and precious few hints at genuine satisfaction.

I know this sounds harsh, but believe me, *being a writer* can damage your mental and possibly your physical health.

Please don't for a moment interpret this as an attack on those people in the literary world who make their ways with integrity, humanity and a sometimes astonishing patience in the face of boorish catastrophe. What I am trying to convey is the mental and emotional impact which the public demands now made upon a writer can sometimes still have in my life, and which undoubtedly threw me considerably off balance when I began a career in print. Or, more accurately, careering in print – bear in mind that I was barely in my mid-twenties when my first book was published. I was also underendowed with common sense, and an introvert.

Perhaps it will be helpful to begin with a small, relatively gentle example of the emotional assault course which seemed to walk, hand in pocket, with the heady promise of becoming a published writer. To this end, I will describe, in as far as I can remember, my first visit to a London publisher.

I can't say that I arrived a wee Scotch waif, licking the pavements for traces of precious metals. I had been in London before, but I hadn't been in this part of London before and this part of London was obviously considerably better off than I was. I felt out of place. I would go as far as to say that I felt short. The weather was also unseasonably hot, so I felt sticky, out of place and short.

I also felt confused, as I had done for several months. A year earlier, a small Scottish house had published my first book, a collection of (occasionally rather raw) short stories. The book had advanced me £450 and sunk quietly away. Only to reappear months later, winning awards and surprising nobody more than me.

An element of the surreal now crept into my life and refused to leave. Some people I knew stopped speaking to me, some people I didn't started and friendships seemed to shimmer for a few months, becoming distant or somehow not themselves.

I approached the publisher's building knowing that I had quite recently spent hours, after being given one particular prize, wandering across Hyde Park with a cheque in my pocket, repeating 'Well, well, well,' something I never normally say at all. I had also inadvertently made my mother so happy that she cried. For the first time, I was seeing myself described in news-

papers as someone completely unrecognizable. At my grandmother's funeral, one of the principal topics of conversation
had not been her life, but a short story I had written about her
life. I was growing accustomed to the sense that I was in some
way both an unclean moral influence and obscurely vulnerable.

My collection of stories (several rewrites short of the pound)
had been rejected by the very same London publishing house I
was now finally calling on. Why was I going to see them?
Because, after another initial rejection, my first novel had been
accepted by an editorial judgement which I had begun to believe
existed only to politely raise my hopes and then, equally courte-
ously, stub them out. At the back of my mind I was sure that I
would arrive only to be told I was the butt of an elongated practical joke and should now leave the building and kindly take my
dreadful manuscript with me.

As I approached what seemed to be the appropriate address,
I worried about the possible humiliations to come. I did not
(and still do not) in any way resemble what I would think of as
a novelist. I did not know the things that a novelist surely
should. I couldn't imagine what these things might be and had
therefore been unable to learn them in advance. I was certain
that any forthcoming conversations would prove me to be not
only a notwriter and notnovelist, but also an ignoramus with a
loose grasp on even quite simple spelling when placed under
pressure.

And then I couldn't find the entrance. Because I am an ignoramus with a loose grasp on even quite simple spelling when
placed under pressure.

I had, of course, allowed myself more than ample time for my
journey – expecting transport emergencies and direct intervention from the hand of God which, as a good Scot, I knew must
have been raised against me by now for the sheer presumption
of my whole notwriterly position. In the event, I arrived
unscathed but massively early.

Nevertheless, the minutes dribbled away and I became
increasingly disturbed as I circled the block, looking for anything which might conceivably be the way in. I hadn't been
warned that, to the uninitiated, the front door of this particular

company looks quite like a fishmonger's.

This meant that I eventually stumbled my way in through the service entrance in a gesture which was kindly interpreted as a nod in the direction of singularity, not to say secrecy, rather than nervous ignorance. I braced myself for whatever opportunities I would be offered next to prove my idiocy really convincingly.

Instead, I might have realized that, because the publishing world is used to people who are clever, or who wish to be clever, and is constantly anxious to cause no detectable offence, even demonstrations of utterly crass stupidity will be analysed for signs of obscure meaning. On the day in question, I may well have appeared to be on the brink, either of requesting paramedical attention, or of producing an exceptionally complex personal subtext. Probably both.

At this point I was charitably propelled towards a Business or Working Lunch, the cost of which I remember was almost equal to my weekly wage at the time. This fact alone adversely affected my ability to swallow.

I did not, naturally, understand the basis on which a Working Lunch is founded. I came from a family where we ate at lunchtime because we were hungry and we ate out at lunchtime with other people because we liked and/or were related to them.

The Working Lunch may well be about hungers and likings and relations, but they will all be of the Business kind. Your co-diner may like your work, but not you, or the reverse, may be hungry for a success you could represent, or may seek simply to establish the relations necessary for efficient collaboration. Motivations, power-plays and subtle inquisitions may break around your head like shrapnel, or you may dawdle away an afternoon telling stories, improving a friendship and coincidentally discovering something useful in what you think.

On that day I had no experience of such culinary Work, or of eating with strangers in restaurants where waiters with dubious French accents read you the menu to save you the burden of reading it yourself. I was not in any condition to be hungry or even capable with food. I was also unused to flailing silently for any salient or mentionable details from my life with which I might make a sensible sentence.

I asked for one soup, was given another – which was very unpleasant – and ate it as a kind of apology for my existence. I was treated kindly, but this only made my position more alarming – there I was, wasting someone's time to no apparent purpose (we were surely not celebrating the acceptance of my novel, the merits of which entirely escaped me) and yet I could make no adequate reparation or response.

I do now enjoy eating with people with whom I also work. I have begun to learn that nice people are nice to work with and nasty people are not, and that four or five minutes shared with them and a tricky vegetable or two will sort the human from the less human very well. I have learned that writing is human first and a business second and that even its business element can be conducted in an atmosphere of dignity, civilization and humanity. It just took me a long time and a great deal of indigestion to discover that this was possible.

The first few years of my gradual slide closer and closer to the terror of self-employment and reliance on my ability to put one word after another were consistently filled with food-related guilt. Would I, at some point, have to buy all these people a lunch in return? How should I handle a buffet when my hands shook and I was nauseous? Why did anything involving puff pastry always explode?

In fleeting moments of reconciliation with my cutlery, the people worried me. When I was met by complete strangers with warmth and enthusiasm, did this gush of friendliness have any basis in reality? Was everyone insincere? Was anyone sincere? Was anyone not obviously in a position of monstrous power over me? Who was I?

And by that I do mean that I had begun to wonder who I was. Partly, this was because I found myself, more and more often, in completely alien circumstances. I could grasp no points of reference. Meanwhile, I encountered further unrecognizable photographs of A. L. Kennedy, unrecognizable profiles of A. L. Kennedy, petrifying reviews of A. L. Kennedy's work. I no longer had any idea of what or whom to believe and I had not yet developed the kind of confidence or clear-headedness which would have allowed me to ask for help. Some of my friends were a massive comfort, but adrift in the world of writing, I began to identify increasingly with the melting witch at the end of *The Wizard of Oz*.

To pursue the theme of dissolving identity a touch further, I will return to that first afternoon of feeding at my publisher's expense. The day was rounded off with an hour or so of enthusiasm (from a photographer) and embarrassment (from me). I then came face to face for the first time with an individual opinion of me – not my work, me. The possibility of the author's anonymity began to shrivel. The procurer of my lunch presented me with five possible pictures of myself – all developed with sickening speed, all virtually the same and all more than a little grim. The final choice – or illusion of choice – would be mine. This was what A. L. Kennedy would look like: one of five variations on glum. I didn't really warm to A. L., but a trick of framing did seem to imply that she had slightly larger breasts than my own. I found this oddly consoling.

Or perhaps not. I spent two or three years turning up to give readings from my work and being asked if I had a ticket for the event. I could not be recognized from my photograph. A. L. was me, but I was not, it seemed, A. L.

Now and again something completely intoxicating would happen. Perhaps someone would ask me to sign a book which I had written. *A book which I had written,* that was something to consider. I even once saw someone in a bookshop *buying* my book. I was becoming a writer, slipping forward to the point where I would be paid for doing exactly what I wanted to, paid to celebrate existence and joy. I should have been very happy. I was quite well aware that I have few, if any skills, that I am virtually unemployable, that if I wasn't a writer, I wouldn't really be anything else, that my job is clean, indoor, has no particular risk of industrial injury. Many people have no job at all, never mind one that they like. I repeat, I should have been happy. Instead, I felt lonely, exposed, fraudulent and very guilty that I couldn't just say thanks very much for my outrageous luck and be done with it. But I couldn't do that, not yet.

I was stuck in a position where I took myself seriously, met apparently sane people who took me even more seriously and then took all of that taking, even more seriously. Worse, I then swooped about myself for signs of unhealthily rampant ego. Naturally, I got the signs all wrong. I went on an interior search and destroy mission in all the areas which would have allowed me to enjoy what was enjoyable in my situation and to thank people for their interest – real or feigned. I began to disassemble myself for fear that I would become an egomaniac. Meanwhile, my ego flourished clandestinely, in the shape of my steadfast belief that any of this mattered a damn, anyway. Of course books and reading and passion and writing and humanity and enlightenment matter, but my own involvement with any of those things is really very small and, in many ways, none of my business. I am in no position to decide on my own scale – even if all the world asks me to. And it doesn't. I am not important, not in that way.

And one of the other major things I got wrong? I forgot that a writer writes. Even if *being a writer* intervenes severely, as soon as I set myself to the page, there is no room for ego, for scales and judgements, there is only the familiar mercy of inspiration and joy of discovery. If *being a writer* is the illness, then *writing* is the cure. I had to learn that, no matter what, I should attempt to keep a grip on my work, keep my concentration exercised and take as little as possible of the other nonsense to heart.

It was very important that I should do this, before I lost myself entirely. I had been trying to understand professional, but completely contradictory, opinions of myself and my work – most of them not written for my information. I had been bombarded by images and impressions of myself which were not me. I had been told by strangers I had only just met that they were *afraid* of me. I had seen my relatives both delighted and wounded by the side-effects of my profession. Eventually, I had to surrender, radically redefine my priorities and either laugh at my role in it all, or let it drive me very literally crazy. I chose to laugh. I still do. Sometimes the conscious effort required to raise even a grin can be quite great, but it is worth it in the end, believe me. And I don't forget that my position in life is actually very fortunate.

I am now at a stage in my work where I can mostly concentrate on the writing and, occasionally, fumble at the elements of the writer's life which are pleasant. Every now and then, I can put on the kind of things that A. L. wears and go out and take advantage of a public persona invented for me by the usual chain of inter-referential newspaper articles and the five variations on glum. I play a part, a role which conveniently allows me to put that necessary sliver of distance between me and too much of being taken seriously.

I can't even remember why I chose A. L. Kennedy as a name, rather than the full Alison Louise Kennedy, but the abbreviation has finally borne useful fruit. A. L. Kennedy is apparently a touchy, secretive and puritanical creature – hard to get at, never mind get on with. But she can also stand being taken seriously for days at a time, bless her. *I* can then take her off and put her away, almost unscathed. A. L. – the glum and temperamental – also tends to get a little more elbow room than I would and sometimes that's no bad thing. She allows me to travel and to meet some very pleasant people, some of whom I work with and some of whom I simply like. Sooner or later, they get to know who *I* am, because I do and because this is only practical.

My process of coming to terms with my profession has taken a number of years and will no doubt continue for many more – mainly because I can be astonishingly hard of thinking. My work process is very self-contained and I am comfortable with this, but there have been times when I have made myself more lonely than necessary within the larger context of my work. I am trying to adjust to a position which is, perhaps, more relaxed and more tolerant of company. I am also still trying to counteract the negative effects which the A. L. phenomenon can produce. The familiar journey from insularity and doubt towards something more open and comfortable takes the standard couple of steps forward and one step back.

I love writing and, on the good days, I can love being a writer. Both these parts of my life represent a certain degree of mental risk, but both of them offer rewards which have already exceeded my imagination.

And sometimes A. L.'s not so bad – she has a very nasty sense of humour which we both do our utmost to enjoy. To paraphrase Emeric Pressburger, our situation is hopeless but not serious.

ALISON FELL
In the Event of Plane Crash, Burn These Diaries

For my counsellor, Annette Elliot

Voices. They come periodically: that is, every month. Just after, or sometimes accompanied by, sex, dreams, poetry. The message is punitive. You aren't allowed. You're worth nothing, less than nothing, deserve nothing. And nothing you will have. I listen incredulously. Chalk up my achievements. *But but but. BBC Scotland just made a programme on my work and my story was on the radio last week and, Christ, what about the American book tour coming up?* Bad move. Red rag to a bull, in fact. I should know by now that fighting back only makes things worse. Cheek the teacher and you'll get a good belt, that's how it always was in Scotland. I should know by now that I can't win this one.

Lucky for me that I know the voices are housed in the rooms of my head, and don't waft about the ether or issue from flying saucers. I'm perfectly aware that I contain parties who are periodically at war.

Disorder in the outlying provinces: the dishes sulk in the sink.

Diplomats would negotiate, would try to foster dialogue between oppressor and oppressed. Equalize the balance. I've tried that. Exchanged views frankly and fruitlessly. I know by now I'm facing a tyrant, and the trouble is she's a tyrant I'm very attached to.

For she is the rule of nonsense and Hallowe'en, winter's first witch-gift, the debt come due.

Be sneaky, then. Play dead, play doggo. Want nothing, have

nothing, be nothing. Be above suspicion. Ascetic. Lonely. Pure. Thin. Deprived. Tiny. Vanishing. Shrink to a pinhead. Don't exist, in fact. (Or fiction.) Make no move, be blameless, be no bother. Don't be rival, but helpmeet, martyr, status angelic, status unimpeachable. Relinquish the fire in the belly, nest-eggs, the love of lilacs, so that they can't be taken away. Scourge yourself like some medieval penitent, and perhaps you won't be condemned out of hand. Not loved, mind you, but at least not punished.

In the event of plane crash etc., burn these diaries.

This is how the words go baldly where none have gone before:

OK, I give in, stop fighting, surrender. I'll say 'you win'. Will that do? The triumph of the will, absolute. Are you satisfied with that, does it make you happy? That I've stopped talking back, stopped trying. I'm inert now, does that please you? Does it please you that I want nothing except your pleasure? That I'll do anything to ensure it? That I'm yours to do what you like with, so do what you will, mould, make, save, control, protect. Be right in every respect, for obedience is my only pleasure. If it pleases you I comply completely, for ever and ever . . .

The face I offer you, the hurt like a sun in my chest, asking, will you speak back to me?

The postures of compliance, of course, are as imaginary as the postures of rebellion. All this is shadow-boxing. The protagonists are fabulous wraiths; the Empress has no clothes and should be laughed off stage. Strange how we hark back to lost loves and disasters, to a time when words themselves were an anachronism. Instincts can't answer back any more than bees can.

I say Empress because the critical voice is always female, a vengeful mother-in-the-head. My real mother is a real old lady who lives 12,000 miles away and no longer has the power to give me what I need, refuse it, deny, punish, or lay down harsh conditions. Nor (I hope) would she want it. But the mother-in-the-head, that dazzling tyrannical creature, is a great deal more difficult to dethrone. And kills people, real people, in the imperfect present. Poets, often. Plath, for instance.

In her dark green satin, the holly-angel has sharp nails.

She's a shape-shifter, too. Say that the strategy of self-abasement works for the imaginary infant, and the lady is temporarily placated, like the Goddess of prehistory, by this ritual sacrifice. In the uneasy truce that follows there's a little peace, a little bliss, a little writing. But already she's casting around for fresh meat, for another victim. And this will be the girl, now, with her dreamy aspirations – another occupant of the overcrowded house of psyche, and another rival to be routed. Her breasts are budding, her eggs, she is preparing to bleed, even to be beautiful. The girl-part senses the danger, suspects that a boy would be safer, being other, being the object of mother's desire, being consort, admirer. There is only one queen in this palace, and no princesses, certainly not this one with her languor and luxury, her craving for compliments, her excitable exhibitionism. How brightly she wants to shine!

How swiftly
something that can't be mapped
takes hold,
senseless and necessary,
a constant sideways shimmying
of the minute skirts of light,
and from the no-less-bright
air everything
falling

Yet even the desire, so harmless in itself, smacks of criminality. The mother-in-the-head will not lend an ear, smile gently, admire, accept or sanction. Far from it. Periodically I dream of daughters dying of leukaemia (no blood), of daughters disturbed, naked, flaunting themselves. Nine years old, ten. Desperate for attention.

She wants to say she is not word alone
but material, sewn from satin and fire,

a red lava of blossom which pours down
like birdsong on the ever-open ears of the dead

All this is imaginary. If envy was material once, it has long since lost its sting. The trouble is that in the real present I do receive attention, if not the exact attention the girl once craved. There are readings, book launches, talks, interviews, cameras. In this business only the seriously eminent can hide themselves away from the Gaze, while the rest must say their prayers and just get on with it.

Take readings, for instance. I'm not talking here about the nervous first or second, but the twentieth, thirtieth, fiftieth. You have dressed up, made an effort, even got a bit excited about it. On the train you're beginning to presume that you deserve the attention, even that you have a perfect right to claim your share. You risk liking your shoes, your hair, your work, your battered leather jacket. You cross your fingers and step on stage, feeling almost like a contender. Don't get too excited, though. Don't shine too brightly. For the mother-in-the-head has entered the audience and moves malevolently among them, stirring up censure. Turning a thoughtful look to a hostile frown, and an idle stare to a merciless criticism of your shoes, hair, work, presumption. You soldier on, tell her to bugger off, fight the feeling that you're really in for it. You absolutely will not tremble. It would even be comical, if you weren't the one facing the judge and jury. For wanting too much, for getting above yourself, you're accused and found guilty of gross immodesty.

All this is imaginary. My real mother is a real old lady who lives 12,000 miles away and no longer has the power to envy, deny, rival. I alone allow the invasions, give the prohibitions houseroom. Periodically I dream of unwanted guests, stroppy lodgers, Japanese squatters. Of not having a square foot I can safely call my own. An ineffectual landlady, I dream of evicting them. Perhaps poets' minds are simply too elastic, suggestible, always slipping promiscuously in and out of images, forms. Vulnerable to occupation by absolutely anything.

Today, prehistoric, like the terrapins,

these little sundials with shadows
that move so slowly

I need a shell, and to be slow sometimes. Sometimes hiding from the voices is the only way. Let the arrows bounce off, and keep the good things snugly inside, where they can't be snatched or scorned. Stow the feminine safely away on a shelf. Play dead, in fact, pretend to be doing nothing, going nowhere at all. Periodically prose becomes impossible, too linear, its aim too apparent; novels stop in their tracks, refusing the progression of past present future. You've already tried calling on the animus to protect you, that internal lover who forms a bridge between the inner and outer worlds, but he seems weak or asleep or broken, and won't stand up for you.

You could even call it the soul, this shy bridegroom, silver
fellow who must be summoned from a long way off

Do male writers have to duck and dive this way, I wonder? I think of Proust in his seclusion, I think of Emily Dickinson raking in the everyday unknown, ekeing her limbs across the wet green weave of the garden.

'Our Summer made her light Escape
Into the Beautiful'

Evasion. Were they hiding from too many incursions, sensing an overload, keeping things out? It seems that the voices Emily sought to escape were masculine, societal, the external codes of the father. Is the female voice more destructive because it is deeper-seated, and formless in its forbidding? A real room, a real door to shut: these seem to have afforded Emily enough protection. She lived spinsterly, pursuing 'the largest need of the intellect', and let nothing stand in the way of her explorations.

I think of her in her wild white bonnet, owning the foreign
shine of the morning. Becoming, growing into – I believe she
knew it – God's raspberry-tree, his strangeness.

Tom Pow
Black Daffodils

Black as scoops
of oil, heavy
as gannets' heads,
there's never a vase
to hold them.

Their waxen stems
are black as their roots,
as the rich
black soil that
fed by ashes
grew them.

Stare into
their glossy eaves,
your face
like a fossil
fresh as tar
stares back.

Black daffodils
               shine
like any others
but don't carol,
don't dance
in the breeze; in fact
as often as not
are solitary,
though common
enough to fulfil
the name: common
black daffodil.

Nor do their black
heads trumpet

to the heart
in the way
of the yellow.
Black daffodils
                shine
like any others
but that's an end
to their giving.

Gathered
by your bedside,
snug in ready moulds
of darkness, you hear
drawn to their always
open mouths
the hanging fruits
of night – the screeching
of cats, the train's
explosive roar;
its tender, your own
attraction to black.

You dare not sleep
lest you wake
an effigy, weeping across
your chest a delta
of black daffodils
and Magritte
their patron saint
standing there, his brush
on the palette already
dipped in black.
'Darling,' you say,
'are you sleeping yet?'

Try them now
against a snow field.
See how
all things are pulled
to them: cattle,

fences, barns –
large or small –
the horizon,
language itself,
till it seems
we all live
in the throat
of a black daffodil.

But that's simply
speculation. All
we know is: these are
the black daffodils
and we must hold to them
for they have a spring-
time too. They are
ours and a gift
like any other.

MELVYN BRAGG
Out of My Mind with Terror

They began when I was about thirteen and continued upwards of two years, at times intensively. They faded away slowly, but still at eighteen or nineteen I was apprehensive that they might return, and in force. They did, briefly, at the end of my twenties, but since then I have been spared.

Usually they came at night. I cannot recall the first time, but I do remember the first onslaught. My parents kept a pub and they would be downstairs from about five-thirty p.m. until after eleven p.m. I would have been out at choir practice, the Scouts, swimming, playing football, whatever, and come back to take it on. Having eaten a quick snack in the bar kitchen downstairs, I would go up to my bedroom – I would be alone in the flat above the pub. I would know that it was waiting for me, but I had no alternative but to go upstairs, though I would feel distraught.

I used to say my prayers then and yet I never mentioned this fear in them. For one thing, that would have been to extemporize, and the prayers I said were set ones, spoken twice on Sundays in church and most mornings in school assembly. There was no room for individual additions except to bless parents and relations, but that was somehow allowed for. What was not allowed was to tell anyone what was happening.

I cannot remember before or since being anything like as terrified. I remember the fact of it now, and even a little digging into memory gives off something of the taste of it. I would simply lie in bed waiting for it to happen, screwing up my eyes as tight as possible, hoping that I would be felled by instant, merciful sleep or somehow left alone. When I was, the relief the next morning was momentary before the fear began to build again.

What happened was this. Not *part* of me, but *what I was* left the boy's body on that bed and went above – it seemed to the corner of the ceiling next to the window. It hovered there. It stayed there. It, that thing, that object, was me. The huddle on the bed was controlled by it. There was no will in the boy's body. There was only, as it were, a holding state uninhabited, save for a possessing aura of terror. Whether the terror was in the body or in that thing which, at times, I thought I could make out and describe, I do not know. But the experience was terror.

If the thing moved away then the body would be finished. It would be no more, because that thing not only controlled the body but gave it life. The desperate fear was – would these two fuse again or not? What did this presence want the body to do besides lying inert and being a void? Somehow an invisible help line would be thrown and the two would come together – and usually by that time I was exhausted and went into sleep of a sort.

This became the secret obsession of my life over those years. The noise from the pub downstairs, which could be lulling or, sometimes on Fridays and Saturdays, rather threatening, would often be a help. But when the pub closed and my parents had cleared up and settled downstairs for their final talk, the silence intensified the dread.

On spring and summer nights they would often go out for a walk after they had cleared up. I wanted to rush down and beg them not to after the cheery 'We're just off for a bit of fresh air', but of course I would have been ashamed to have done that. I dared not. Left alone was the worst possible state. And so I would track their walk. I knew the route. I would try to time it. I would try to 'be' with them.

Down Burnfoot past Scott's, where they used to have the funeral horses, to Joe Hill's on the corner with a shed in the garden where he slept for his asthma. Then into Birdcage Walk, along the cinder track past the allotments, with the pigeons silent as the pub, and on to the West Cumberland Farmers' warehouses. I feared I was always ahead of them and forced myself to slow down. Past Toppins field, where I used to sledge and where I used to play when I lived in Council House Yard. Toppins field, with its great beech tree and its bomb shelters dug in the war. Then the Redmaynes clothing factory where my mother had worked as a girl.

Then they would turn into Station Road opposite the factory and slowly up the hill back into the middle of the town, left around Blue Bell corner, past Tickle's Lane and Plaskett's Lane and down towards the pub. I was always ahead and so I'd go over the route again trying to pick out more and more details until I heard them coming down the hill and, finally, the key turned in the lock and there would be some comfort.

These experiences, or attacks, were never anything other than utterly terrifying. I have read other people describing analogous experiences in terms of happiness and hope; that was never mine. In its most intensive period, they began to happen in the classroom, on the street, everywhere, and I seemed to spend my entire time constructing strategies to evade them or endure them.

It was impossible to talk to anyone about it. My parents could not have been better or kinder, but it was inconceivable that I could discuss this with them. How would I describe it? What would I, literally, say?

It has taken me this long to be able to write about it openly and autobiographically, although it was part of the main character in my first novel – when I was twenty-five – unconsciously as it were.

I was still convinced that I had never admitted to it when, consciously, I made this state part of the underpinning of the main character in a later novel when I was in my late forties. But it was when I found myself referring to it in a recent interview about religious belief, in which the possibility of a duality and a soul was introduced, that I wanted to begin to put on paper something of that experience.

I could not talk to my parents, as I have said. I was not ill, so there was no need of a doctor. It was totally off the radar as far as friends were concerned. I just had to get through it, although at the time I thought simultaneously both that it would never end and that this attack could be the last.

I am sure that there are a number of plausible explanations. We know that people with an amputated arm can be driven to a frenzy at the pain in their missing fingers. We know from those who have been almost dead but just 'returned' that similar experiences to mine are not uncommon. A. J. Ayer described one such most vividly.

There are fantasies within the human condition and in the casebooks of many analysts – Oliver Sachs is just one example – which furnish explained instances of circumstances much more bizarre. I am sure that materialists of consciousness will bring forward proof and so on. And there is the undeniable, unpredictable pressure of adolescence.

But at the risk of building far too much on this slender base of personal experience, my current thinking is that what I experienced is evidence of a duality, of a split, in Christian terms, of a distinction between body and soul.

It is relevant perhaps, and it could take away from my case that I was brought up as a strong Christian and the religious experience was, with me – as is common – especially strong in early adolescence. But the solidity of the thing which was undoubtedly outside my body, and the number of times it happened, and most importantly, the fact that it *was* the life, the intelligence as it were, is something I cannot, and do not want to, deny.

I'm prepared to be told that this evidence is too personal and too slight, but for what it is worth I hold on to it and find in it a duality which magnetizes my earlier, schooled, received faith.

Perhaps these experiences would have faded away on their own, but at about fifteen I realized that I had to attack them. At the same time I was not doing well at school and I knew that I had to study or leave and get work. I began to overwork and to write and to do as many other things as I could manage. Most importantly, I stayed in that bedroom studying on a chopped-off table which was wedged between the bed and the wardrobe. This was a conscious attempt to face up to it, in the very place where I had experienced it most violently and frighteningly. Gradually, I grew a bit stronger, although even in my late twenties I could feel fragile and vulnerable.

It is something that I would like to understand more. I would also like to gather up the determination to attempt to go through that experience again, but that will take a build-up of energy and nerve which another part of me says it would be foolish to do. To seek to uncork a part of the past now blessedly gone would be not only painful but dangerous.

Doris Lessing
Dialogue

The building she was headed for, no matter how long she delayed among the shops, stalls, older houses on the pavements, stood narrow and glass-eyed, six or eight storeys higher than this small shallow litter of buildings which would probably be pulled down soon, as uneconomical. The new building, economical, whose base occupied the space, on a corner lot, of three small houses, two laundries and a grocer's, held the lives of 160 people at forty families of four each, one family to a flat. Inside this building was an atmosphere both secretive and impersonal, for each time the lift stopped, there were four identical black doors, in the same positions exactly as the four doors on the nine other floors, and each door insisted on privacy.

But meanwhile she was standing on a corner watching an old woman in a print dress buy potatoes off a stall. The man selling vegetables said: 'And how's the rheumatism today, Ada?' and Ada replied (so it was not *her* rheumatism): 'Not so bad, Fred, but it's got him flat on his back, all the same.' Fred said: 'It attacks my old woman between the shoulders if she doesn't watch out.' They went on talking about the rheumatism as if it were a wild beast that sunk claws and teeth into their bodies but which could be coaxed or bribed with heat or bits of the right food, until at last she could positively see it, a jaguar-like animal crouched to spring behind the brussels sprouts. Opposite was a music shop which flooded the whole street with selections from opera, but the street wasn't listening. Just outside the shop a couple of youngsters in jerseys and jeans, both with thin vulnerable necks and untidy shocks of hair, one dark, one fair, were in earnest conversation.

A bus nosed to a standstill; half a dozen people got off; a man passed and said: 'What's the joke?' He winked, and she realized she had been smiling.

Well-being, created because of the small familiar busyness of the street, filled her. Which was of course why she had spent so long, an hour now, loitering around the foot of the tall building. This irrepressible good nature of the flesh, felt in the movement of her blood like a greeting to pavements, people, a thin drift of cloud across pale blue sky, she checked, or rather tested, by a deliberate use of the other vision on the scene: the man behind the neat arrangements of coloured vegetables had a stupid face, he looked brutal; the future of the adolescents holding their position outside the music-shop door against the current of pressing people could only too easily be guessed at by the sharply aggressive yet forlorn postures of shoulders and loins; Ada, whichever way you looked at her, was hideous, repulsive, with her loose yellowing flesh and her sour-sweat smell. Etc, etc. Oh yes, et cetera, on these lines, indefinitely, if she chose to look. Squalid, ugly, pathetic . . . *And what of it?* insisted her blood, for even now she was smiling, while she kept the other vision sharp as knowledge. She could feel the smile on her face. Because of it, people going past would offer jokes, comments, stop to talk, invite her for drinks of coffee, flirt, tell her the stories of their lives. She was forty this year, and her serenity was a fairly recent achievement. Wrong word: it had not been tried for; but it seemed as if years of pretty violent emotions, one way or another, had jelled or shaken into a joy which welled up from inside her independent of the temporary reactions — pain, disappointment, loss — for it was stronger than they. Well, would it continue? Why should it? It might very well vanish again, without explanation, as it had come. Possibly this was a room in her life, she had walked into it, found it furnished with joy and well-being, and would walk through and out again into another room, still unknown and unimagined. She had certainly never imagined this one, which was a gift from Nature? Chance? Excess? . . . A bookshop had a tray of dingy books outside it, and she rested her hand on their limp backs and loved them. Instantly she looked at the word *love*, which her palm, feeling delight at the contact, had chosen, and said to herself: Now it's enough, it's time for me to go in.

She looked at the vegetable stall, and entered the building, holding the colours of growth firm in her *heart* (word at once

censored, though that was where she felt it). The lift was a
brown cubicle brightly lit and glistening, and it went up fast.
Instead of combating the sink and sway of her stomach, she
submitted to nausea; and arrived at the top landing giddy; and
because of this willed discoordination of her nerves the enclosed
cream-and-black glossiness of the little space attacked her with
claustrophobia. She rang quickly at door 39. Bill stood aside as
she went in, receiving her kiss on his cheekbone, which felt
damp against her lips. He immediately closed the door behind
her so that he could lean on it, using the handle for a support.
Still queasy from the lift, she achieved, and immediately, a
moment's oneness with him who stood giddily by the door.

But she was herself again (*herself* examined and discarded) at
once; and while he still supported himself by the door, she went
to sit in her usual place on a long bench-like settee that had a
red blanket over it. The flat had two rooms, one very small and
always darkened by permanently drawn midnight-blue curtains,
so that the narrow bed with the books stacked up the wall
beside it was a suffocating shadow emphasized by a small
yellow glow from the bed lamp. This bedroom would have
caused her to feel (he spent most of his time in it) at first panic
of claustrophobia, and then a necessity to break out or let in
light, open the walls to the sky. How long would her amiability
of the blood survive in that? Not long, she thought, but she
would never know, since nothing would make her try the
experiment. As for him, this second room in which they both sat
in their usual positions, she watchful on the red blanket, he in
his expensive chair which looked surgical, being all black
leather and chromium and tilting all ways with his weight, was
the room that challenged him, because of its openness – he
needed the enclosed dark of the bedroom. It was large, high,
had airy white walls, a clear black carpet, the dark red settee,
his machine-like chair, more books. But one wall was virtually
all window: it was window from knee height to ceiling, and the
squalors of this part of London showed as if from an aeroplane,
the flat was so high, or seemed so, because what was beneath
was so uniformly low. Here, around this room (in which, if she
were alone, her spirits always spread into delight), winds

clutched and shook and tore. To stand at those windows, staring straight back at sky, at wind, at cloud, at sun, was to her a release. To him, a terror. Therefore she had not gone at once to the windows; it would have destroyed the moment of equality over their shared giddiness – hers from the lift, his from illness. Though not-going had another danger, that he might know why she had refrained from enjoying what he knew she enjoyed, and think her too careful of him?

He was turned away from the light. Now, perhaps conscious that she was looking at him, he swivelled the chair so he could face the sky. No, this was not one of his good days, though at first she had thought his paleness was due to his dark blue sweater, whose tight high neck isolated and presented his head. It was a big head, made bigger because of the close-cut reddish hair that fitted the back of the skull like fur, exposing a large pale brow, strong cheekbones, chin, a face where every feature strove to dominate, where large calm green eyes just held the balance with a mouth designed, apparently, only to express the varieties of torment. A single glance from a stranger (or from herself before she had known better) would have earned him: big, strong, healthy, confident man. Now, however, she knew the signs, could, after glancing around a room, say: Yes, you and you and you . . . Because of the times she had been him, achieved his being. But *they*, looking at her, would never claim her as one of them, because being him in split seconds and intervals had not marked her, could not, her nerves were too firmly grounded in normality. (*Normality?*) But she was another creature from them, another species, almost. To be envied? She thought so. But if she did not think them enviable, why had she come here, why did she always come? Why had she deliberately left behind the happiness (word defiantly held on to, despite them) she felt in the streets? Was it that she believed the pain in this room was more real than the happiness? Because of the courage behind it? She might herself not be able to endure the small dark-curtained room which would force her most secret terrors; but she respected this man who lived on the exposed platform swaying in the clouds (which is how his nerves felt it) – and from choice?

Doctors, friends, herself – everyone who knew enough to say
– pronounced: the warmth of a family, marriage if possible,
comfort, other people. Never isolation, never loneliness, not the
tall wind-battered room where the sky showed through two
walls. But he refused common sense. 'It's no good skirting
around what I am, I've got to crash right through it, and if I
can't, whose loss is it?'

Well, she did not think she was strong enough to crash right
through what she most feared, even though she had been born
healthy, her nerves under her own command.

'Yes, but you have a choice, I haven't, unless I want to
become a little animal living in the fur of other people's
warmth.'

(So went the dialogue.)

But he had a choice too: there were a hundred ways in which
they, the people whom she could now recognize from their eyes
in a crowd, could hide themselves. Not everyone recognized
them, she would say; how many people do we know (men and
women, but more men than women) enclosed in marriages,
which are for safety only, or attached to other people's families,
stealing (if you like) security? But theft means not giving back
in exchange or kind, and these men and women, the solitary
ones, do give back, otherwise they wouldn't be so welcome, so
needed – so there's no need to talk about hanging on to the
warmth of belly fur, like a baby kangaroo, it's a question of taking one thing, and giving back another.

'Yes, but I'm not going to pretend, I will not, it's not what I
am – I can't and it's your fault that I can't.'

This meant that he had been the other, through her, just as
she had, through him.

'My dear, I don't understand the emotions, except through
my intelligence, *normality* never meant anything to me until I
knew you. Now all right, I give in . . .'

This was sullen. With precisely the same note of sullenness
she used to censor the words her healthy nerves supplied like
love, happiness, myself, health. All right, this sullenness meant:
I'll pay you your due, I have to, my intelligence tells me I must.
I'll even be you, but briefly, for so long as I can stand it.

Meanwhile they were – not talking – but exchanging information. She had seen X and Y and Z, been to this place, read that book.

He had read so-and-so, seen X and Y, spent a good deal of his time listening to music.

'Do you want me to go away?'

'No, stay.'

This very small gift made her happy; refusing to examine the emotion, she sat back, curled up her legs, let herself be comfortable. She smoked. He put on some jazz. He listened to it inert, his body not flowing into it, there was a light sweat on his big straining forehead. (This meant he had wanted her to stay not out of warmth, but for need of somebody there. She sat up straight again, pushed away the moment's delight.) She saw his eyes were closed. His face, mouth tight in an impersonal determination to endure, looked asleep, or –

'Bill,' she said quickly, in appeal.

Without opening his eyes, he smiled, giving her sweetness, friendship, and the irony, without bitterness, due from one kind of creature to another.

'It's all right,' he said.

The piano notes pattered like rain before a gust of wind that swept around the corner of the building. White breaths of cloud were blown across the thin blue air. The drum shook, hissed, steadily, like her blood pumping the beat, and a wild flute danced a sky sign in the rippling smoke of a jet climbing perpendicular from sill to ceiling. But what did he hear, see, feel, sitting eyes closed, palm hard on the armrest for support? The record stopped. He opened his eyes, they resolved themselves out of a knot of inward difficulty, and rested on the wall opposite him, while he put out his hand to stop the machine. Silence now.

He closed his eyes again. She discarded the cross talk in her flesh of music, wind, clouds, raindrops, patterning grass and earth, and tried to see – first the room, an insecure platform in height, tenacious against storm and rocking foundations; then a certain discordance of substance that belonged to his vision; then herself, as he saw her – at once she felt a weariness of the spirit, like a cool sarcastic wink from a third eye, seeing them both, two little people, him and herself, as she had seen the vegetable seller, the adolescents, the woman whose husband had rheumatism. Without charity she saw them, sitting there together in silence on either side of the tall room, and the eye seemed to expand till it filled the universe with disbelief and negation.

Now, she admitted the prohibited words love, joy (et cetera), and gave them leave to warm her, for not only could she not bear the world without them, she needed them to disperse her anger against him: Yes, yes, it's all very well, but how could the play go on, how could it, if it wasn't for me, the people like me? We create you in order that you may use us, and consume us; and with our willing connivance; but it doesn't do to despise . . .

He said, not surprising her that he did, since their minds so often moved together: 'You are more split than I am, do you know that?'

She thought: If I were not split, if one-half (if that is the division) were not able to move in your world, even if only for short periods, then I would not be sitting here, you would not want me.

He said: 'I wasn't criticizing. Not at all. Because you have the contact. What more do you want?'

'Contact,' she said, looking at the cold word.

'Yes. Well, it's everything.'

'How can you sit there, insisting on the things you insist on, and say it's everything?'

'If that's what you are, then *be* it.'

'Just one thing or the other?'

'Yes.'

'Why? It's true that what I think contradicts what I feel, but . . .'

'But?'

'All right, it's all meaningless, with my mind I know it, it's an accident, it's a freak, but all the same, everything gives me pleasure all the time. Why should it be a contradiction, why should it?'

'You don't see it as a contradiction?'

'No.'

'You're living on the fat of your ancestors, the fat of their belief, that's all.'

'Possibly, but why should I care?'

'A fly buzzing in the sun,' he said. His smile was first wry and tender, then full of critical dislike. The criticism, the coldness of it, hurt her, and she felt tears rise. So today she could not stay long, because tears were not allowed, they were part of the other argument, or fight, a personal one, played out (or fought out), finished.

She was blinking her eyes dry, without touching them, so that he would not see she wanted to cry, when he said: 'Suppose that *I* am the future?'

A long silence, and she thought: Possibly, possibly.

'It seems to me that I am. Suppose the world fills more and more with people like me, then –'

'The little flies will have to buzz louder.'

He laughed, short but genuine. She thought, I don't care what you say, that laugh is stronger than anything. She sat in silence for the thousandth time, *willing* it to be stronger, feeling herself to be a centre of life, or warmth, with which she would fill this room.

He sat, smiling, but in an inert, heavy way, his limbs seeming, even from where she sat across the room, cold and confused. She went to him, squatted on her knees by his chair, lifted his hand off the black leather arm-piece, and felt it heavy with cold. It gave her hand a squeeze more polite than warm, and she gripped it firmly, willing life to move down her arm through her hand into his. Closing her eyes, she now made herself remember, with her flesh, what she had discarded (almost contemptuous) on the pavement – the pleasure from the touch of faded books, pleasure from the sight of ranked fruit and vegetables. Discoloured print, shut between limp damp cotton, small voices to be bought for sixpence or ninepence, became a pulse of muttering sound, a pulse of vitality, like the beating colours of oranges, lemons and cabbages, gold and green, a dazzle, a vibration in the eyes – she held her breath, willed, and made life move down into his hand. It lay warmer and more companionable in hers. After a while he opened his eyes and smiled at her: sadness came into the smile, then a grimness, and she kissed his cheek and went back to her place on the rough blanket. 'Flies,' she said.

He was not looking at her. She thought: Why do I do it? These girls who come through here for a night, or two nights, because he needs their generous naïveté, give him no less. I, or one of them, it makes no difference. 'I'd like a drink,' she said.

He hesitated, hating her drinking at all, but he poured her one, while she said silently (feeling adrift, without resources, and cold through every particle of herself): All right, but in the days when our two bodies together created warmth (flies, if you like, but I don't feel it) I wouldn't have asked for a drink. She was thinking: And suppose it is yours that is the intoxication and not mine? when he remarked: 'Sometimes when I've been alone here a couple of days I wonder if I'm not tipsy on sheer . . .' He laughed, in an intellectual pleasure at an order of ideas she was choosing not to see.

'The delights of nihilism?'

'Which of course you don't feel, ever!'

She saw that this new aggressiveness, this thrust of power and criticism (he was now moving about the room, full of energy) was in fact her gift to him; and she said, suddenly bitter: 'Flies don't feel, they buzz.'

The bitterness, being the note of the exchange they could not allow themselves, made her finish her few drops of liquor, making a new warmth in her stomach where she had needed a spark of warmth.

He said: 'For all that, it seems to me I'm nearer the truth than you are.'

The word *truth* did not explode into meaning: it sounded hard and self-defined, like a stone; she let it lie between them, setting against it the pulse that throbbed in the soft place by the ankle bone – her feet being stretched in front of her, so she could see them.

He said: 'It seems to me that the disconnected like me must see more clearly than you people. Does that sound ridiculous to you? I've thought about it a great deal, and it seems to me you are satisfied with too little.'

She thought: I wish he would come over here, sit by me on this blanket, and put his arm around me – that's all. That's all and that's all. She was very tired. Of course I'm tired – it's all the buzzing I have to do . . .

Without warning, without even trying, she slipped into being him, his body, his mind. She looked at herself and thought: This little bundle of flesh, this creature who will respond and warm, lay its head on my shoulder, feel happiness – how unreal, how vulgar, and how meaningless!

She shook herself away from him, up and away from the settee. She went to the window.

'What are you doing?'

'Enjoying your view.'

The sky was clear, it was evening, and far below in the streets the lights had come on, making small yellow pools and gleams on pavements where the tiny movement of people seemed exciting and full of promise. Now he got himself out of his machine-like chair and came to stand by her. He did not touch her; but he would not have come at all if she had not been there. He supported himself with one big hand on the glass and looked out. She felt him take in a deep breath. She stood silent, feeling the life ebbing and coiling along the pavements and hoping he felt it. He let out his breath. She did not look at him. He took it in again. The hand trembled, then tensed, then set solid, a big, firmly made hand, with slightly freckled knuckles – its steadiness comforted her. It would be all right. Still without looking at his face, she kissed his cheek and turned away. He went back to his chair, she resumed her place on the blanket. The room was filling with dusk, the sky was greying, enormous, distant.

'You should get curtains, at least.'

'I should be tempted to keep them drawn all the time.'

'Why not, then, why not?' she insisted, feeling her eyes wet again. 'All right, I won't cry,' she said reasonably.

'Why not? If you feel like crying.'

She no longer wept. But once, and not so long ago, she had wept herself almost to pieces over him, her, their closeness which nevertheless the cold third, like a cruel king, refused to sanction. She noted that the pulse moving in her ankle had the desperate look of something fighting death; her foot in the dusk was a long way off; she felt divided, not in possession of herself. But she remained where she was, containing her fragmentation. And he held out his fist, steady, into the glimmer of grey light from the sky, watching it exactly as she looked at her own pulse, the stranger.

'For God's sake turn the light on,' she said, giving in. He put out his hand, pressed down the switch, a harsh saving light filled the room.

He smiled. But he looked white again, and his forehead gleamed wet. Her heart ached for him, and for herself, who would now get up deliberately and go away from him. The ache was the hurt of exile, and she was choosing it. She sat smiling, chafing her two ankles with her hands, feeling the warmth of her breathing flesh. Their smiles met and exchanged, and now she said: 'Right, it's time to go.'

She kissed him again, he kissed her, and she went out, saying: 'I'll ring you.'

Always, when she left his door shut behind her, the black door which was exactly the same as all the others in the building except for the number, she felt in every particle of herself how loneliness hit him when she (or anybody) left.

The street she went out into was unfamiliar to her, she felt she did not know it. The hazy purple sky that encloses London at night was savage, bitter, and the impulse behind its shifting lights was a form of pain. The roughness of the pavement, which she knew to be warm, struck cold through the soles of her sandals, as if the shadows were black ice. The people passing were hostile, stupid animals from whom she wished to hide herself. But worse than this, there was a flat, black-and-white two-dimensional jagged look to things, and (it was this that made it terrifying) the scene she walked through was a projection of her own mind, there was no life in it that belonged there save what she could breathe into it. And she herself was dead and empty, a cardboard figure in a flat painted set of streets.

She thought: Why should it not all come to an end, why not? She saw again the potato face of Fred the vegetable seller whose interest in Ada's husband's illness was only because she was a customer at his stall; she looked at Ada whose ugly life (she was like a heave of dirty earth or some unnameable urban substance) showed in her face and movements like a visible record of thick physical living. The pathos of the adolescents did not move her, she felt disgust.

She walked on. The tall building, like a black tower, stood over her, kept pace with her. It was not possible to escape from it.

Her hand, swinging by her thigh, on its own life, suddenly lifted itself and took a leaf off a hedge. The leaf trembled: she saw it was her fingers which shook, with exhaustion. She stilled her fingers, and the leaf became a thin hard slippery object, like a coin. It was small, round, shining, a blackish-green. A faint pungent smell came to her nostrils. She understood it was the smell of the leaf which, as she lifted it to her nostrils, seemed to explode with a vivid odour into the senses of her brain so that she understood the essence of the leaf and through it the scene she stood in.

She stood fingering the leaf, while life came back. The pulses were beating again. A warmth came up through her soles. The sky's purplish orange was for effect, for the sake of self-consciously exuberant theatricality, a gift to the people living under it. An elderly woman passed, mysterious and extraordinary in the half-light, and smiled at her. So, she was saved from deadness, she was herself again. She walked slowly on, well-being moving in her, making a silent greeting to the people passing her. Meanwhile the dark tower kept pace with her, she felt it rising somewhere just behind her right shoulder. It was immensely high, narrow, terrible, all in darkness save for a light flashing at its top where a man, held upright by the force of his will, sat alone staring at a cold sky in vertiginous movement.

She moved steadily on, on the rhythm of her own pleasantly coursing blood. With one hand, however, she secretly touched the base of the tower whose shadow would always follow her now, challenging her, until she dared to climb it. With the other hand she held fast to the leaf.

ESTHER FREUD
For No Reason

I was sitting on the top deck of a No. 15 bus, willing it on along the Edgware Road, when for no reason, no reason at all, I began to drown. A wave came up and hit me and in my terror I put my head between my knees and moaned. Two girls looked over at me, giggling and alarmed, and to avoid them I pulled open a window. People need air, I told myself, it's normal to be short of breath, but the fear, the abnormal fear was rising, numbing my mouth and curdling my guts and so I ran downstairs and jumped out into the street.

I stood swaying on the pavement, wondering what to do. I was meeting Anthony outside a cinema on Oxford Street and I had to get to him and tell him that I wouldn't, couldn't see the film. I looked round for a taxi, but the traffic was moving at a crawl, and so instead I walked along beside my bus, and finding that I didn't feel much better, I got back on. I stayed downstairs this time, near the open door, pushing my heart down, checking that my teeth were still safely in my head and waiting to arrive.

Anthony, reliable and early, warmly dressed and smiling, was standing on the street. I ran towards him, babbling that I needed to go home, but he shook his head and waved the tickets at me. 'I've paid for them.' And for a moment I considered opening up my wallet and buying my way out. 'Don't give in to it,' he smiled when I tried to explain and, taking my hand, we walked into the red plush of the cinema.

I slipped into the Ladies to run my hands under the tap. Far away I felt the water rushing and then beside me, grinning, was a little boy, playing with the dryer, and for a second as I smiled at him, a great roll of relief spread over me, and I was back inside my life. 'Did you enjoy your film?' I asked him. The boy looked up at me and closed one eye. He rolled his top lip against his teeth, about to answer, when his mother bustled out, half-fastened, from her cubicle and whisked him off.

The advertisements swam in, too loud and close, and just before the film was due to start Anthony began to shift out of his seat. 'I'll get some popcorn.' And then I knew I couldn't stand it. 'I'm going to have to leave,' I said, and I walked out through the padded doors, up the velvet steps and out into the night.

Anthony had left his car in a special place behind the YMCA. A narrow street that seemed to have been overlooked by other parkers. As we walked towards it, side by side, not touching, he asked me to explain. He asked me questions, obviously put out, and instead of using words, I buckled my knees and pretended to be sick, keeling over, retching, so that he had to catch me seconds from the ground.

I'd proved how bad things were, to him and to myself, and there was silence as he drove me home.

I sat in the bathroom, my back against the radiator, cradling the phone. I knew no one could help me. I pulled off my boots and peeled away my socks. They were red and white in over-the-knee stripes, and would not be worn again. I thought of the roast peppers that I'd eaten, soaked in garlic oil, the mouthwash that I'd used to take away the taste for sweets, and tried to find a clue, a reason. I slipped into a bath, the water slid over my body, the heat failed to get through, and then, giving up, I lay down on my bed. Anthony stood over me. 'Is there anything I can get you?' He leant down to remove my earrings and his fingers, claustrophobic, made me want to flail. But I clenched my teeth and closed my eyes, because one day, maybe tomorrow, I'd feel better, and then I'd need him again.

Later when I went downstairs he was sitting in an armchair watching television. It was a programme about Francis Ford Coppola and as I came into the room they showed a field of chickens. They'd buried them, packed up to the neck in sand, their heads turning in confusion, their coxcombs trembling, and then with one great blast they blew them up. I saw their little ragged necks spin through the air. 'Oh, God,' I had my hands over my ears, 'switch it off.'

Anthony turned it down.

I stood over the kettle waiting for my camomile tea and then, as if to justify my outburst, 'Why couldn't they use chickens that were already dead?'

'It's the Vietnam War for Godsake!' But he kept the volume low.

I pressed myself against the bathroom radiator, the hot panels heating up the towelling of my back. I shut the door over the thick lead of the phone and dialled. 'Kate?' Even my voice was strange to me.

'What's wrong?'

I'd eaten lunch with her that day, talking and laughing, dissecting Anthony, Anthony and Tim, making ourselves dizzy with the circle of our lives. She'd only left so I could get ready for the cinema. 'Something's happened,' and I could hear her prepare to pounce. 'It's not Anthony,' I added quickly, 'he's downstairs, it's . . .'

'What then?'

'Something terrible . . . on the bus. I was just sitting there . . .'

It was difficult to explain.

'I was absolutely fine. Just sitting there, not thinking about anything when . . .' And I caught sight of the striped socks, slung against a wall, and the bottle of green mouthwash which I'd never use again.

'Take a sleeping pill,' Kate soothed. 'And get straight into bed.' But I was too frightened to let anything else in. And so I sipped my tea and let the radiator burn stripes into my back.

Kate knew a girl whose sister saw a therapist. A woman named Carina who lived in Primrose Hill. 'She changed her life,' the girl told Kate, and Kate rang me with her number.

Carina was cool and homespun and had two chairs that faced into the room. She sat and rocked on pale runners, smiling into space while I twisted round to try and make her see. 'I'm stuck,' I said, 'trapped up inside my head.' And I wished that I could cry. Carina asked if I'd like to lie down. I stretched out dutifully.

'If there had been a reason . . .' I began, but she took hold of my feet and held them and I waited, suspended in mid-air to see just what would happen. Nothing happened and I froze over with embarrassment, wondering whether it was up to me to call a stop.

Carina worked from home and had a separate door straight into the basement. The door was always open by a hair, so that I could push it with my fingertips to find her waiting in the room. One day, after a month or so, I found the door was shut. I knocked politely, waited, and then I knocked again. I walked up on to the pavement and shuffled back and forth. After ten more minutes I thought I'd try her real front door. The bell rang through the house and it occurred to me just then I could take this opportunity to leave, slip off round the corner and run down to Chalk Farm tube. Why was I waiting, stubborn on the street, for something that I didn't want? She may have changed someone's sister's life, but for me she was too slow, too calm and her sentences had a disconcerting habit of drifting off before the end.

Sometimes I caught her staring at me, round and pale, grounded in her chair, and it made me feel light as a bird, twittering on air, rattling like bottle tops on string. But the door had opened and a man was peering out. 'I had an appointment with Carina?' And the man smiled a professional smile and asked me to come in.

They'd been having a late breakfast. Plates were scattered on the table and a half-eaten brioche was smeared with jam. The man introduced himself as Erik. He looked fresh from bed and he wasn't wearing shoes. We waited in silence while someone moved about downstairs. 'You can come through now,' he said and I was ushered down into the basement.

'So.' Carina took her seat in her carefully placed chair. Our gaze crossed halfway across the room. 'How are you today?' I smiled a small embarrassed smile, but she was waiting for me to speak.

'Well,' I began, and I felt her begin to rock. She forgot about me, she forgot about me . . . her runners squeaked and I wanted desperately to laugh.

'How am I?' I tried to concentrate. 'I'm still . . .' and remembering myself the panic rushed in, fizzing in my head and I asked to use the bathroom.

The avocado bath was full of water. I tested it for heat and found the water was still warm. There was a layer of oil collecting on the surface. Lavender. And now that I had proof I felt much better. She did forget about me, I smiled with relief, and I pressed my head against the mirror.

'It's so embarrassing,' Kate laughed with me over Erik, the avocado bath and the state of her friend's sister who thought Carina was a help. But I was frightened. 'Please God,' I whispered daily, 'let me get back, let me get back to normal.' And I moved right through my life, amazed that people walked and talked, lifted spoons up to their mouths and showed no signs of fear.

Out of good manners and to divert her from the truth I went twice more to Primrose Hill. I didn't want her to get the wrong idea. 'I feel much better, it's probably a good time to stop.' Carina looked concerned. 'If you're sure.' And to ease the situation I said I'd probably be in touch quite soon.

If there had been a reason, I tortured myself, tracing that last journey by bus. My nonchalance amazed me now, sitting on the top deck, thinking about nothing. Only vaguely dreading the film. If I'd been in a car it might not have happened. I'd have been concentrating on gears. Red and green lights. I rolled the striped socks into a ball and pushed them out of sight. I glanced warily at peppers, and never let my brain go soft, terrified that if I let my guard down for a moment the wave would rise up and overtake me.

'I'm all right,' I whispered as I went about my day, forcing myself to interviews, to lunches, to parties and at least once a week, for Anthony's sake, through the terrifying hell mouth of the cinema.

And then one day I bumped into an old friend. I was in a café on the Portobello Road trying to avoid garlic.

'Hi.' It was Melissa, blonde and radiant, in red. 'How are you?'

'I'm fine,' My spirits sagged.

Melissa plumped herself down, 'You're doing so well, congratulations, and I hear Anthony is wonderful.'

We sat talking at the café window, drinking tea and looking out into the street.

'Do you fancy walking through the market?' But Melissa glanced down at her watch.

'I've got an appointment at two,' she said, 'and I don't want to be late.'

I laughed. When had Melissa ever been on time?

But she lowered her voice. 'I'm seeing someone actually,' and she blushed into the blonde roots of her hair.

'Has he changed your life?' I joked.

But Melissa stopped with one arm caught up in a sleeve. 'I'd say.' And she kissed me warmly on each cheek.

'I bumped into Melissa. She looked fantastic.'

'Really?' Kate was with us in a queue at Whiteleys, waiting to see a film. 'What's she up to?'

'Actually she was just off to see a shrink.'

Kate and Anthony were silent, scanning the times and prices of the various films.

'But you're all right now, aren't you?' Kate whispered as we nudged through to find our seats, and Anthony squeezed my ice-cold hand.

Melissa warned me it was miles away. 'I'd drive if I were you.' She also said her man was unconventional. 'He wouldn't do for everyone.' But I'd already decided he would have to do for me.

John Sotherton lived in the suburbs above Wood Green. It was a rented house with windows sealed against the cold and from outside I could see the stretch of clingfilm billowing behind the frames. I remembered Melissa saying he would only charge what you could afford. There was a sign fixed to his door. 'Please do not ring the bell unless you have an appointment. Please do not deliver free newspapers or trade cards. We do not buy anything from door-to-door salespeople. We do not wish to be converted to any religion.' I read it as I rang the bell.

John Sotherton was dressed in a tweed suit and tie. He was older than I'd expected, and he looked kind. He led me into a book-lined room with handmade shelves put up at random and stacked with paperbacks. I sat down on a worn-out sofa, adjusting myself between the springs, and he sat opposite on a chair.

I looked down at my hands, and he leant towards me with both feet on the floor.

'So how are you?' he asked kindly, and with a sudden surge of pity for myself tears welled up and stung my nose. John shifted out of his seat and pushed a box of tissues at me. I could tell, just like an ordinary person, he longed for me to stop.

'And the worse thing is,' I sobbed, 'everything's going rather well.' I cried some more and watched him squirm uncomfortably on his chair. 'If there was a reason for what happened,' and I described the wave and how it took up all my time just keeping it at bay.

'There's always a reason,' he insisted and I looked hopefully across and blew my nose.

He told me about a businessman who was unable to sign public cheques, a patient of his who couldn't go anywhere on the tube, a young man who pretended to his father that he didn't have a car as nice as his. 'There's always a reason,' and he drew a graph in the air between us. 'If your anxiety level is here,' he pointed to the middle of the chart, 'it will take something fairly big to bring it up to here,' his finger sped up to the top, 'and if it's here,' he moved right up and smiled at me, 'then any little thing can send it brimming over.'

'But what happened on the bus . . .' I tried to explain the drowning.

'A normal panic attack,' he assured me and I almost laughed, normal, normal, and I thought of Carina and the sideways glance.

'So you don't think I'm beyond hope?' And he smiled with me and said I was going to be all right.

'You just have to be a bit careful with yourself, that's all.' And he pointed to the bottom of the graph.

'I'm going to be all right, I'm going to be all right,' I told myself, as I negotiated the way home, concentrating on the gears, the red and green lights, and I wondered if Anthony would forgive me for turning down the chance to sit through *Die Hard 2*.

II

Black Dogs

U. A. FANTHORPE
Walking in Darkness

For Rosie who gets me through, and Drs B., C., and R.

It would be a comfort to have evidence of something wrong: a broken leg, a bandage, even a cough. But nothing shows, except perhaps the pallor and the pill bottle. And, in the early stages, no one can tell, except the people who know you best, who may notice a slowness. Maybe it's because there is nothing to show that you feel so ashamed about it. An honourable scar is one thing; a defection, a failure to be fully human, is quite another. You don't want people to know; you won't tell friends what the trouble is; you stay indoors; you keep, if you can, to your bed.

I don't suppose for a minute that I'm fooling you. 'You' isn't *you*; it's me. The 'it' is depression.

Usually I enjoy writing, and sit down to it happily. This time I'm profoundly unwilling, because I have to bring out into the open something that frightens me so much that I've never tried to understand it. As I've experienced it, it comes prowling out of darkness, itself a thing of darkness, and disables me for a time. Then, unpredictably but mercifully, it crawls off my back and goes away. I know some things about it, since it's been around me now for thirty years, and other things I've learnt from doctors and from friends. But it will always, for me, have an element of black magic about it, so such help as I can offer concerns living with the darkness rather than understanding its temperament. Writing about it is also hard because it's of the nature of the illness that, once it has gone, I forget all about its ways. Only when it returns, I remember: *Ah, that's just how it was*. But in between, I'd forgotten.

As an explorer of darkness, I should tell you my qualifications. How far have I been? My qualification is the usual one, that of being a patient, one who endures, to whom things are done by other people. I've been a patient, on and off, for thirty

years, but never in a sensational way. I've never been admitted
to a hospital, never had ECT (though I was offered it once),
never even had Prozac. I was generally able to go on working,
even to go on writing, while the darkness lasted, though there
was one bad patch when I couldn't. The drugs I've had have
been the unexciting sort: Tryptizol and Parnate. Parnate I hated.
Quite apart from the fact that it played havoc with my bowels,
life is made so difficult if one is a peripatetic poet, and mustn't
eat OXO, Bovril, Marmite, broad bean pods, pickled herrings,
yoghurt, any kind of alcohol, or cheese. Some of these things are
fairly easily avoided (I got strange looks from kind hostesses
when broad bean pods were mentioned); but it's surprising how
many people can't say for sure if they've included cheese in that
delicious casserole . . . In the end, Dr B., most recent in a line of
kind and painstaking doctors, from Gloucestershire to Merthyr
Tydfil to Bristol, decided to try Priadel (lithium carbonate), and
after seven years this still seems to be working. I now have the
smallest possible dose, but – and I see this as an indication that
I'm at last beginning to learn – I no longer try to drop everything I'm prescribed the moment I begin to feel better.
Something, however small, has been understood.

Not an interesting case, you see. Just a case. The only thing I
have of value to offer is that I seem, though rather raggedly, to
have survived thirty years of walking in darkness, and have on
the way discovered a few coping strategies. I hope you won't
need them, and in any case they may not work for you,
but . . . When depression hits me, the last thing I want to do is
see the doctor, because it seems hard to define anything as
'wrong'. When I have finally made myself go, and the doctor
has slotted me back into a medical definition again, the reactions are odd: relief at knowing where I am again and what I
have to do, but at the same time resentment that this has
happened again, the same symptoms, prescriptions, general
fears, and drearinesses.

Again I find myself waking miserably early, even before the
summer birds; again I find music unspeakably painful; again my
speech becomes slow, and my arms seem grotesquely long;
again I'm afraid to go out, because people will see at a glance

that there's something wrong, and shun me; I can't face the garden because, although in one part of my brain I know the blackbirds are just making their usual evening calls, I'm convinced that the cats are after them and that it's my fault; above all, my vocabulary shrinks to such an extent that the only word I'm really at home with is 'sorry'.

It isn't like this all the time. Towards evening the cloud starts to lift, and if I have something demanding to do in front of an audience, I can bring it off so that they won't suspect. Afterwards, of course, it's worse.

As for getting through time, I have several specifics: sleep is first and best, and unquestionably has the healing properties that Shakespeare describes. Closely linked is Radio 4, with its benign voices; with any luck they will be my sleeping pill, but in any case they tell me of a saner world, which some day I'll rejoin. And there's reading. Normally I read anything at any time, but when I'm depressed the only kind of book I can face deals with climbers in the Himalayas. I suppose their struggles with height and cold are a bearable parallel for my difficulties. During this hibernation there's a struggle taking place about my identity. 'This is not the real me!' I claim, viewing the inert, drugged, cowardly, hopeless body. It feels as though there must be an involuntary element of acting in it, as though by shamming depression I'm avoiding something, but it's not the 'real me' who is doing the shamming. The real me is fine, upstanding, seven feet tall and fearless. This self-consciousness about the self doesn't help.

One of the worst problems is other people, especially the ones who are kindest and most understanding. Their goodness makes me want to cry; imaginative tenderness is one of the hardest things to live with when you're depressed, and yet I suppose that without it I should lose my (very faint) desire to live altogether. Being grateful all the time takes such energy. Of course, they don't *want* you to be grateful – just to get better. You can't do the one, and the other makes you feel worse. When I'm badly depressed I long above all things to be a prisoner. I imagine this as a life where you don't make choices, where the pattern of life is plain and involuntary. Life in depression is like this anyway, but it retains the illusion of choice. If you had to do the sad things you are doing because someone had ordered that you should, indeed because you'd deserved it, the despair might (you think) go.

And then, so subtly that at first I don't realize it, the thing begins to clear. People can be faced again, books read, jobs done. There seems no reason for its going. Kind Dr C., who is now dead, believed the best cure for depression was hope. 'Remember,' he said to me, in his most forceful way, 'it is a self-limiting disease. It will go.' And so it does, as if it's got bored with me and wants to toy with somebody else.

And now the hard part. What is the use of all this? (I have the sort of economical housewife's mind that feels there should be a use for everything.) To make a complete use of depression, I'd need to remember very clearly what it was like after it's disappeared, and that seems impossible. I doubt, anyhow, whether I'd want to. But I do seem to retain enough awareness of the dark to have an abnormal response to the light. When I was small I acquired an immense fear of the dentist; but afterwards, coming out of the surgery, things seemed for half an hour or so wildly beautiful, strange, echoing. It isn't possible to live at that edge of sensation all the time, but quite often, now, I do. The dark makes the colours brighter. And I think I see what people's faces are really saying, and listen more attentively to what people say. They seem clearer, and more remarkable, than they were before the darkness. As Isaiah assures us, 'The people that walked in darkness have seen a great light . . . Upon *them* hath the light shined.' He didn't mean the depressed, but I think it holds good for them too.

This poem was published in 1982. With low cunning I hid it among poems about the illnesses of other people, hoping no one would be perceptive enough to see that it was mine. Now, however, I've acquired enough courage to admit that, yes, this is me, and this is how it seems. I also have the experience to be sure that, yes, the darkness does come to an end, and when morning comes, even in our climate, it might even be a fine day.

Inside

Inside our coloured, brisk world,
Like a bone inside a leg, lies
The world of the negative.

It is the same world, only somehow
Conviction has dribbled out of it,
Like stuffing from a toy.

A world of hypnotic clocks and unfinished
Goblin gestures. Nothing moves in a landscape
Fixed in hysteria's stasis.

This is the hushed network of nightmare.
You have lost touch with the sustaining
Ordinariness of things.

Suddenly the immense and venerable
Fallacies that prop the universe
Fail, the colossal flickering fabric
Which we must believe in so that it can be
Goes out.

Here malevolence is routine, the shadow
Is real and the world is shadow.
Here the happy-ever-after crumples
Into a rheumatoid hic-iacet.

Here the appalling and unexpected
Disaster is expected. Here the blood
Screams whispers to the flesh.

And here the alien wanders
Endless benighted streets where innocent households
Laugh behind blinds and believe in tomorrow
Like the milkbottles at the door.

WILLIAM STYRON
Darkness Visible

When I was first aware that I had been laid low by the disease, I felt a need, among other things, to register a strong protest against the word 'depression'. Depression, most people know, used to be termed 'melancholia', a word which appears in English as early as the year 1303 and crops up more than once in Chaucer, who in his usage seemed to be aware of its pathological nuances. 'Melancholia' would still appear to be a far more apt and evocative word for the blacker forms of the disorder, but it was usurped by a noun with a bland tonality and lacking any magisterial presence, used indifferently to describe an economic decline or a rut in the ground, a true wimp of a word for such a major illness. It may be that the scientist generally held responsible for its currency in modern times, a Johns Hopkins Medical School faculty member justly venerated – the Swiss-born psychiatrist Adolf Meyer – had a tin ear for the finer rhythms of English and therefore was unaware of the semantic damage he had inflicted by offering 'depression' as a descriptive noun for such a dreadful and raging disease. Nonetheless, for over seventy-five years the word has slithered innocuously through the language like a slug, leaving little trace of its intrinsic malevolence and preventing, by its very insipidity, a general awareness of the horrible intensity of the disease when out of control.

As one who has suffered from the malady in extremis yet returned to tell the tale, I would lobby for a truly arresting designation. 'Brainstorm', for instance, has unfortunately been preempted to describe, somewhat jocularly, intellectual inspiration. But something along these lines is needed. Told that someone's mood disorder has evolved into a storm – a veritable howling tempest in the brain, which is indeed what a clinical depression resembles like nothing else – even the uninformed layman might display sympathy rather than the standard reaction that 'depression' evokes, something akin to 'So what?' or 'You'll pull out of it' or 'We all have bad days.' The phrase 'nervous breakdown' seems to be on its way out, certainly deservedly so, owing to its insinuation of a vague spinelessness, but we still seem destined to be saddled with 'depression' until a better, sturdier name is created.

The depression that engulfed me was not of the manic type – the one accompanied by euphoric highs – which would have most probably presented itself earlier in my life. I was sixty when the illness struck for the first time, in the 'unipolar' form, which leads straight down. I shall never learn what 'caused' my depression, as no one will ever learn about their own. To be able to do so will likely for ever prove to be an impossibility, so complex are the intermingled factors of abnormal chemistry, behaviour and genetics. Plainly, multiple components are involved – perhaps three or four, most probably more, in fathomless permutations. That is why the greatest fallacy about suicide lies in the belief that there is a single immediate answer – or perhaps combined answers – as to why the deed was done.

The inevitable question 'Why did he [or she] do it?' usually leads to odd speculations, for the most part fallacies themselves. Reasons were quickly advanced for Abbie Hoffman's death: his reaction to an auto accident he had suffered, the failure of his most recent book, his mother's serious illness. With Randall Jarrell it was a declining career cruelly epitomized by a vicious book review and his consequent anguish. Primo Levi, it was rumoured, had been burdened by caring for his paralytic mother, which was more onerous to his spirit than even his experience at Auschwitz. Any one of these factors may have lodged like a thorn in the sides of the three men, and been a torment. Such aggravations may be crucial and cannot be ignored. But most people quietly endure the equivalent of injuries, declining careers, nasty book reviews, family illnesses. A vast majority of the survivors of Auschwitz have borne up fairly well. Bloody and bowed by the outrages of life, most human beings still stagger on down the road, unscathed by real depression. To discover why some people plunge into the downward spiral of depression, one must search beyond the manifest crisis

– and then still fail to come up with anything beyond wise conjecture.

The storm which swept me into a hospital in December began as a cloud no bigger than a wine goblet the previous June. And the cloud – the manifest crisis – involved alcohol, a substance I had been abusing for forty years. Like a great many American writers, whose sometimes lethal addiction to alcohol has become so legendary as to provide in itself a stream of studies and books, I used alcohol as the magical conduit to fantasy and euphoria, and to the enhancement of the imagination. There is no need either to rue or to apologize for my use of this soothing, often sublime agent, which had contributed greatly to my writing; although I never set down a line while under its influence, I did use it – often in conjunction with music – as a means to let my mind conceive visions that the unaltered, sober brain has no access to. Alcohol was an invaluable senior partner of my intellect, besides being a friend whose ministrations I sought daily – sought also, I now see, as a means to calm the anxiety and incipient dread that I had hidden away for so long somewhere in the dungeons of my spirit.

The trouble was, at the beginning of this particular summer, that I was betrayed. It struck me quite suddenly, almost overnight: I could no longer drink. It was as if my body had risen up in protest, along with my mind, and had conspired to reject this daily mood bath which it had so long welcomed and, who knows? perhaps even come to need. Many drinkers have experienced this intolerance as they have grown older. I suspect that the crisis was at least partly metabolic – the liver rebelling, as if to say, 'No more, no more' – but at any rate I discovered that alcohol in minuscule amounts, even a mouthful of wine, caused me nausea, a desperate and unpleasant wooziness, a sinking sensation, and ultimately a distinct revulsion. The comforting friend had abandoned me not gradually and reluctantly, as a true friend might do, but like a shot – and I was left high and certainly dry, and unhelmed.

Neither by will nor by choice had I become an abstainer; the situation was puzzling to me, but it was also traumatic, and I date the onset of my depressive mood from the beginning of this deprivation. Logically, one would be overjoyed that the body had so summarily dismissed a substance that was undermining its health; it was as if my system had generated a form of Antabuse, which should have allowed me to happily go my way, satisfied that a trick of nature had shut me off from a harmful dependence. But, instead, I began to experience a vaguely troubling malaise, a sense of something having gone cockeyed in the domestic universe I'd dwelt in so long, so comfortably. While depression is by no means unknown when people stop drinking, it is usually on a scale that is not menacing. But it should be kept in mind how idiosyncratic the faces of depression can be.

It was not really alarming at first, since the change was subtle, but I did notice that my surroundings took on a different tone at certain times: the shadows of nightfall seemed more sombre, my mornings were less buoyant, walks in the woods became less zestful, and there was a moment during my working hours in the late afternoon when a kind of panic and anxiety overtook me, just for a few minutes, accompanied by a visceral queasiness – such a seizure was at least slightly alarming, after all. As I set down these recollections, I realize that it should have been plain to me that I was already in the grip of the beginning of a mood disorder, but I was ignorant of such a condition at that time.

When I reflected on this curious alteration of my consciousness – and I was baffled enough from time to time to do so – I assumed that it all had to do somehow with my enforced withdrawal from alcohol. And, of course, to a certain extent this was true. But it is my conviction now that alcohol played a perverse trick on me when we said farewell to each other: although, as everyone should know, it is a major depressant, it had never truly depressed me during my drinking career, acting instead as a shield against anxiety. Suddenly vanished, the great ally which for so long had kept my demons at bay was no longer there to prevent those demons from beginning to swarm through the subconscious, and I was emotionally naked, vulnerable as I had never been before. Doubtless depression had hovered near me for years, waiting to swoop down. Now I was in the first stage –

premonitory, like a flicker of sheet lightning barely perceived depression's black tempest.

I was on Martha's Vineyard, where I've spent a good part of each year since the sixties, during that exceptionally beautiful summer. But I had begun to respond indifferently to the island's pleasures. I felt a kind of numbness, an enervation, but more particularly an odd fragility – as if my body had actually become frail, hypersensitive and somehow disjointed and clumsy, lacking normal coordination. And soon I was in the throes of a pervasive hypochondria. Nothing felt quite right with my corporeal self; there were twitches and pains, sometimes intermittent, often seemingly constant, that seemed to presage all sorts of dire infirmities. (Given these signs, one can understand how, as far back as the seventeenth century – in the notes of contemporary physicians, and in the perceptions of John Dryden and others – a connection is made between melancholia and hypochondria; the words are often interchangeable, and were so used until the nineteenth century by writers as various as Sir Walter Scott and the Brontës, who also linked melancholy to a preoccupation with bodily ills.) It is easy to see how this condition is part of the psyche's apparatus of defence: unwilling to accept its own gathering deterioration, the mind announces to its indwelling consciousness that it is the body with its perhaps correctable defects – not the precious and irreplaceable mind – that is going haywire.

In my case, the overall effect was immensely disturbing, augmenting the anxiety that was by now never quite absent from my waking hours and fuelling still another strange behaviour pattern – a fidgety recklessness that kept me on the move, somewhat to the perplexity of my family and friends. Once, in late summer, on an airplane trip to New York, I made the reckless mistake of downing a scotch and soda – my first alcohol in months – which promptly sent me into a tailspin, causing me such a horrified sense of disease and interior doom that the very next day I rushed to a Manhattan internist, who inaugurated a long series of tests. Normally I would have been satisfied, indeed elated, when, after three weeks of high-tech and extremely expensive evaluation, the doctor pronounced me totally fit; and I *was* happy, for a day or two, until there once again began the rhythmic daily erosion of my mood – anxiety, agitation, unfocused dread.

By now I had moved back to my house in Connecticut. It was October, and one of the unforgettable features of this stage of my disorder was the way in which my own farmhouse, my beloved home for thirty years, took on for me at that point when my spirits regularly sank to their nadir an almost palpable quality of ominousness. The fading evening light – akin to that famous 'slant of light' of Emily Dickinson's, which spoke to her of death, of chill extinction – had none of its familiar autumnal loveliness, but ensnared me in a suffocating gloom. I wondered how this friendly place, teeming with such memories of (again in her words) 'Lads and Girls', of 'laughter and ability and Sighing, / And Frocks and Curls', could almost perceptibly seem so hostile and forbidding. Physically, I was not alone. As always Rose was present and listened with unflagging patience to my complaints. But I felt an immense and aching solitude. I could no longer concentrate during those afternoon hours, which for years had been my working time, and the act of writing itself, becoming more and more difficult and exhausting, stalled, then finally ceased.

There were also dreadful, pouncing seizures of anxiety. One bright day on a walk through the woods with my dog I heard a flock of Canada geese honking high above trees ablaze with foliage; ordinarily a sight and sound that would have exhilarated me, the flight of birds caused me to stop, riveted with fear, and I stood stranded there, helpless, shivering, aware for the first time that I had been stricken by no mere pangs of withdrawal but by a serious illness whose name and actuality I was able finally to acknowledge. Going home, I couldn't rid my mind of the line of Baudelaire's, dredged up from the distant past, that for several days had been skittering around at the edge of my consciousness: 'I have felt the wind of the wing of madness.'

Our perhaps understandable modern need to dull the saw-tooth edges of so many of the afflictions we are heir to has led us to banish the harsh old-fashioned words: madhouse, asylum, insanity, melancholia, lunatic, madness. But never let it be doubted that depression, in its extreme form, is madness. The madness results from an aberrant biochemical process. It has been established with reasonable certainty (after strong resistance from many psychiatrists, and not all that long ago) that such madness is chemically induced amid the neurotransmitters of the brain, probably as the result of systemic stress, which for unknown reasons causes a depletion of the chemicals norepinephrine and serotonin, and the increase of a hormone, cortisol. With all of this upheaval in the brain tissues, the alternate drenching and deprivation, it is no wonder that the mind begins to feel aggrieved, stricken, and the muddied thought processes register the distress of an organ in convulsion. Sometimes, though not very often, such a disturbed mind will turn to violent thoughts regarding others. But with their minds turned agonizingly inward, people with depression are usually dangerous only to themselves. The madness of depression is, generally speaking, the antithesis of violence. It is a storm indeed, but a storm of murk. Soon evident are the slowed-down responses, near paralysis, psychic energy throttled back close to zero. Ultimately, the body is affected and feels sapped, drained.

That fall, as the disorder gradually took full possession of my system, I began to conceive that my mind itself was like one of those outmoded small-town telephone exchanges, being gradually inundated by floodwaters: one by one, the normal circuits began to drown, causing some of the functions of the body and nearly all of those of instinct and intellect slowly to disconnect.

There is a well-known checklist of some of these functions and their failures. Mine conked out fairly close to schedule, many of them following the pattern of depressive seizures. I particularly remember the lamentable near disappearance of my voice. It underwent a strange transformation, becoming at times quite faint, wheezy and spasmodic – a friend observed later that it was the voice of a ninety-year-old. The libido also made an early exit, as it does in most major illnesses – it is the superfluous need of a body in beleaguered emergency. Many people lose all appetite; mine was relatively normal, but I found myself eating only for subsistence: food, like everything else within the scope of sensation, was utterly without savour. Most distressing of all the instinctual disruptions was that of sleep, along with a complete absence of dreams.

Exhaustion combined with sleeplessness is a rare torture. The two or three hours of sleep I was able to get at night were always at the behest of the Halcion – a matter which deserves particular notice. For some time now many experts in psychopharmacology have warned that the benzodiazepine family of tranquillizers, of which Halcion is one (Valium and Ativan are others), is capable of depressing mood and even precipitating a major depression. Over two years before my siege, an insouciant doctor had prescribed Ativan as a bedtime aid, telling me airily that I could take it as casually as aspirin. The *Physicians' Desk Reference*, the pharmacological bible, reveals that the medicine I had been ingesting was (a) three times the normally prescribed strength, (b) not advisable as a medication for more than a month or so, and (c) to be used with special caution by people of my age. At the time of which I am speaking I was no longer taking Ativan but had become addicted to Halcion and was consuming large doses. It seems reasonable to think that this was still another contributory factor to the trouble that had come upon me. Certainly, it should be a caution to others.

At any rate, my few hours of sleep were usually terminated at three or four in the morning, when I stared up into yawning darkness, wondering and writhing at the devastation taking place in my mind, and awaiting the dawn, which usually permitted me a feverish, dreamless nap. I'm fairly certain that it was during one of these insomniac trances that there came over me the knowledge – a weird and shocking revelation, like that of some long-beshrouded metaphysical truth – that this condition would cost me my life if it continued on such a course. This must have been just before my trip to Paris. Death, as I have said, was now a daily presence, blowing over me in cold gusts. I had not conceived precisely how my end would come. In short, I was still keeping the idea of suicide at bay. But plainly the possibility was around the corner, and I would soon meet it face to face.

What I had begun to discover is that, mysteriously and in

ways that are totally remote from normal experience, the grey drizzle of horror induced by depression takes on the quality of physical pain. But it is not an immediately identifiable pain, like that of a broken limb. It may be more accurate to say that despair, owing to some evil trick played upon the sick brain by the inhabiting psyche, comes to resemble the diabolical discomfort of being imprisoned in a fiercely overheated room. And because no breeze stirs this cauldron, because there is no escape from this smothering confinement, it is entirely natural that the victim begins to think ceaselessly of oblivion.

MARY LOUDON
Blocking the Writer

Writing came to me by accident. It is a slightly more complicated story than this, but when I was twenty I met an Anglican
nun called Stella who was to become a close friend. One year,
and many conversations, later, I asked her why she had chosen
such an unorthodox life. At the time, I was reading Theatre
Studies at university, and my fifteen-year-old intention of pursuing a career on the stage was on the wane. When Stella sat
down under an apple tree in the convent orchard and told me
why she had chosen the contemplative Benedictine life over a
modern one I abandoned all thoughts of the theatre.

Overnight, I had discovered what I wanted to do. It was certainly not to join a religious order; I wanted to write a book
about why women become nuns, because I couldn't even begin
to understand why anyone would. Suddenly, in the form of a
book idea, along came everything I'd ever wanted: adventure
and exploration and escape and freedom and structure. On my
own terms. I had always loathed restrictions, and I hated being
a student, felt that university life was like some awful giant team
game. I hated being told what to write and how to write it, was
livid with the tutor who told me that I was 'clever but not an
academic. You think sideways.' I decided to take it as a compliment and ticked off the days until I could leave. It was a marvellous countdown. From the age of three I had been waiting to
run my own life.

As I limbered up for what was to be one of the most liberat-
ing experiences of my life, I found myself feeling increasingly
cramped in other ways. I left university full of plans for my
book, but in reality my life was utterly dominated by the
deterioration of a long, complicated and very fraught relationship with my boyfriend of the time. We had been together since
I was at school and, rather predictably for a twenty-one-year-
old fresh out of university, instead of doing the decent thing and

ending it honourably, I decided to go to India where, again rather predictably, I fell in love with someone completely different. While this provided the necessary catalyst for change (and eventually a happy new relationship), nothing had prepared me for the fury of the messy and overdue break-up that was waiting for me at home.

I thought I would feel relief, but I felt anger. I thought I would feel free, but I felt hostage to guilt and enormous resentment. I felt (unnecessarily, for everyone makes mistakes in love) incompetent and ashamed. I felt (irrationally, for I had had as loving and secure an upbringing as one could wish for) rootless. I grew up in a small community where I was regarded as my father's daughter, then moved into another one where I was my boyfriend's girlfriend. Now, for the first time in my life, I felt I had no frame of reference. I was just Mary, and having longed for that, having longed to escape from these associative forms of identification, I found that once I had done so I felt anchorless. Mary was a writer-in-waiting, no more. It should have been enough but it wasn't. In a manner so explosive that it surprises me even now, I fell to pieces.

People talk about breakdowns, but I'm never sure what they mean. Even clinical definitions vary considerably. Since childhood, the term 'breakdown' has always produced in my mind an image of someone buckling at the knees and collapsing on the floor. Perhaps the reality is more like a vehicle breakdown, a grinding to a standstill. Certainly, when life as I knew it fell away, I ground to a standstill. I had no idea how to move forward, still less where I wanted to be. I knew I had an idea for a book and that I wanted to write it, but I felt substantially reduced and consumed with inertia. An overwhelming need for sleep exacerbated my feelings of hopelessness, while keeping me from doing anything positive about them. In its physiological responses to mental distress, my body seemed to be pushing and pulling at the same time, keeping the heart and mind stuck between opposing forces, inhibiting progress of any kind.

Normally full of energy, I was awash with apathy. Normally optimistic, I was heavy with gloom. Normally confident, I was riven by guilt, shame and anger. Normally bold, I was gripped by fear. I was frightened that I had wasted my life. I was frightened that I was going to be punished by fate for my mistakes. I was frightened that I would never experience peaceful love. I was convinced that I had no future, or at any rate not one worth staying around for. A wasteland of days unfolded, giving way only to the demands of sleep obscured by relentless dreams. Dreams are especially pernicious when you are depressed: only seconds long, they can wreak havoc for hours. If they are good, if they are full of fancy, it is exhausting to wake up to a less agreeable reality. If, on the other hand, they trawl your subconscious for your worst fears or most painful memories, they are equally dispiriting.

I became too frightened to sleep and was prescribed sleeping pills and anti-depressants. Together, these produced dizziness, exhaustion, a ringing sensation in the ears (I was convinced that I could hear bells, day and night), and vivid hallucinogenic nightmares. I hallucinated when falling asleep too, convinced that the wardrobe was falling on me and that the door was advancing across the room. I thought that the floor was breathing and the walls were bleeding. I dreamt of being trapped in a rotating tunnel, walking past rows and rows of glass cases, each of them containing identical photographs of my earlier self. I dreamt that I was stuck before a pair of open electric doors which closed automatically each time I attempted to walk through them. Once, I dreamt that I was standing in an airfield, watching jets nose-dive and crash to the ground as the sky turned purple. 'Help me!' I cried to a man standing by my side, 'the world's ending!' 'I can't,' the man replied, as he metamorphosed into a baby before my eyes. 'You shrank me.' Every morning I awoke saturated with aimlessness.

By day, I couldn't take in the simplest information. I couldn't read a paper or a book, or watch television. I love music passionately, but it was a long, barren six months before I listened to any. For a while, maybe a month or so, I couldn't really sustain a conversation, was reduced to mumbling apologies: 'I'm sorry, I just can't take this in.' I remember asking someone to repeat herself three times when she offered me a cup of tea, and then answering like a drunk, my speech slurred.

I became physically clumsy. I dropped things, walked into doors, tripped on stairs. I lost things, or forgot where I'd put them. When buying a new railcard, I had to look on my driving licence for my date of birth: I couldn't even remember the year I was born. This strange amnesia seemed to arise from what felt like an almost physical barrier against information being either received or transmitted by me, and loss of memory was just as likely to occur over something integral to my sense of identity (like my date of birth) as it was over something trivial.

I tried to reduce the chaos. Every day for two months I turned to my writing for help, believing that I might be able, on paper at least, to govern the confusion, contain the pain, give shape to the disorder. Every day I failed, finding myself locked out of my imagination by a wall of fear and inertia. Eventually, I would give in and curl up on the sofa, defeated. I don't think I thought about much, I was too depleted to do so. I slept intermittently, waking up with cramp. I was more than housebound, I was roombound, confined to my study by irrational fear of anything beyond it. I barely went near the kitchen during the day because an empty kitchen somehow looked like death to me. I wasn't hungry anyway. I lost an enormous amount of weight, twenty pounds, which I didn't need to do. At five feet eight inches, and eight stone, I was the perfect size for the catwalk. I have never looked so ill or so unattractive in my life.

When life became unbearable I would escape to my endlessly kind and comforting parents. The escape itself was a hell of a task, though. For someone who is physically active and pretty fearless, I became as good as disabled. I dreaded other people so much that leaving the house became increasingly difficult. Perhaps the natural indifference of strangers merely emphasized my feelings of anonymity, isolation and dislocation. Whatever it was, trips between London and Oxfordshire became dominated by my attempts to avoid contact with other people. I took taxis to Paddington station because I couldn't face the tube, wordlessly paid for my ticket and sat, with my eyes shut or dark glasses on, for the entire journey. I didn't read or look out of the window, and if someone sat next to me I would ignore them completely, or move. I made eye contact with no one, half-believing that if I could not see anyone else then there was some chance that I could become invisible myself.

I have never before or since experienced such a violent desire to vanish. I'm convinced that this wasn't a suicidal urge, although I think it was allied to it. Not once did I think seriously about committing suicide, but I had lost my love of life. Oddly, however, I seemed to be grieving in the abstract and not the particular. I did not want my life to be the way it had been. I definitely did not want my relationship back. I regretted aspects of it, certainly. I felt I'd wasted time, felt I'd demeaned myself by being weak and cowardly and dishonourable, but I was not mourning for the past so much as a perceived absence of future.

They say time is a great healer, and it's a cliché because it's true. But quite apart from the distance afforded by time, and the perspective afforded by distance; quite apart from the support of loving family and friends, the truth is that I became *bored* with feeling so awful. I became bored with tears, bored with exhaustion, bored with misery, bored with regret. I was bored stiff with myself.

Throughout all this, I clung to the idea for my book like a life raft, and somehow it played a large part in my rescue. Soon, misery was replaced by panic, by the thought that I had nearly screwed up. I became obsessed with completing my book. Despite my earlier occasional wish for obliteration, the thought that I might not create something that I could truly call my own was unbearable. There was nothing about my life that anyone who did not know me could look at and say, 'That's what Mary Loudon did,' and the thought appalled me. Terrible really, to discover that the embers of ambition are stoked primarily by a fear of obscurity!

I won a couple of prizes awarded by the Society of Authors; an agent found me; and then she found me a good publisher. I subsidized my paltry first advance with my prize money, wangled my way on to the Enterprise Allowance Scheme for a year as a small business, worked six long days a week and ate a lot of soup. I wrote from eight in the morning until eight at night, stopping only to swim and eat, and occasionally to go out. It was a wonderful two years. I felt as if I had been waiting all my life for something to ignite my entire imagination, and finally something had.

I spent hours and hours alone, day after day after day, and I found to my surprise that I loved it. Even more, however, I loved emerging from my closeted life with something to show for it. I was motivated by the thought of results. On long days, I would urge myself onwards with the thought that contained within my work was something completely new, and completely original, which I wanted to share with others on the grounds that if I enjoyed it then they might. Writing books reminded me of childhood afternoons spent drawing complicated pictures to show to my father when he came home from work. I loved doing the drawings, but it was the anticipation of approval which proved so galvanizing.

'Ambition is the humour most contrary to seclusion,' wrote the French philosopher Montaigne. 'Glory and tranquillity cannot dwell in the same lodgings. As far as I can see, those authors have withdrawn only their arms and legs from the throng: their souls, their thoughts, remain even more bound up with it. They step back only to make a better jump, and, with greater force, to make a lively charge through the troops of men.' I'm not sure who Montaigne's 'troops of men' were for me. Perhaps just anybody out there who cared to take notice. I was definitely conscious of 'wanting to show them', but I never worked out who 'they' were. Not my parents. My brothers and sisters, for all those years of teasing? I don't really think so. The awful university tutor? No, not even her. 'They' could have been 'myself', of course, but from where this need to prove something, to stand up, stand out, and be clapped on the back, emanated, I do not know. All I know is that the desire to write springs from somewhere out of sight, and surprises me every time.

Once my first book was published, life was very exciting. The sudden opening of doors that accompanies even modest success gave me an incredible boost. I was offered a lot of work and with it came an overwhelming sense of validation. But I was not content. It wasn't enough. I still suffered from bouts of brief, but enervating, depression. I was intellectually and creatively fulfilled, but I had stopped being happy at eighteen and now I was twenty-three. The pendulum had not swung all the way back. Was I wrong to expect it to? I went to a counsellor at Relate and said, 'I don't expect you to do anything for me, but I want to be somewhere different and I need someone neutral to bounce some questions off.' She said, 'If that's what you think, then you're halfway there.'

I embarked upon a six-week programme with the counsellor at Relate. It was the best thing I could have done. She was not only well-trained, but calm, kind and intelligent. We made progress. I trained myself as far as possible to save my questions, fears, and occasional despair for my Tuesday morning sessions with her. If anything lasting came out of it, it was my admission to myself that while I wanted to be a writer, and I wanted to be able to write undisturbed, I also wanted to be taken care of by a nice, big, safe man. I knew that if I could not write I would go nuts. I also knew that if writing came to dominate my life to the exclusion of all else I would be desperately unhappy. I realized that this was bound to produce some not inconsiderable conflicts, and I was right.

Over the next five years, I experienced a perpetual tug-of-war, and the theme was always the same. I felt that I had to choose between writing and love, and writing always came first. I made matters excessively complicated for myself, terminating several relationships while continuing, impossibly, to seek security within them. My mid-twenties were punctuated by bouts of sometimes acute misery, invariably generated by the breakdown of love affairs I only half wanted.

In general, as my work prospered my friendships faltered. The absorption I needed in order to write made me extraordinarily selfish. I went out a lot but it was more often than not to some literary do. I nearly lost one of my closest friends through sheer neglect, at a time when she needed me badly. I was busy finishing my second book, working in the evenings and at weekends. She was quietly pleading with me to spend some time with her and I'm ashamed to say that I didn't even notice. It had reached the point when, if people wanted to see me, they generally had to come to supper at my house, and put up with me printing out draft chapters in between courses. It absolutely horrifies me when I look back. I was turning into A Writer; at the expense of everything else.

After my second book was published I experienced a curious malaise. I was tired. I felt lethargic, fed up, generally a bit bleak. I felt that there was something missing from my life. I thought, I'm twenty-seven, I've written two books and lots of book reviews. That's fine, but I don't want to be thirty-seven and the same, only more so. I want to be thirty-seven with a family. It is time, I thought, to find a mate.

I decided I'd better be practical about it. I decided to put my writing second to anything else that mattered to me. My agent would have been horrified if I'd admitted to her what I was up to, but I didn't. I didn't admit it to anyone, actually. ('So, Mary, what are you working on at the moment?' 'Finding a good man.') I decided not to begin writing another book until I felt ready, and to support myself in the meantime by writing articles and book reviews. I said no to work I didn't really want if it threatened to impinge upon my tidier life. It cost me a lot in overdraft fees, but I didn't care. I tied up the loose ends in my personal and professional life. I stopped working in the evenings and at weekends, accepted invitations, took holidays. I made greater efforts with friends. I went to Cornwall for the summer and began writing a novel.

'You've become too London,' said my brother. 'If you want a sensible man, put on some sensible clothes. Try wearing jeans and going on a date with someone quiet instead of having lunch with all these wankers from the BBC.' I wasn't actually having lunch with any wankers from the BBC but it was good advice. Within the year, I met a man I loved and respected and knew I wanted to stay with. (I wore a tracksuit for our first date: rock-climbing under the M40.) Now I am more contented than I've ever been and I wouldn't change it for anything. Still, there's always a catch, and as life gets easier, writing gets harder. Certainly, I am a better and more experienced writer than I was, but the writing itself requires more effort. And while I write more productively than I did, I take longer to get going. My mother says it's age and hormones but I like to think of it in rather more grandiose terms.

I have lost my edge. I care as much about my writing as I ever did, but I care less about the overall trajectory of my career, still less what others may think of me. Producing good work is intrinsic to my happiness, there's absolutely no question of that, but I have lost the frantic desire to please which found expression in the hot spur of quivering ambition. I'm not sorry, for the depressions have more or less entirely disappeared along with it. Writing remains my greatest passion, as well as being the way I earn my living, but these days I don't need to see my existence reinforced in print because I feel as if I truly, properly exist off the page.

I suspect that I will write for ever, but I don't know that for sure as I don't fully understand the creative impulse. I don't know anyone who does. I understand ambition, though, and it is not the same thing. Ambition is rocket-propelled frustration. It may project you upwards, but it can also leave you dangling in space. That's fine if all you want is a view of the world at one remove. But if you want the opportunity to partake, you have to come down. Earth and orbit are incompatible.

Some of what has happened to me is design, much of it is chance, and perhaps all of it is fate. I am twenty-nine now and I find I am looking forward to my thirties with a sense of thrill that is entirely new. 'The only duty we have in life,' said one of the nuns I interviewed for my first book, 'is to become who we are.' I feel as perhaps she would like me to; that at last I am becoming who I am. I certainly feel that I have some sure foundations for the next part of my life. This would mean much less to me if I hadn't experienced what it felt like to believe that I had none, and never would do.

SHEILA MACLEOD
The Art of Starvation

When I gradually began to eat less and less it was with no
thought of slimming in the normally accepted sense of the term.
I know that many girls who become anorexic set out with this
express intention, and may even be able to persuade themselves
that this is the sole cause (whole truth) of their subsequent condition. I know, too, that the stomach, on receiving less and less
food, will shrink and gradually require less and less food at any
one time. If this were indeed the whole truth about anorexia
nervosa, it would be a straightforward medical problem, and
therefore comparatively simple to resolve. But it is not.

The first question to be asked of the slimming thesis is, why
do people, especially young girls, want to become slim? The
answer is, in order to look good or, more bluntly, in order to
become (more) sexually attractive; slimness in our culture being
an essential ingredient of sexual attractiveness. In other words,
to slim is to take a rational decision with a conscious aim in
view. When that aim has been reached, the slimmer will abandon or moderate her strict dietary habits and try to maintain
what she considers to be her ideal body weight. My case, like so
many of those studied in the literature, does not bear out these
facts. What, for instance, would have been the point of my striving towards sexual attractiveness? I was in an all-female establishment, and, even when I was out of it, lived in an almost
exclusively female world. As far as I was concerned, men and
boys constituted a separate species, with whom I had nothing in
common, and the last thing I wanted to do (had I given the matter any thought) was to arouse their interest, which I feared
might be predatory. I had no conscious aim in view. If I had, I
should also have had the sense to know when I had achieved it,
and therefore when to start eating normally again. Although the
slimmer and the anorexic are both to some extent governed by
anxiety, there is an important difference between them.

Slimming is a conscious process; anorexia nervosa (being more than non-eating) a largely unconscious one – at least at the outset. In observing the behaviour of the slimmer and the anorexic, we may read the same text, 'I want to lose weight.' But the subtexts differ. Whereas the slimmer's reads, 'I want to be a sexually attractive woman,' the anorexic's reads, 'I want to shed the burden of womanhood.' Slimming is basically a matter of vanity. Anorexia is much more a matter of pride.

Loss of weight has meanings other than slimness. The most obvious is thinness: anorexics are not slim, but thin, often to the point of appearing almost completely fleshless. An anorexic may tell her friends or parents, 'I'd like to be slim,' and, if pressed for a reason, may reply along the lines of, 'So that I can wear nice clothes, date good-looking boys, and generally have a good time.' These conventionally acceptable statements constitute the apparent text of her behaviour. But the subtext reads somewhat differently: 'I want to be *thin* because I don't like flesh.' Flesh, female flesh, is to the anorexic an imposition from outside and, in extreme cases, an imposition of something swollen, polluted, dirty. Selvini Palazzoli quotes a dream related by one of these latter cases: 'On my way home from the convent I stopped outside the hospital. A woman who had just given birth was being lifted off a stretcher. I was horrified by her swollen and distended stomach. I heard them say that she had been brought to hospital because her belly was still full of urine.' My reaction to female flesh was neither as extreme nor as ignorant as that, and it was only my own, not that of other women, which caused me to feel revulsion. I have described how I looked in the mirror and, seeing myself 'in the flesh', did not recognize myself. My horrified 'That can't be me' soon became a determined 'That won't be me'. But I had no idea how to implement my refusal and, when I began not to eat, it was out of apathy and depression, out of a hopelessness concerning myself (including my body), rather than according to a definite plan.

The inescapable fact is that I didn't want to be a woman, although I was unaware of this at the time. What I did know was that I didn't want to grow up, and my diary records that I confessed as much – when pressed – to my housemistress. To me, the adult world was not a place where the individual could act freely and achieve growth, both in the acceptance of responsibility and in the likelihood of success. To me, it was just another place where I would be pushed around, perhaps even more violently than I had been before. Jung suggests that 'something in us wishes to remain a child; to be unconscious or at most conscious only of the ego; to reject everything foreign, or at least subject it to our will; to do nothing, or, in any case, to indulge our own craving for pleasure or power'. Such a wish, which presumably applies to both men and women, seems as impossible of fulfilment as my determination, 'That won't be me'. And Jung's phrase 'something in us' implies that the wish constitutes only a small element in the psyche – one that is not difficult for a sensible, mature person to reject, once she/he has recognized how unrealistic it is. But for me, it was difficult to reject and, far from being a minor psychic element, became a major obsession. The miracle of anorexia is that this wish can be fulfilled: one does not have to grow up; one does not have to become a woman, even in the biological sense; one can reject all foreign substances, for which food is a metaphor, and subject them to one's will. This is power indeed. Once the process is under way, it all seems easy: the only attribute required is an initial and stupendous effort of will. My non-eating started from positions of helplessness, of hopelessness, of a barely deniable adulthood and an even less deniable womanhood. By the time I had become fully anorexic, all these unwanted or unwelcome positions had been reversed.

At school we were weighed regularly – at the beginning, middle and end of each term – and it had been customary for me to record my weight in my diary on all these occasions. At the beginning of the O level summer term I weighed eight stone three pounds and, if I was pleased at having lost two pounds, I certainly didn't say so. The omission is meaningless: I could well have been delighted, although I can't remember whether I had actually begun to think consciously about weight in terms of stones and pounds at this time. By half-term I weighed seven stone nine pounds, and I suspect it was only then that I became weight-conscious in the literal sense.

During the first half of the term, my diary scarcely mentions food, apart from the occasional comment on the revolting nature of some too-frequently presented dish. This in itself is odd because in previous terms I had often (though not regularly) described meals in detail. As anyone who has ever been confined to a closed institution will know, meals are events: they are the landmarks in each repetitive day, often providing the only elements of novelty or surprise in an otherwise predictable routine. I think I didn't mention food in my diary during this period because I didn't want to mention my own eating habits. Maybe I was worried that someone else would read my diary, but if so this worry could only have been a slight one: I was much too careful to afford anyone the opportunity to snoop. It is more likely that the elements of secrecy and self-deception involved in my behaviour were already so strong that what I was actually doing couldn't be described in words at all, least of all in the incriminating written word. If I had used words, I should have had to think more carefully about what I was doing. I was, so to speak, keeping the secret even from myself. Having recently re-read my own, I have come to the conclusion that diaries furnish the perfect vehicle for self-deception and self-enhancement, provided that, in later years, the reader/writer is incapable of reading between the lines or unable to remember what has been left unsaid. I can remember exactly what I was doing and, out of context, my behaviour seems so harmless that the need for secrecy appears quite mysterious. I was refusing second helpings of food, asking unfailingly for small helpings, and skipping optional meals like tea or Sunday breakfast. It was what was going on in my mind that had to be kept secret, on pain of interference, on pain of ridicule, on pain of punishment and, inevitably, on pain of self-understanding. It was this: the less I eat, the more I am getting away with.

O levels began ten days after the half-term weighing session, and if anyone noticed the drop in my weight, I suppose they attributed it to anxiety over the forthcoming examinations. In fact I wasn't particularly anxious, although my diary is full of the usual teenage moans and groans about the impossibility of absorbing any more information, and the exams themselves are described as 'foul', 'really foul', or, at best, 'not very nice'. I knew very well that I was going to pass them all. And my new-found confidence was not unconnected with my weight loss. I had already achieved something; I had already proved to myself that I was capable of independent achievement. This discovery made it all the more important to me to maintain my behaviour and to maintain it in secret. I told myself that my intention was maintenance of the status quo, but this was at best a half-truth. The truth was that I didn't know how to effect such an aim, and if I found myself eating any more than the minimum – that is, enough for me to remain undetected by the authorities – I considered myself guilty of backsliding, and had to punish myself by eating even less the next day or at the next meal.

After O levels there was still a month of term to go, a month in which I had ample time to devote myself to my obsession. Although I read a great deal, and wrote a great deal, mealtimes were still what kept me going. But whereas before mealtimes had implied some sort of positive interest in eating, their purpose now was the active avoidance of eating, the opportunity to prove to myself that I was still achieving, still winning. I would now ask for very small helpings, eat perhaps a mouthful, and then smear the rest of the food all over the plate, hiding the residue underneath an upturned fork. My diary records such incidents as, 'Had to eat another roll at breakfast, much to my disgust,' or 'M. insisted that I eat another piece of toast, so I walked out in disgust.' (It should be noted that the word 'disgust' is being used in both cases with literal force.) I was becoming more upfront, and not just as far as food was concerned. Instead of withdrawing and being generally anti-social, as I had been, I began to argue with people – teachers and pupils alike – and to disrupt other people's activities for the sake of disruption. Having lost weight, I was beginning to 'throw my weight around'. My diary is full of diatribes against the childishness, laziness, conceit, or inefficiency of others. I had emerged from apathy into active aggression, and my housemistress's report for the term includes the advice, 'Sheila must learn to curb her natural exuberance.' I went home for the summer holidays weighing seven stone six pounds. And at the beginning of the following term I wrote in huge letters on the front of my rough book (regularly inspected by the housemistress), 'Exuberance is beauty'.

So my resolve had not weakened during the holidays. I had spent some time on a camping/cycling holiday with my family in the West Country. I didn't enjoy it, but for me there was one advantage: there were no regular meals, and so no one noticed how much or how little anyone else ate. We shopped in village stores as we went along, and my diary lists items of food bought rather than consumed. At the beginning of the holidays I spent a week with a schoolfriend in London, and towards the end another week with another friend in Bedford. During those two periods my diary makes no mention of food, and I assume I must have eaten more or less normally. During the time I spent at home I seem to have eaten nothing but apples and, if I am to be believed, an inordinate number of them. Only the entry for 15 August reveals some alleviation of my anorexic anxieties in a reaction which is, at the same time, typically anorexic: 'O level results came today. Have passed them all, thank goodness. Cooked huge meal to celebrate. Ate masses.' Because there are no expressions of regret afterwards, I assume I felt entitled to some sort of reward. But for the last two weeks of the holidays I was continually feeling 'sick' and 'shaky', and went back to school, weighing seven stone one pound.

This time – at last – someone must have noticed what was happening to me. The entry for a week later reads: 'Had to go to Hospice. Dr ordered no games, extra rest, milk, butter, cream!! Nothing wrong with me at all really! The housemistress even presented me with a glass of milk at lunch. Ugh! . . . Had to have butter at supper, which I refused to eat. I don't see why I should, if I feel all right . . . Matron said I had to go to bed early for a fortnight. This place is so depressing!' The battle was on, and was to continue for another year. The school authorities decided that my diet was to be strictly supervised, and that I should be weighed every week. At first it was easy enough to evade supervision, and my weight remained stable for several weeks. But at the end of October, a diary entry reads: 'Was weighed and have gained 2 lbs – am now 7 st, 3 lbs! Went to see Dr and was on Gym for 1st time this term. Had to play games too, and felt dead. I wish I were. I hate this place!' I felt I was beginning to lose the battle, and the diary for the remainder of the term is full of expressions of hatred for the school, interspersed with the repeated and heartfelt question, 'Why can't they leave me alone?' By the time I went home for Christmas, I had gained another pound.

Whether or not the school communicated any concern for my health to my parents I don't know. I don't remember that the question was ever discussed at home. My diary for the holidays is, as usual, almost blank, but contains several references to having overeaten and then feeling sick, which served me right. Nevertheless, I went back to school having lost four pounds. I now weighed seven stone, the lowest figure I had yet attained. The general reaction was, 'Anyone who can actually lose weight over Christmas must be ill.' But the doctor could find nothing physically wrong with me, and the notion of seeking psychiatric help doesn't seem to have arisen. I was put back on the diet designed to 'build me up'. This time the supervision was stricter, and it became more difficult for me to pass my butter ration on to someone else, to pour Ovaltine down the sink behind the matron's back, or to dispose of extra food by means of the lavatory. But I had also become more cunning. I think it was about this time (I can't tell exactly because my diary makes no reference at any point to the practice) that I discovered purging. How this happened, I don't remember, but I suppose it was a case of a desperate situation demanding a desperate remedy. I soon found out that if I swigged a mouthful or two of the laxative Cascara Sagrada from the medicine cupboard, I could get rid of the obnoxious feeling of weight and fullness which had been forced on me. The sinking stomach pains which heralded this loss were always welcome to me, and afterwards I would feel triumphantly clean.

It must have bewildered the matron, who watched practically every mouthful I ate, that by the end of term I had lost another two pounds. The diary entries for the Easter holidays are even sparser than usual, but when I went back to school I had lost yet another two pounds. This time the diary entry reads: 'Weighing. 6 st, 9 lbs. It's awful. I must go up.' But of course I didn't think it was awful at all, and was in fact extremely pleased with myself. I pretended to be as puzzled as everyone else was about the nature of my 'mysterious illness'.

Meanwhile I continued the strategy I had been following for the previous two terms: feigning compliance with the authorities and responding cooperatively to their apparent concern, while continuing to eat minimally and to purge in secret. By the end of the summer term I weighed six stone one pound.

Two facts emerge immediately from this resumé. The first is that I felt my battle to be with authority, whether in the form of teachers, matrons, parents, or even nature itself. The second is that, up until this point, I was winning. It seems to me that anorexia nervosa acts as a metaphor for all the problems of adolescence. But instead of meeting each problem separately and assessing it for what it is, the anorexic thinks she has a master plan, designed to solve them all at one stroke. She is convinced that it works; it can't fail. It is like a dream come true. It is euphoria.

When I first came across Szasz's dictum, 'Mental illness is a self-enhancing deception, self-promoting strategy,' I considered it to be a harsh judgement on a suffering fellow creature. But when I substituted 'anorexia nervosa' for 'mental illness' I could see the truth in what Szasz was saying, and realize at the same time that his judgement was not so harsh. After all, if the self is felt to be nothing, any strategy adopted to enhance or promote it, desperate though it may be, is a step towards what most of us would consider to be health, and an action necessary for survival. The anorexic's skinny body proclaims, 'I have won; I am someone now.'

But thinness, as opposed to slimness, also carries connotations of weightlessness and emptiness. The subtext to be read in that skinny body is, 'I am weightless/worthless; I am empty/ nobody. This is what my behaviour is all about.' The strategy works by means of paradox, a paradox which has ultimately to be resolved through some sort of fusion between the apparent text and the subtext. But in the first, euphoric phase of the disease, only the apparent text is granted recognition by the anorexic.

I have said that the anorexic starts from a position of helplessness and hopelessness, and I have tried to demonstrate that this was so in my case. As my weight decreased, so did my helplessness. Anorexia provided me with the illusion that I was in control, not only of my body and my own status within the community, but of that community itself and, finally, of the biological processes which others around me were powerless to influence. In short, I became convinced of my own omnipotence. The conviction started from my body and the discovery that no one could prevent me – if I were determined enough – from treating it as I wished. I had discovered an area of my life over which others had no control. And although the subtext of my increasing thinness (which I chose to ignore) read, 'I am doing this because I feel so helpless that not even my own body belongs to me,' the apparent text read to me, and increasingly to others, 'My body is my own and I can do what I like with it.' At first I was exhilarated to be able to make such a statement. I had considered my body to be lumpy, untidy, anomalous, and entirely unsuited to the person within. My behaviour had accordingly been unstructured: I was lazy, untidy, uncommunicative, forgetful, and generally inefficient. But when I managed to convert my body into something trim and neat, my personality changed too. I became lively, hard-working, and so well-organized that I found inefficiency in others deplorable.

My diary, in my pre-anorexic days, often refers to a 'weight of depression' which I felt myself to be carrying around. Once I became anorexic, that weight vanished with my flesh. My step lightened, I was full of energetic high spirits, and during the summer term I even became keen on playing tennis, which I would practise with the assiduousness I had formerly devoted to the piano. At night I would often get up and go for long walks in the school grounds, especially when the moon was full and I felt particularly restless, enjoying the silence and solitude of the woods. I don't remember ever being afraid, and I would boast of my nocturnal activities to a few close friends, who were duly impressed. As far as the physical aspect of this sort of behaviour is concerned, the apparent text read, 'My body is strong and healthy, super-healthy, despite your insistence that I am ill.' But, as Bruch has pointed out, anorexics tend to deny fatigue, and my diary is full of complaints such as, 'felt dead tired'. So the subtext of my behaviour could be interpreted as, 'I feel weak and tired, but I'm damned if I'm going to admit it, because that would only prove you right.' Far from making any such admission, I became more and more fanatically energetic as the disease progressed.

If my body was now trim and neat, redeemed from the excrescences of flesh, it was also clean. When I reached six and a half stone or so, my periods stopped. I mentioned this to no one for two practical reasons: one was that I loathed swimming, and if I pretended that I was still menstruating, signing the little red book every four weeks, I should be able to evade an unpleasant experience for at least one week out of four; the other was that I feared further reprisals might be taken against me. It was easy enough to deposit the unused sanitary towels in the school dustbins during my nocturnal wanderings. But the main reason for my silence was that secrecy and deception had by then become second nature to me. I didn't want my periods to start again. That I had managed to stop them was a major achievement on my part. Instead of growing up, I had, as it were, grown down, and thus reversed a natural biological process. I was no longer a woman. I was what I wanted to be: a girl. I was what I felt unconsciously I had never had a chance to be: a little girl.

I rejected womanhood, not because I preferred manhood, but because I preferred girlhood. At the time my idea of manhood was personified as someone who had to work hard at a job he hated in order to support not only himself, but other people whose very existence he resented; someone who was forever having to make difficult decisions and take frightening initiatives, both of which ended in frustration; and someone who might be called upon to fight in wars (National Service was then still in operation) and kill people. This was not an attractive proposition, but my idea of womanhood was hardly preferable.

In her attempt to ascertain why anorexia nervosa is a girls' rather than a boys' disease, Selvini Palazzoli emphasizes the manner in which the adolescent girl 'is exposed to lewd looks, subjected to menstruation, about to be penetrated in sexual embraces, to be invaded by the foetus, to be suckled by a child, etc.'. I find this emphasis generally correct in that it describes what the anorexic girl believes to lie in store for her as a woman: a passive role, a position of helplessness, a loss of self. It is what she has experienced already, but with the addition of responsibility, pain, and bodily suffering exemplified in the bearing of children and the shedding of blood.

When I was anorexic I had only dim feelings of resentment as to how my body was destined to be used, and the thought of anything as positive and specific as penetration never entered my mind. Incredible as it may seem, I never thought about sex at all, and didn't even masturbate: starvation reduces libido. However, I now see my very sexlessness as a flight from sexuality, and mainly *my own* sexuality. I think I was afraid that, once I recognized it, it too might get out of control – just like my body in general. On the conscious level, sexuality was to me only one of the responsibilities of adulthood: as far as the sexual act itself was concerned, I simply didn't want to know, as a child who is exposed to sexual information at an age when she/he feels incapable of absorbing it will not want to know. And I use the word 'responsibilities' rather than 'pleasures' because whereas no one had ever discussed with me the possible pleasures of sexuality, the responsibilities of adulthood had been habitually stressed, both at home and at school. With the weight of my flesh, I had also shed the weight of responsibility.

It seemed to me obvious at the time that to be a child was safer and easier than to be adult and that, specifically, to be a girl was safer and easier than to be a woman. As far as I was concerned there were two types of women, the true type and the failed type. The true type, as personified by my own and other mothers, was destined to bear child after child, some of whom could be miscarried, some of whom could die, and all of whom were a perpetual source of worry and expense. This true type, having found her man, was forced to accept that biology was indeed destiny. But I couldn't accept any such thing. The failed type of woman, as personified by most of the teachers at school, had been unable to find a man. All the same, they were no freer, no happier, than the true type. It was generally assumed among the pupils that our teachers, being women, would have preferred to be fully sexual, childbearing beings. But instead they were 'dried-up old spinsters', miserable biological failures. At that stage in my life I couldn't take any kind of failure, and so this latter model of womanhood was as unacceptable to me as the former. I think too that because I had postponed rather than rejected sexuality, the latter model was even less acceptable. But, for the time being, the rejection of womanhood had to be complete.

When I looked in the mirror and told myself, first, 'That can't be me,' and later, 'That won't be me,' what I was seeing was a woman. In my rejection of the image I saw I was making a statement, the apparent text of which read, 'I don't want to look like (be) that.' And I think I was right to make the equation between 'look like' and 'be' because a woman *is* what she looks like. That she is so is essentially an untruth, but it is at the same time a socially undeniable fact, even today, although it was probably a more widespread one twenty-odd years ago. It is also a fact which should be given careful consideration in the attempt to determine why it is that girls rather than boys tend to become anorexic. When a man looks in the mirror, he can tell himself, 'You may be an ugly old devil, but you're brilliant/successful/ virile.' When a woman looks in the mirror, she sees the totality of her being: because of the social brainwashing to which she has been subjected, the mirror seems to tell her more than it can tell a man. And so my subtext read, in part, 'I can't cope with this; I'm not going to be any good at it.' The flight from womanhood was linked with the flight from failure, the fear of which had practically been bred into me.

Thus far the subtext had a certain logic, but fear (or, rather, anxiety) can lead to panic, and the second part could have been expressed as, 'I don't want to be a woman because I would rather be myself.' On the face of it, this was an illogical statement, but by becoming anorexic I refuted logic. When I eventually weighed under six stone and looked at myself in the mirror (which, in common with other anorexics, I did a great deal) I saw someone beautiful: I saw myself. No matter what anyone else thought or said, I was beautiful: I was myself. The clearer the outline of my skeleton became, the more I felt my true self to be emerging, like a nude statue being gradually hewn from some amorphous block of stone. This is the distortion of perception referred to by Bruch, but I must add that in my case I see it less as a long-standing perceptual difficulty than as a consequence of my general state of confusion as to my self-image. To see my starved self as beautiful was to dissipate a large part of this confusion: I was, literally and metaphorically, in perfect shape.

The distortion of perception extended itself to areas other than my body. Having disposed alike of unwanted flesh and unwanted menstruation, I had become pure and clean, and therefore superior to those around me. I was so superior that I considered myself to be virtually beyond criticism. The intellectual form of superiority was the one most accessible to me both at home and at school. At home it was a simple matter for me to parade my learning in front of my sisters, stressing my more advanced academic achievements at every possible opportunity, and remaining quite oblivious to their assessment of me as an insufferable little prig. My attitude to my mother was similar: I would feign amazement at her ignorance of the intricacies of the Punic Wars, while at the same time snobbishly correcting her pronunciation or her misapprehensions of social niceties.

With my father I had more difficulty: all I could do with him was to argue about literature, citing my teachers' opinions as being more up-to-date and therefore more valid than his own. At school I worked hard, spending most of my time in the library. Anything less than a straight A disappointed me, and even when I had clearly gained the best grade in the class – a slightly alleviating factor – I still told myself that it wasn't good enough. My reading was not confined strictly to the syllabus, and my book-list for the period shows that I was prepared to read around it. As I remember, I was even readier to advance in

class the theories of, for instance, F. L. Lucas on the decline of
the Romantic ideal, or E. M. Y. Tillyard on poetry direct and
oblique, while suspecting that none of the other girls (or perhaps even the teachers) had read the books in question. People
were impressed – maybe too easily. I didn't fully understand
everything I read, and although the apparent text of my behaviour was, 'Look at me – how learned and knowledgeable I am,'
the subtext was something more like, 'I'm trying frantically
hard to learn and to understand, despite my stupidity. Give me
some credit. Tell me I'm not so stupid.' The book-list also
shows that I read Virginia Woolf, Aldous Huxley, Samuel
Butler, Maxim Gorki, Henry James, Samuel Beckett, and so on.
I have always been a quick reader and my capacity, not to say
my voracity, was generally admired. I felt good. But perhaps I
was as oblivious at school as I was at home to the sneers or the
impatience of others. At the euphoric level of the disease, the
anorexic perceives only what she wants (needs) to perceive.
Anything else would only threaten her hard-won sense of
unique achievement.

From this stage I proceeded to a more general sense of superiority, which can only be described as moral. At school I would
follow certain rules in an ostentatious manner (while breaking
others in secret) and become severe, even morally censorious,
towards those who lapsed from my hypocritically high standards. Most of these rules, I should point out, were petty, auto-
matic ones relating to punctuality or tidiness and can generally
be described as 'going by the book'. At home I 'rationalized'
(the word used in my diary) the kitchen cupboards, according
to a system in which items most frequently used were most
accessible, and vice versa. I cleared out the forgotten corners
which exist in every family home, sending old clothes to jumble
sales, and asking boy scouts to collect useless piles of old newspapers and magazines. I tried to take over the kitchen, but in
this I was thwarted by my father who had his own ideas about
food, and who would keep interfering and making a mess,
whereas I preferred to clear away and wash up as I went along.
Whenever I did succeed in preparing a family meal, I insisted
that everyone eat whatever was placed on her/his plate. Serving

large helpings, I ate nothing myself and my abstinence was only
another proof of my moral superiority. The apparent text of my
behaviour, openly declared, read, 'I'm superhuman. I don't need
food,' and the subtext, admitted only to myself and ignored as
far as possible, read, 'I'm starving.' Similarly, the apparent text
of my obsessive orderliness read, 'Form and order make for efficiency, and efficiency makes for a well-structured, meaningful
life,' while the subtext read, 'Unless I impose some form and
order on life, I shall lose control, chaos will ensue, and life will
become meaningless.' My twin obsessions were food and order.

It is at this point that the analogy between anorexia nervosa
and hysteria, which Freud saw as separate from and possibly
opposed to the obsessional neuroses, seems to break down,
along with Dally's separation of the two as different forms of
the disease. Both terms may be outmoded by now, but I think
that in view of what I have already said about gender confusion
and gender avoidance in my own case, they may not be entirely
unhelpful. In Freudian terms, I had taken upon myself the
typically female neurosis of hysteria along with the typically
male one of obsessiveness. Nevertheless, it is Adler rather than
Freud who sums up for me what was happening at this stage of
the disease. Delineating his theory of retreat into illness as a
means of obtaining power, he wrote, 'Every neurosis must be
understood as an attempt to free oneself from a feeling of infe-
riority in order to gain a feeling of superiority.' Although I
denied being ill and scorned to make the demands for attention
usually employed by invalids or malingerers, there is no doubt
that I was by this time making a bid for power. The sense of
superiority I gained was essentially related to control and, eventually, to the triumph of the will. The apparent text of superiority read, 'I am in control. I can influence events and people. I
am all-powerful. My will is supreme.' But the subtext, wilfully
suppressed, read, 'I'm terrified that I have no control over
events, over other people, over myself. Everything is arbitrary
and therefore meaningless.'

It amazes me now how little of this subtext was legible to
those around me. I suspect that my parents simply took my
word and my active behaviour as proofs of my essential health,

and that my non-eating was something I would grow out of and could therefore be ignored. The possibility that I might starve myself to death was never raised: instead I was scolded for looking like a scarecrow, and my mother told me that she was ashamed to be seen with me. At school I was told by the matron that I would die if I continued to lose weight. I didn't believe her: my sense of superiority had extended itself to include a conviction of my own immortality. But I humoured her, agreeing that she and I should cooperate in order to save my life. Thus I deceived her into thinking that she had scared me, and that I would take the necessary steps to ward off fatality. Outwardly it must have seemed that I had overcome my emotional difficulties and, apart from the mysterious phenomenon of my continuing thinness, had become a bright, helpful, well-adjusted member of the school. I told myself that I was happy, that I was free at last. In a way I was happy: I had achieved something, I was winning for the first time in my life, and I had a strong sense of myself as a differentiated individual. But the combined subtext of my behaviour showed that this was far from being the whole truth about my psychic state.

As for being free – to be in thrall to a ruling obsession is hardly to exist in a state of freedom. I thought I was doing what I, and I alone, wanted to do, but my pursuit of academic superiority shows that I was still striving to be the person my parents wanted me to be. And my excessively tidy and authoritarian behaviour shows that I was striving to be the person the school wanted me to be. Up to a certain point I was succeeding in both roles, driven as I was towards success by anxiety and the fear of failure. In reality, I was back where I had started – in a position of helplessness and hopelessness – but with one important exception. I now had something I could call my own: my disease, my unique neurosis, which I perceived as my thinness. The connection with neurosis was not unconscious, nor yet fully conscious in the sense that I could have expressed it verbally, but it was, in being unique, all-pervasive. Perhaps this may help to explain the determination of the anorexic to go on starving herself: without anorexia, I should have been nothing. I know that I had no intention of stopping the procedure, whatever anyone said or did to influence me. I was determined never to give in.

Margaret Drabble
Umbrella of Darkness

When I was a child of nine or ten years old, I was so depressed that I used to wish I could die in my sleep. I remember going to bed saying to myself, 'Enough of that, enough of that,' and wishing I might never wake again. In the morning I would surface to such anxiety, darkness, and oppression that I could hardly believe I could endure the day. And what was all this about, what was it *for*?

There was nothing in my external circumstances to inspire such precocious suffering. I was the second child of a middle-class family in suburban Sheffield, attending a nice Junior School for Girls, and I think I had some friends. Outwardly, my life was normal enough. I worked hard at my lessons, I read a lot of books. I went riding on Friday afternoons, I ate and slept. My only noticeable oddity was a severe stammer, but I didn't cope with this too badly. I was an ordinary skinny little girl with pigtails and wrinkled ankle socks. But over me hung this black cloud, this umbrella of darkness.

I recall that I had convinced myself that I had committed what I called 'the sin against the Holy Ghost'. I didn't know what this was, but I had heard or read somewhere that it was unpardonable, and therefore I was convinced that I had committed it. We were not a religious family. My mother was a professed atheist and my father was a half-hearted member of the Church of England who eventually became a Quaker, partly because he couldn't bring himself to believe in the Resurrection of the Body. So hell-fire was not a threat that dangled over us. Where and why I picked up this particular fear I still don't know. In early adult life I came to believe it was connected with sexual guilt (masturbation, or some forgotten or repressed trauma), but now I'm not so sure.

Whatever the cause, the effect was real. I moped, I wept, lumps of my hair dropped out. My parents could see I was

miserable: my mother's view was that I was paying the price for
my overdeveloped 'intelligence', that I would always be 'sensitive' and 'vulnerable', and that I'd have to put up with it until
my real life matched my inner aspirations. My father was more
practical. I remember one dreadful interminable afternoon he
said to me, 'Why don't you go to the cinema down the road and
see *The Count of Monte Cristo*?' I looked at him, full of
reproach. How could *that* help? 'Go,' he said, 'go. It will take
you out of yourself.' So I went, and it did. I had two hours of
relief. And gradually, through such strategies, I began to learn
to trick myself out of depression; I began to learn to deceive my
own worse self. I can still do it. I am really very good at it now.
Sometimes months go by and I forget that I have ever been
depressed.

My parents were sensitive to my misery, as they were both
depressives themselves. But they might easily never have
noticed. Parents and teachers don't notice that anything is
wrong, until extreme symptoms – bouts of weeping, bed wetting, night fears, school refusal, unnatural silence, and withdrawal – draw attention to some deep-seated problem. We tend
to think of childhood as a happy time, the best days of our lives,
a time of hope and play and fun and irresponsibility: we notice
the intense griefs of childhood but expect them to be as short-
lived as the pain of a bruised knee. Children are forever falling
off bicycles and banging their heads or howling over bleeding
elbows or broken toys or refused treats, and we expect them to
recover and forget.

When I had my first child, in 1961, at the age of twenty-one,
I knew a bit about English Literature and nothing at all about
children. I worried myself sick about breastfeeding and weaning
and sterilizing bottles, I read my Dr Spock in tears whenever the
baby wouldn't eat or sleep, and I didn't know whether it was
good or bad to let him into our bed when he cried in the night.
I muddled through, on a mixture of Spock, instinct, and old
wives' tales, but I was acutely aware that a baby isn't a resilient
rubber toy but a person in the making, and that parents play a
lasting part in that making. Crisis came later when we discovered that he had a heart lesion: for years the threat of

illnesses, infections and operations hung over us, displacing normal anxieties about everyday disasters as my imagination leapt to the worst possible scenarios.

This experience resulted in my novel *The Millstone*, in which the heroine, Rosamund, makes a similar discovery. Her child, unlike mine, has to undergo heart surgery, and she hands the baby over confidently to the nurses. All goes well, but once the operation is over, Rosamund begins to worry about the future:

> It was only when I got home that I began to be preoccupied by certain details . . . What would Octavia think when she woke up in hospital? Would she be in terrible pain? Would they feed her properly? Would she cry? Earlier it had seemed presumptuous to have considered these questions, but now their importance swelled minute by minute in my mind . . . Lord knows what incommunicable small terrors infants go through, unknown to all. We say they forget, because they have not the words to make us remember. We cannot stand the injustice of life, so we pretend that a baby can forget hours spent wrapped in newspaper on the floor of a telephone kiosk, the vicious blows of the only ones that might have loved it, the sight of its unsaved brothers in a blaze of oil stove flames.

Infants do suffer, in the mind as well as in the body. Looking back, it is clear to me now that my knowledge of this came not only from first-hand observation but also from reading of the discoveries of the pioneers of child psychotherapy, Anna Freud, Melanie Klein, Donald Winnicott, and Dr John Bowlby. All of these stressed the fears, terrors, and needs of very small children, and their work has resulted in general changes of attitude, as well as in the rescue of individual cases. Bowlby in particular was a great influence on my generation, and much of Rosamund's fear and eventual courage in *The Millstone* was Bowlby-inspired. He wrote of the emotional deprivations of children with no reliable mother or mother figure, and of the lasting damage caused by sudden, unexplained or prolonged separations.

We all want to be perfect parents, and find it hard to face the knowledge that, often for reasons quite beyond our control, we have not even been 'good enough' in a particular relationship or over a particular crisis. I remember my own mother saying to me, in her old age, recalling that dreadful period of guilt and terror which I suffered at the age of eight or nine, 'I failed you then. I couldn't comfort you at all.' It wasn't like her to admit failure, and I respected her for it, although late in the day.

One of the most common precipitating causes of depression in childhood is maternal depression. I heard a child psychotherapist describing this pattern, and suddenly the probable causes of my own childhood depression became blindingly clear: of course, I was depressed because my mother was depressed. This is the kind of thing one has always both known and not known. The two concepts would seem to be naturally linked. The child of a depressed parent feels protective, responsible, yet powerless: the infection takes before the child is old enough to develop resistance, and the depression is often linked to an unexpressed and inexpressible rage. The child has no strong person to kick against, it dare not even try to destroy the weak and depressed mother, so it takes the suffering upon itself. This seems an entirely convincing scenario. Back in 1936, Anna Freud observed that 'Maternal depression at any point during the first two years after birth may create a tendency to a similar depressive mood in the child.'

The child is father of the man. My mother was mother to my gloom. Babies are dangerous: they bring danger to their mothers, they receive danger from them. But despite the high-risk business of living, most children develop normally. Every baby is a new beginning, a new chance to break the old doomed pattern. We all hope that somehow our children will be freed of the worst of the family bad blood, and will take nothing on into the future with them but the good, the new, the hopeful. They have, after all, a new chance: a new set of genes with all the strengths and qualities of the partner that the Life Force chose for us. With any luck, they really will do better. This is why we smile when we see a new baby.

The parents of all depressed children have to cope with feelings of inadequacy and rejection – and as they are often themselves depressed, the cycle of misery continues, the sense of fail-ure is handed on like a baton. (Some families actually become *proud* of their gloomy heredity.) I have become a convert to intervention and an admirer of the patience and skills of the professionals. I know it can be argued that depression is creative, that it is the pearl in the oyster, that it makes great writers, great artists, great thinkers. But then I think of my mother, swallowing anti-depressants until her dying day, and greeting me as I took her morning tea in bed with a cloud of dark, black, infectious misery, and I think, No, that was not good, that was not creative, that was probably not even neces-sary. The suffering we depressives inflict on ourselves and oth-ers is in part avoidable, and we can do our best to make sure that our sour grapes don't set our children's teeth on edge.

III

Shrinks

WENDY COPE
Learning to Be Myself

I liked my new analyst from the first moment I set eyes on him. A balding, middle-aged American, dressed in a dark, baggy suit, he clearly had no interest whatever in being trendy. He seemed kind, honest, and trustworthy – a good man. Through all the battles that were to follow, I never seriously doubted that this was so.

It was just as well that I took to him, because the circumstances in which we began working together were far from ideal. The previous year, desperate for some help but unable to pay much out of my teacher's salary, I had applied to the London Clinic of Psychoanalysis, where the fees vary according to the patient's income. After a diagnostic interview, the clinic agreed to take me on. My condition was described, in a letter to my GP, as 'fairly severe chronic depression'. I had to wait a few months before I was assigned an analyst, but I felt better already, just to know there was hope.

Then came the false start. My first analyst was a trainee, working under supervision. After I had been seeing him for three months, he decided not to continue with his analytic work. Not my fault, I was assured repeatedly. There was concern at the clinic about the possible effect on me of losing my analyst, especially as my father had died less than two years earlier. I was designated a 'casualty' and given a more experienced analyst, the American, a classical Freudian. It was, I think, understood that he was taking on a difficult job.

To begin with I was well behaved. Still very much the obedient child, I was anxious to work out what the rules were, do everything right, and be the best patient ever. Five times a week I arrived punctually, lay on my back on the couch, did my best to free-associate, and avoided looking at the shrink. Somehow, in the course of my first analysis, I had formed the impression that you weren't supposed to say 'hello' or 'goodbye', so I didn't. I just shuffled in and out of the room with downcast eyes.

One day he commented on this. It was funny, he said, that I never looked at him. Didn't I ever feel like sitting up for a while or walking round the room? I was horrified. Certainly not. It was against the rules, wasn't it? Perhaps, he suggested, you should try it some time.

Weeks, maybe months, later, I did. I sat up and looked at him and nothing terrible happened. Next day, I didn't lie down at all. I sat there and chatted to him, just like a normal person, and I liked it. It was all much more friendly and relaxed. He let this go on for a few days before mentioning that maybe, now the barrier was broken, I should lie down for a bit and free-associate. I didn't feel like doing that.

'Is it a rule? Have I got to?' I said.

'Well, the general rule is that most of the time the patient should lie on the couch.'

'What if I don't? You can't make me.'

'Nope,' he replied, as neutrally as possible, 'I guess you'll just go on sitting up for a while.'

It was ages before I lay down again. Several times every session, he would say to me, 'You should lie down,' and I would smile gleefully. I was getting a real kick out of being bad.

Gradually I became more daring. Sometimes, instead of sitting on the couch, I would go and sit on a chair at the other side of the room. I took books out of his bookcase and read what was written on the flyleaves. I wandered around and had a look at what was on his desk.

The adult part of me was aware that he was maintaining a delicate balance between approval and disapproval. I knew that he knew that this disregard of 'the rules' was a good thing. If he'd been too benign, however, I might have felt the need to do something worse. There may have been times when he was genuinely worried that the analysis was becoming a bit too unconventional – I couldn't be sure. Occasionally I threatened to do something really bad, like taking all my clothes off or not paying the bill, but it never came to that.

What did eventually emerge, along with the innocent mischief, was a lifetime of repressed aggression. In my adolescence I had been afraid to fight with my parents, for fear of killing my elderly father. As I grew bolder, the poor old shrink copped the lot. From being an excessively nice, polite patient, reluctant to say the word 'bald' in case it hurt his feelings, I developed into a harpy, who hurled at him any and every insult that came to mind. Over the years I called him fat, old, boring, ridiculous, stupid, incompetent, a fascist, a philistine, a thick Yank who couldn't use the English language properly, and much, much more. I regularly accused him of wasting my time and money, completely failing to understand my problems, and ruining my life. By now an aspiring writer, I made a special song and dance about his ignorance of contemporary poetry, culminating in a spectacularly vicious outburst on the day I discovered he hadn't heard of Sylvia Plath. It was the final straw, I was never coming back, I was going to go to the clinic director and tell her he was useless and ask for a different analyst.

I don't, now, think it would have mattered all that much if he hadn't heard of Shakespeare either. What mattered was that I was learning, in a way that must sometimes have been very disconcerting for him, to be myself. In time, as well as finding out how to be horrible, I also learned to flirt with him and be seductive and, most difficult of all, to tell him I loved him. Towards the end of my analysis, the insults became a joke – the nastier the remark, the more it made us laugh. Nowadays, when I go back and see him, we both seem to be laughing all the time.

In the space available I have only been able to provide the merest glimpse of what went on over ten years. I still have problems, I still get depressed sometimes, I am still neurotic. But when people ask me, 'Did it work?' I answer 'Yes'. I am much happier than I could possibly have been without it.

1986

MARIE CARDINAL
The Words To Say It

The little cul-de-sac was badly paved, full of bumps and holes, bordered by narrow, partly ruined sidewalks. It worked its way like a finger between private houses of one or two storeys, pressing one against the other. The little street stopped at iron gates overgrown with scraggly vines.

The windows revealed no sign of life within. It might have been the country; nevertheless it was the heart of Paris, in the XIVth arrondissement. There were not the extremes of poverty or wealth here, only the petite bourgeoisie, hiding their valuables, their woollen socks even, in chinks, behind toothless shutters, rusted gutters, decrepit walls, the plaster flaking off in scales. Yet the windows were barred and the doors were solid.

This quiet corner of the city must have dated back fifty years, for there was a modernistic feeling in the mismatched architecture of the dwellings. Who lived here? Seeing these particular glass doors, door frames, these vestiges of decorative finish work, it could be said that some retired artists ended their careers behind these façades, hack painters, old opera singers, ancient virtuosos of the stage.

For seven years, three times a week, I travelled this little street on foot to the end, as far as the gate on the left. I know how the rain falls here, how the inhabitants protect themselves from the cold. I know how, in summer, a life which is almost rustic establishes itself with geraniums in pots and cats sleeping in the sun. I know how the days go in this cul-de-sac, and the nights, too. I know that it is always empty. It is empty even when a pedestrian hurries towards one of the entrances or a driver is pulling his car out of a garage.

I can no longer remember what time of day it was when I first entered the gate. Did I see only the abandoned state of the small gardens? Did I feel the gravel on the narrow path? Did I count the seven narrow steps to his door? Did I take in the fieldstone wall while waiting for the door to open?

I don't think so.

On the other hand, I saw the little dark-skinned man who gave me his hand. I saw that he was very slight, very formally dressed and very distant. I saw his black eyes, which were smooth as nail heads. I obeyed him when he asked me to wait in a room which he revealed by opening a curtain. It was a dining room done in the manner of Henri II in which the furniture – the table, chairs, buffet, and sideboard – invaded almost the entire space, impressing the newcomer, which I was, with its carved wood, sculpted with little gnomes and ivy, its contorted columns, its copper trays and Chinese pots. This ugliness was not important. What was important to me was the silence. I waited, on the watch, tense, until I heard the sound of the double doors opening to the right of the curtain – a space for two people – then the opening of the door in the vestibule, a voice murmuring: '*Au revoir, Docteur,*' no answer, and the door closing. Again, muffled movement in the direction of the front door; seconds later, the parquet creaking under the rug, the cold air coming in – a sign that the door remained ajar – then some incomprehensible noises. Finally, the curtain was lifted and the little man had me enter the office.

Here I am seated in a chair in front of his desk. He is leaning back in a black leather armchair to the side of the desk, so that I am forced to sit sideways to look at him. Against the wall facing me are shelves full of books, into which is fitted a brown sofa with a bolster and a little cushion. The doctor is waiting for me to speak.

'Doctor, I have been ill for a long time. I ran away from a private sanatorium to come to see you. I can't go on living this way.'

He showed me with his eyes that he listened attentively, that I could continue.

Prostrate as I was, withdrawn into my own universe, how to find the words which would flow between us? How to construct the bridge which would join the intense to the calm, the clear to the obscure, which could span this sewer, this river filled with decomposing matter, this treacherous current of fear, that separated the doctor and me, the others and me?

I was ashamed of what was going on inside of me, of this uproar, of this disorder, of this agitation; no one should look, no one should know, not even the doctor. I was ashamed of the madness. It seemed to me that any other form of life was preferable. I was sailing endlessly in extremely dangerous waters full of rapids, falls, wreckage, turbulence, while having to pretend that I was effortlessly gliding on a lake like a swan. The better to hide myself, I closed off all the orifices: my nose, my ears, my mouth, my vagina, my anus, the pores of my skin, my bladder. The better to block these openings, my body produced materials in abundance, certain of which thickening to the point of no longer being able to pass, creating a block, others of which, on the contrary, flowing without stopping, preventing anything from entering.

'Can you tell me about the treatment you have been under, specialists you have been to?'

'Yes.'

About that I was able to speak: I could enumerate the doctors and the remedies, I could tell about the blood, about its soft and tepid presence for more than three years between my thighs, the two curettages I had had to stop its flow.

The bleeding, with its variations in rate of flow, was familiar to me. This anomaly was reassuring because it was real, it could be measured or analysed. I loved to make it the centre of my illness. And really, could such constant losses not be frightening? What woman would not have been driven insane to see her own sap run? How could one not be exhausted by the surveillance without respite of this secret spring, nagging, observable, shameful? How to avoid using the blood to explain that I could no longer live with others? I had stained so many easy chairs, straight-back chairs, sofas, couches, carpets, beds! I had left behind me so many puddles, spots, spotlets, splashes, and droplets, in so many living rooms, dining rooms, anterooms, halls, swimming pools, buses, and other places. I could no longer go out.

How not to speak of my joy on the days when it seemed to dry up, only to show itself in its brownish traces, brownish, then ochre, then yellow? On those days when I wasn't ill, I was able to move about, to see, to get out of myself. The blood was finally going to creep back into its tender sac and stay there as before for twenty-three days. With this end in mind I used to try to exert myself as little as possible. I handled myself with the greatest possible precaution: not to hold the children in my arms, not to carry the groceries, not to stand too long before the stove, not to do the laundry, not to wash the windows. To move in slow motion, quietly, so that the blood would disappear, so it might stop its horrors, I would stretch out with my knitting, while watching over my three babies. Furtively, with a gesture of the arm, quick and adroit from habit, I went to check my condition. I knew how to do it in any position, so no one would notice it. Depending on the circumstances, my hand would slip down to my pubic hair, tough and curly, to find the warm, soft, moist place of my genitals, only to quickly take it away again. Or else it would slip just as easily up the valley between my buttocks and thighs, and suddenly plunge into the deep, round hole, only to quickly re-emerge. I would not look at my fingertips right away. I would withhold the surprise. And what if there was nothing there? Sometimes, there would be so little on it that I had to scratch hard with my thumbnail the skin of my index finger and my middle finger in order to produce an almost colourless sample of the secretion. A sort of joy would come over me: 'If I don't make even the smallest possible movement, it is going to stop completely.' I would be motionless, as if asleep, hoping with all my strength to become normal again, to be like others. Again and again I made those calculations at which women are so adept: 'If my period ends today, the next one will be on . . . Let's figure it out. Does this month have thirty days or thirty-one?' Lost in my calculations, in my joy, in my dreams, until that strong and precise caress, very secret, very tender, would surprise me with a clot carried along by the blood.

The dense, rushing lava, descending from a crater, invades the hollows, tumbling down, hot. And the heart was beginning to pound again and the anxiety returned, and the hope disappeared while I was running towards the bathroom. The blood already had the time to reach my knees, even my feet, flowing from me in thin streams of beautiful, vivid red. So many years spent in perpetual waiting, obsessed by the blood.

I had seen I don't know how many gynaecologists. I know exactly how to put my buttocks on the edge of the examining table, my legs outspread in the raised stirrups. The entrails offered open to the heat of the lamp, to the eyes of the doctor, to the fingers gloved in transparent rubber, to the beautiful yet frightening steel of the instruments. I would close my eyes or stare obstinately at the ceiling while being probed by the specialist. Raped.

All that – it seemed to me – vindicated my troubled mind, made it acceptable, less suspect. They wouldn't put a woman in an asylum just because she was bleeding and it terrified her. As long as I would only speak about the blood, only the blood would be seen, not what it masked.

So it was, that I was sitting near the doctor, in the calm of that baroque house, at the foot of the silent, dead-end street, gentle and obedient, as my blood ought to have been, in the hollow of my belly. I was unaware that this place and this man were the starting point of everything.

* * *

I must think back to find again the forgotten woman, more than forgotten, disintegrated. She walked, she talked, she slept. To think that these eyes saw, that these ears listened, that this skin felt, filled me with emotion. It is with my eyes, my ears, my skin, my heart that that woman lived. I look at my hands, the same hands, the same fingernails, the same ring. She and I. I am she. The mad one and I, we have begun a completely new life, full of expectations, a life which can no longer be bad. I protect her; she lavishes freedom and invention on me.

In order to tell about the journey, the birth, in effect, I have to remove myself from the mad one, to keep her at a distance, to split myself in two. I see the mad one hurrying in the street. I know the effort she makes to seem normal, to stop the fear behind a glance. I remember her as she used to stand, her head hunched between her shoulders, sad, at once absorbed by the growing agitation within and by the armour descending over her eyes, so nothing could be seen! Above all, not to fall in the street, not to be grabbed by the others, not to be taken to the hospital. She trembled to imagine she could no longer stifle the madness, whose swelling tide would one day breach the dikes and overflow, making her shudder and groan.

The route she travelled grew more curtailed. And then one day, she no longer went into the city. After that, she had to limit the space in which she moved within the house. The traps multiplied. In the final months before she was handed over to the doctors, she could live only in the bathroom, a sombre white-tiled room, barely lit by a window in the form of a half-moon fanlight cut out of the shutter and almost totally obstructed by the branches of a large pine tree which scraped against the window on windy days. A clean room smelling of antiseptic and soap. No dust in the corners. Her fingers slid across the tiles, as if on ice. No decomposition, no fermentation. Nothing but that material which doesn't rot, or else rots slowly so as to convey no idea of putrefaction.

It was between the bidet and the bathtub where she felt most secure when she could no longer master her internal functions. It was there where she hid while waiting for the pills to take effect. Curled up like a ball, heels against buttocks, arms holding the knees, strong, tight against the chest, nails dug so deep into the palms of her hands they eventually pierced the skin, her head rocking back and forth or side to side, feeling so heavy, the blood and sweat was pouring out of her. The Thing, which on the inside was made of a monstrous crawling of images, sounds, and odours, projected in every way by a devastating pulse making all reasoning incoherent, all explanation absurd, all efforts to order tentative and useless, was revealed on the outside by violent shaking and nauseating sweat.

I think the first time I went to see the psychoanalyst was in the evening. Or was I still nostalgic for those late sessions at the foot of the dead-end street, sheltered from the cold, from the others, from the mad one, from the night? One of those sessions when I was aware of coming into the world? An opening up of the mind was making the pathway larger, more accessible, I understood. The mad one was no longer this woman who went to hide her trembling in the toilets of bistros, who bled on the sidewalks. The sick one who didn't want to be touched, to be looked at or to be spoken to. I began to accept her, to love her even.

In the beginning, I had come to the cul-de-sac with the idea of putting myself in the care of a doctor who would not hospitalize me. (I knew that psychoanalysts do not readily put their patients in the hospital.) I was afraid of being put away as I was afraid of the operation which would have removed my organs. I'd run away from a sanatorium to come here, but I thought it was too late and that I would have to return to the hospital. I thought it was inevitable, especially since the Thing had by then acquired the trappings of a hallucination. Moreover, I had decided against speaking of it to the doctor. I thought if I spoke of it, he would send me back there. In certain moments, the presence of a living eye, looking at me, really there, but existing only for me (that I knew), seemed to me to be the evidence of genuine insanity.

I was thirty years old. I was in good health. Yet I could be locked up for fifty years. But for my children, I might let myself go completely, stop fighting, perhaps, for the struggle against the Thing was exhausting. More and more, I was tempted by the medication that delivered me to a nothingness which was dull and sweet.

Ever since I was a little girl, I had said to myself: One day I'm going to have children. Full of new life and strong, they had come into the world, each one different from the other. They were growing up well. I loved their laughter, I loved to sing to them.

Then, disaster. The Thing had come back again and would no longer leave me. It absorbed me so completely that it had become my only preoccupation. There was a time when I believed I could live with the Thing, the way others live with only a missing eye or leg, with a stomach disorder or with kidney trouble. Certain drugs relegated the Thing to a corner from which it did not budge any more. I was able to listen, to speak, to get about. I could go out and take a walk with my children, do the shopping, make them desserts, and tell them stories which would make them laugh. Then the effects of the drugs wore off more quickly. So I took a double dose. Then a triple dose. And one day, I woke up a prisoner of the Thing. I saw innumerable doctors. The blood began to flow without stopping. My eyesight was growing weaker. I lived in darkness, everything becoming imprecise and dangerous. My head was hunched between my shoulders, my fists were clenched tight in a defensive posture. My pulse went up to 130 to 140 beats per minute, all day long. I believed that my rib cage was going to break, my heart was going to spring out, palpitating, for everyone to see. Its agitated rhythm exhausted me. It seemed to me that the others could hear, and I was ashamed.

I had acquired involuntary obsessions, two gestures which were repeated a thousand times a day: checking the flow of blood, and taking my pulse, furtively, so no one could see. I didn't want to hear anyone say, 'What is going on, you don't feel well?' My blood and my pulse were two barometers of my illness, two symptoms which could sometimes allow me to say, when I could no longer stand it: 'I am about to have a heart attack. I have cancer of the uterus.' And the waltz of the doctors would begin again. And death was ever more present with its putrid liquids, its disintegration, its worms, its gnawed bones.

Now I have it in mind to tell the story of my illness and am accorded the privilege of the supplicant to describe the awful images and painful sensations which procured for me the memory of past events. It seems to me that I am a director with his camera attached to the end of an immense arm, capable of descending to shoot close-ups and of drawing back in order to take in the action of the scene. So it is for this first visit I see Paris lit up at night in autumn (was it in autumn?) and, in Paris, the Alesia district, and in this district the dead end, and on the dead end the little house, and inside the little house the softly lit office where a man and a woman are speaking, and this woman, on a couch, curled up, like a foetus in the womb.

But at that time, I didn't know that I had hardly begun to be born again and that I was experiencing the first moments of a long period of gestation lasting seven years. Huge embryo of myself.

I'd told the doctor about the blood and the Thing which made my heart pound. I knew I wouldn't speak of the hallucination. I was going to speak of the last days in the hospital. Then I'd have told everything.

The doctor listened attentively, yet nothing in particular in my long recitation caused him to react. When I was through conjuring up the scenes of anguish in the bathroom, he asked me: 'What do you feel when apart from your physical malaise?'

'I'm afraid.'

'Afraid of what?'

'I'm afraid of everything, afraid of death.'

In truth, I didn't really know of what I was afraid ... I was afraid of death, but I was also afraid of life which contained death. I was afraid of the outside, but I was also afraid of the inside which is the opposite of outside. I was afraid of the others, but I was also afraid of myself who was other. I was afraid, afraid, afraid, fear, FEAR, FEAR. It was everything.

Fear had relegated me to the alienated of this world. My family, from which I had hardly emerged, had again secreted its cocoon around me, tighter, more and more opaque, as the illness progressed. Not only to protect me but also to protect themselves. Madness is unacceptable in a certain class; it must be hidden at any cost. Madness among the aristocracy or the lower classes is regarded as eccentricity or as a defect which can be explained. But in the newly powerful middle class, it is not admissible. When the madness comes from inbreeding or poverty, it may be understood. But when it comes out of a comfortable life where there is good health and that poise conferred by money decently earned, in such a case, it is a disgrace.

At the beginning they murmured to me, 'It is nothing, you are nervous. Rest, get enough exercise.' In the end it turned into an imperative: 'You are going to see the doctor. So-and-so is a friend of your uncle's and a great neurologist.' The great specialist friend had ordered a course of treatment 'under medical supervision'. They had reserved a room for me high up in my uncle's sanatorium.

A room was set up in the attic with a big bed, the walls covered in fabric depicting a restful country scene. The shepherdess with her sheep and crook, the gnarled tree with its trunk and olive leaves. Shepherdess, sheep, tree. Soothing repetition of a pattern. A screen covered in the same fabric hid a comfortable toilet with its white porcelain angles rounded, reassuringly. Opposite, a table and chair and a small dormer window opening on to a line of trembling poplars, apple trees planted four in a square, one at the centre, fields of grain stretching to the horizon.

Was the restful scene in my room at the hospital or at home? Was the restful scene on the fabric printed with large flowers with pulpy stems? Was there fabric on the walls, or was it painted a glossy blue? I no longer know how I got there or who drove me. I can recall the narrow wooden stairs leading up to the room. I can remember the proportions of the room and its furnishings, the window, the toilet.

I must have undressed, put on new pyjamas, gotten into the soft, freshly made bed, stretched out, allowing my blood pressure and pulse to be taken, delivering myself over to the medication. Meanwhile, I closed my eyes in order to continue my internal struggle as I was outwardly letting myself go: I had stretched my body out at full length, my arms resting on the taut sheets, my hands open. Outside, I was normal. Inside, I had to calm my heartbeat. They put on the arm band. I heard the quick puff of the ball they squeezed to inflate it, I felt it clasp me tighter and tighter, then I cringed a little from the contact with the cold metal disc placed in the crook of my arm. The doctor had insisted on taking my blood pressure, which was very low; they had taken it every four hours before giving me my pill. It was all the same to me if my blood pressure was so low. What I really cared about was my pulse, the insane beating of my heart. The procedure of taking my blood pressure gave me a little time to try to calm myself. They took off the arm band. Near me someone was moving.

Who was it? My uncle? The specialist friend? Someone else?

I don't know. At the time, I was so taken up with trying to control myself in the war against the Thing that my vision was warped. I felt I was going blind, I was navigating by radar. Some kind of instinct kept me from colliding into people and things.

Finally, I felt the ends of the four fingers pressing against the inside of my wrist. Four soft little balls. They had no need to grope. Scarcely had they touched the zone of my pulse than the blood, churned up by the Thing, made me fight them. Hardly had the fingers felt the beating of the heart when they amplified it and made it resound throughout every part of my body. Ninety, one hundred, one hundred ten, one hundred twenty, one hundred thirty, one hundred forty ... In vain I hid the Thing, in vain, I shut everything up in order not to let it out, though it knew very well how to reveal itself through my veins and my skin. The bastard, it was there, it made fun of me, it would not obey me, it was beating like a maniac against fingers which let go. Now they knew. Again, someone moved about, making small inoffensive bustling noises.

'You are going to take your pill now. Only a quarter of a pill, four times a day for a week. Then the dose will be increased. It will do you good.'

It was a woman who spoke, short, thin, with white hair. I saw in her eyes that she had taken in the message transmitted through the fingers. She knew.

I took the minuscule quarter pill and the glass of water she handed me, and I made it seem as if I were swallowing normally. There were weeks when I could no longer swallow the undiluted pills. My throat was so constricted, nothing would go down. I had the impression that I was suffocating whenever I tried to swallow. I closed my eyes and indicated by my attitude that everything was all right, I wished to rest. The small portion of the pill stuck in my throat. It was enormous, like a block. They went out.

Immediately I sprang towards the sink to spit it out, my fingers down my throat, provoking the spasms which would deliver me. Finally the little yellowish triangle came up, covered with phlegm, saliva, and ropy mucus. (Was the morsel of pill yellowish or pinkish? Was it the colour of a pearl?) I was sitting on the bidet, trembling from head to toe, my forehead against the cool, hard edge of the sink. Time had no meaning. I don't know how long I stayed there without moving. I remember taking out the tampon that stopped the blood, which I began to watch gently flowing, drop by drop, rocking back and forth, all the while knowing very well that at that same time I was rocking the Thing. The drops of blood flattened out and became slightly diluted in the moisture on the white porcelain, eventually making a narrow, winding path right to the drain. It was an activity to watch the blood work its way out of me; it had a life of its own now, it could discover the physics of earth-bound things, weight, density, speed, duration. It kept me company and at the same time was delivered over to the indifferent and incomprehensible laws of life.

The Thing had won. There was only it and me from now on. We were finally shut in alone with our secretions – blood, sweat, mucus, pus, saliva, and vomit. It had driven away my children, the animation in the street, the lights in the shop windows, the sea at noon when there are small waves, lilacs in bloom, laughter, the pleasure of dancing, the warmth of friends, the secret exaltation of study, long hours of reading, music, the arms of a loving man holding me, chocolate mousse, the joy of swimming in cool water. All I could do was curl up in the bathroom at the sanatorium, there where it was cleaner, trembling in my own sweat. I shivered so that the sound of my teeth chattering made an idiotic clatter like machinery.

Luckily, the steps of the little stairway creaked. At the slightest noise, I would go back to bed and lie down as usual. I didn't like the woman with white hair and I never spoke to her. She carried in my meals on a tray and gave me the pills after taking my blood pressure and my pulse. I couldn't eat. I threw what I could of it down the toilet, the rest I threw down into the gutter which ran along the edge of the tiled roof under my window. I do not remember whether the time was short or long, any more than I do the difference between night and day. I was a prisoner. I looked out the window to consider whether or not I would be killed if I jumped. Yes. There were four floors to the ground below. But the roof hid what was down there. Would I crash into the glass enclosure or into the shrubs? I did not want to kill myself in this way. Moreover, death made me afraid, while at the same time it held out the only means of getting rid of the Thing.

I don't know how many days had gone by when I was seized by a violent need to escape. More than a week in any event, since the morning (I'm sure it was in the morning) the woman had me take half a pill, and I remember very well that I was supposed to take a quarter of one for a week and then a half.

Suddenly, I realized that I was in my bed, lying on my back like other people, and that my face was showing. That surprised me: there were so many months when I could only live, whether awake or asleep, in the foetal position, my body hidden under the sheets. While at the same time as I verified this change, I felt a heaviness at the nape of my neck, as if the base of my skull was weighing me down and my brain was made of lead. Then it came to me that this heaviness, though well defined, had been there for some time. At the same time, I recognized that the Thing was not the same any more, agitated, breathless, weak; it had become thick, gelatinous, sticky. It was not so much the fear that inhabited me as the despair and the disgust. I didn't want any of it. I don't know what instinct made me prefer the exhausting struggle with the Thing when it was enraged to coexistence with it when enfeebled, sticking to me with nause-ating abandon.

In the course of the morning – my head more and more painful and heavy, buried in the pillow – I made a connection between my present condition and the pills. I was reminded of a conversation between the psychiatrist friend and my uncle. They spoke of a new treatment, of a 'chemical electroshock', difficult to control but promising much better results than the standard electric shock treatment. They held forth in front of me as if I were a piece of furniture. And the fact is that at that point, I had taken absolutely no interest in what they were say-ing. I thought simply that the door was shut. I was going to be locked up, which was as it should be since I was incapable of living like the others, incapable of bringing up children. I couldn't take it any more. I wanted them to deliver me from fear, from the Thing, whatever the cost.

However, on this particular morning in the sanatorium, I had figured out that the price was going to be enormous and that I did not want to pay it.

It was decided! I wasn't going to take any more of their disgusting pills. When the lady came I would pretend to swallow the pill and instead would spit it all out the window. In the gutter!

And that is what I did.

* * *

For the twelve o'clock medication, I was sitting up in bed. The nurse came in.

'Good morning.'

'Good morning. It looks as if you're feeling better today.'

'Yes, I feel better.'

The blood pressure, the pulse, the glass of water and the half a pill on a little tin tray. For several days, it was no longer worth the trouble to delay it. I swallowed normally. The half-moon wedged cleverly under my tongue against my teeth, while the water went down.

A smile, and she was gone. The pill in the gutter below.

Now it is afternoon. I am standing in the bathroom: 'It's a nice day.'

'Yes, it's a beautiful day,' the nurse said.

'I want to see my uncle, I feel like going out.'

'Take it easy, I don't think it's possible. Not in the middle of the treatment.'

'Could I see my uncle? I feel like reading.'

'Certainly.'

The blood pressure, the pulse, the pill down the gutter. Several minutes later my uncle appears: 'So it seems you're feeling better, you want to read! I brought you some magazines and detective stories.'

'I'd like to get a little exercise. Could I go for a walk on the grounds tomorrow?'

'I have to ask the doctor who's treating you.'

'Call him. I know it would do me good. I want to do it.'

'I'll call him; anyway, he's supposed to come and see you the day after tomorrow.'

'I'm not going to stay here all the time without moving. You know I'm feeling much better.'

A big smile. He is sitting at the foot of my bed. He hardly dares to look at me.

To give himself something to do, he studies my chart on which every day they put down my blood pressure, my pulse and the doses of medicine that have been given me. He knows it by heart. The nurse takes it down to him every morning.

'You look better. I'm really happy.'

* * *

'Your doctor has given his permission. You can go out for a walk tomorrow. He is very pleased that your condition is improving so rapidly. It seems this new treatment sometimes has the opposite effect on patients; it makes them listless, it gives them migraines. The nurse will go with you. Your aunt has asked if you would like to have dinner with us.'

'No, not tonight thanks. I've already had dinner and I'm going to sleep. I would rather tomorrow if the walk goes well. Thank her for me. She'll understand, won't she, if I don't come?'

'Of course. You know, she never doubted for a second you'd come out of it in a hurry. It is not in the nature of the family. You were too exhausted to want to raise your children alone. That is all. Her chief concern is for your mother, who is wild with anxiety. You know how fond they are of each other. They spend the whole day on the telephone. Your poor mother doesn't even have the energy to go out. The children exhaust her.'

'I'm going to feel better very soon. You must reassure her. It's not going to drag on.'

'You know, what I'm going to say about it . . . it is mostly for your mother's sake. The poor woman has been through enough, she deserves a rest . . . I am talking to you like a . . . grown-up. You're not going to make a mountain out of a molehill.'

'No. No. I understand what you're saying but I'm going to get over it, I know it. I really do feel like I'm getting better.'

'Goodnight, my grown-up.'

He kisses me on the forehead and leaves.

I don't want to think about my mother. I don't want to think about my children . . .

Then everything is confused. The Thing is taking hold of me with such ferocity. I don't think I am strong enough to fight it for very long without any drugs to help me, without anything; I am defenceless. And yet, I am getting past it.

I went out without the nurse. I ran in the fields (I try to remember if the wheat was high, but am unable to). I got my friend on the telephone: 'Promise me to come tomorrow at this time? At the junction of the main road and the little one, where there's a sign for the sanatorium, one kilometre before the village on the left.'

'You can count on me, I'll be there.'

In the evening, sitting in front of the TV between my uncle and my aunt, for I had decided I would go there after all, it seemed to me that we were in an enormous aquarium. They were the gentle fish peacefully feeding on seaweed and I was an octopus.

Above all my aim was not to provoke them, not to do anything to displease them, not a word, not a gesture.

I didn't know that I was never going to see them again. I knew only that I was about to deceive them and that it upset me. Especially these two, who were the most successful branch of the family. In abandoning them, I was abandoning the Good. But that was the road I had decided on. Thinking about it, I had never been normal like them. I might just as well disappear and release them from having to deal with me.

The following day the car was there. We started up right away and I was able to let myself go, body trembling, teeth chattering.

'Are you sick? What do you want me to do?'

'Nothing, nothing. You can do nothing for me. Take me to

Michèle's. Don't worry, I'll get over it. Call the sanatorium later, tell them I am safe, that they mustn't look for me. But don't tell them where I am. I don't ever want to see them again.'

The next day I entered the cul-de-sac for the first time. Who called the doctor? Did I call him? Was it Michèle? I no longer know. She knew him and I had heard of him. I must have called him myself. (At Michèle's place, I got hold of some tranquillizers and managed to stifle the Thing.) I just don't know.

There, I had told it all.

I had wanted to talk about the blood and yet it was above all the Thing about which I had spoken. Was he going to send me away? I didn't dare look at him. I felt all right there, in that small space talking about myself. Was it a trap? The last of them? Perhaps I shouldn't have trusted him.

And then he said: 'You were right not to take those pills. They are very dangerous.'

My whole body relaxed. I felt profound gratitude towards this little man. Perhaps there was a path between myself and another. If only it were true. If only I could talk to someone who would really listen to me!

He continued: 'I think I can help you. If you agree, we can begin an analysis together starting tomorrow. You would come three times a week for three forty-five-minute sessions. But, should you agree to come here, it is my duty to warn you, on the one hand, of the risk that psychoanalysis may turn your whole life upside down, and, on the other hand, that you will have to stop taking all medication right now, whether for your haemorrhages or for your nervous system. Not even aspirin, nothing. Finally, you must know that an analysis lasts at least three years and that it will be expensive. I'm going to charge you forty francs a session, that is to say one hundred twenty francs a week.'

His manner of speaking was serious and I felt he wanted me to listen to him and to think about what he was saying. For the first time in a long time someone was addressing me as if I were a normal person. And for the first time in a long while I was behaving like a person capable of assuming responsibilities.

Then I understood that little by little they had taken all these responsibilities away from me. I was no longer a nothing. I began to think about this situation and about what he had just said. How could my life turned upside down be worse than it was? Perhaps I would get a divorce because it was from the time of my marriage that the Thing established itself inside me. Never mind, I'll get a divorce or I won't get a divorce. Besides this, I couldn't see what else could be changed in my life.

As for the money, that was more difficult; I didn't have any. I lived on the money my husband earned and what my parents gave me.

'I have no money, Doctor.'

'You will earn it. You will have to pay for your sessions with the money you have earned yourself. It is better that way.'

'But I can't go out, I can't work.'

'You'll manage. I can wait three months, six months until you find a position. We can arrange something. What I want is for you to know that you will have to pay me and that it will be expensive. The sessions you miss will be paid for the same as the others. If it doesn't cost you one way or another, you won't take the analysis seriously. This is common knowledge.'

His tone of voice was dry enough, as though he was someone involved in a business transaction. Not any commiseration in his voice, nothing of the doctor or the father. I didn't know that in agreeing to begin immediately, he was taking three more hours a week out of his own life which was already invaded by his patients. He made no allusion to the additional fatigue or to the fact that he was making an exception because he saw how ill I was. Not a word of it; on the contrary. On the face of it, it was a simple bargain. He was taking a risk, he was allowing me to choose. And yet, he knew that but for him, there were only two solutions for me: the psychiatric hospital or suicide.

'I agree, Doctor. I don't know how I can manage to pay you, but I agree.'

'Very well, we'll begin tomorrow.'

He took out a little notebook and he showed me the days and the hours when I had to come.

'And what if I haemorrhage?'

'Do nothing.'

'But they already put me in the hospital for this, they gave me transfusions, curettages.'

'I know it. Do nothing, I will expect you tomorrow . . . There is one thing I want to ask you, however: try not to pay attention to what you know of psychoanalysis; try to avoid any reference to this knowledge; find equivalents for the words in the psycho-analytic vocabulary which you have learned. Everything you know can only hold you back.'

It was true that I believed that I knew everything about intro-spection and that, in the core of my being, I felt this treatment would have no more effect on me than cauterizing a wooden leg.

'But, Doctor, what is the matter with me?'

He made a vague gesture of the hand, as if to say: 'What use is diagnosis?'

'You are tired, troubled. I believe that I can help you.' He took me to the door. 'Goodbye, Madame, I will see you to-morrow.'

'Goodbye, Doctor.'

WILL SELF
Dave Too

'Perhaps . . .' Dr Klagfarten leaves this word dangling for a while – he likes to do that, 'perhaps the blackbird is the real object of your sympathy. After all, it cannot leave the room, whereas you can.'

'Perhaps.' I don't leave the word dangling. I leave it crashing, falling to the floor between us, the iterative equivalent of a wildebeest, shot in slo-mo, after being shot with a high-velocity rifle bullet, and collapsing in undulations of muscle and dust, crumpling on to the hard, deathly ground.

Dr Klagfarten tries another tack. 'I'd like to see you again this afternoon, about another matter – you recall, I mentioned it yesterday?' How typical of the man, that 'recall'.

'Yes, yes, of course.' I'm struggling to my feet. I sit facing Dr Klagfarten for these sessions, inhabiting a low armchair of fifties ilk, wooden arms, cushioned base underslung with rubber straps. Dr Klagfarten sits some way off, behind a white, wooden table which does service as his desk. He's a thin man, quite bald, with an expressive, sensitive face. His lips are alarmingly sensual for a middle-aged psychiatrist. He twists them constantly this way and that in a *moue* of intense, emotive contemplation. He's doing it now. Doing it as he says, rising from behind the table, 'Well, see you at three this afternoon then.' And I sort of hunch up, half turn on my way to the door and go 'Y'mf' by way of assent.

What does Dr Klagfarten want, in the midst of his carpeted enclave? That's what his consulting room is like – a carpeted enclave. A modern room, cream of wall, thick of pile. And that pile, after a session of curdling monologue, seems in danger of creeping up the walls, providing further insulation, further deadening. What does he want of me? To slide my hand beneath the curiously thick and defined lapel of his jacket? To caress the front of his shirt; unbutton it, bend, slide tongue and lips in; seek out a depressed, sweaty nipple? Is that what Dr Klagfarten wants?

I woke this morning with the radio burbling in my ear. If I'm alone – which I am more and more nowadays – I always sleep with it on, so that the World Service mixes with my dreams. So that I dream of a riot of headscarved Dr Klagfartens, stoning Israeli soldiers in the Gaza Strip. As I came to consciousness a politician was being interviewed. 'We have to make some terms for the long term,' he said, and then later he also said, 'I'm going to sit down and think about it – I think.' There's something about these broadcast contexts that does it to people, makes them repeat themselves. It's as if, halfway through their sentence, they lose some sense of what it is to be themselves, they flounder in the very moment of articulation, asking, 'Who am I? Who the fuck am I?' And the only answer that comes back is that they are the person who has just said 'actually' or 'term' or 'policy' or 'whatever', so they have to say it again. Are compelled to say it again.

Dr Klagfarten's consulting room is in the old administration building. It's a blocky thing of weeping concrete and square, green-tinted windows, which project out, as if the interior of the structure were swelling, slowly exploding. As I cross the car park I look over my shoulder, once. Dr Klagfarten stares down at me from his window. He lifts a hand and carefully swivels it at the wrist, suggesting the possibility of valediction. And as he does this a great gout of chemical smell, like air freshener, comes into the back of my throat. I gag, turn, walk on.

Dave is waiting for me in the café – as he said he would. He's a very tall, very jolly man, and I think of him as my closest friend. 'Howdy!' he cries as I come in through the door. The café is a long, tunnel-shaped room. Near the back a counter is set on the right, and on the very edge of this a Gaggia huffles and burbles, sending out little, local weather systems. Dave is under one of these clouds. 'Howdy!' he cries again. Maybe he thinks I haven't seen him, or maybe he's just reminding himself that he's Dave.

I can't blame him for that. It's such a common name, Dave. There are two other Daves who are usually in the café at this

time of the morning. Dave and I call them, respectively, Fat
Dave and Old Dave, by way of differentiating them both from
him and from each other. Fat Dave, who's the owner's rather
dim-witted brother, mans the Gaggia. He's a barrel of a being
with a bucket for a head. He wraps an apron around his
abdomen, ties it with a cord as tight as a ligature, and leaves his
big, white arms bare. These are constantly in motion, scooping,
twisting and pulling at the Gaggia. It looks as if he is deftly, but
without much feeling, making love to the coffee machine.

Old Dave is an altogether grimmer figure. He sits, face down
to his racing paper, a roll-up made from three strands of
tobacco stuck on his lower lip. He never says anything. We only
know his name because from time to time Fat Dave will refer to
him in passing, thus: 'Yairs, Dave there used to . . .' or 'Y'know
Dave over there, he could tell you a thing or two about . . .' It
seems that this is the fate of these two particular Daves. To be
caught, their sembled identities bookending the café, leaning
into one another's being.

My Dave is eating a full English breakfast. The eggs have
been turned so that a small skin of white has coagulated over
the yolk. It has the aspect of a cast over an eye. Dave looks up
at me as I sit down opposite him, smiles, then looks down,
spears the yolk with his fork, spears a bit of bacon with same,
tucks the whole, gnarled mass into his mouth. 'Yungf',' he says,
and then, 'have you seen her?' I sigh. 'No, yungf'-yungf', tell
me, have you?'

I shrug, unexpressively, 'Oh yeah. Oh yeah, I have.'

'And?' He's sawing at the fried bread.

'She understands . . . sort of. She, she accepts that maybe I
have to . . .' I can't bear to say this, it's so *trite*, 'have to . . . find
out who I really am. I feel so . . . well, you know, we've talked
about it. I feel so amorphous, so shapeless, so *incoherent*. I
don't feel as if I know myself any more. Especially after a morning like this, when I'm up early and talking to Dr Klagfarten
before I'm awake, before I've had an opportunity to, sort of,
boot up my identity, become who I really am –'

'Yes, yes, of course, I know what you mean entirely,' Dave
has set his knife and fork down, he's kneading one hand with

the other, he's completely engaged in the matter, abandoning himself to the discourse – perhaps that's why I like him so much. 'I sometimes feel the same way myself, exiguous, wavering, fundamentally peripheral –'

'And full of fancy words, ha!' We both laugh, our shared laugh, my wheezing giving a windy accompaniment to his percussive ho-ho-hos. And in the moment of this laugh I'm at one with Dave, I feel a real kinship with him. I feel he and I are essentially similar, that no matter what differences may arise between us, of belief, of intent, we will share the same basic character. It's only with Dave that I feel comfortable discussing Dr Klagfarten – or rather, discussing what Dr Klagfarten and I discuss.

It's odd, because I'm sensitive about the therapy, and sensitive about my relationship with Dr Klagfarten, who, far from being a distant or impersonal presence in my life, is actually well known in some of the circles I move in. But predictably, it was Dave who ran into him socially. He was at a party in Davyhulme given by some zoologists. According to Dave, Dr Klagfarten was very jolly, drank deep, and sang revolutionary songs in a fine, warm baritone, much to everyone's enjoyment. I find this clip of Dr Klagfarten at play difficult to reconcile with the benign severity he always evinces towards me. I even find it hard to imagine Dr Klagfarten as being anything but a shrink. How could anybody whisper lovers' endearments to him? What could they call him? Klaggy? Farty? The mind boggles.

Lovers' endearments. *Her* endearments. I don't feel I deserve them. Or perhaps worse – I don't quite believe they're directed at me. When Velma looks at me with what are meant to be loving eyes, I see too much comprehension, too much calculation. It's as if she were looking at my face in a spirit of having to do something with it, make it work.

I sign to Fat Dave that I want a double espresso, and turn back to Dave.

'I am going to see her – this afternoon.'

'I thought as much,' Dave bends back down to his breakfast, I am gifted a top view of his head, the island of grey-blond hair marooned on the apex of his skull, like a negative image of a monk's tonsure. 'I couldn't believe that you'd just let it ride, let her go out of your life.'

'No, it's true, but y'know, Dave, the same applies –'

'The same applies?'

'To her, to Velma. Even when I'm with her, and we've made love . . . Well, no, *especially* when we've made love, especially at that moment when I roll away from her, see her face blanched, emptied by orgasm, wrung out. Then I don't know who she is –'

'You don't know who you are –'

'That goes without saying, but I don't know who she is either. She . . . she could be *you* for all I know.'

'Double espresso?' says Fat Dave, holding the cup in front of me. Out of the corner of my eye I can see Old Dave light his roll-up with a lighter so buried in his calloused, chipped, yellowing fingers that the flame seems to issue directly from flesh. 'Double espresso?'

'Whassat?'

'Double espresso?' Fat Dave is still standing over me. Has he forgotten that it was I who placed the order, from this very seat, not three minutes ago? I scrutinize his face for traces of irony. I know that Fat Dave feels less fondness for me than he does for his namesake. But Fat Dave doesn't have the contrast control necessary to express irony – he's only looking *at* me.

'Yeah – that's mine.'

Dave observes all this with a wry smile puckering up his long, equine face. His visage is really a series of crescent shapes: long, droopy earlobes; large droopy eyes; cheeks nearing jowl; and straight lines, in the form of fine wrinkles, that experience, twiddling his knobs, has Etch-a-Sketched alongside the crescents. Dave's countenance, I realize for the first time with an access of minor dread, is composed entirely of Ds, letter Ds, Ds for 'Dave'. Dave is, in fact, initialled all over. Like some ambulatory stick of rock, he carries his ascription written on his body. Written *through* his body, for I feel certain that were I to excavate, dig into one of these fleshly Ds, I would find that it was bred in the bone.

My Dave is, I like to think, a kind of Ur-Dave, a primary

Dave. His Daveness, his Davidity, his Davitude, is unquestion-
able. In a world with so many Daves, Daves running, Daves
walking, and Daves standing, desolate, crumpled betting slips at
their feet, it's infinitely reassuring to feel that within my grasp
is some part of the essential Dave.

But that essential Dave is now talking, wheedling his way
back into my thoughts. I tune to this very Dave frequency:
'. . . went back with her. She went into the bedroom. To be
frank I was a bit pissed. She called me after about five minutes.
I'd poured myself a generous snifter. She keeps a bottle of
Calvados in her desk . . .' He always speaks in these short sentences. A Moog speech synthesizer – with the 'Hemingway' button permanently on. '. . . on the bed. She's wearing a red, rubber
dress. The video is on. A Californian pol of some kind is giving
a press conference. She was writhing. He was saying something
impassioned –'

'Dave –'

'She said, "Come here." But I was watching the pol, who had
pulled out a gun. It was quite clear that this was real. All shot
by a live-action news camera. He put the gun in his mouth. Big
fucker – long-barrelled Colt –'

'Dave, you –'

'I look from the screen to the bed. She's got her hand up
under the rubber dress. She's playing with herself. On screen the
pol just does it. Blows –'

'Dave, *you told me this yesterday*!'

'– his brains out.'

Silence in the café. I realize I've shouted. A hiss of steam from
the Gaggia, a small cloud floats over me, sends shadows racing
across the sward of Dave's face. I look up to where a peg board
is affixed to the pine cladding. A peg board with plastic letters,
detailing the café's fare. I scan the lettering, picking out As, Vs,
Es, and, of course, Ds.

Why did he do that? Repeat himself like that. It undermines
my whole sense of him. The fact that he could repeat himself so
comprehensively, sentence for sentence. It must mean that he
didn't register whom he was talking to. He didn't know that he
was talking to me. He does, after all, have a lot of friends, Dave.

And it's often remarked upon how sympathetic he is, how warm, how caring. But it's also true that this quality has to be spread about a bit; a margarine of feeling.

'I have to go now.'

'But –'

'No, really. Velma. I'm going to see her. I told you.'

'Are you sure about . . . I mean that it's a good idea?' He's half rising. Bobbing slightly in the awkward, rigid gap between banquette and bolted table. With his horsey head, painted-on hair, and simian arms, he looks puppet-like to me. He isn't in any sense a real Dave, this Dave. How could I be so fooled? His very posture suggests thick, yet invisible threads running up, through the ceiling tiles, to the spatulate fingers of a giant Dave, who squats above the café, trying to coax dummy Dave into a semblance of humanity. 'Are you seeing Dr Klagfarten again today?' His brow is corrugated with ersatz angst.

'What's it to you?' I'm plunking a handful of change down on the table, rising to leave.

'Oh, come on . . . I'm only concerned for you . . .'

He's concerned. Hell, *I'm* concerned. We're all fucking concerned. We're united in concern, wouldn't you say? United like so many stickle-bricks, pressed together to form a model society. From the door of the café I turn. All three Daves are in the same positions, frozen. Fat Dave his hand on the big knob of the Gaggia's handle; Old Dave nodded out over *Sporting Life*; dummy Dave still deanimate, dangling. I raise an arm, and in imitation of Dr Klagfarten swivel a palm.

I walk swiftly, listening to the arguments of my conscience: pro-Dave and anti-Dave. I know I've been stressed recently. Dr Klagfarten says I shouldn't look to any one of the several therapies we are applying for succour. Rather, I should try and apprehend them as a manifold entity that cushions and constrains me. But even so – there just is an objective creepiness, a not-quite-rightness about Dave at the moment. Far from finding his very Daveness reassuring this morning, it has instead gravely unsettled me. I can't stand duplication. It *is* replication.

I'm heading back past the old administration building. It's

not the most direct route to Velma's house, but I have a kind of urge to make contact again with Dr Klagfarten, if only in the most glancing way. Looking up, I see that a drape or curtain has been pulled across the window of his office. It reminds me of Dave's egg. If a fork like a prop for a Magritte painting were to be plunged through the window of Dr Klagfarten's office, a gush of yellow neurosis would undoubtedly ooze out.

My route to Velma's takes me across the park. As I enter, between cast-iron gates, the sun at last begins to seep through the clouds. I keep my speed up, concentrating on the internal dispositions of muscle, flesh, and bone; feeling my shoes as flexible, overall callouses, attached at heel and toe.

By the brackish, oily carp pond, in the very centre of the park, a small, wooden bridge is marooned on the impacted earth. Squirrels flow about, grey rivulets of rodent. The hacked and husbanded woodland here is filtering the lax sun, making for bad dappling. At a fence of waist-high, wooden pallisades, two young men stand, feeding pigeons and crows.

If not foreign – they ought to be. They both wear expensive overcoats of lambs' wool, or cashmere. Their hair is too glossy, too dark, too curly. Even from some fifty yards away I can see the sideburns that snake down from hairlines to jawlines. They are both wearing gloves. I don't like birds at the best of times, and the pigeons and crows in this town are getting quite obese. We don't need types like these coming into our park and feeding them expensive peanuts.

The pigeons and crows rear up so. And they're so big. Today, their bipedalism makes them humanoid to me. In their greasy, feather capes of grey and black, they might be avine impersonators, hustling a sexual practice founded on fluttering and paid for in peanuts.

As I draw level with the two men, one turns away from the fence, scattering peanuts and pigeons from his gloved hands. 'See you, Dave,' says his companion, but not with any real feeling. Dave glances at me, once, but with an unexpected acuity, as if reading me. He strides away in front, kicking up small sprays of old leaves, mould, and twigs. It's clear that he is uncomfortable, that he wishes to put some distance between us. I quicken my pace.

I caught him by the octagonal, wooden gazebo, used by the park staff as a place to brew up teas, and stash their tools. He was unexpectedly heavy-set, his body fluent like a waterfall beneath his soft overcoat. There was a nasty, ungainly struggle, which reflected badly on both of us. There was no symmetry, no choreography to our bestial growls and spasmodic cuffs. He went down to his knees, hard and fast, an enthusiastic convert to nonconsciousness.

There was mush on the mattock. I hefted it. It felt so light, so buoyant. I resisted an urge to hurl it up, into the blueing sky, to watch it rise to the heavens, rotating slowly on its own axis, like the transmogrified tool in *2001*.

His wallet was made from slightly furry-feeling leather. Possibly pigskin. Credit cards, business cards, driving licence, kidney donor card, all were in the name of Jonathan D. Sczm. I wondered about the D. Did it stand for David, or was Dave merely Sczm's nickname? Did it matter now?

Velma answers the door looking very grey, very drawn. She only opens the door a fraction, just far enough for me to appreciate how very grey, how very drawn she is. 'You look rather rough,' she says, 'and your jacket's all torn.'

'What's this?' I reply, gesturing, taking in the crack, the vee, of Velma. 'I'm not hawking anything here, Velma, you can take the chain off.'

'I'm – I'm not sure I can do that, I don't think I want you to come in. Dave called me from the café – he said you were in a bit of a state.'

'Oh, for fuck's sake!' I lean against the brickwork, and awkwardly kidney-punch the intervening air. I'm doing my best to affect an air of complete naturalness – but I have the idea it isn't working.

'Dave said you had an appointment with Dr Klagfarten for three this afternoon.'

'Yeah.'

'After Dave rang, I called Dr Klagfarten. He says it would be fine if you wanted to go back there now, have a word now. He said –'

'What? What did he say?'

'He said you might be a bit upset – upset about me . . .'

'You, Velma?' I'm looking at her now, and I can see the tears burgeoning in her eyes. 'You? Velma?' She shakes her head.

'Not Velma, not any more, not Velma, not –' and she's sobbing now, the sobs slotting into a cycle, an hysterical cycle which she breaks, crying, 'D-Davina! Davina! That's my name! Davina!'

I'm quite taken aback by my own sang-froid. I straighten up, adopt a conciliatory but vaguely imposing demeanour. Davina is still sobbing, but subsiding. 'When you say your name is Davina now, do you mean that you've changed it by deed-poll?'

'I've applied, yes.' She's composing herself.

'How long will it take?'

'About six weeks.'

'And until then?'

'Well, you encourage the people who know you to address you as you would prefer to be addressed,' she's regained her composure altogether. 'In a sense that's what it is to have a name at all. A name is, after all, simply a certain common ascription.'

'Which in your case is – ?'

'Dave.'

'Dave?'

'That's right.'

Dr Klagfarten stands with his back to me, looking out over the rooftops. The yellow-tinted glass imparts a slight, bilious whine to his voice, as he says, 'You are finding this business of the ubiquity of the name Dave unsettling, hmm?'

'Not exactly, no.' I am, for the first time since I left Dr Klagfarten's office two hours ago, at ease. He turns from the window and retreats behind his desk. He smiles at me and gives the endearing, lip-twisting *moue*.

'How would you feel if I told you that the blackbird which flew down your chimney last week was called Dave?'

'Both incredulous – and curious.'

'So, this Dave thing isn't entirely awful –'

'I just don't see why it has to be Dave.'

'Well, Colin Klagfarten would be patently risible, like Ronald MacDonald. Dave Klagfarten has both resonance and assonance.'

I take some time out to consider this proposition. Dave goes on smiling benignly. He likes silences, he thinks that you find yourself in the context of silence, that whether or not silence is experienced as an absence or a presence, gives you a litmus test for your own identity.

'You aren't telling me,' I say eventually, 'that it all begins with you?'

'No, no, of course not. This is a non-causal singularity – of that much I'm certain, although it jibes unpleasantly with your particular brand of alienation, of depersonalization. Still, the fact that the biblical David was the individual who most completely realized the theocratic ideal of the Israelites, and that the yearning for his return became a matter of almost Messianic fervour . . .' a shrug, another *moue*, '. . . well, it doesn't seem to stretch the analogy that far to suggest that this new pattern of emergent Daves represents something similar, a secular ultramontanism, perhaps?'

'But it is *Daves*, not David.' I know I'm nit-picking, but I can't help it.

'Oh, come on, what's in an id? Look, I think you'd feel a lot better, I think we could consider easing off on the Parstelin, I think it might be a breakthrough. You know, we could even collaborate on a paper –'

'If I was –'

'If you were –' He's nodding, smiling, every fibre of his body exhorting me to say it, which I do:

'Dave too.'

JANICE GALLOWAY
The Trick Is to Keep Breathing

ooo

The kitchen is bright, even at this time in the morning. Yellow walls and white woodwork. Inside the white cupboard, a big green box silts at the corners, leaving snuff trails on the floor of the shelf. Family Size Economy Green Label (Strong) Tea. I have no entitlement to a family-size box but it cuts costs: I drink a lot of tea. There is powdered milk in a plastic container shaped like a milkbottle and a white cylinder of saccharine. The cupboard always smells of Green Label even though there are plenty of other things in there. I once made a list of them and memorized it, just to see if I could. Two tins of soup, dehydrated potato, several jars of beetroot, table jelly, powdered custard, pineapple chunks, packet sauces (cheese and parsley), and the tea things. They all smell of tea. This morning, there's a note as well:

HEALTH VISITOR 12.30

so I phone school and say I won't come. They never ask why: they're used to it by now.

Friday morning 10.23
There's a lot to do before she comes but it's a set routine so I don't need to think. It just uses my body and runs itself, hands picking up the cloth and wiping taps after I rinse the emptied cup. I begin cleaning the house.

I can't stop getting frantic about the house being clean and tidy for people coming. I used to watch my mother when I was a teenager and think I'm never going to do that: it's so pointless. I'd tell her things I'd read in books, that my mind was going to be more important than the thickness of the dust on my man-

telpiece and she'd zoom the hoover too close to my feet shouting SHIFT to drown me out. I thought I knew something. I
looked down my nose at the windolene sheen of my mother's
house and knew better while my mother revved the hoover in
the background and told me I was a lazy bitch.

I clean the kitchen till my hands are swollen from cold water,
red as ham. My knuckles scrape and go lilac till the kitchen
looks like they do on TV and smells of synthetic lemons and
wax. I worry about the living room. It never looks right. I try
not to worry. I try to be grateful since it took me long enough
to get here, haggling with tiny-minded Mr Dick from the
Housing Authority. Every fourth house in this estate is empty.
Kids break the windows and the council have to pay to repair
and maintain them empty so the rents go up all the time. Every
time the rent goes up more houses become empty, some
overnight. But Mr Dick said there were difficulties in my getting
tenancy. They have to make this fuss so you know who's boss.
There were rent arrears. I wasn't liable but Mr Dick explained
if I paid them it might ease the aforementioned difficulties. I
said I hadn't got the money.

Mr Dick looked me right in the eye.
    Try to be a little more cooperative. We're bending over back-
wards. You're not helping yourself, creating difficulties. Strictly
speaking, we're under no obligation to house you at all, not
when you were never registered as tenant. We needn't do anything at all, strictly speaking. There has to be a bit of give and
take. We're bending over backwards you know, bending over
backwards.
    I said I was sorry about all the contribution they were having
on my account and appreciated how good they were being. But
I didn't have any money. Surely they understood I had all sorts
of debts and expenses at a time like this. Besides the place did-
n't have a dustbin. Did he expect me to pay for no dustbin?
    Mr Dick made his eyes go very small.
    There was certainly one there when Mr Fisher became resi-
dent, Miss Stone. Oh yes, there was certainly a dustbin on the

premises.

His eyes almost disappeared.

I suggest you know more about the whereabouts of this dustbin than you say. And the washing line, Miss Stone.

I paid for the missing things and they gave me back the keys. I got the house.

It's too big really. There are four rooms. One is decorated as a bedroom and the others randomly. There isn't enough furniture to go round. The two armchairs are covered with sheeting. Dust puffs up from underneath when someone sits on them or if they move, really old chairs. The curtains don't meet and are blue. The shelves are his: something to do before we went on holiday. That's why they're not finished. They asked for a receipt to prove the shelves were new, then let me have the benefit of the doubt. His wife didn't want them anyway. The shelves are white, complete enough to house the record player, books, magazines, and the phone. The pile of records are mostly his. The Bowie poster hides wine stains where I threw a glass at the wall. A wee accident.

I rearrange things, placing chairs over the bald patches of the rug, sweeping the boards. It never looks as good as I'd like.

By twenty past I'm running along the twisty road between the houses to the shop for biscuits. She likes biscuits. I get different ones each time hoping they are something else she will enjoy. I can't choose in a hurry. I can't be trusted with custard creams so deliberately don't get them. Chocolate digestives are too expensive. I wait for too long in the queue while a confused little kid tries to bargain for his father's cigarettes with the wrong money, so I have to run back clutching fig rolls and iced coffees and nearly drop the milk. I get flustered at these times, but I know I'll manage if I try harder. These visits are good for me. Dr Stead sends this woman out of love. He insisted.

I said, I'm no use with strangers.

He said, But this is different. Health Visitors are trained to cope with that. He said she would know what to do; she would find me out and let me talk. *Make me* talk.

HAH

I'm putting on the kettle, still catching my breath when she comes in without knocking and frightens me. What if I had been saying things about her out loud? I tell her to sit in the living-room so I can have time to think.

Tray

jug

sweeteners

plates

cups and saucers

another spoon

christ

the biscuits
the biscuits

I burst the wrap soundlessly and make a tasteful arrangement. I polish her teaspoon on my cardigan band. No teapot. I make it in the cup using the same bag twice and take it through as though I've really made it in a pot and just poured it out. Some people are sniffy about tea bags. It sloshes when I reach to push my hair back from falling in my eyes and I suddenly notice I am still wearing my slippers dammit.

Never mind. She smiles and says

(Well!)

This is to make out the tea is a surprise though it isn't. She does it every time. We sit opposite each other because that's the way the chairs are. The chairs cough dust from under their sheets as she crosses her legs, thinking her way into the part. By the time she's ready to start I'm grinding my teeth back into the gum.

HEALTH VISITOR   So, how are you/how's life/what's been

                                    happening/anything interesting to tell me/
                                    what's new?
PATIENT   Oh, fine/nothing to speak of.

I stir the tea repeatedly. She picks a piece of fluff off her skirt.

HEALTH VISITOR   Work. How are things at work? Coping?
PATIENT   Fine. [Pause] I have trouble getting in on
                                    time, but getting better.

I throw her a little difficulty every so often so she feels I'm
telling her the truth. I figure this will get rid of her quicker.

HEALTH VISITOR   [Intensifying] But what about the day-to-day?
                                    How are you coping?
PATIENT   OK. [Brave smile] I manage.
HEALTH VISITOR   The house is looking fine.
PATIENT   Thank you. I do my best.

This is overdone. She flicks her eyes up to see and I lower mine.
She reaches for a biscuit.

HEALTH VISITOR   These look nice. I like a biscuit with a cup of
                                    tea.

We improvise about the biscuits for a while, her hat sliding back
as she chews. She doesn't like the tea. Maybe she eats so many
biscuits just to get rid of the taste.

HEALTH VISITOR   Aren't you having one? They're very good.
PATIENT   No, thanks. Maybe later. Having lunch soon.

She goes on munching, knowing I don't want her to be here/
that I do want her to be here but I can't talk to her.

This is the fourth time we have played this fucking game.

                                          *

The first time was worst. I went through the tea ceremony for five minutes then tried to get the thing opened up.

What are you supposed to come here for? I said.
  She just looked.
  What's it for? What are we supposed to talk about?
  She said, I'm here to help you. To help you try to get better. I'm here to listen.
  But I don't know you from a hole in the wall. I can't do it.
  She said, You can tell me anything you like. I assure you it goes no further and I've heard it all before.

I could hear my own breathing. I knew Dr Stead was doing his best for me and that was why she was here. I had to try. It was reasonable. I swallowed hard. I can't remember what I said now. Whatever it was, I was in mid-flow, keeping my eyes low because I couldn't look her in the eye. When I finished, nothing happened. I looked up.

She was dunking a ginger nut. I watched her hand rocking back and forth, getting the saturation just right. At the crucial moment, she flipped the biscuit to her mouth, sucking off the soaked part, her tongue worming out for a dribble of tea. It missed. The dribble ran down to her chin and she coughed, giggling. And I had forgotten what I had to say. I knew if I opened my mouth something terrible would dribble out like the tea, gush down the front of my shirt, over shoes and cover the carpet like
like
like

She sucked her teeth and leaned closer, whispering.
  She knew how I felt. Did I think doctor hadn't given her case notes? She knew all about my problems. Did I want her to tell me a true story? Her niece had an accident on her bike once. And she thought, what'll happen if Angela dies? What'll happen? But she prayed to God and the family rallied round and they saw her through to the other side. That's what I had

to remember. She knew how I felt; she knew exactly how I felt.

She keeps coming anyway. I make tea and fetch biscuits and we forget all about that first little hiccup. This time she eats only the coffee biscuits so I make a mental note. No more fig rolls. The way I'm coiled is getting uncomfortable. One foot has gone to sleep and my tea is coated. I put it down on the rug and straighten up.

HEALTH VISITOR   [Alert to the change] Nothing else to tell me, then?
PATIENT   No. Nothing special.

She looks blank and vaguely disappointed. I am not trying.

PATIENT   I have a friend visiting tonight. That's all.
HEALTH VISITOR   Anyone special? Going out?
PATIENT   Just the pub, have a few drinks, that kind of thing.
HEALTH VISITOR   Lucky girl. I can't remember the last time someone took me out. Lucky.

She smiles and stands up but guilt is spoiling the relief. I get more guilty as she waddles towards the door, tumbling crumbs from the folds of blue coat, fastening up one top button, ready for outside. My temples thunder as she touches the door and something buzzes in my ear.

You Always Expect Too Much.

The exhaust rattles till she curves out of sight, struggling against her bulk and the need to turn the wheel.

I rub out the creases on the chairs where we have been sitting then take the crockery through and crash it into the sink. One of the red cups has a hairline crack along the rim, fine but deep enough to cut if it wanted. I throw the cup in the bin in case the person it cuts is not me. I lift the biscuits still on the plate and crush them between my hands into the bin. The opened packets follow. They only go soft. The wrappers crackle with life in the recesses of the liner so I let the lid drop fast and turn on the taps to drown it out. They run too hard and soak the front of my shirt. There isn't time to change. I get my coat and run like hell for the stop.

        ooo

TESCO's. Red neon all the way to the other end of the precinct, pointing the way to lights, rows of pretty boxes, pastels and primaries, tinsel colours; tins, sealed packets, silver polythene skins begging to be burst. I get dry and warm just thinking about the supermarket. It makes me feel rich and I don't need to think. I can spend hours among the buckle-wheeled trolleys, fruit and fresh vegetables, tins of blueberry pie filling, papaya and mango, numbing my fingers on bags of frozen broccoli and solid chocolate gateaux. The bakery, near the scent and the warmth of the fresh rolls and sugared pastries. The adrenalin smell of coffee drifts and draws towards the delicatessen, the wedges of Edam, Stilton, and Danish Blue. But never too long in one place. I don't encourage buying. Sometimes, I get baking things: sugar and flour, dried fruit and tubs of fat, maybe cherries, ginger and peel. Mixed spice, cinnamon, eggs. Or I go to the drinks aisle and read the labels over and over, teasing myself with which one I'll buy. It's always the same one in the end.

Afternoon is easiest. Rush time makes me confused and anxious. In the afternoon, I feel I belong. There may be a new magazine: full of adverts and recipes, clothes and thin women. A new horoscope. I get excited when I see a new cover smiling over the chewing gum and chocolate at the checkout racks. I buy the magazine and fold it carefully inside my shoulderbag, then walk the length of the precinct, echoing with the ring of my heels, avoiding the skateboards. The end of the mall needs careful handling because people finishing work don't look where they're going. Like clockwork toys. There are days when this makes me furious (I can't get over the inefficiency): other times it makes me depressed. As though I'm trapped in a coop full of hens for the slaughterhouse. Today, the important thing is not to think about the Health Visitor and just keep moving. I lied. No one is visiting tonight. Or tomorrow night. They did once but not now. I told a lie. I tell lies all the time.

At the end of the precinct, a security guard opens the doors with a leather glove and offers me a sweetie. I smile and take it. Round the corner I drop it in a plastic bin shaped like a rabbit. Bobby the Bunny says Keep Your Country Tidy.

LUDOVIC KENNEDY
On My Way to the Club

My psychological problems first showed themselves in physical form soon after I took up my job at Government House, Newfoundland: the manifestations were insomnia, stomach pains, sweating in hands and feet, and general lassitude. The Canadian naval doctor who examined me called my ailment 'soldier's heart', a stress condition brought about by three years of the war at sea. It plagued me on and off while I was in Newfoundland but paradoxically when I returned to sea in the autumn of 1944 it vanished. After the war, however, at Oxford and Ashridge, and before and after my marriage, it returned and became something I had to learn to live with; and I sought no cure for it because there did not seem to be one.

One evening in London, having run out of sleeping pills, I approached a local doctor for a prescription. First, though, he questioned me; and when he handed me the prescription, gave me the name of a psychiatrist whom he thought I ought to see. At that time my knowledge of psychiatry was hazy. However, I went along as suggested and was told by the psychiatrist that it was not 'soldier's heart' I was suffering from but an anxiety neurosis. In that case, I asked, how was it that when I went back to sea where I might be blown up at any moment, the symptoms disappeared? Because, he said, it was not anxiety about death that was unconsciously troubling me but doubts about my ability to cope with my personal life. At sea in the war the Navy provided me with bed, board, uniform, transport, and a daily routine; a personal life hardly existed.

This was the first of hundreds of visits I made to psychiatrists in the course of the next twenty-five years, and which altogether cost a small fortune. During that time I always endeavoured to hide what I was experiencing from the outside world; and it was only when people said, as they occasionally did, 'Cheer up! It may never happen!' that I knew I had not been entirely successful. Some of the initial psychiatric interviews were quite painful because, in answer to questions about my childhood, I had to relate the nightmare of my early relationship with my mother. Although then in my thirties, I still felt a residue of guilt and shame about it; and it was my reluctance to accept and articulate what had happened, allowing it to stay locked in the unconscious, I was told, that was a principal cause of the neurosis. Disappointingly, though, when I did come to accept the situation and could talk about my mother without embarrassment, the symptoms continued – indeed it is only in the last fifteen years or so that I have been free of them. This has led me to wonder if all I ever gained from the hours spent and the fees paid was a degree of self-discovery; and that had I never bared my mind to any psychiatrist I might have gained the self-discovery and outlived the neurosis anyway. It is a question I have heard others pose. I kept on going back because I always hoped I would eventually feel physically better; but in twenty-five years I rarely did. So are analysts and psychiatrists anything more than father confessors, sounding-boards, whose reputations for healing are largely illusory?

Two incidents stand out from those twenty-five years. The first occurred at a time when the pains and lassitude had become so acute that on many days I was reduced to sitting slumped in a chair, staring into space for hours on end, unable to concentrate on anything. To counter this I was prescribed a course of electric shock therapy. After the third treatment, when I had come round from the anaesthetic, I experienced what psychiatrists call an abreaction; that is to say, I burst into floods of tears, clung to a nurse who was standing by and told her she was the only woman who had meant anything to me in my life. It was a rum thing to do; but she didn't bat an eyelid. For about a week or ten days afterwards I felt a new man, refreshed and invigorated, and thought my neurosis had gone for ever. Then the symptoms returned.

The other incident took place during one of my twice-weekly interviews with a distinguished Jungian analyst whom I had been seeing for several years. My father always told me never to recount my dreams to anyone as, while they might be fascinating to me, they were dead boring to anyone else. But this man could never have enough of my dreams. I had to write them down each morning as I woke (it's amazing what one remembers doing that) and then he interpreted them (trains were wombs, etc.) in his consulting room.

Usually I sat in a chair opposite him, but one afternoon, having for once no dreams to offer, I was told to lie on the couch and indulge in 'free association', i.e. shut my eyes and tell him whatever came into my mind. I did as he asked, but nothing came. After a few minutes I said, 'I'm sorry, but my mind is a blank,' to which he replied, 'Don't worry. Just relax and wait for something to come. It will.' In another few minutes I saw a white cloud. 'I see a white cloud,' I said. He made no comment but I hardly expected it. Presently I saw a lamppost. It was black. 'I see a black lamppost,' I said, and then, 'The black lamppost is underneath the white cloud.' I was aware this sounded like something from a foreign language phrase book, but felt that precision was important. More time went by, the cloud and the lamppost vanished and their place was taken by a herd of trotting pigs. 'I see pigs,' I said, 'a whole lot of pigs, and they're trotting.' I said this quite excitedly because there were so many and I wasn't expecting them. Again no comment, and now something made me turn and open my eyes.

I saw a figure with head back and mouth open, deep in slumber. Although surprising, I did not have it in my heart to blame him; what I had been saying was enough to make anyone nod off. I rose and, so as not to disturb him, tiptoed to the door. The click of the handle woke him. 'Good heavens!' he said. 'I *am* sorry.' He was obviously terribly embarrassed. 'You may not believe this,' he said, 'but this is the first time this has ever happened.' I was sure he was telling the truth and yet I did find it hard to believe. When you consider the sort of sludge in the way of dreams and fantasies and happenings that patients dredge up from the unconscious every day and which, hour upon hour, week in week out, psychiatrists have to force themselves to listen to, it is a wonder to me that any of them manage to stay awake at all.

FAY WELDON
A Gentle Tonic Effect

'What did you say your name was?' asked Morna Casey. 'Miss Jacobs? Just Miss? Not Doctor or anything? Well, *chacun à son goût*. But tell me, do you need planning permission, or can anyone just set up in their front room and start in the shrinking business?'

Morna Casey frowned at what she thought might be a hangnail, and looked at her little gold watch with the link chain, and waited for Miss Jacobs' reply, which did not come.

'I have very little time for people who go to therapists,' added Morna Casey. 'I'm sorry, but there it is. It's so sort of self-absorbed, don't you think? I can't stand people who make a fuss about nothing. If it wasn't that my dreams were interfering with my work, I wouldn't be here.'

Still no response came from Miss Jacobs: she did not even lift her pencil from the little round mahogany table at her side.

'You charge quite a lot,' observed Morna Casey, 'for someone who says so little and takes no notes. But if you can get away with it, good for you. I suppose on the whole people are just mentally lazy; they employ analysts to think about them rather than do it themselves.'

Morna Casey waited. Presently Miss Jacobs spoke. She said, 'This first consultation is free. Then we will see whether it is worth both our whiles embarking on a course of treatment.'

'I don't know why,' said Morna Casey, 'but you remind me of the owl in "Squirrel Nutkin".'

A slight smile glimmered over Miss Jacobs' lips. Morna Casey noticed, of course she did. She had declined to lie down on the leather couch, with her head at Miss Jacobs' end, as patients were supposed to do.

'I suppose,' acknowledged Morna Casey, 'it's because I feel like Squirrel Nutkin, dancing up and down in front of wise old Owl, making jokes and being rude. But you won't get to gobble me up: I'm too quick and fast for the likes of you.'

Morna Casey was a willowy blonde in her late thirties: elegantly turned out, executive style. Her eyes were wide and sexy, and her teeth white, even and capped. She wore a lot of gold jewellery of the kind you can buy in duty-free shops at major airports. Her skirt was short and her legs were long and her heels were high.

'I went to see a doctor,' said Morna Casey, 'which is a thing I hardly ever do – I can't stand all that poking and fussing about. But the nightmares keep waking me up; and if you're going to do a good job of work it's imperative to have a good night's sleep. I've always insisted on my beauty sleep – when Rider was a baby I used ear-plugs: he soon learned to sleep through.'

Rider was Morna Casey's son. He was seventeen and active in the school potholing club.

Morna Casey leant forward so that her shapely bosom glowed pink beneath her thin, white, tailored shirt. She wore the kind of bra which lets the nipples show through.

'The fool of a doctor give me sleeping pills, and though I quadrupled the dose it still didn't stop me waking up screaming once or twice a night. And Hector wasn't much help. But then, he never is.'

Hector was Morna Casey's husband. He was head of market research at the advertising agency where Morna worked. She was a PR executive for Maltman Ltd, a firm which originally sold whisky but had lately diversified into pharmaceuticals.

'Helping simply isn't Hector's forte,' said Morna Casey. 'You ask what is? A word too crude for your ears, Miss Jacobs, probably beyond your understanding; that's what Hector's forte is. I first set my eyes on Hector in a pub one night, eighteen years ago. I said to my then-husband, "Who's that man with the big nose?" and Hector followed us home that night and we haven't been apart since.'

Miss Jacobs looked quite startled, or perhaps Morna Casey thought she did.

'People say, "Didn't your husband mind?" and I reply, "Well, he didn't like it much but what could he do?" ' said Morna

Casey. 'He moved out, which suited me and Hector very well. It was a nice house: we bought him out. Hector's one of the most boring people I know: he has no conversation apart from statistics and a very limited mind, but he suits me OK. And I suit him: he doesn't understand a word I say. When I tell him about the dreams, all he says is, "Well, what's so terrible about dreaming that?" It was the doctor who suggested I came to see you: doctors do that, don't they? If they're stumped they say it's stress. Well, of course I'm stressed: I've always been stressed: I have a difficult and demanding job. But I haven't always had the dreams. I told the doctor I was perfectly capable of analysing myself thank you very much, and he said he didn't doubt it but a therapist might save me some time, and time was money, which is true enough, and that's the reason I'm here. At least all you do is poke about in my head and not between my legs.'

Miss Jacobs took up her notepad and wrote something on it.

'What's that?' asked Morna Casey, nastily. 'Your shopping list for tonight's dinner? Liver? Brussels sprouts?'

'If you lie down on the couch,' said Miss Jacobs, 'you wouldn't see me writing and it wouldn't bother you.'

'It doesn't bother me,' said Morna Casey. 'Sorry. Nothing you do bothers me one little bit, one way or another. And nothing will make me lie down on your couch. Reminds me of my father. My father was a doctor. He smoked eighty cigarettes a day and died of lung cancer when he was forty-three and I was seventeen. He'd cough and spit and gasp and light another cigarette. Then he'd inhale and cough some more. I remember saying to my Uncle Desmond – he was a doctor too – "Do you think it's sensible for Daddy to smoke so much?" and Uncle Desmond replied, "Nothing wrong with tobacco: it acts as a mild disinfectant, and has a gentle tonic effect." I tend to believe that, in spite of all that research – paid for by the confectionery companies, I wouldn't be surprised – about the tobacco–lung cancer link. It's never been properly proved. The public is easily panicked, as those of us in PR know. My father enjoyed smoking. He went out in his prime. He wouldn't have wanted to be old.

'But I'm not here to waste time talking about my father. When you're dead you're dead and there's no point discussing you. I'm here to talk about my dream. It comes in two halves: in the first half Rider is miniaturized – about twenty inches long – and he's clinging on by his fingertips to the inside of the toilet, and crying, so I lean on the handle and flush him away. I can't bear to see men crying – and at seventeen you're a man, aren't you? That part of the dream just makes me uneasy; but then out of the toilet rise up all these kind of deformed people – with no arms or two heads or their nerves outside their skin and not inside so they have a kind of flayed look – and they sort of loom over me and that's the bit I don't like: that's when I wake up screaming.'

Morna Casey was silent for a little. She stretched her leg and admired her ankle.

'I think I understand the first part of the dream,' said Morna Casey presently. 'I gave birth to Rider in the toilet bowl at home. I wouldn't go to hospital. I wasn't going to have all those strangers staring up between my legs, so when I went into labour I didn't tell a soul, just gritted my teeth and got on with it, and it ended up with Hector having to fish the baby out of the water. Now Rider climbs about in potholes – he actually likes being spread-eagled flat against slimy rock faces, holding on with his fingertips. His best friend was killed last year in a fall but I don't worry. I've never worried about Rider. What's the point? When your number's up, your number's up. Sometimes I do get to worry about the way I don't worry. I don't seem to be quite like other people in this respect. Not that I'd want to be. I guess I'm just not the maternal type. But Rider grew up perfectly OK: he was never much of a bother. He's going to university. If he wants to go potholing that's his affair. Do we stop for coffee and biscuits? No? Not that I'd take the biscuits but I do like to be offered. Food is an essential part of PR. The laws of hospitality are very strong. No one likes to bite the hand that feeds them. That's one of the first things you learn in my job. You should really seriously think about it, Miss Jacobs.'

Morna Casey pondered for a while. A fly buzzed round her

head but thought better of it and flew off.

'I don't understand the second part of the dream at all,' said Morna Casey presently. 'Who are all these deformed idiots who come shrieking out of the toilet bowl at me? I really hate the handicapped. So do most people only they haven't the guts to say so. If there'd been one single thing wrong with Rider – an ear out of place, oesophagus missing, the smallest thing – I'd have pushed him under, not let Hector fish him out. Don't you like Rider as a name? The rider of storms, the rider of seas? No one knows how poetic I am: they look as I go by and whistle and say, there goes a good-looking blonde of the smart kind not the silly kind, and they have no idea at all what I'm really about. I like that. One day I'm going to give it all up and be a poet. When Hector's old and past it I'm going to push him under a bus. I can't abide dribbly old men. When I'm old Rider will look after me. He loves me. He only clambers about underground to make me notice him. What he wants me to say is what I've never said: "I worry about you, Rider." But I don't. How can I say it? It isn't true.'

Miss Jacobs raised an eyebrow. Morna Casey looked at her watch.

'I have a meeting at three-thirty,' said Morna Casey. 'I mustn't let this overrun. I'm on a rather important special project at the moment, you may be interested to know. I'm handling the press over the Artefax scare.'

Artefax was a new vitamin-derivative drug hailed as a wonder cure for addictions of all kinds, manufactured by Maltman and considered by some to be responsible for a recent spate of monstrous births; though Maltman's lawyers had argued successfully in the courts that, as the outbreaks were clustered, the Chernobyl fallout must be to blame – particles of caesium entering the water table in certain areas and not in others.

'So you'll understand it's all go at the moment,' said Morna Casey. 'We have to restore public confidence. Artefax is wonderful, and absolutely harmless – you can even take it safely through pregnancy; you're not addicted to anything, and all it does is have a mild tonic effect. Our main PR drive is through the doctors.'

Morna Casey was silent for a little. Miss Jacobs stared out of the window.

'Well, yes,' said Morna Casey presently. 'I see. If I changed my job the dreams would stop. But if I changed my job I wouldn't worry about the dreams because it wouldn't matter about the job, would it? All the same, I might consider a shift in career direction. I don't really like working for the same outfit as Hector. It does rather cramp my style – not that he can do much about it. I do as I like. He knows how boring he is; what can he expect?

'There's a good opening coming up,' said Morna Casey, 'or so I've heard on the grapevine, as head of PR at Britnuc; that's the new nuclear energy firm. I think I'd feel quite at home with radioactivity: it's like nicotine and Artefax – in reasonable quantities it has this gentle tonic effect. Of course, in large quantities I daresay it's different. But so's anything. Like aspirin. One does you good, two cure your headache, twenty kill you. In the Soviet Union the spas offer radioactive mud baths. Radon-rich, they say. They're very popular.

'Thank you for the consultation, Dr – sorry, Miss – Jacobs. I won't be needing you again. I'm much obliged to you for your time and patience: though, of course, one can always do this kind of thing for oneself. If I ever give up PR I might consider setting up as a therapist. No planning permission required! A truly jolly *pièce de* rich *gâteau*, if you ask me.'

And Morna Casey adjusted her short, taupe skirt over her narrow hips and walked out, legs long on high heels, and Miss Jacobs, whose hand had been hovering over her appointment book, put down her pencil.

Benjamin Zephaniah
Family Values

Reds are in yu beds
Banks are in de red
Bombs in de city
Taxes burn
Crime rates soar
Hospitals fight
Schools rebel
Water kills
Cops kill,
Cover-ups uncovered
Neo-Nazis rise
Pension funds not trusted
Talks fail
War looms
An yu hav de cheek to call me
A
Problem
Child.

Adam Phillips
The Disorder of Uses;
A Case History of Clutter

> *I think your analysis is right as far as it goes but if com-*
> *pleted leaves no word which is at all meaningless.*
>
> William Empson, *A Note on a Commentary*
> *on Hart Crane's 'Voyages III'*

All psychoanalyses are about mess and meaning, and the links
between them – about the patient's and the analyst's relationship to disorder, and their mostly unconscious fantasies of what
disorder might entail: something orgiastic, something violent,
something inchoate, something longed for and feared. If our
lives have a tendency to get cluttered, apparently by themselves
but usually by ourselves, most accounts of psychoanalysis have
an inclination to sort things out. A kind of pragmatic clarity is
considered a virtue in psychoanalytic writing; it always has a
how-to ingredient; as though its genre was the instruction
manual. The raw material of psychoanalysis – the unconscious
desire that is personal history – may be wildly unreasonable, but
there are eminently sensible vocabularies for summing it up.

Psychoanalysis, in the more empirical British tradition and
the more ego-psychological American tradition, aims to clarify
things; it is impressed by the lucidity it promotes without
acknowledging that this supposed lucidity is itself an effect of
language. Psychoanalytic theory – and, indeed, its highly ritual-
ized practice – has an aversion to clutter. Its categories of
pathology are always fantasies of disorder (there is, for
example, a well-known diagnostic category called a character
disorder, as though character could be anything else).
Psychoanalysis, of course, wants us to be interested in – indeed,
wants us to reappropriate, to re-dream – whatever we are keen

to get rid of. And yet, in all its versions, it promotes the intelligibility of system; it repudiates chaos.

So, in the inevitable to and fro we might prefer between idealizing order and idealizing disorder, clutter has rather an ambiguous status. It has the paradoxical implication of being something which may have no intrinsic, or discernible, order or pattern, and yet of being something that people make, wittingly or unwittingly, determinedly or helplessly. It invites us, in other words, to do something puzzling, or even uncanny; that is, to make meaning – as in, just say something about – the absence of pattern. Clutter, like all the orderly disorders we can describe in language, tantalizes us as readers of it. We can't be sure whom the joke will be on if we say something intelligible or persuasive about it.

It is obviously unpromising to try and imagine representation without structure, or games without rules. (If clutter was a game, how would you learn to play it?) And yet our virtual passion for learning rules – if only by breaking them – lures us into situations where we can't apply them. All the now infamous psychoanalytic categories – hysteria, obsessionality, narcissism – are, among other things, parodies of rule-making. The obsessional neurotic, for example, in classical psychoanalytic theory, has an addiction to the clutter of order to conceal his instinctual life from himself. Winnicott's 'false-self personality', in his words, 'collects demands' to clutter up his life: to baffle and evade his desire, to protect but to starve his true self. If psychoanalysis is necessarily about the inevitable passions of losing and finding, about the terrors of the absence of meaning and desire, it is worth wondering how clutter is made, and what clutter can be used to do. It is, as everyone knows, a lot of work that makes a lot of work. Looking, say, at the clutter of one's desk, it can sometimes seem the apotheosis of that wish that Freud saw as so insidious, the wish to frustrate oneself. But as the psychoanalyst Michael Balint once remarked, talking about defences, anyone who is running away from something is running towards something else. By the same token, when we are talking about clutter we should remember that anything that stops something happening is making something else possible, that if you lose something you might find something else in the process of looking for it. Indeed, this may be the only way you can find something else.

So in this case history of clutter my first image – my emblem for the story – is the picture that mothers (not so often fathers), frequently conjure up for me of their adolescents' bedrooms. When they want to give a full account of how impossible their child is, the adolescent bedroom is *the* symptomatic scenario. This story is set in the cross-fire between the parents' view of the adolescent's bedroom and the adolescent's view of the adolescent's bedroom. The adolescent, it should be noted, rarely complains about the parents' bedroom.

The person I want to write about, a painter in his early thirties, referred himself to me because he thought he was becoming 'mildly agoraphobic'. It was, he said, difficult to be sure because, obviously, he spent most of his time at home painting. He was not, he thought, a loner, but had, ever since early adolescence, a passion for painting. He had a world of friends and a girlfriend; he knew something about psychoanalysis and it was clear to him, as far as he knew, that he did not especially have relationship problems. As he said, what 'people call relationship problems should just be called relationships'. I couldn't help agreeing, while also assuming that he was locating something about desire – about his link with other people – in his apparent symptom. His mild agitation about going out, and in particular the way he found himself steering clear of wider open spaces like parks and the countryside, had made him wonder, as he put it, 'what there was out there that he didn't want to see'.

Since, perhaps unsurprisingly, he thought of his fear in visual terms, I asked him if he could see any links between this fear and his work. When I asked him this in our first meeting a curious thing happened. He said, 'When you asked me that I suddenly had a very strong image of that famous photograph of Francis Bacon's studio, and I remembered thinking when I first saw the picture, "How could he find anything in all that mess?" '; and then he paused and said, as an afterthought, 'And his pictures are so uncluttered.'

I said, entering for some reason into a seminar on Francis Bacon, 'Yes, it's odd, isn't it? The paintings are uncluttered but rather claustrophobic.'

And he replied, rather amazingly to me, 'You feel like the figures can't get out, but Bacon got them into it, so presumably he could get them out.'

There was a pause then, and I had so much to say that I couldn't think of anything to say. It was as though we had suddenly done a lot and there was too much already. The word I want to use now, of course, is clutter; but, as it turned out, a sense of impossible excess was to be integral to this man's predicament, and so the predicament he would put me in.

What I did say was, 'Are you worried that I might get you out of painting?'

And he replied, 'I will be in a mess if I come here with agoraphobia and you cure me of painting!'

As is often the case, I think, when people fear that psychoanalysis will destroy their talent – and symptoms are a talent, if only for survival – they are often having to manage a very powerful wish to be cured of it. One of the things this man had struggled with since adolescence was a great fear of – and intimidation by – other people's envy of his talent. One of the ingredients in what he began to call his 'space fear' was that when he went out people would know what he had just painted and would want to attack him, or to spoil it, or stop it being finished. He was, as it were, staying at home to protect his children. We established, in short, that he had only begun, or begun again, to feel hemmed in when he was becoming successful. It was to be perhaps his only revelation in the treatment that it is possible to make envious attacks on oneself. That no one is more envious of one's gifts than oneself.

A lot of our conversation was about how space works, how one can make it work, how one finds the space one needs, and how often making the right space is the point, all else follows from there. The frame makes the picture; as he said, 'Without it you wouldn't know where to stop, or start.' We could link this with the unframed quality of life outside his flat. And by the same token we talked a lot about the filling of space – indeed that one can make space by filling it, as though space was simply an idea to house things in – and of the difference between filling space and filling time. He had never thought of himself as someone who filled time, but of course, being a painter meant he was, in a sense, filling space all the time.

Psychoanalysis only begins, in any sense, to work when people begin to be impressed by their symptoms. It was the links between his present, apparently mild, symptoms and the initial dilemmas my patient found himself in when he began painting as a fourteen-year-old boy that brought the analysis to life. Faced with an empty canvas, in short, he would 'clutter it all up', and then he wouldn't be able to do anything with it. In his very eagerness, the way he painted stopped him painting. It was as though painting was too exciting, or too illicit, or too something, and he needed the clutter to stop what he thought of as the real painting happening. After all, what would he find himself painting if he didn't clutter up the canvas? The earliest sexual fear he could remember himself having – and it was painting that turned up for him when sexuality did – was of premature ejaculation. There was something he desperately wanted and something he had to get out of as soon as possible. And someone he must refuse to satisfy.

It is perhaps one of the most useful, indeed pleasurable, Freudian insights that the way we defend ourselves tells us, in disguised form, what it is we desire. If clutter was the obstacle to desire, it was also an object of desire. Clutter may not be about the way we hide things from ourselves but about the way we make ourselves look for things. It is, as it were, self-imposed hide and seek. I may clutter up my canvas or my studio to stop myself working – to sabotage the process – or I might do it to make myself, or force myself, to work in a different way. The problem with not being able to bare frustration is that you never notice the paradoxical nature of your acts. That to frustrate one version of the self is always to gratify, to promote and to re-find another version.

One of the reasons that Bacon had been so important to my patient – apart from the fact that he was powerfully affected by the paintings, even as a child – was because he had, in fact, shown him the way out of this problem of cluttering up his canvases. In an interview my patient had come across, Bacon spoke about his now famous untechnique of, at a certain point, throwing paint at the canvas. When he had first read this, he said with his own almost unwitting irony, 'everything fell into place'. Not only did this idea fit with a whole nexus of – then adolescent – intellectual passions: Gide's gratuitous acts, Breton's random writing, the chance and indeterminacy of John Cage's compositions; in other words, a passion for loopholes, for ways of abrogating self-control in the service of contingencies. It also fitted in with one of his own techniques for the uncalculated, which I imagine was an adolescent reworking of a childhood game. Little children often like dropping things behind them as a way of making them disappear. My patient, aged about fourteen, had invented a new way of dressing in the morning. For obvious and not insignificant reasons he could only do this during the holidays, when he wasn't going to school.

He invented this new method one morning when he couldn't decide what to wear. He took a lot of clothes out of his cupboard, dropped them over his shoulder behind him, and took what came to hand, irrespective of whether it matched or, indeed, of whether he liked it. But as important was the fact that his method depended on accumulation. That is to say, in his view, it got better the longer he did it. The more clothes that piled up over time on the floor of his room, the better it was. When he bought new clothes he would drop them on the floor, pick up the bundle of clothes, and drop it over his shoulder so they would be properly mixed in. To begin with, his, as he called them, 'bohemian parents' were amused by this; but eventually his mother cracked. 'But you can't find anything in this room,' she would say to him quite sensibly, to which he would reply, in one way or another, that that was the point. He would say to his mother, 'Our clothes should come and find us,' which seemed rather profound to me. Sometimes, he acknowledged to himself, it was extremely frustrating not being able to find something that he was looking for; but this was more than compensated for by the way he could both discover things he didn't know he was looking for, and, of course, the way that he would find himself wearing such apparently unusual combinations of clothes. Of course, as he now conceded, it wasn't all quite as random as he then liked to think – he was, after all, still selecting his clothes, but from a different way of organizing them.

Part of the freedom of being fourteen – or at least the freedom one has to fight for – is the freedom to sleep-walk, the freedom, that is to say, to do things in one's own way. This is why psychoanalysis can be so disruptive for adolescents – indeed for anyone – because at its worst it forces a pattern. It can make the links that should be left to find their own way. It had never occurred to my patient, until we started talking, that there was a link between the problem he was having with his painting and what he called his 'mess-dress' method. By, as he put it, cluttering up his paintings it was as though he couldn't paint; by cluttering up his room he could dress in his own way. One was apparently a problem, one was a solution. Something that worked for him in one area of his life was felt to be a kind of sabotage in another area. It is often true in psychoanalysis that solutions can be found by mapping one area of a person's life on to another, apparently disparate, one. When it came to dressing, clutter was useful to him; it was exactly what he needed, and so he deliberately made a mess. When it came to painting, it seemed to take him over; he was making it but he couldn't get away from it. Ordinarily one might think one person's clutter is another person's . . . what? Pattern, beautiful object, whatever. For this man, from one psychoanalytic point of view, there was an unconscious project to keep these two selves separate. The self that dressed and the self that painted had to be kept apart. When he dressed he could make, at least from his point of view, a good mess. When he painted he made a bad one.

Clearly, a lot could be made of this, in psychoanalytic terms. In this splitting of himself he managed to keep the destructive mess-making away from his parents; 'No one,' as he once said to me, 'gets hurt if you fuck up a painting . . . except yourself.' Or you could think that his elaborate, quasi-obsessional ritual of spontaneous dressing, exactly the same as cluttering up his canvases, was in fact an anxiety about allowing himself to fantasize, to really elaborate the thought of his desire. Faced with a wardrobe or a canvas, he might start imagining – owning up to – his dreams of what he wanted, who he wanted to be, what of himself he might want others to want. If paint, like clothes, was for him, at an unconscious level, a covering up, then what were the catastrophes associated with nakedness? What would he have been doing, what would he have been thinking about, if he had neither got dressed nor painted? If one was to be a crude old-style Freudian, in other words – not an uninteresting thing to be – one might think of clutter as a reaction formation against some simple crudities. Think how cluttered – how complicated and confusing – one's mind, or indeed one's conversation, can become faced with someone we desire.

All of this, to some extent, and at different times, seemed pertinent to my patient. But I want to consider some more specific questions. Firstly, what's a good mess? Which might mean, from whose point of view is it good (or bad), and what are the unconscious criteria for deciding? In one mood I might think despairingly, 'This room is too cluttered.' In a different mood I might take it for granted, find it rather cosy, be impressed by being the kind of person who lives in creative chaos, and so on. What makes clutter work for us, and how does it when it does? A good life, one might say, involves making the messes you need.

We may be able to tolerate, and even enjoy, our own mess, but nothing tests our feelings for other people more than our feelings about their mess. Indeed, our relationship to what we think of as the other person's disorder – or their disordering of us – is a picture, a synecdoche, of our relationship to them. Where we experience other people as disorder can be where we experience them as other; can be where we experience them. In this sense, clutter is other people, they get in our way. So it's always worth wondering when we think someone is ruining our life what we imagine our life uncluttered by them would look like. I think all this is relevant because our relationship to clutter – what we identify as clutter, when we use the word – has a history. And personal history is always co-constructed, is always made in the context of relationship. So we may wonder, at the start, with whom did we first experience what we think of now, or even thought of then, as clutter? How did we learn it, and how were we taught it? Two different things.

My patient, growing up, as he said, with 'bohemian parents', had clearly spent some of his childhood longing for what he thought of as 'an ordinary home' like some of his friends had. It was, of course, only by going to other children's houses that he began to realize that there were other worlds. And of course, his friends found his home, crowded as it usually was with things and people, incredibly exciting. 'We are ramshackle but we are comfortable,' his mother would apparently say, sounding like someone from a Bloomsbury novel. What my patient thought of as an ordinary home was one in which meals were regular and on time, and one in which the adults made more time for the children. As he remembered it, it was as though other people's 'more normal' homes crystallized something that he had always felt but never quite realized: that he experienced his life as something of an obstacle course. A lot of things seemed to get in his way. The freedom of his parents' household could be sometimes just a mess for him.

At home there had been both too much space – the space created or imposed upon him by his parents' own absorbing preoccupations, which left him, he thought, too much to himself – and too little space – the house seemed cluttered with its unpredictable population of people and its various artefacts. And this was another ingredient of his present agoraphobia. Outside, with all that space, and no one keeping an eye on him, what might happen to him? This in turn was the passive version of a more frightening question: what might he do? The neglect he had felt at home had left him feeling uncontained; this was then, in adulthood, displaced on to the outside world, as a fear of freedom.

When he cluttered up his canvases as an adolescent he was inevitably doing several things at once. At a documentary level it was a representation of the clutter he experienced his home as, a clutter that could preclude his freer expression of himself.

What he had, to some extent, suffered passively at home – his parents' chaos – he now actively inflicted on his canvas. There was a strong Oedipal current here; that is what the parents do – they prohibit, they baffle one's desire. None of our parents gave us enough freedom, gave us the freedom we needed and deserved, which was the freedom to make them our partners. But also the clutter at home suited him – he could exploit it as part of his defence against his own desire. He could become addicted to the obstacles to his desire rather than to the objects of his desire. He could protect himself from his own delirium of wanting. The rage of frustration can be more comforting than the derangement of desire.

But, as is often the case, the solution is as interesting, as inventive, as the problem. When, following the lead of another father, Francis Bacon, my patient started throwing paint at his canvases, he was, as he put it, 'making a mess of the mess'. It wasn't, exactly, that he needed to unclutter his canvas, but rather that he needed to find a different way of cluttering it up. What mattered then was simply that it worked. His coming for psychoanalysis meant we could think about – in relation to his presenting symptom – what made this new kind of clutter work for him. 'While you're working in a certain way,' Bacon said in an interview, 'you try to go further in that direction, and that's when you destroy the image you had made, an image that you will never retrieve. That's also when something unexpected suddenly appears: it comes with no warning . . . What's most surprising is that this something, which has appeared almost in spite of oneself, is sometimes better than what you were in the process of doing.' Bacon is saying that whatever destroys the image takes its place. That the act of ruining something produces something else. That the spoiled thing can not only – though not always – be better than the original thing, it can also be, indeed can't help but be, utterly unpredicted; in that sense, unique, unprecedented. That only by absolutely losing something – 'an image that you will never retrieve', as Bacon says – do you get the surprising thing.

Chambers Dictionary defines clutter as: 'A clotted or confused mass: a disorderly accumulation: confusion . . . to clog with superfluous objects, material, etc.' What Bacon suggests – without superstition – and, indeed, what my patient found, was that the disorderly accumulation of throwing paint, the act that could clog the picture with superfluous material, could also disclose something new, something that paradoxically was closer to one's heart by being beyond one's design. Clutter, as chaotic accumulation, could be both a thwarting and a source of revelation. One might think of the difference as being two different kinds of unconscious work. The good mess and the bad mess – the mess that can be used, and the mess that stultifies; it may be a more productive distinction than the one between clutter and pattern. Our vocabulary of disorders, by virtue of being a vocabulary, a grammar, is always glib.

In her wonderful book, *On Not Being Able to Paint*, Marion Milner refers to a kind of personal aesthetic she discovered for herself through what she called 'free drawing', the visual equivalent of free association, the kind of doodling one might do in an idle moment:

> One thing I noticed about certain of my free drawings was that they were somehow bogus and demanded to be torn up as soon as made. They were the kind in which a scribble turned into a recognizable object too soon, as it were; the lines drawn would suggest some object and at once I would develop them to make it look like that object. It seemed almost as if, at these moments, one could not bear the chaos and uncertainty about what was emerging long enough, as if one had to turn the scribble into some recognizable whole when in fact the thought or mood seeking expression had not yet reached that stage. And the result was a sense of false certainty, a compulsive and deceptive sanity, a tyrannical victory of the common-sense view which always sees objects as objects, but at the cost of something else that was seeking recognition, something more to do with imaginative than common-sense reality.

Milner counsels us to be wary of the pre-emptive imposition of patterns, of the compulsive sanity of reassuring recognitions, of what we might be doing when we are too keen to clear up clutter. Clutter, that is to say, may be a way of describing either the deferral that is a form of waiting, or the waiting that is a form of deferral. Our eagerness for recognition can be a self-blinding.

IV

Substances

ZOË HELLER and ROY PORTER
The Chemistry of Happiness

November 15th

Dear Roy,

When we spoke on the phone, you suggested that it was my duty, as an 'addict and advocate' of Prozac, to start off this correspondence. I'm not sure that I can produce the cheerleaderly zeal suggested by that phrase. However, I'll give it a go and leave you to judge whether our positions are sufficiently opposed to constitute an argument.

I was put on Prozac by a psychiatrist in New York, eight months ago. I have been subject to bouts of depression for as long as I can remember, but at the time, I had been seriously depressed for at least a year and was finding it increasingly difficult to function normally. In a very short space of time after I had started taking the drug – three weeks, I guess – my behaviour and outlook underwent a significant change. To name some of the most tangible results: I stopped lying in bed in the middle of the day. I stopped crying all the time. I began to entertain visions of my future that were, if not entirely rosy, then at least not entirely gloom-laden. Perhaps most significantly, I found myself able to halt the chain reaction of morbid anxieties that, in my depressive state, was frequently set off by the most minor of incidents. (In the US, and, so far as I know, in the UK too, Prozac has been officially approved for the treatment of serious depression and of obsessive-compulsive disorder. The connection between these two ailments is interesting to me because depression has always struck me as obsessional in nature: instead of being merely sad, one becomes *obsessively* sad, *compulsively* fretful.)

A brief word about the chemistry: Prozac is the first of a new generation of anti-depressants known as selective serotonin re-uptake inhibitors, or SSRIs. Its development was based on the theory that depression is related to the decreased concentration of certain neurotransmitters – among them, serotonin – in the brain's synapses. Instead of doing their job – i.e. carrying impulses from one nerve cell to another – the neurotransmitters in a depressed person are being 'taken back' into the transmitting cell and destroyed by certain enzymes. Previous antidepressants have worked by attempting to inhibit this 're-uptake' process. Prozac is simply the first drug to target the re-uptake of serotonin, without affecting the other transmitters. Prozac doesn't seem to be more effective at relieving depression than previous drugs: its rate of success is in the same 65 to 70 per cent range. It is just easier to take and it gives rise to fewer side effects.

Since it was introduced in 1987, a number of fairly nutty claims have been made on Prozac's behalf. In his book, *Listening to Prozac*, the American psychiatrist Peter Kramer claims that Prozac might give rise to a new era of 'cosmetic psychopharmacology', enabling people to 'extend social popularity, business acumen, self-image, energy, flexibility, sexual appeal' as they wish. While it seems perfectly likely that a person overcoming a bout of depression may find that he or she feels more attractive and on the ball (people in the depths of depression are not, generally speaking, a lot of laughs at cocktail parties), the implication that such benefits may be enjoyed by non-depressives – that Prozac can be used as a generalized personality-enhancer – seems to me highly suspect. Such claims encourage the impression that Prozac is a self-indulgent American fad. Certainly, Prozac has been used to fuel a fond American faith in the perfectibility of life, but it seems unfair to condemn a drug because of some of the inappropriate causes it has been made to serve.

The chances of anyone who is not authentically depressive staying on Prozac, for any length of time, seem slim. Prozac doesn't lend itself easily to recreational purposes. Some people report a mildly speedy effect during the first few weeks, but this is the sort of buzz you might get from drinking too much coffee. And though the adverse side effects – nausea, headaches, diarrhoea, night sweats, and so on – are fewer than with earlier anti-depressants, they are still not much fun.

Am I entirely happy to be taking Prozac? Not really. I have as much puritan distaste for the idea of being reliant on a drug as the next woman. If the effects of Prozac had been even slightly less dramatic, I think I would have probably given it up by now. It has been pointed out to me by fellow Prozac-eaters that if I suffered from diabetes, I would have no scruples about injecting myself regularly with insulin. The problem is that the relationship between levels of serotonin and depression is nowhere near as scientifically established as the relationship between insulin and diabetes. More than that: depression itself is much more difficult to define and quantify than diabetes. I have friends who question whether my depression was sufficiently chronic to warrant pharmaceutical intervention. I'm not sure. All I can say for certain is that I was miserable for a long time and now I'm not. Where fresh air, exercise, therapy, vodka, and iron pills all failed, Prozac seems to have done the trick.

Yours,
Zoë Heller

November 22nd

Dear Zoë,
Funny thing, serendipity. Your Prozac thoughts reached me just when all the talk here was about drugs and depression. As I write, Britain is glued to the sad case of Leah Betts, who took her first Ecstasy tablet at her eighteenth birthday party, fell into a coma and died – accompanied by tabloid hysteria.

Just as the story broke I happened to be paying a visit to my ex-stepdaughter, also eighteen, who's just gone off to university. The conversation turned to 'substances'. For her the issues were clear as crystal. Cigarettes and dope were one thing: all her generation smoked ('in moderation'); it was their way of coping and relaxing (lung cancer? well, you only live once). But Ecstasy and 'hard drugs' were a different story. They were cultish – don't mess with those things, she told me, you never know what they might do to your head, especially mixed with alcohol. And Prozac? Never heard of it!

It was intriguing chatting to someone so near to myself yet so far (a whole generation), and swapping our lines on what were once called 'good scenes' and 'bad trips', with respect to what goes into our bodies. And all right, it's time to out myself: I knock back the coffee and the Chardonnay, counteract with Nurofen and vitamin C, and still slaver over roast beef – 'Oh, please, Roy, do try to break yourself of the habit,' she implores, 'it's so bad for you, with all the mad cow disease.' Ashamed, I gaze at my boots and remember Astrov as Sonya begs him to lay off the bottle.

The other thing buzzing round my mind when your letter arrived was the Princess Di television interview, particularly the bit where she came clean about her old bulimia and self-mutilating behaviour. Pressures had built up, depression deepened, and the bingeing had served both as symptom and relief – all that before she'd undergone treatments (pre-Prozac, I guess) to break those harmful habits. I watched, reflecting: I've never binged and puked myself, I've never slashed my wrists, I've never lain in bed all day so gripped by leaden-eyed despair that I just can't stir; I've never popped a Prozac. What do I make of this? Do I say: there but for the grace of God . . . ? Do I think: thanks to this, that and the other, I'm 'normal'? (Thanks to *what*? – because I came from a loving family? Because through some fluke my serotonin and dopamine levels make me Mr Meridian?) Or do I say: look at yourself and admit: when it comes to obsessions, over-compensation, displacement behaviour, and the rest, you've got enough on your case notes to confine the average neurotic to the also-rans?

All that's by way of prologue to explaining why I feel so unsure about Prozac. There's an old argument going round in the UK that runs like this: Prozac must be a bad thing because it's a quick fix. Happiness, as the worthy John Stuart Mill pronounced, isn't something you can patent or purchase; there are no chemical short cuts. The proper thing to do is to stiffen your upper lip and fight the good fight; through will-power and character you will achieve autonomy – and maybe just a smidgen of cheer.

Well, that's not an objection I buy: that brand of muscular individualism was all too often Victorian hypocrisy dolled up to mask the smugness of the successful. And anyway, it's humbug, because we all harbour some fix of our own, some private addictions that keep us going. All of us make secret deals with our minds and bodies – another swig for Dutch courage, a Mars bar sugar fix now (work it off later). Even that most earnest of Victorians, Thomas Carlyle, was hooked on his baccy and gingerbread (now *there's* a new one). One man's Prozac is another man's poison, so we should all pick our own poison – and never forget that opium kept Thomas de Quincey writing for fifty years.

But it *would* bother me if Prozac (or anything else) were to be accepted as some kind of pleasure principle panacea, bringing to pass Huxley's *Brave New World* fears. Sure, millions are stressed and depressed, but that may be because we live in times in which anxiety and anger are the right responses – even healthy ones. Social disintegration, job insecurity, ceaseless pressures, the devaluing of all that's decent by the 'greed is good' philosophy: all these spread distress and menace our sanity. And if that's so, we ought to pause before opting to sweeten the system by swallowing stimulants or sedatives. That's not to say we should yell 'Stop the world – I want to get off' like gaga hippies. But if it's the way things are that makes us depressed, surely what we need is not chemicals but change: politics, not happy pills.

So answer me this question. What we Brits are hearing from America is that the Prozac revolution is now snowballing well beyond helping the individual, into a sort of national nostrum. *Prozac Nation* is no longer confined to Elizabeth Wurtzel's arty fast-lane fantasies: our papers are now talking of ten million Americans on the better-than-well pill and of eight-year-old addicts. Or is this just another panic cooked up over here to make you lot all seem as mad as Manhattan? Reassure me! Please!
Roy Porter

November 25th

Dear Roy,
I thought you were kidding when you first called me a Prozac-addict, but since you have used the term 'addict' again, in reference to the mythical hordes of eight-year-old Prozac-eaters, I think I should risk pedantry and clear this up. Prozac is not an addictive drug. (By the way, it is just silly to place cigarettes, gingerbread and Prozac under the same naughty-but-nice heading. Cigarettes are poison by any objective standard and gingerbread patently is not.) My larger objection, however, is to your take on depression. You talk about your own neurotic behaviour and wonder why you shouldn't be considered a suitable candidate for Prozac. I don't know you well enough to be certain, of course, but I'd guess that none of your symptoms are sufficiently severe to indicate chronic depression or obsessive-compulsive disorder. In other words, Prozac isn't meant for people who feel a bit down in the dumps, or who fret about things too much. Those feelings, as you suggest, are the occupational hazards of being human and any effort to banish them permanently from human experience would not only be sinister, but doomed to failure.

By the same token, Prozac cannot and isn't meant to replace political action by pacifying people who have rational, material reasons for discontent – for example, the homeless, the jobless, or the recently bereaved. Unlike you, I do agree with Mill that happiness cannot be purchased or patented. But Prozac doesn't purport to make you happy; it merely counters a chemical predisposition to being unhappy. Prozac takers are still subject to the normal human share of sadness, anger, and anxiety; it's just that those feelings tend to have specific causes rather than being perpetual, irrational states of mind.

Clearly, when one starts talking about 'rational' and 'irrational' unhappiness, one is treading on very dodgy ground: who, after all, is to define what constitutes the 'irrational' blues? As I acknowledged, clinical depression is a much woollier medical concept than, say, diabetes. I don't think that this diagnostic vagueness has led to quite the Prozac-frenzy in the

US that you speak of, but yes, I am quite certain there are Prozac takers, here and in the UK, who would be better off in therapy, or doing aerobics. One psychiatrist I recently met at a party gleefully informed me that he had taken to dispensing Prozac as a sort of marital aid for couples who weren't getting on with each other. He had found it particularly useful, he said, in treating 'nagging wives' and their 'self-righteous husbands'. This struck me as a very misguided and frivolous use of the drug. (Whatever 'benefits' he claimed to have witnessed seemed much more likely to do with the fact that the couples in question were talking sensibly to each other, than with increased concentrations of serotonin.)

I suspect, however, that the medical establishment's love affair with Prozac is peaking and that, sooner or later, passion for the new wonder drug will give way to a more sober assessment of what it can and can't do. Like Valium – once hailed as the housewives' saviour – Prozac will cease to be the latest craze and take its rightful place in medicine's pharmacological armoury. Reassuring enough?

Best wishes,
Zoë Heller

November 28th

Dear Zoë,
Points taken! And I certainly don't want to be a dog in the manger. But my problem – because I earn my living as a historian – is that I'm haunted by the past.

As long ago as 1700, a pre-Prozac wonder drug was being praised. 'Providence has been kind to us beyond all expression in furnishing us with a certain *relief*, if not a remedy, even to our most intense pains and extreme miseries,' trumpeted the great Scottish physician George Cheyne. It had no side effects, no drawbacks, and doctors prescribed it with abandon. It was opium.

A century later, they'd wised up a bit, but fortunately

pharmacologists had by then extracted from the divine but dangerous poppy a positively non-addictive extract: morphia, perfect for quelling pains and soothing troubled souls. Luckier still, the hypodermic syringe was invented in about 1850, so that doctors could prescribe morphine to the millions who could then inject it for themselves. It was, as one practitioner put it, 'the greatest boon given to medicine since the discovery of chloroform'. The predictable crop of morphine-dependent 'dope fiends' appeared. But the medics soon solved that problem by coming up instead with heroin, touted as far safer than morphia; and then with cocaine, which the young Sigmund Freud (among others) liberally prescribed to wean his patients off their morphine habit.

History keeps on repeating itself, so I'll cut a long story short and zoom to the present. In about 1950 the psycho-pharmacological revolution was proclaimed. Psychiatrists claimed that, thanks to new psychotropic drugs, mental illness would be a thing of the past by the year 2000. Now we know such drugs turned thousands into zombies. In the 1960s the new pill for people who were down was Valium. Unlike the widely prescribed amphetamines, the new tranquillizers (the drug companies reassured us) were absolutely non-habit-forming. What's more, just like those other two miracle drugs of the times, the Pill and Thalidomide, they had (so it was said) positively no side effects.

The historian's perennial temptation is to deal the Judgement card, turning the past into the great punisher, and parading precedents proving that whatever you do, you'll pay for it. All that Horsemen of the Apocalypse stuff – we had a bellyful with Aids – is obviously best avoided. But the sobering fact remains: over the centuries the panaceas promoted by the doctors and puffed by the drug firms have had a nasty way of creating unforeseen side effects and dependencies. Prozac, I grant, might just be different; we may have the unbelievably good luck to be living at precisely that moment when, for the first time ever, a wonder drug really lives up to its promise; but short memories are dangerous.

I have no doubt that Eli Lilly's scientists have run all possible trials, and will put their hands on their hearts and swear Prozac is non-addictive. But that's been said of so many smart drugs in the past that it can't be worth the paper it's written on until we have some decades of experience to judge by. Prozac's just coming up to eight years.

And that brings us back to the dreaded 'A' word. You're quite right to resent the term 'Prozac addicts', because 'addict' conjures up all kinds of images – junkies shooting up in toilets or groaning in the gutter. In truth, we'd all be better off if the demon image of the 'addict' were towed out to sea and sunk. This talk is mainly the fantasies of twisted tub thumpers; or, when real, such addicts are essentially the offshoots of criminalising legislation and punitive attitudes. I go along with those who maintain that today's 'drug problems' are more the product of public attitudes towards drugs than the substances themselves; that the 'war against drugs' mainly profits politicians, police, and pushers; and that a key step towards solving drug problems lies in decriminalisation.

So if I have reservations about Prozac, it's not because I have a banning mentality – far from it. My fear is that, like all other wonder drugs, Prozac will prove a double-dealer. Or let me put it this way. You say Prozac isn't meant for people who are just down in the dumps. Quite right. But then we're told that ten million Americans are on Prozac and the numbers are soaring. Does that mean that ten million Americans are profoundly depressed? Or that *use* has already turned to *abuse*? In the end, it's not the Prozac that worries me, it's why it's been seized upon like a new salvation.

Cheers,
Roy Porter

December 8th

Dear Roy,
The medical establishment is a little more wary than it once was, and the procedures for testing new drugs are rather more

sophisticated. But you are right, of course: to meddle with one's internal chemistry is not – and will never be – risk free. I have tried to measure the risk of taking Prozac against the known discomfort of depression and have ended up opting for the former. The point is: I have opted. You, on the other hand, seem to be taking a rather mealy-mouthed line. You say you don't want to turn the past into 'the great punisher', but what then, is the point of the precedents you cite? Play Cassandra by all means, but at least do it with some conviction: tell us we should take Prozac off the market at once. Tell the chronic depressive whose life has been dramatically improved by Prozac that you don't want him taking the drug any more. Otherwise, what are you doing, except hedging your bets? ('No, no, I'm not saying you *shouldn't* – but don't say I didn't warn you . . .')

It is also only fair to point out that most of the drugs you mention, in your list of wonder-cures-gone-horribly-wrong, continue to serve, in some revised form, useful medical purposes. Morphine may not have been 'the greatest boon given to medicine' but it certainly makes dying from cancer a lot less grim than it once was. This was what I meant when I suggested that, sooner or later, the Prozac-frenzy would die down and the drug would find its proper value. Should ten million Americans be on Prozac? I would think not (although I'd still like to know where you got that figure). Should doctors be responsible and restrained when prescribing drugs, particularly new ones? Yes. Should patients be encouraged to take an active interest in their own health and the pills they put in their own bodies? Yes. Should we appreciate that much of what is now branded 'dysfunction' is merely the necessary stuff of being human? Yes. But do I plan to stop taking my beautiful, green and white, 20mg pill every day? As my cab driver said to me this morning, when I gave him a twenty-dollar bill to pay a three-dollar fare – no freaking way.

Best wishes,
Zoë Heller

December 10th

Dear Zoë,
But what you say doesn't follow. If I say something may be dangerous, it doesn't commit me in the next breath to trying to ban it. John Stuart Mill sorted that out over a century ago, and I'll stick by his defence of personal liberty any day. In any case, the social consequences of all sorts of prohibition are usually counter-productive.

There's a difference between choosing to dice with danger and pretending that at last we've got something that's risk free – the message that seems to waft across from the Prozac pushers.

Let me suggest a compromise: why not have an unseen but implied *Surgeon General's History Warning* on every pack of Prozac (and cigarettes, and bourbon, and whatever), saying 'On Your Own Head Be It.' That'll make sure the imp of the perverse stays alive and kicking.

Be warned, be well, beware – and keep taking the tablets.
Roy Porter

SIMON ARMITAGE
The Stuff

We'd heard all the warnings; knew its nicknames.
It arrived in our town by word of mouth
and crackled like wildfire through the grapevine
of gab and gossip. It came from the south

> so we shunned it, naturally;
> sent it to Coventry

and wouldn't have touched it with a barge pole
if it hadn't been at the club one night.
Well, peer group pressure and all that twaddle
so we fussed around it like flies round shite

> and watched,
> and waited

till one kid risked it, stepped up and licked it
and came from every pore in his body.
That clinched it. It snowballed; whirlpooled. Listen,
no one was more surprised than me to be

> cutting it, mixing it,
> snorting and sniffing it

or bulking it up with scouring powder
or chalk, or snuff, or sodium chloride
and selling it under the flyover.
At first we were laughing. It was all right

> to be drinking it, eating it,
> living and breathing it

but things got seedy; people went missing.
One punter surfaced in the ship-canal
having shed a pair of concrete slippers.
Others were bundled in the back of vans

and were quizzed, thumped,
finished off and dumped

or vanished completely like Weldon Kees:
their cars left idle under the rail bridge
with its cryptic hoarding which stumped the police:
'Oldham – Home of the tubular bandage.'

Others were strangled.
Not that it stopped us.

Someone bubbled us. CID sussed us
and found some on us. It was cut and dried.
They dusted, booked us, cuffed us and pushed us
down to the station and read us our rights.

Possession and supplying:
we had it, we'd had it.

In Court I ambled up and took the oath
and spoke the addict's side of the story.
I said grapevine, barge pole, whirlpool, chloride,
concrete, bandage, station, story. Honest.

ROSIE BOYCOTT
A Nice Girl Like Me

From the outside it is an unobtrusive building. You pay highly
for the exterior discretion. Inside it's a bit like a ship. You go
upstairs to the dining room, even further upstairs to the rooftop
balcony. The inside corridors have no windows and are permanently lit by harsh strip-lighting. Our floor was the upper
ground, which meant we were just above street level. The windows of our rooms only opened six inches upwards or downwards, thus preventing patients sneaking out for a quick one at
a pub called the Chelsea Potter, which was tantalizingly situated
across the street.

Alcoholism is no longer classed as a mental illness, but is
described as an illness; not because it can be caught, like a virus,
but because it has an observable set of symptoms. Articles about
alcoholism in popular magazines always set out a series of questions, and end with the remarks, 'If you say yes to any two or
three of the above then you have a drink problem.' If you are
drinking in the morning, drinking to run away from something
frightening, drinking when you're already drunk, having memory blackouts and so on, then that is not normal drinking. On
the other hand it may not mean that you are necessarily
alcoholic.

The definitions of alcoholism are as varied and numerous as
the doctors who have devoted their lives to studying the subject.
My doctor was a believer in the works and studies of Jellinek,
in whose honour the unit in which I currently resided was
named. Loss of control due to drinking, on a regular basis,
means you're alcoholic. As a medical definition, it's a good one.
I've known people who can drink half a bottle of Scotch a day
and not come to any apparent mental harm. They may get a bit
slurry, but their behaviour is not antisocial, they don't pass out
like flies who've suddenly been squirted with Black Flag and
their inner calm does not degenerate into alcoholic paranoia.

They are, however, harming their bodies.

Over what is a 'safe' amount to drink, there is also endless debate. Women, with smaller bodies and smaller livers, can drink far less. But people's constitutions vary and what can poison one can be tolerable to another.

Alcohol itself is ether. Chemists call it ethyl alcohol and what we drink is ether with flavourings for taste. Ether reduces the activities of the nervous system, and in small quantities this creates the 'high', since your inhibitions are lifted. You get sexier, happier, funnier, and so on. I know the magic of the first few drinks as well as anyone. After the first few, when the alcohol cuts deeper into the brain, your judgement becomes severely impaired, senses numb, stumbling starts because you are cutting off the motor controls which govern your body. As judgement goes, belligerence, anger, and lies may emerge. Finally you can numb the brain so much that you pass out. You also have blackouts.

Blackouts are the only piece of irretrievable human memory known to man. You can subject an alcoholic to sodium pentathol, to hypnosis, to any of the tricks which are supposed to bring back deeply buried thoughts. No luck. Later in my stay in the clinic, I met an American doctor who then worked for the US Navy. Alcoholic pilots were his speciality. He had treated men who could remember leaving their hotels in London's Gloucester Road at nine in the morning, and the next thing they could remember was walking into another hotel in Manhattan. Three hundred lives in their hands in between and 3,000 miles at 30,000 feet. No joke.

The body, as well as the mind, suffers from alcohol excess through liver disease, pancreatitis, heart disease, gastric inflammation, malnutrition, and brain damage. Most are reversible if you stop in time, though each on its own can kill if left to run riot with constant supplies of booze. There is no escaping the fact that alcoholism is a fatal disease. Quite how many fatalities it actually causes is impossible to pinpoint, since a respectable city gent who dies of heart failure at his desk is going to be recorded as leaving this planet as a result of a heart attack. His widow is not going to want a doctor to stick on his death certificate that his premature death was caused by copious quantities of alcohol which had weakened his heart, built up fatty deposits around it, and caused that fatal seizure.

No alcoholic will survive to end his days naturally. It may be a car accident, it may be cirrhosis, it may be internal haemorrhaging due to the wearing down of the skin surrounding the oesophagal veins until they become so worn that they literally burst open and flood your blood right into the wrong places: stomach, lungs, and life.

Day patients often joined the group sessions. Later on, during my fourth day in the clinic, a middle-aged blonde, wearing a bright red polyester suit, came hesitantly into the room.

'Anne,' she cried, her prematurely lined face breaking into a smile.

'Shelagh!' Anne leapt up from her seat and they embraced.

'What are you doing here?' they both asked simultaneously.

'I've been here for two weeks. It's really working this time,' said Anne.

Shelagh looked at her friend encouragingly. 'Great,' she said, 'I'm checking in tomorrow.' The two women had met in another clinic in London. This was my first introduction to the phenomenon of clinic-hopping. The boozer tries one after the other, in the hope of finding some cure, and always seems to end up relapsing. The concept was grossly depressing, but it also had its funny side.

The doctor came in. 'Hello there, Shelagh,' he said and smiled brightly at her. 'You're coming in tomorrow?'

Shelagh looked glum. 'Andrew can't stand it any more. The kids are in a state. The gardener found ten empty vodka bottles in the potting shed.'

Her hands were shaking. She twisted her fingers together in her lap.

'I had a disaster in the house too. I passed out and when I came to I'd forgotten where I'd hidden the bottle. The maid came to do the washing and when she turned on the machine there was this awful noise. I'd hidden the vodka in there. It wrecked the kids' clothes and Andrew says we've got to have a new washing machine.'

The doctor looked at the floor. Shelagh had been his patient for two years and success, so far, was elusive. 'How long did you stay off this time?' he asked her gently.

'Under a week. I can't seem to manage it. Andrew's threatening to leave me. I feel so useless.'

'But what about the children?' asked Brian. 'Aren't they an incentive to stay sober?'

'They don't need me,' she said sadly, 'neither does Andrew. No one does. I've tried having a maid, and not having a maid, so that I have something to do, then I find I can't even make the effort to make the bed in the morning.'

She looked tragic and frightened. She was overweight, badly dressed for someone with a great deal of money, and always wore the same pair of plastic, imitation patent-leather black shoes. Her tights usually had a ladder in them. She bit her fingernails. But her hair was always immaculate.

'Do you have to go out, entertain?' Brian asked.

'No, Andrew doesn't ask people to the house any more . . . he daren't. But I never drink in public.'

'Same as you, Anne, though not you, Rosie,' said the doctor. A difference between the generations: older women only drank in private, younger ones got drunk sometimes, at least, in public.

Very few marriages survive alcoholism. It's a hard statistic that whereas only one in ten alcoholic husbands are left by their wives, nine out of ten husbands eventually leave their alcoholic wives. Taylor coughed gently. 'I can't imagine what I would do if my wife was drunk all the time.'

'My wife left me because I drank,' said Brian. 'Well, it was one of the reasons.'

'I suppose the man I really loved left me because of the booze,' I added. I hadn't confronted that fact before, only suspected it, and immediately shut it out.

'Pauline, my wife,' said Raju to Shelagh, 'nearly left, but then she started going to Al-Anon and somehow got me to go too.'

'Well, what are you doing here?' Shelagh snapped back.

'Impulse!' The word came out staccato. It was Raju's

favourite word, and his only explanation to account for his presence in a booze clinic after being off the stuff for one year.

'No such thing,' retorted Shelagh, who was recovering from her bout of self-pity.

There was a silence.

'How was the year without booze?' I asked Raju.

'OK,' he said. Raju worked as an anaesthetist in a West Country hospital, so his alcoholism was a potential killer not only to himself, but to others too.

'How did you cope with going to parties?' I asked.

'OK,' he replied again. The question was silly anyway. Raju and I had nothing in common, bar the booze.

'Does the fact that you're asking about going to parties mean that you're starting to see that you'll have to give up drink?'

Brian turned towards me. I shrugged, noncommittally.

'Do you yet admit that your life has been fucked by booze?' I nodded.

'And you want it to go on?'

'No, of course not,' I said crossly. 'Why would I be here if . . .'

'How many times have you tried to stop?' asked the doctor.

'None. Well, that's not really true. I've tried cutting down,' I added.

'And it hasn't worked,' interrupted Anne.

'Sometimes, yes, sometimes it has,' I muddled on, defensively.

Every drunk is different. It took Anne half a bottle of sherry to pass out, it took Brian a couple of bottles of vodka. What we had in common was an addiction to booze, and a sense of worthlessness in our lives. No one could pinpoint the magic line where we stopped being 'social drinkers' and became alcoholic, but we all publicly or secretly knew that we were there. Our lives were in a mess, were being run by the bottle. That doesn't mean being drunk all the time, either. In my case, I would go for long stretches, sometimes weeks, sometimes months, drinking normally. At least, that's how it appeared. I wasn't drinking normally, because I would be anxious near lunchtime, anxious around 6.30, anxious to make sure there was always wine for dinner. But in terms of quantity, I was actually drinking no more than William. Except at times. Loneliness, misery, a sense of no purpose to my life would come rushing up and I knew the answer. Drunkenness was a shield against pain, against the failure of too many dreams, against a sense of spiritual confusion. But what had started out as a protection racket, my third mad lady (the drinking me) taking care of the inner baby, was no longer working. Now it was no longer possible to see what problems stemmed from booze and what were problems in themselves.

I remembered endless visits to a Harley Street shrink, who probed, at great expense, into reasons for my drinking. He thought, and many people do, that if he could ever crack the reason, then the booze problem would disappear. 'See if you can manage to have more orgasms,' he'd once said. 'Did you see your father in the bath when you were a baby?' He thought that if I got fucked better then I'd stop drinking. I'd discuss this problem with him quite seriously, but for only one reason: it kept the conversation away from my growing dependence on alcohol. By the time I got up to leave his office, he'd smile, I'd smile, and then I'd scamper to the off-licence or the pub. My weekly visits to the shrink were a sanction to drink.

I snapped out of my reverie to find the doctor asking me a question.

'I'm trying to get you all to write your life stories,' he said. 'No one has bothered to do it so far, but since you're a journalist maybe you can sit down and write something, or take notes, and then tell us.'

William brought my typewriter into the clinic that night. He had been a faithful visitor, but I was finding it hard to deal with any visits. I was reverting to a childlike state: accepting help for the first time in my life made me vulnerable, shaky, and shy. The growing friendship between me and my fellow patients was becoming increasingly valuable. We were finding out each other's habits, who liked which TV programmes, who had sugar in their tea, which newspapers people liked to read.

The absurdities of the other patients (and of ourselves) presented an absorbing soap opera. The clinic, like it or not, was fast becoming my home. That night, I carefully cleaned off my eye make-up and applied moisturizer to my face. It's absurd, I thought, but I don't want to be anywhere else until . . . until when? I didn't know the answer. It wasn't like checking into a hotel. You arrived only when you had no alternative.

VICKI FEAVER
Pills

For God's sake take your pills!
He had to hurl her against the bathroom wall
before she'd be silent.
He wanted peace in the house.
He wanted her tame, grateful, faithful,
to eat from his hand
the little yellow pills
that turned everything grey
as a sea fret: butter, strings of marmalade,
crumbs crusted round the children's mouths
like grey sand. *Take three tablets*
three times a day. She'd push them up
with her tongue between teeth and cheek,
spitting them into the sink. After a few days,
when the mist rolled back, she'd strain her neck
craning to comprehend the blue space
birds moved in, limitless, filled
with twitterings and cries.
She'd kneel on the lawn,
skirt soaked, rediscovering
the shades of grass: each blade –
like the seconds lost –
separate, sharp, drawing blood
from her thumb. She'd gaze at oranges
as people gaze at statues of Christ
on the Cross: the brilliant rinds –
packed with juice, flesh, pips –
exploding like grenades,
like brains, like trapped gases
at the surface of the sun.

SHARON OLDS
19

When we took the acid, your wife was off
with someone else, there was a hole in your bedroom
wall where the Steuben wedding owl
had flown from one room right into another,
I was in love with your best friend
who had gone into a monastery
after he'd deflowered me,
so when we took off our clothes, it felt almost
like family, you came, under my
palm, I could feel the circular ribs of your
penis, I came with my legs wrapped around your
leg, even with my toes pointed
my feet reached only halfway down
your calf, later I was lying on the bathroom
floor, looking up at you, naked, you were
6' 6", a decathlete,
my eyes followed the inner curve of your
leg up, up, up,
up, up, up, up.
Weeks later, you would pull a wall-phone
out of a wall, and part of the wall,
the wires like ripples of vesicle; you would
cross the divider in the middle of the night
and drive us against the traffic a second, going
60, crying, I could hardly hear what you were
saying about the barbed wire
and your father and your balls,
but that night, we stayed up all night,
not going all the way,
making love now and then, and
talking like a slumber party – since I
wasn't in love with you, your beauty made me

happy, we chattered, we chatted naked, you
told me everything you liked
about my body – and you liked everything –
even the tiny goose-flesh bumps
around my hard nipples,
you said the way to make love to me
would be from behind, with that long angle, your
forefinger drew it gently, the deep
hairpin curve of the skinny buttocks, you
said it the way I imagined a brother might
give advice to a sister, your fingertip
barely missing my – whatever in love one would
call the asshole, you regarded me with a
savouring kindness, from some cleft of sweetness in the
human you actually looked at me and
thought how I best should be fucked. *Oooh.*
Oooh . . . So there was something to be done with me,
something exactly right, you looked at me
and saw it,
willing not to be the one
who did it – all night, you pleased me
and protected me, you gazed at my body and un-
saw my father's loathing, pore by
pore on my skin you closed that old man's eyes.

ELIZABETH YOUNG
Mother Can Take It

A memoir

L's JOURNAL

*First time I smoked H was in the lavatory at the China
Fleet Club, in Wanchai, Hong Kong.*

*I'd been trying to score some weed and, after making the
smoke sign to a rickshaw driver, I bought a HK$10 wrap
of H. He showed me how to smoke it.*

*Pinch the end of a Camel filter until some tobacco fell
out, empty half the wrap in, twist up the paper again, tap it
to settle the grey powder down into the cigarette.*

*In the loo I sucked greedily, holding down the smoke.
Thick grey coils of it, talcum scented, writhed away from
the tip of the cigarette.*

*Back in the bar I nursed a half pint of San Miguel which
I'd suddenly got no use for.*

*My experience of drugs at that time was limited to grass
in South Africa and Mombasa, and Rangoon Red in
Singapore.*

*Feeling a sudden urge to be out of the bar I left my drink
and took a rickshaw to the Peak Tramway. I caught the
ascending car with seconds to spare.*

L was still a teenager when he first took smack in China. He
wrote about it in his notebook, not long before his death. He'd
been trying to remember things.

All I have left now is two plastic bags. One contains his notebooks and letters, address books and sketchpads. The other is
full of photographs. The pictures he took are obsessive, repetitive. Many of them are townscapes, showing what is obviously
a Northern city; dull, rain-streaked, old-fashioned. Narrow

streets, hills of tumbledown terrace houses, net curtains, puddles in the road.

The other photos are of young boys with soft hair and wary eyes. They look uneasily into the camera, uncertain as to whether to smile. They hold syringes in the air, needle up, flicking the barrel, trying to settle the bubbles. Some of them are unconcernedly naked, apart from a leather belt wound tightly round the upper arm, making the veins stand out in relief.

('He's got pipes on him like the Pompidou Centre!' L boasts one evening in a London pub, rolling up the boy's sleeve to show me. The boy is bashful, unresisting. He looks at L and smiles lovingly. L is getting old. His teeth are almost gone. He has started wearing a soft-brimmed grey hat. His cheekbones stand out like adzes. It is a summer night. Other teenage boys drift up gently, wearing heavy, unseasonal overcoats. One of them has a piebald mongrel on a string. 'That one works double-shifts. They always throw more cash if you've got a pup along.' They start producing bags of stolen goods, stowing them under the wooden table. Sirloin steak and candy kisses from Marks and Spencer, piles of shining books from Foyles and Zwemmers. 'Hmmm, well,' says L. 'Don't just stand there, our Mark. Get a drink. Mek yerself at home. And one for the lady. What would you like, m'dear?')

L always had this Fagin aspect. I remember reading somewhere that Fagin was the real hero of *Oliver Twist* because he took all those children off the street and gave them a purpose.

The town in the photographs lies west of the Pennine Hills. Peter – L – was born there in 1947. That was his home and he always returned to it. He went back there to die. He left London just a few days before the end, in the deepest part of winter, as 1991 became 1992. We spoke on the telephone every day after he'd gone but soon he didn't know who I was.

L's parents were well into middle age when he was born.

'You were never wanted, you know.' That was what his next-door neighbour, Mrs MacDonagh, told him one day.

'After that,' L said, 'everything seemed to fall into place.'

His parents had each served about twenty years in the Army

before they met. His mother's pregnancy – and probably the conception too – was entirely accidental. His Scottish maternal grandparents, shamed and horrified, forced the reluctant couple into marriage. They retired from the Army and L's father built a small, grim house for them.

'They were that cruel,' said L, shortly before he died. 'I could never understand it.'

L wrote of a cold house, run on military lines. Carbolic soap, Bronco lavatory paper, thick skin on tepid milk at bedtime. They wondered aloud, he said, how they could ever have bred 'such a wee shit-bag'. His mother had one of those forties fox furs that were worn draped over the shoulders. It had the traditional shiny boot-button eyes and sharp little yellow teeth. As a child L was terrified of it. One afternoon his mother brought it down from the bedroom and chased him with it till the little boy was near crazy with fear.

'They just wanted to make trouble for somebody they hadn't encouraged to be alive at all. Ian and Myra – what a fucking pair.'

L was largely brought up by Mrs MacDonagh-next-door. He loved her. Her husband was part-owner of one of the town's chemists, MacDonagh and Ellis. After he grew up it was the one local chemist that L would never rob. He sent his best mate to do it instead.

He would usually pop in to see her in the mornings. 'Oh, Peter,' she'd say. 'Them vandals have been back. We've bin cleaned out.'

'Oh, aye, Mrs Mac? That's terrible.'

'This town's a changed place.'

He didn't feel good about it but there was no point muddying the different streams of your life. You'd only end up with shrinks and counselling and detox groups, all the crap they go in for now, and he couldn't be doing with any of that.

There is a photograph of L smiling – too knowing to look ironic – beneath one of those large, tin advertisements that used to hang on city walls. It says YOUR CHEMIST IS ROUND THE COR-NER. A helpful, pointing hand indicates the direction, just above the address.

When L was five or six his mother died. His father married a woman L always called 'that slag' and they moved westwards, to the sea. As soon as he reached school-leaving age, that slag enlisted him in the Royal Navy. He was sent away at the age of sixteen.

By the time L returned to the North in 1970 everything had changed. The dreary, brown uncut moquette carpet of the fifties had been rolled up and put away in an attic. The town was full of kids in T-shirts and bell-bottoms hanging around the cobbled courtyards of the pubs in the sun and frightening the old folk. 'Time' had been called for the traditional North of clogs and lamplighters. The last cotton mills closed down and although the docks, the river, and the canal looked the same there was less and less work to be had on them. The Northern teenagers who'd come of age in Wilson's candy-floss Britain had no time for all the hippy-dippy shite that was dizzying the rest of the world. They fastened on the heart of the matter – the drugs – with all the wolfish intensity of a generation released for ever from a lifetime's drudgery in factory and mill.

L returned with a fixed sexual identity and a lot of tattoos – he even had one on his belly-button, a squiggly thing somewhere between a comma and a sperm – and became notorious. He was shooting speed which made him pernickety and he looked after his flat – a basement in a crumbling wedding cake of a house surrounded by a jungle garden – with a combination of amphetamine obsession and Navy-trained meticulousness. He shared the flat with Billy, a headless man-sized dummy with stuffing shooting out his neck. Billy had huge muscles, emphasized with strokes of paint. His legs too were painted brown, to simulate sunburn. Once he had been part of an open-air tableau under an umbrella at Happy Mount Park, Morecambe.

L was constantly planning trips to Morecambe to sell drugs, or to Wigan for Northern Soul Night, but usually he stayed at home and shot more speed, sometimes dripping blood neatly on to the spotless tiles. He kept his works taped tidily to what was probably a syringa bush in the garden.

The local – hastily formed – Drugs Squad knew L well.

Dear Sir,

I refer to your letter dated 15th June, concerning property taken from your room at 43, Moon Street, ——.

I wish to inform you that this property is stored at Drug Squad Office, Heysham and if you contact the office on your release the property will be returned to you against signature. Yours faithfully, (scrawl) Chief Superintendent.

A lot of people died in those years and a lot of people went mad.

L's JOURNAL

To my surprise the lock clicked off and I slipped inside. It was a long, narrow lavatory and he sat, like an unstrung puppet, blond hair hanging over his face, his trousers pushed down exposing his groin, legs apart as far as the trousers and width of the loo would allow, probing away at the vein in his groin with a syringe full of vivid pink liquid.

Between his legs lay bloodied tissues, needles, swabs, and two foil squares.

I knew I had to move quickly to get a taste. I shouted his name over and over and finally he looked up and shaking the hair away from his face gasped and gulped. 'How the fucking hell did you get in here?'

'Can I have some, eh? C'mon,' I pleaded and to my surprise he indicated the remaining tablets.

'How many?'

'Tek 'em, tek 'em.'

I took 'em. I knew I'd still got to move fast, so did a hurried crunch of two of the three and a half I'd got, shook the powder up in a works and banged it in, wheezing as the wave of prickling hit my lungs.

I used to think it was the silicon base of the pills blocking the fine blood vessels of my lungs but a friend with a Double First in Chemistry and a raging habit told me the effect was 'purely pharmacological'.

The Northern kids seemed to run at night, in packs. From disco to dive to late licence, to offie. The girls were through their dyke phase with their cropped heads and fistfights. Their big boots clattered over the cobbles, the dawn chorus of another century. The Pendle Witches still walk the barren land outside town. There were babies buried all over the moors. Everyone knew. The boys tried to outdo one another in pharmacological psychosis. Sex was mainly dancing. Otherwise it dwindled before the crazed clash of gender politics in the pub or a sudden scream and crash of ampoules shattering on a floor. Think on.

'Oh, what a night – late September back in . . .'

L's JOURNAL

His torso and his arms were an appliqué of nick tattooing, knife scars, and burnt patches like raffia mats. When I returned my books had been torn asunder and scattered round the room.

'I sucked my little brother off but he didn't come in my mouth,' he shrieked.

'Why not?'

'Cos he wasn't OLD ENOUGH!!!'

I was glad to laugh, believe me, the atmosphere was electric. He raved off into the night. Later I heard he'd been put away. It was happening all the time, people burnt up on re-entry.

I met L when I was passing through the North in 1975. He heard I had a first edition of Kenneth Anger's recently published *Hollywood Babylon* and came round to look at it. I lent it to him and never saw it again. L was as extreme a bibliophile as you could find. At the time we grew up an unhappy childhood was not a public thing, a focus for therapy and discussion and social workers, but a private agony, often alleviated by a desperate amount of reading. Later, reading had taken L around the world where he'd seen little but the greasy interiors of industrial vessels or a brutality to which he occasionally alluded. It doesn't take much imagination to enlarge a voracious consumption of books into one of drugs. The two experiences are very similar. Especially smack – Tin Tack, Plastic Mack – which makes the world go away in a very similar manner. L was never mercenary enough to be a real drug dealer so his life was always a precarious spider's web of small-time theft, fucked-up Giros arriving late, tide-over loans and minuscule drug haggling – 'Two of them for one of these, go on, mek it three.'

L and his friends were always in and out of nick – 'It's amazing how being inside can give you an entrée, isn't it? Especially the circles we move in,' he wrote. Stupid, small-time charges – possession of drugs, possession of stolen goods – which meant that those most vulnerable were always being swept up, uselessly, pointlessly in other raids, like the wretched dolphin in tuna nets. Very soon I was visiting him in Preston Gaol, a blackened, archaic Victorian workhouse, tastefully situated beside a new motorway where the north winds spun down the lanes to rage and tear at the prison. 'What a fucking hole. Like Siberia in winter and so lonely.'

Actually he always adjusted well to institutional life, particularly as the prisons, like everywhere else, responded to Western policies of drug prohibition by becoming increasingly saturated with them. He worked as librarian. 'The first few days I were here,' he said, 'I just couldn't understand it. There was one cell that no one went near. No one spoke to the inmate. He didn't dare come out to eat. It was like he was on Rule 43 only he weren't. The screws had to shove his meals through his door. No one ever saw him. I were dead puzzled and eventually I ask the Senior Librarian what's up wi' the guy. Is he some sort of fuckin' leper or owt? "Oh no," says the Librarian. "That's the Preston Cat Strangler." '

By the end of his life L was up on his forty-seventh book-stealing charge. This one made *The Times*.

THIEF WAS OBSESSED BY
SMELL OF BOOKS

A trainee bookbinder with an obsession for books
was put on probation for two years yesterday after
giving an undertaking in the Central Criminal Court

that he would stay away from bookshops.

P – L –, aged 44 of Stepney, East London, who admitted stealing three astrology books from a central London bookshop in March, said he could keep out of trouble if he was not tempted by the smell of books. 'I don't miss them as long as I don't get a whiff of them,' he said. 'If I could go into a library that would suffice.'

Astrology? For resale only. By this time, of course, L had Aids so they weren't going to put him in prison. Too expensive.

During the eighties L spent more time in London. Eventually he was given a council bedsit round Royal Mint Street in the Minories, at night little changed in its blackness and silence from a century earlier when Jack had whispered to the whores. It was a big, airy room, overlooking the railway, and once Billy the headless torso was installed and the books and compilation tapes placed in their neat piles, it looked very like his previous flat, as neat and fastidious as ever. Did he really only have two homes in nearly half a century? Yes. Otherwise it was always squats and friends and burned-out houses.

At the beginning of the eighties I hired L to come and paint my new council flat. I would pay him in cocaine. My boyfriend dealt it. L rarely saw coke, it being so expensive. The decor ended up beguilingly spontaneous, tastefully *au courant* in its stripped-down minimalist look, garnished by the sprays of blood on the walls. We just sat on the stairs and shot all the coke, this being before the days of the Aids panic in needle park. He later undertook to be my housekeeper, tutting like an old maid as he scratched his initials into the gunk on the cooker. 'The glory that was grease! You could do a Bolero on this fuckin' floor too. To the ice, m'dear! And over and back . . . and again!' He laughs, starts coughing and spits into the sink. 'I'll mek us a cuppa.'

But, accustomed to popping round to see people in the North, he hated to use the telephone and so would just turn up. And then he would push you. For a bath, to borrow a book, for

money, for another cup of tea, to have a fix – I'd given up
needles so we'd start arguing. It always ended in screaming
rows and L's lacerating insults. He did this to all his friends,
tested them and tested them as if he had to know how much
they could take. And most took it and never held a grudge. L
had to live entirely without safety nets and it is hard for most
people to imagine this. No heating. The plumbing goes. The
kitchen window gets punched out. Who pays the plumber?
Who pays the glazier? But no one put up with him out of pity.
They did so because they loved him. He made them laugh. That
was it. (But think what it's like in this cold, tight-arsed country
for the drifter bereft of charm. Dennis Nilsen's cooking pot?)
The loyalty and devotion of his friends – and there were many
closer than myself – make a nonsense of all those theorists, their
mouths clogged with shit, who insist that there can be nothing
but betrayal and selfishness among criminals and drug users.

L grew older. He lost his hair, took to wearing the hat and
acquired that ghostly, seamed, old junkie look. His boyfriends
stayed the same though, always Northern teenagers, fluttering
around him like little drunken butterflies, hustling, scrounging,
ducking, and diving. L became less sexual and more avuncular,
although there were still days when 'There was so much dried
come lying around this morning I could have gone to a Fancy
Dress Ball as a GLAZED DOUGHNUT!' He had only had one
great, shattering love affair in his early life, with a beautiful,
intelligent redhead – long gone – but he was very loving towards
his boys, all of whom had nicknames – The Shadow, The
Fledgeling, The Kitten, Donkey Wanger ('Drum my upraised
face with your meat truncheon'). He liked them sulky. He liked
them sultry. He liked big dicks. There was the inevitable shrinking from judgement – from thought – on the morality of L
involving these kids in his life. The inexorable diffidence of
deviance. Throw stones? Who gets stoned first? Then you can
laugh again. One friend could in a couple of hours make contradictory assertions on the subject, if he bothered to: 'L has a
great capacity for corruption'; 'L has a strict working-class
morality.' It is safe to say that all the little chickens had shown

a marked disinterest in the straight and narrow long before they ran into L, otherwise they would never have done so. He showed them great concern, writing endlessly and exhorting them to treat the more dangerous drugs with care: 'Be sensible for your old Uncle Fester – he who loves you dearly. Please, Caution! EAT THE FUCKERS!'

L was killed not by sex or by drugs but by insane legislation. Although he liked speed he was primarily a junkie. Since 1968 heroin has been almost completely unobtainable legally for addicts in Britain. The American system of methadone maintenance was adopted. L, like most junkies, hated methadone and turned to the black market, to the streets, to the crime and the dirty needles and the disease to get the drugs he wanted. This enforced lifestyle created the conditions wherein Aids was passed on between drug users. If L had been able to get clean heroin on prescription when he needed it, his life – and probably his death – might have been different. L *was* a sufficiently extreme case to get heroin prescribed for a while (Diamorphine injection 30mg. Two to be administered daily), but the doctor ministering unto him was tracked down by a television crew and his life made difficult by those who have an economic interest (clinics, counsellors, doctors, shrinks, highlevel corruption in industry, finance, and God knows where) in keeping the methadone madness underway and the junk on the streets. As he aged, in common with many lifetime junkies, L could no longer summon the resources to acquire heroin, which is expensive. If it were available legally, people might not find themselves burnt-out and exhausted in mid-life from hustling for their drug, with no employment record – only a criminal one – and no future prospects just at the point when many of them start to 'age out' and lose interest in the drug anyway. I don't mean that L would have had a straightforward and conventional life, just that things would have been a lot easier if drugs had not outlawed him. He was no big-time criminal. He just wanted to get by, in his way. As heroin became more inaccessible he started shooting instead the very much cheaper and more lethal tranquillizer benzodiazepine, which he used in

the form of sleeping pills named Temazepam. He called them
'eggs', for their shiny, gelatinous look and the way you could
suck the liquid out of the capsule with a spike. 15mg ones were
bright yellow and looked like egg yolks. 30mg ones – he called
them 'double yolkers' – were dark green. He also started drinking more, again a common reaction as junkies get too old to
hustle for their drugs – and that didn't help.

L's deterioration was very sudden. Aids, one year from diagnosis to death. He knew he'd probably got it but had put off
having a test. Drugs were his first love and by this time I don't
think he was capable of endangering other people sexually nor
would he have wished to. He was not lethal. But, in the spinning months before the diagnosis, as he coughed more and
became even more gaunt, the needles were around. Always.

He had nearly completed his HND in bookbinding around
the time of diagnosis. Although, as he pointed out to me – more
than once – there were no jobs whatsoever in the field, so what
then? 'I never thought I'd make old bones,' he said.

The first time I went to see him in the London Hospital, they
had, with characteristic sensitivity, put him in a ward of men
with leg injuries, largely cab drivers. L made no secret of his
condition and these burly men, hair sprouting like rain forests
along their shoulders beneath their string vests, were all of a
twitter at having L in their midst. I arrived to hear him screaming at one of them, 'If you don't turn that flamin' telly off this
fuckin' instant I'll be *straight* over into yer bed and I'll have my
tongue *right* down that gorgeous gullet!'

L never lacked courage. He was not self-pitying. During that
year he became increasingly skeletal and the sores on his feet
and legs made it hard to walk. He struggled to college nearly
every day. Only occasionally in letters did he allude to the nightmares they inflicted on him – 'Screaming nerves – change of
medicine from AZT to DDI which *didn't* agree with me at all.
So I took the whole coffin-sized box back to the clinic and said,
"Forget it – if you'll poison me with this why won't you give me
the smack?" What a performance a girl has to go through.'
Even then they withheld the morphine and heroin until it was

too late to matter. He never did like doctors – 'Those stuck-up middle-class cunts working off their guilt on us.'

L did speak kindly of some of the hospices he was in – although he left one when a visit from Princess Di was imminent. L had never been a morbid or ghoulish person and descriptions of suffering were rare: 'Abscesses, thrombosis, phlebitis. It took two nurses two hours from nine-thirty p.m. to eleven-thirty p.m. to find a vein suitable for a cannula (a thick, flexible needle with another one which slips inside it) and get it in and the blood flowing. I was shagged out completely (so were they!) and covered in plasters.' Generally he preferred to talk or write about happier things. 'Fuck the pressure. Still, Mother can take it – it's great to be tucked up in bed, a supply of eggs, a spoon of Tin Tack, the odd can of Tennants, Radio 4 and the World Service, a good book or three. A blessed comfort.' He could still manage a J. Arthur, he said.

L needed very little to make him happy – he wasn't greedy – and it seems cruel that so much of it was withheld or made so hard for him. As he said, 'I've lived off fuck-all so long.'

L didn't want to die any more than anyone else once he knew he was going to. He'd never been suicidal or even depressive but like many people whose life gets fumbled in the first half he was careless with it. But some of his friends who were not yet under sentence seemed to care far, far less than he had ever done. They really didn't seem to mind whether they lived or died, or more probably they never thought about it but just went on and on, grinning blindly into the steady, relentless slap and suck of the media tide. Rubbers, shame, shock, horror, HIV, ARC, syndrome, euphemism, synonym, antonym – it all seemed to ebb away from them just as the sea withdrew further every year – in horror or indifference – from their northwest coast.

The beginning of the end blew in from the North. L knew he was sick. He had a good idea of what it was but he hadn't been to see a doctor yet. He always went up North for Christmas and this year was spending it with a man he'd known for some time. Too long perhaps. This guy was a veterinarian who liked to do operations on his penis. Or best of all he liked his young, stoned boyfriends to do the ops. He lived with his current boyfriend Al in a sort of Quonset hut somewhere on the Yorkshire side of the Pennine Way. The first night they had their friends in – L described it as 'the speeding of the five thousand' – but the rest of Christmas was to be given up to arcane delights with L as spectator. 'You wouldn't believe the state of this house,' L wrote. 'The veg racks are *crammed* with capsicum, tomatoes, lettuce, carrots, *everything*, all well rotten – as if Howard Hughes had done the shopping.'

L wrote the rest down in his notebook, sporadically. The vet had to explain the procedure to him.

L's JOURNAL

He indicated a plate in an old medical book which lay open on the table between us.

'I've already been through all this with Al. Tomorrow, when we go down to the surgery, this is what I hope to be able to do.'

The picture was of a prick, cut away to show the components. His eyes twinkled over the tops of his half-moon shaped glasses as his finger pointed out and named them, the Latin flowing easily. 'Now this body of tissue here is the corpus spongeosi as you can see from this cross section. It's surrounded by three kinds of tissue and they keep everything together.'

He chuckled to himself happily. He was looking forward to the operation he'd been promised as a Christmas treat. Across the room, his boyfriend, swinging a joint from his fingertips to shake the tobacco down, winked at me and flashed a quick smile.

'What's happened is that on the last operation I had done, afterwards two of the outer sleeves grew together, so when I get a hard-on now my willy bends to the right and up which is all right for what Al and I get up to but if I ever put it in a woman again I might damage her internally.'

'What were the other operations?'

He needed no prompting. In seconds he was standing

*over me, jeans pulled down, underwear ditto, with his
bunch in his left hand, his right being used to pull his large
though still soft prick until the extent of the scarring and
cicatrizing could be seen. It looked like a Cumberland
sausage.*

*'This is the one that Al did last year. THAT one has been
fine, haven't had any trouble there, but look, here's where
it's grown together, this lumpy bit here.'*

*Even the most cursory inspection revealed that all was
not well. For although still soft, under the ridged and
lumpy surface you could feel an area the size of a ten-pence
piece which was obviously two if not three of the 'inner
tube' sleeves he'd described earlier, fused together into one
dick-distorting knot.*

*'What's this patch here?' I said, indicating what at first
seemed to be an area of surface veins but on closer inspection with fingertip was found to be a kidney-shaped area of
puckered and hairy skin.*

*'Ah now, that's where I had to have a skin graft when
another operation went wrong. I didn't do this one myself.
That skin was taken from my scrotum, that's why it's hairy,
you can see the similarity. Look!'*

*He took up a couple of fingerfuls of scrotum. He'd had
some of his balls grafted on to his prick!*

'Are you using gas tomorrow?'

*'No. Local. And we'll want some sandwiches, pork pies,
meat pies, cans of lager, there's tea and coffee at the
surgery, better take some milk. I'll get the video camera
down.'*

So off they went. L and Al liberally sample the medicine cabinet
at the surgery. The video is set up and Al, the boyfriend, begins
hacking away. L feels sick. He has a terrible cold, slowly sinking towards a deadly pneumonia. He goes off to make a cup of
tea and returns to discover Al—

L's JOURNAL

*Sitting behind the bathroom door, naked except for a
towelling robe, his cock a gruesome spectrum of bruised
and varicosed meat from where he'd been hitting the dorsal
vein. 'Can't seem to get a hit anywhere else.' The shells of
double yolkers littered the floor about him, mostly 'blown'.
After washing the sore on his prick thoroughly with a can
of Fosters, Al went back to carry on the operation.*

L felt wretched and forlorn. The great spotlights in the surgery
were making his head ache. He didn't want to watch so he kept
making cups of tea. He couldn't get a picture of the vet's tool
box out of his head. It was a chrome box with a hinged lid filled
with what seemed to be craft knives but *as I quickly realized on
closer scrutiny, peering close down into the clear reddish fluid
in which they lay, they were scalpels.* He had to struggle not to
think – about his sickness, about their sickness. *Later they put
my single bed next to their double bed so I wouldn't feel lonely.*
When he got home to London L went to the hospital and had
the Aids test.

I never thought I would miss someone so much. L had an ill-
deserved reputation for misogyny and it was true if you
objected to hearing women described as 'Little miss smelly fish-
bag whore' or 'A rancid-snatched shag cow' you had better stay
out of his way. Or if you were squeamish about a vivid, graphic
way of expressing a horror of menstruation. This was someone
with a mouth so foul he managed to get fired from a radical
bookshop for his language. But L chose his friends regardless of
sex. What he didn't like was femininity – not the external femininity of clothes and scent and make-up on either men or
women, although he was by nature butch in appearance, but
the internal femininity that convinced a woman that she was
different, special and probably morally superior. He hated self-
righteous feminists. He liked non-political dykes. L's indifference to politics kept him away from much that happened in the
years of post-war gay politics but he always felt that his own
homosexual state was not only natural but superior and that
most men, however straight they seemed, must really be homo-

sexual. He was out all his life. He never backed down, never apologized, and never compromised his integrity on the subject. He wrote to young boyfriends telling them about gay history, gay writers and artists. He writes to his young lover, Jay, 'Oh my pretty pretty' and tells him that 'Red Indian gays were revered as special people in touch with their gods – they dressed in women's clothing and looked after the young and were respected' – conducting a gentle epistolatory education between the screeds of pornographic illustrations. Teeth and pricks and dogs and bums and more teeth.

I have a photograph of him hitching North way back in the seventies, holding up a sign saying 'Honk If You're Gay.' I hope he scored for the ultimate ride. The car slicing northwards like a knife, celebratory pink and golden ribbons whipping in the slipstream like the unravelled DNA of all possible possibilities, as bright and brave and unforgettable as that first sure touch upon the knee.

'Do you still use that pig's grease on your nipples, Liz?' someone roars from behind me in a long Christmas queue at Marks and Spencer. L carries on as the queue inches forward, blenching, to enumerate my (bestial) sexual tastes, ending, 'We should never have got married, you slag – all that stuff's too gross for me!' He's waiting round the corner with a steak and some oranges beneath his black leather jacket.

'Bet that made their Christmas.'

'Mmm. It's my local branch actually.'

'Well, I nevah! It's my No Cash 'n' Carry ectualleh.'

'What you got? Protein for once, I see.'

'Build me up. Not that I need it. Well, not all of me. Heh! I allus told you it were a whopper. Remember the time – Missed yer chance, dintch'a?! Buy us a drink then. Buy us a Guinness.'

Down Camden High Street. Into the autumn, into the dusk.

L went back North a few days before his death. His last – and longest – affair was with another teenage angel-face, Jay, a skinny child doll with soft red curls. Jay stayed till the very end, crying, laughing, crying, holding L's hand, whispering how much he loved him. He died with the old year, in the deepest, darkest part of winter. I have never been to his grave. The bereavement counsellors and all the rest say you should do stuff like that to face up to the reality of death but I won't. I don't want to. As it is, I know he's in a cemetery but when I picture it I just seem to hear L's words: 'All human life is there. And the rest of it.'

With deepest thanks to
Howard Downes and Tony Carricker.

V

Storms

SALMAN RUSHDIE
The Harmony of the Spheres

In the time of the Jubilee the writer Eliot Crane, who had been suffering from what he called 'brainstorms' of paranoid schizophrenia, had lunch with his wife, a young photo-journalist called Lucy Evans, in the Welsh town of R., where she was working on the local paper. He looked cheerful, and told her he was feeling fine, but tired, and would go to bed early. It was the paper's press night, so Lucy was late getting home to their hillside cottage; when she went upstairs Eliot wasn't in their bedroom. Assuming that he was sleeping in the spare room, so that she wouldn't disturb him, she went to bed.

An hour later Lucy woke up with a premonition of disaster and went without getting dressed to the door of the guest bedroom; which, taking a deep breath, she opened. Half a second later, she slammed it shut again, and slumped heavily to the floor. He had been ill for more than two years, and all she could think was *It's over*. When she started shivering she went back to bed and slept soundly until morning.

He had sucked on his shotgun and pulled the trigger. The weapon had belonged to his father, who had put it to the same use. The only suicide note Eliot left after perpetrating this final act of macabre symmetry was a meticulous account of how to clean and care for the gun. He and Lucy had no children. He was thirty-two years old.

A week earlier, the three of us walked up a beacon hill in the Borders to see the Jubilee bonfires flowering along the spine of the country, garlanding the darkness. 'It doesn't mean a "good fire",' Eliot said, 'though I grant there's an element of that in the word. Originally it was a fire made of bones: the bones of dead animals but also, fee fi fo fum, human remains, the charred skeletons my dears of *yuman beans*.'

He had wild red hair and a laugh like an owl's hoot and was

as thin as a witch's stick. In the firelight's bright shadow-theatre
we all looked insane, so it was easier to discount his hollowed-
out cheeks, the pantomime cockings of his eyebrows, the mad-
sailor glitter in his eye. We stood close to the flames and Eliot
told dread tales of local Sabbats, at which cloaked and urine-
drinking sorcerers conjured devils up from Hell. We swigged
brandy from his silver hip flask and recoiled on cue. But he had
met a demon once and ever since that day he and Lucy had been
on the run. They had sold their haunted home, a tiny house in
Portugal Place, Cambridge, and moved to the bleak, sheep-
smelly Welsh cottage they named (with gallows humour)
Crowley End.

It hadn't worked. As we shrieked at Eliot's ghost stories, we
knew that the demon had traced the number on his car number-
plates, that it could call him any time on his unlisted telephone;
that it had rediscovered his home address.

'You'd better come,' Lucy had called to say. 'They found him
going the wrong way on the motorway, doing ninety, with one
of those sleep-mask things over his eyes.' She had given up a lot
for him, quitting her job on a London Sunday paper and settling
for a hicksville gazette, because he was mad, and she needed to
be close.

'Am I approved of at present?' I'd asked. Eliot had elaborated
a conspiracy theory in which most of his friends were revealed
to be agents of hostile powers, both Earthly and extraterrestrial.
I was an invader from Mars, one of many such dangerous
beings who had sneaked into Britain when certain essential
forms of vigilance had been relaxed. Martians had great gifts of
mimicry, so they could fool yuman beans into believing they
were beans of the same stripe, and, of course, they bred like
fruit-flies on a pile of rotten bananas.

For more than a year, during my Martian phase, I had been
unable to visit. Lucy would phone with bulletins: the drugs were
working, the drugs were not working because he refused to take
them regularly, he seemed better as long as he did not try to
write, he seemed worse because not writing plunged him into
such deep depressions, he was passive and inert, he was raging

and violent, he was filled with guilt and despair.

I felt helpless; as one does.

We became friends in my last year at Cambridge, while I was involved in an exhausting on-off love affair with a graduate student named Laura. Her thesis was on James Joyce and the French *nouveau roman*, and to please her I ploughed my way through *Finnegans Wake* twice, and most of Sarraute, Butor, and Robbe-Grillet too. One night, seized by romance, I climbed out of the window of her flat in Chesterton Road, balanced precariously on the windowsill and refused to come back inside until she agreed to marry me. The next morning she rang her mother to break the news. After a long silence, Mummy said, 'I'm sure he's very nice, dear, but couldn't you find someone of, you know, your own kind?'

Laura was humiliated by the question. 'What do you mean, my own kind?' she yelled down the phone. 'A Joyce specialist? A person five feet and three inches tall? A woman?'

That summer, however, she got stoned at a wedding, snatched the glasses off my face and snapped them in two, grabbed the wedding-cake knife to the consternation of the bride and groom, and told me that if I ever came near her again she'd slice me up and pass me round at parties. I blundered myopically away from her and more or less fell over another woman, a grey-eyed fellow-alien in granny glasses named Mala, who with a straight face offered to drive me home, 'since your optical capability is presently reduced'. I didn't discover until after we married that serious, serene Mala, non-smoking, non-drinking, vegetarian, drug-free, lonely Mala from Mauritius, the medical student with the Gioconda smile, had been propelled in my direction by Eliot Crane.

'He'd like to see you,' Lucy said on the phone. 'He seems less worried about Martians now.'

Eliot sat by an open fire with a red rug over his knees. 'Ahoo! The space fiend boyo!' he cried, smiling broadly and raising both arms above his head, half in welcome, half in pretend surrender. 'Will you sit down, old bug-eyed *bach*, and take a glass before you have your evil way with us?'

Lucy left us to ourselves and he spoke soberly and with apparent objectivity about the schizophrenia. It seemed hard to believe that he had just driven blindfolded down a motorway against the traffic. When the madness came, he explained, he was 'barking', and capable of the wildest excesses. But in between attacks, he was 'perfectly normal'. He said he'd finally come to see that there was no stigma in accepting that one was mad: it was an illness like any other, *voilà tout*.

'I'm on the mend,' he said, confidently. 'I've started work again, the Owen Glendower book. Work's fine as long as I keep off the occult stuff.' (He was the author of a scholarly two-volume study of overt and covert occultist groups in nineteenth-and twentieth-century Europe, entitled *The Harmony of the Spheres*.)

He lowered his voice. 'Between ourselves, Khan, I'm also working on a simple cure for paranoid schizophrenia. I'm in correspondence with the best men in the country. You've no idea how impressed they are. They agree I've hit on something absolutely new, and it's just a matter of time before we come up with the goods.'

I felt suddenly sad. 'Look out for Lucy, by the way,' he whispered. 'She lies like a whore. And she listens in on me, you know. They give her the latest machines. There are microphones in the fridge. She hides them in the butter.'

Eliot introduced me to Lucy in a kekab house on Charlotte Street in 1971, and though I hadn't seen her for ten years I recognized at once that we had kissed on the beach at Juhu when I was fourteen and she was twelve; and that I was anxious to repeat the experience. Miss Lucy Evans, the honey-blonde, precocious daughter of the boss of the famous Bombay Company. She made no mention of kisses; I thought she had probably forgotten them, and said nothing either. But then she reminisced about our camel races on Juhu beach, and fresh coconut-milk, straight from the tree. She hadn't forgotten.

Lucy was the proud owner of a small cabin cruiser, an ancient craft that had once been a naval longboat. It was pointed at both ends, had a makeshift cabin in the middle and a Thorneycroft Handybilly engine of improbable antiquity which would respond to nobody's coaxings except hers. It had been to Dunkirk. She named it *Bougainvillaea* in memory of her childhood in Bombay.

I joined Eliot and Lucy aboard *Bougainvillaea* several times, the first time with Mala, but subsequently without her. Mala, now Doctor Mala, Doctor (Mrs) Khan, no less, the Mona Lisa of the Harrow Road Medical Centre, was repelled by that bohemian existence in which we did without baths and pissed over the side and huddled together for warmth at night, zipped into our quilted sacks. 'For me, hygiene-comfort are Priority A,' said Mala. 'Let sleeping bags lie. I-tho will stay home with my Dunlopillo and WC.'

There was a trip we took up the Trent and Mersey Canal as far as Middlewich, then west to Nantwich, south down the Shropshire Union Canal, and west again to Llangollen. Lucy as skipper was intensely desirable, revealing great physical strength and a kind of boaty bossiness that I found very arousing. On this trip we had two nights alone, because Eliot had to return to Cambridge to hear a lecture by a 'top man from Austria' on the subject of the Nazis and the occult. We saw him off at Crewe station and then ate a bad meal ,in a restaurant with pretensions. Lucy insisted on ordering a bottle of rosé wine. The waitress stiffened contemptuously. 'The French for red, madam,' she bellowed, 'is *rouge*.'

Whatever it was, we drank too much of it. Later, aboard *Bougainvillaea*, we zipped our sleeping bags together and returned to Juhu beach. But at a certain moment she kissed my cheek, mumured 'Madness, love', and rolled over, turning her back on the too-distant past. I thought of Mala, my not-too-distant present, and blushed guiltily in the dark.

The next day, neither of us spoke of what had almost happened. *Bougainvillaea* arrived at a one-way tunnel at the wrong time; but Lucy didn't feel like waiting three hours for her right of way. She ordered me to go ahead with a torch along the narrow towpath inside the tunnel, while she brought the boat on behind me at a crawl. I had no idea what she'd do if we met anyone coming towards us, but my journey along the slippery, broken towpath required all my attention, and anyway, I was only the crew.

Our luck held; we emerged into the daylight. I had been wearing a white cricket sweater which was now bright red, stained indelibly by mud from the tunnel walls. There was mud in my shoes and in my hair and on my face. When I wiped my sweating forehead a lump of mud fell into my eye.

Lucy whooped in triumph at our illegal success. 'Made a lawbreaker of you at last, bloody wonderful,' she hollered. (As a youth, in Bombay, I had been notoriously Good.) 'You see? Crime does pay, after all.'

Madness. Love. I remembered the rosé and the tunnel when I heard about Eliot's high-speed escapade. Our adventures aboard *Bougainvillaea* by night and by day had been as dangerous, in their way. Forbidden embraces and a wrong-way journey in the dark. But we weren't shipwrecked, and he wasn't killed. Just lucky. I suppose.

Why do we lose our minds?

'A simple biochemical imbalance,' was Eliot's view. He insisted on driving home from the Jubilee bonfire, and as he accelerated through blind corners on lightless country roads, various biochemicals surged, off-balance, through my veins as well. Then, without warning, he braked hard and stopped. It was a clear night with a moon. On the hillside to our right were sleeping sheep and a small fenced-off graveyard.

'I want to be buried here,' he announced.

'No can do,' I answered from the back seat. 'You'd have to be dead, you see.'

'Don't,' said Lucy. 'You'll only give him ideas.'

We were teasing him to conceal the quaking within, but Eliot knew we had registered the information. He nodded, satisfied; and accelerated.

'If you wipe us out,' I gasped, 'who'll be left to remember you when you're gone?'

When we got back to Crowley End he went straight to bed without a word. Lucy looked in on him a while later and reported that he'd fallen asleep fully clothed, and grinning. 'Let's get drunk,' she suggested brightly.

She stretched out on the floor in front of the fire. 'Sometimes I think everything would have been a lot easier if I hadn't rolled away,' she said. 'I mean, on the boat.'

Eliot met his demon for the first time when he was finishing *The Harmony of the Spheres*. He had quarrelled with Lucy, who had moved out of the doll's house in Portugal Place. (When she came back to him she found that in her absence he had not put out a single milk bottle. The massed bottles stood in the kitchen, one for each day Lucy and Eliot had been apart, like seventy accusations.)

One night he woke at three a.m., convinced of the presence downstairs of something absolutely evil. (I remembered this premonition when Lucy told me how she woke up at Crowley End, certain that he was dead.)

He picked up his Swiss army knife and descended, stark naked (as Lucy would be naked, in her turn), to investigate. The electricity wasn't working. As he neared the kitchen he felt arctically cold and found that he had acquired an erection. Then all the lights went crazy, switching themselves on and off, and he made the sign of the cross with his arms and screamed, '*Apage me, Satanas*.' Get thee behind me, Satan.

'Whereupon everything went back to normal,' he told me. 'And, below decks, limp.'

'You didn't really see anything?' I said, slightly disappointed. 'No horns, or cloven hooves?'

Eliot was not the hyper-rationalist he claimed to be. His immersion in the dark arts was more than merely scholarly. But because of his brilliance, I took him at his own estimation. 'Just open-minded,' he said. 'More in heaven and earth, Horatio, and so forth.' He made it sound perfectly rational to sell a haunted house double-quick, even to lose money on the deal.

*

We were the most unlikely of friends. I liked hot weather, he preferred it grey and damp. I had a Zapata moustache and shoulder-length hair, he wore tweeds and corduroy. I was involved in fringe theatre, race relations and anti-war protests. He weekended on the country-house circuit, killing animals and birds. 'Nothing like it to cheer a fellow,' he said, winding me up. 'Blasting the life out of one's furry and feathered friends, doing one's bit for the food chain. Marvellous.' He gave a party the day after Edward Heath won the 1970 election – 'Grocer Turns Cabinet Maker', one newspaper declared – and mine was the only long face there.

Who knows what makes people friends? Something in the way they move. The way they sing off-key.

But in the case of Eliot and me, I do know, really. It was that old black magic. Not love, not chocolate: the Hidden Arts. If I find it impossible to let go of Eliot's memory, it is perhaps because I know that the seductive arcana which drove Eliot Crane out of his mind almost ensnared me as well.

Pentangles, illuminati, Maharishi, Gandalf: necromancy was part of the *zeitgeist*, of the private language of the counter-culture. From Eliot I learned the secrets of the Great Pyramid, the mysteries of the Golden Section, and the intricacies of the Spiral. He told me about Mesmer's theory of Animal Magnetism (*A responsive influence exists between the heavenly bodies, the earth and all animated bodies. A fluid universally diffused, incomparably subtle, is the means of this influence. It is subject to mechanical laws with which we are not yet familiar*) and the Four Trances of Japanese spiritualism: *Muchu*, that is, ecstasy or rapture; *Shissi, Konsui-Jotai*, or a coma; *Saimin-Jotai*, a hypnotic state; and *Mugen no Kyo*, in which the soul can leave the body behind and wander in the World of Mystery. Through Eliot I met remarkable men, or at least their minds: G. I. Gurdjieff, author of *Beelzebub's Tales* and guru to, among others, Aldous Huxley, Katherine Mansfield, and J. B. Priestley; and Raja Rammohun Roy and his Brahmo Samaj, that brave attempt at making a synthesis of Indian and English thought.

Under my friend's informal tutelage, I studied numerology and palmistry and memorized an Indian spell for flying. I was taught the verses that conjured up the Devil, *Shaitan*, and how to draw the shape that would keep the Beast 666 confined.

I never had much time for gurus back home where the word came from, but that's what Eliot was, I confess with a blush. A mystical teacher in English translation; say it g'*roo*.

Reader: I flunked the course. I never experienced *Muchu* (much less *Mugen no Kyo*), never dared speak the Hell-raising spells, or jumped off a cliff, like some Yaquí *brujo*'s apprentice, to fly.

I survived.

Eliot and I practised putting each other under hypnosis. Once he implanted the post-hypnotic suggestion that if he should ever say the word 'bananas' I must at once remove all my clothes. That evening, on the dance floor at Dingwall's club with Mala and Lucy, he whispered his fruity malice into my ear. Rumbling, sleep-inducing waves began to roll heavily over me and even though I tried hard to fight them back my hands began to undress me. When they began unzipping my jeans we were all thrown out.

'You boys,' Mala said disapprovingly as I dressed by the canal, swearing loudly and threatening dire revenges. 'Maybe you should go to bed together and we all can go home and get some rest.'

Was that it? No. Maybe. No. I don't know. No.

What a picture: a double portrait of self-deceivers. Eliot the occultist pretending to be an academic, with me, more prosaically, perhaps, half-lost in occult love.

Was that it?

When I met Eliot I was a little unhinged myself – suffering from a disharmony of my personal spheres. There was the Laura episode, and beyond it a number of difficult questions about home and identity that I had no idea how to answer. Eliot's instinct about Mala and me was one answer that I was grateful for. Home, like Hell, turned out to be other people. For me, it turned out to be her.

Not Martian, but Mauritian. She was a ninth-generation child of indentured labourers brought from India after the black exodus that had followed the end of slavery. At home – home was a small village to the north of Port Louis, and its largest edifice was a small white Vishnu temple – she and her family had spoken a version of the Indian Bhojpuri dialect, so creolized over the years as to be virtually incomprehensible to non-Mauritian Indians. She had never been to India, and my birth and childhood and continued connections there made me, in her eyes, ridiculously glamorous, like a visitor from Xanadu. *For he on honey-dew hath fed, And drunk the milk of Paradise.*

Even though she was, as she put it, 'from science side', she was interested in writing, and liked the fact that I was trying to be a writer. She took pride in 'Romeo and Juliet of Mauritius', as she called Bernardin de St Pierre's *Paul et Virginie*; and insisted that I read it. 'Maybe it will influence,' she said, hopefully.

She had a doctor's unsqueamishness and practicality, and like all people 'from arts-side' I envied her knowledge of what human beings were like on the inside. What I had to imagine about human nature, she gave every appearance of knowing. She wasn't a big talker, but I felt that in her I had found my rock. And the warm dark tides of the Indian Ocean rose nightly in her veins.

What angered her, it seemed, was Eliot, and my closeness to him. Once she was installed as my wife – we honeymooned in Venice – her unease prompted what was, for her, a major speech. 'All that mumboing and jumboing,' she snorted, full of science-side contempt for the Irrational. 'So phoney, God! Listen: he comes round too much, it's bad for you. What is he? Some English mess-head, only. Get my drift, writer sahib? I mean, thanks for the intro etcetera, but now you should drop him, like a brick.'

'Welsh,' I said, very surprised. 'He's Welsh.'

'Doesn't matter,' snapped Doctor (Mrs) Khan. 'Diagnosis still applies.'

*

But in Eliot's enormous, generously shared mental storehouse of the varieties of 'forbidden knowledge' I thought I'd found another way of making a bridge between here-and-there, between my two othernesses, my double unbelonging. In that world of magic and power there seemed to exist the kind of fusion of world-views, European Amerindian Oriental Levantine, in which I desperately wanted to believe.

With his help, I hoped, I might make a 'forbidden self'. The apparent world, all cynicism and napalm, seemed wholly without kindness or wisdom. The hidden realm, in which Sufis walked with Adepts and great secrets could be glimpsed, would show me how to be wise. It would grant me – Eliot's favourite word, this – harmony.

Mala was right. He couldn't help anyone, the poor sap; couldn't even save himself. In the end his demons came for him, his Gurdjieff and Ouspensky and his Crowley and Blavatsky, his Dunsany and his Lovecraft long ago. They crowded out the sheep on his Welsh hillside, and closed in on his mind.

Harmony? You never heard such a din as the ruckus in Eliot's head. The songs of Swedenborg's angels, the hymns, the mantras, the Tibetan overtone chants. What human mind could have defended itself against such a Babel, in which Theosophists argued with Confucians, Christian Scientists with Rosicrucians? Here were devotees praising the coming of Lord Maitreya; there, bloodsucking wizards hurling curses. And lo, there came forth Millenarians crying Doom; and behold, Hitler arose brandishing his fylfot, which in his ignorance or malignity he gave the name of the symbol of good: *swastika*.

In the throng besieging the sick man of Crowley End, even my personal favourite, Raja Rammohun Roy, was just another voice in the cacodemonic crowd.

Bang!

And, at last, silence. *Requiescat in pace.*

By the time I got back to Wales, Lucy's brother Bill had called the police and undertakers and had spent heroic hours in the spare room cleaning the blood and brains off the walls. Lucy sat sipping gin in the kitchen in a light summer frock, looking dreadfully composed.

'Would you go through his books and papers?' she asked me, sounding sweet and distant. 'I can't do it. There may be enough of the Glendower thing. Someone could pull it into shape.'

It took me the best part of a week, that sad excavation of my dead friend's unpublished mind. I felt a page turning; I was just starting to be a writer then, and Eliot had just stopped being one. Although in truth, as I found, he had stopped being one years ago. There was no trace of a Glendower manuscript, or any serious work at all. There were only ravings.

Bill Evans had stuffed three tea chests with Eliot's typed and scribbled papers. In these chests of delirium I found hundreds of pages of operatic, undirected obscenities and inchoate rants against the universe in general. There were dozens of notebooks in which Eliot had dreamed up alternative personal futures of extraordinary distinction and renown, or, alternatively, self-pitying versions of a life of genius-in-obscurity ending in ago-nizing illnesses, or assassination by jealous rivals; after which, inevitably, came recognition by a remorseful world of the great-ness it had ignored. These were sorry reams.

Harder still to read were his fantasies about us, his friends. These were of two kinds: hate-filled, and pornographic. There were many virulent attacks on me, and pages of steamy sex involving my wife Mala, 'dated', no doubt to maximize their autoerotic effect, in the days immediately after our marriage. And, of course, at other times. The pages about Lucy were both nasty and lubricious. I searched the tea chests in vain for a loving remark. It was hard to believe that such a passionate and eager man could have nothing good to say about life on earth. Yet it was so.

I showed Lucy nothing, but she saw it all on my face. 'It wasn't really him writing,' she consoled me mechanically. 'He was sick.'

And I know what made him sick, I thought; and vowed silently to remain well. Since then there has been no intercourse between the spiritual world and mine. Mesmer's 'influential fluid' evaporated for ever as I plunged through the putrid tea chests of my friend's mad filth.

Eliot was buried according to his wishes. The manner of his dying had created some difficulties regarding the use of consecrated ground, but Lucy's fury had persuaded the local clergy to turn a blind eye.

Among the mourners was a Conservative Member of Parliament who had been at school with Eliot. 'Poor Elly,' this man said in a loud voice. 'We used to ask ourselves, "Whatever will become of Elly Crane?" And I'd say, "He'll probably make something halfway decent of his life if he doesn't kill himself first." '

This gentleman is presently a member of the Cabinet, and receives Special Branch protection. I don't think he realized how close he came to needing protection (against me) on a sunny morning in Wales long ago.

But his epitaph is the only one I remember.

At the moment of our parting Lucy gave me her hand to shake. We didn't see each other again. I heard that she had remarried quickly and dully and gone to live in the American West.

Back home, I found that I needed to talk for a long time. Mala sat and listened sympathetically. Eventually I told her about the tea chests.

'You worked him out, no need to remind me,' I cried. 'You knew his insides. Imagine! He was so sick, so crazy, that he fantasized all these frenzied last-tango encounters with you. For instance, just after we got home from Venice. For instance, in those two days I was alone with Lucy on *Bougainvillaea*, and he said he had to go to Cambridge for a lecture.'

Mala stood up and turned her back on me, and before she spoke I guessed her answer, feeling it explode in my chest with an unbearable raucous crack, a sound reminiscent of the breakup of log jams or pack ice. Yes, she had warned me against Eliot Crane, warned me with the bitter passion of her denunciation of him; and I, in my surprise at the denunciation, had failed to hear the real warning, failed to understand what she had meant by the passion in her voice. *That mess-head. He's bad for you.*

So, here it came: the collapse of harmony, the demolition of the spheres of my heart.

'Those weren't fantasies,' she said.

BENEDICTA LEIGH
The Catch of Hands

One winter afternoon in 1968, I went upstairs and lay on my
bed and began to cry with such force that I thought I might
never stop, and went on crying for a long time and with a thin
pain inside me that I couldn't identify, but that had a keen comfort to it that I was glad of. After about three-quarters of an
hour, however, the doctor was sent for because it was assumed
that such crying must portend something wrong with me, and
blubbered with unbecoming tears, I stumbled down to see him
in the drawing room. Dr Q. was a nice man who did not know
me well, since I was very seldom ill, and at that time I still had
considerable confidence in the medical profession. He questioned me kindly, murmured something about a menopausal
breakdown and depression, prescribed tablets, and suggested a
visit from his colleague, a psychiatrist.

This colleague, Dr Y., a nice shabby exhausted man, came a
few days later, also questioning me and making several
erroneous assumptions I did not correct. However, in view of
his tart rejoinders in twelve years' time, it is worth noting that
he then considered me hypersensitive and markedly altruistic.

The suggestion that I should spend a few days in a mental
hospital I did not feel was inviting or necessary, despite his
additional statement that mental hospitals were much improved
and even quite nice these days. And he smiled reassuringly.

I believed him, since he seemed a nice man, but settled for
out-patient shock treatment, and tranquillizers. And since I was,
as he described me, seriously disturbed, I accepted both, though
not without a rattle of nerves in my stomach, which, as it
happened, would last for the ensuing eighteen years at least.

I rang the friend with whom I had arranged to go to the theatre, and told her I had now become a mental patient, that I was
both disturbed and tranquillized, that if this was what the
change of life was like, I didn't want to know. I said that what

I desperately needed was a bit of real crying, but no one would let me, and I wept a little into the telephone, rather hating the way I suddenly couldn't manage, and wondering why, and I said I couldn't come, unless I stopped being a mental patient in the next hour. She said she was very sorry, but she wasn't altogether surprised, and had I perhaps never got over the boy? I said, 'I don't know what you're talking about. Have a nice time,' and put the receiver down.

When I had my electroconvulsive therapy, we took the puppy so that he could destroy the hospital grounds while I was in the hospital. The staff were charming, and the shock treatment could have been a great deal nastier, and produced, first of all, a predictable but short-lived amnesia and a somewhat misleading state of euphoria. And for me, something else. As the euphoria cleared, small, further pockets of recall invaded the stock I had already, some of which were unfamiliar, as though they were not mine, but belonged perhaps to times before mine. I didn't take it seriously, since I had had a few strange experiences in my childhood which had not proved particularly significant, but put them by, bought loose-leaf paper and pens, and wrote for about three hours every day for days, giving the results to our beloved ex-au pair girl, Laila, to type, which she did, neither questioning nor commenting. I was, she now says, extremely shaky, and very unwilling to let her come into the house. I felt a good deal better, but the puppy felt rather worse, since he was largely unwalked and lay curled and watching me reproachfully, his blanket chewed to shreds.

The stockpile of memory grew, kept in order by the mental docketing that I had always used, and the recall needed only an occasional *aide-mémoire* to open some box or other – a sound, perhaps, or a colour, or a piece of music, or best of all a texture. And all these had been discovered when I was a child truanting my thoughts away from the bang and flitter of flies on the hot schoolroom window and finding a useful freedom from it.

So I was better, they said, probably because they believed in tranquillizers and not in writing, the cradle that always rocked me. And they said on no account would a good cry or proper talking with friends *ever* do. Shock treatment, sleeping pills and tranquillizers, they said, would be just the thing.

Electroconvulsive therapy, at best a somewhat hazardous treatment, did not, of course, produce more than a superficial effect on my unhappiness, the cause of which I had buried so deeply that even I myself could not identify it. It had, however, unexpectedly provided me with a sharper perception of what my hive of recall contained. As to the drugs and their adverse effects, they merely masked my symptoms. Such drugs were not so sophisticated when I was nursing, and their prime use was then in calming the patient in order to encourage communication, and not as an end in themselves.

Nonetheless, to an extent I seemed better both to myself and to others. That is to say that whenever I saw Dr Y. I answered, though listlessly, that yes, I was rendered insensible each night by Mandrax, and that I was eating reasonably well. The enquiry as to whether I was still turning things over in my mind always perplexed me, since that, I assumed, was the function of a mind. However, in order not to disappoint him, I returned an evasive reply.

The world turned a little, and I was forty-seven and standing in the kitchen with a gut full of tranquillizers in 1969. And I said, 'I am forty-seven,' as I had said, 'I'll be thirty next birthday,' to the boy-o and felt that cold rill of air on my shoulder in the flat. I was fine though, now, and slammed and latched my mind and locked it.

Something happened. Something happened as I stood there that quite emptied me of all other bits and pieces, and could not be described, nor comfortably believed. I was alone then, and it was quite an ordinary day, and dim, and what happened was not exactly outside myself, yet not altogether inside my perception either. It was an immediate experience, with a difference to it, so that words could not be happily used.

It seemed to happen within my senses, as though they had opened out, and peeled back to take an explosion of consciousness that I felt, and saw and heard. There were plangent colours and music, all of light and fire that poured into me a perilous knowledge and goodness, and a joy and beauty intense enough to give me a hope almost fulfilled.

It was as though I had pulled back a curtain from the beginnings of the world and my own life was stretching and contracting to take the newness and the flowering in me. I felt strong and light, as though I might fly, and as tired and drained as if I had flown over deserts and seas. A consuming happiness filled me.

If this was a heralding, then I will keep its truth and substance in my journeying thoughts for ever.

It is not possible to say how long this experience lasted, or if it would have been apparent to an onlooker. It may have been of the duration and appearance of a *petit mal*, but since I was alone I could not tell, and it was years before I was able to investigate this or the experience that followed. I could not move immediately, and felt exhausted, although there was in me a great happiness.

I went upstairs and lay down, and played carols on my tape recorder. I felt quickened, and drew and wrote, as though my life had perhaps knit together a little, and I went down to see my children, and saw that upon the forehead each had a black circle. I was frightened and kissed them, and felt it must mean the Black Death, and that I expected it.

When I went up to my room again, it was changed. Where my side of the bed had been, there was a narrow palliasse covered with rough, brown material, canvas perhaps, and I lay down upon it, but with difficulty, for I seemed ill. There was very little light over that side of the room, but I could see something on the other side, perhaps a rush light or tallow dip, but most of the room was dark.

I was in terrible pain, and dying, but I do not know what it was with me. I had swellings and a fever, and I was restless. All the time I could hear the regular knocking of wood on wood, as though something were being built outside that had to do with my dying. I was not a woman any more, but a boy of about twenty, and deathly ill. I was wearing some sort of long shirt, perhaps dark green, bulky, and round my head I felt there was something golden, I do not know what, but I felt a kind of charge run through me. There was a young man sitting at the end of the bed looking at me, and that is how you sat last time,

but I don't know if it was you. You look different and I am
dying. Am I at last that boy you always wanted me to be? Then
take me with you. Take me. The charge inside me lit and darkened.

But I don't know if it was you, and though I sometimes think
of you sitting there, just as you did before you died, my life desperately and horribly changed from that moment, and I felt only
fear, and the trail of corruption for the next eighteen years.

The ambulance came for me in the early evening, and took me
to the hospital, and since Dr Y. had told me that mental
hospitals were perfectly acceptable nowadays, I felt as settled as
was possible in the circumstances.

Upon arrival, it did not appear unpleasant, and I did not, at
that moment, feel in the least apprehensive. Although I had only
been in hospital twice in my life, I had after all done five years'
nursing, and could see no reason for disquiet.

Certainly I felt a sudden sprinkle of nerves when I went into
the day room, but I dismissed it as natural. The general impression of grubbiness was less easy to accept, but I assumed it was
my imagination.

The female patients' day room was on the second floor, and
led into their dormitory. I sat there. 'Go and sit next to the
duchess,' I was told, and I sat next to a woman who was obsessively embroidering.

There was something disturbing in the atmosphere, and an
anxiety that eventually generated itself to me, and I was not too
deeply drugged to feel a sharp physical fear, and to be aware of
the smell that accompanied it – dirty lavatories and corruption
under a wrapper of solace.

For some reason, I felt then and later that it was important
that I should never show fear, whatever happened. All I knew
was that there was something bad about this place, and for that
reason alone, I began to shake, and wonder if I might ever get
out, and wonder that this place was called a hospital.

I was violent. They said I was violent and that was why they
knocked me about. Two male nurses knocked me about,

knocked me about, I fell on the floor, I couldn't speak or breathe or struggle, just fell on the floor, fell down and lay there. They were quite big men, I was frightened, I fell down, some sound coming from me, I blacked out, my cheek against the floor, the green carpet, I blacked out.

At the Enquiry they said that I was violent, they had to knock me about. They said there were no witnesses. They said that at the Enquiry. I was forty-seven and my life began to black out when I heard this.

They can say anything.

From that first incident a tumult of nerves was set up in my stomach which could not be quelled. Wickedness is often sensed before it is encountered, even when it is shielded by a louche respectability.

I don't know how I got into the cell or when I was thrown there, but I felt as though I were coming out of an anaesthetic, and my belly crept and swam as I got to my feet. I was wearing a white gown, wet and cold, and was taut with fear. It seemed to me that I could die in this place. My head cleared a little, but I felt stiff and strange. The wall in front of me was covered in obscene and explicit graffiti, usual in public lavatories but hardly to be found in hospitals, and a bubble of sick burned in my throat, and weakly threaded down the front of my gown.

Stupidly, I believed that I could simply open the door, walk out, and tell the world about this place, and I tried.

The door was irrevocably locked, no one answered my shouting, and I began to shake with a terror I had never felt before, and which has followed me in nightmares ever since. I tried to force my hand through a hole near the keyhole, as I would do throughout the night, each time pulling it back stitched with splinters. Three weeks later the splinters were still there.

In the cell was a bed, and a tiny window high up which I tried to crawl up to. Sometimes an eye looked at me through the peephole, but no one answered or in any way communicated with me, and, my guts liquid with fear, I screamed all night, knowing that now I might never escape and that no one would come. I screamed until I could not scream any more, and then lay on the bed and prayed every prayer I had ever known from the nursery onwards. I thought of my grandparents and Chichester Cathedral, and fell into a thin sleep. I felt that for the first time I was with wicked people, and wondered what else they might do to me, and perhaps to others.

I woke suddenly an hour or two later with the need to pee, and shouted, banged on the door and the wall, too frightened to feel anything, and empty of all but a desperate panic, like a dog in a thunderstorm. No one came and I wet the bed. I slept again, cold and with shallow nightmares, waking every few minutes in the same maw, the central light still blazing down on me. I wanted to die, longed for it, wished it quickly done. I did not feel I could go on pretending to be brave, and did not know that the fear of this hospital would drag after me for over eighteen years after I had left.

I apologized for wetting the bed when the night sister let me out next morning. She seemed the only human being on the staff and was shocked at my blood-spotted hand.

And I ran down the corridor in my white gown, and away down that corridor again in all my waiting nightmares, thinly screaming for help, humanity, for God, and for my safe child-hood and a sworn advocate's hand to drag on and know best for me. For my changing life, so reasonable for many other women, had slipped from that reason into the clamminess of dread.

Round the room sit the patients, looking ahead, not speaking, sometimes smoking, and I with them with empty desperation, because I know I have to take care what I say and behave myself. Weighing up the time lopped away between injection and injection, tablet and tablet is impossible, and I know only that I surface from each drug till the next in that web of apprehension that is now part of me. Meals I sometimes remember, and once I said the Winchester Grace, Benedictus Benedicat, as a prayer.

I am lying on my bed in the dormitory. Light comes through a fanlight over the door to the day room where the night sister sits knitting.

I am a mental patient and I lie where I am put, on the top of my bed in the dormitory, my mind half rubbed out by drugs. No one will ever believe me again and I want my mother. My stomach is rancid and my senses sprawl, but some of us are asleep, us mental patients. The stupor keeps only a handhold on me, but suddenly when I see him I shake it free, and am shocked sane but no, no I see him at once – the kind male nurse – no Mummy, no Mummy, say no no no.

He put his hand between my legs, pushing and fumbling into my cunt, said, 'Is this what you want? Is it?', took my hand and made me hold his cock, no no, take away my memory that is dirtied take it, take it, my life unfastens me.

Lovers do such things with love and joy, wonderfully weeping for the little death to crown their divine agony.

But now I can never, will never – cannot love again, nor will I ever feel safe. Inside me is the shout, and outside me is the bleak whimper of an animal, pulled from me, and take me home, take me, take me. The shadow slips away to his covert, but my skin creeps still, and I am marked as prey, since I am gentry, a captive, and have wet myself with fear. And I know that nothing need ever be heard of me, nothing revealed.

They said there were no witnesses. At the Enquiry they said there were no witnesses.

I did not run away that night, but later – later – after – running, running, running, through the grounds, a great arc of red leaves on the grass and ran and ran but didn't know where, and fast, as fast as I used to be when I was a sprinter, running for a safe place that would hold me safely and gently, where no wickedness could get me. But the dream of footsteps behind me stopped my breath back into my throat, and they found me and, terribly, brought me back and thought it amusing.

But the night of the dormitory I could not move, and lay awake half the night staring into the pale dark, and when my husband visited me, once more I did not say anything, just asked if I could go home, and when they would not allow it, could only make that whine again that animals make. And we sat, and the other patients sat and sat. I felt sorry for them, but my own sick fear numbed me too much to feel more than anxiety for their duck and glance. We were all impaled by silence.

I was in the hospital for three weeks and in a continual state of fear, particularly when I had to take off my clothes for an X-ray. I was frightened of being alone with the man who gave me an intelligence test, and although a brush with what was probably an electroencephalograph seemed innocuous, I trusted no one throughout my sojourn.

Most of the time I sat silently in the room, like the other patients. Sometimes I went down to the men's day room, since they were pleasanter and seemed to like me.

I was standing in the female patients' day room when I heard the voices. There were only two of them, and they came from about eight feet away from me and about ten feet above the floor. One of them said, 'You are going to have to be braver than you have ever been before,' and the other said, 'You're going to have to do it yourself.'

They were quite objective, and I accepted them, although it was the only time I had ever heard voices, nor did I hear them again. It has taken eighteen years for fulfilment.

Florence Nightingale, of course, heard voices four times, wisely remaining mum and merely recording the information in one of her little notes. Fulfilled in due time.

For the ensuing weeks of my captivity, my conduct was impeccable, because I was too frightened to behave in any other way, and because I felt I must be discharged if I were to survive. I took my pills, talked to the other patients, even smiled at the staff and eventually discharged myself with the help of a young male patient who filled in the form for me.

And I went home. I was dirty. My trousers and jersey were the ones I was wearing when I had arrived at the hospital, and now they smelt of fear, of sweat, of sick, and of pee. The ugliness and terror of that time would darken my senses for years, and tablets procure my silence.

At home I described what had been done to me, but quickly, with revulsion, the sides of my mouth sticking together. My own house seemed alien, and loneliness still sliced into me, sending me to the lavatory with the taste of bile in my throat, as it had for the last week of my captivity. I remembered the cigarette butts swimming in shit in the hospital and retched and thought of how I had sat on those rank lavatories with shit pouring out of me and felt that no one would save me. I felt I had no being, for shock wipes your brain clean, and since I did not know I was in shock, there was no one else to recognize it, and soon I felt as unprotected as I had at the hospital. I knew how my condition should be treated, but could not do for myself what I had done for the soldiers I had nursed, and the clammy horror plastered itself to my mind.

I could not recover from the remembered fright that short-changed my life. I would not see friends, and would rather cross the road than encounter a man. I lost interest in everything, and was too afraid to answer the front door until we had had a peephole put in it. I no longer liked or trusted doctors, and in my consciousness forever swung a constant re-enactment of the hospital. Nothing quickened me, and love was no longer beautiful, but ugly and frightening.

Since psychiatry seemed the only treatment for my state, a barricade of complicity met me the moment I left the hospital, and I was forbidden to talk of the ordeal and immediately silenced with drugs. My inner scream for help echoed back at me as it had done in the cell, and after a while, I knew I was being held incommunicado. My instincts and principles, once healthy and defined as apples, were peeled and I could trust no one.

I cut my wrists. I cut them because I was a coward and I cut them because I was thoughtless. I looked sharp and bought the razor blades the day before, and I looked sharp and made certain the house would be empty. I felt lonely and guilty but I was not at all afraid, and I had two baths, one for getting clean and one for getting dead, and washed my hair and put on quite a lot of scent.

I thought, into whose hands do I commend my spirit, for God's sake? Who will love me? Who will be there? And the thread of scarlet sprang against my wrists and aridly stopped, and I began to weep for the struggle and the failure. I thought, you failed, and you've buggered up people who love you, and I got out of the pink bath water but still struggled and sawed, and meanly bled.

I sat on the sofa and wept and lit a cigarette and picked up the telephone and said, 'I'm sorry – I've – I'm sorry –' and great, bloody tears banged down on my dressing gown, and I wiped them away with the heel of my hand like I did over the egg you boiled me, boy-o. But I didn't think of you. You were dead.

Ambulance drivers are impatient with failed suicides, they give you little shoves and say, 'Come along, dear.'

I commended my spirit into the hands of a short, clean, manicured psychiatrist who would not allow me to speak, did not wish me to say I still felt dirty from that place because that was nonsense, and you shouldn't attempt suicide for such a ridiculous reason. I tried to explain the other reasons that were attached to it, but he didn't like that because I might have betrayed a sensibility and a knowledge that he would not care for. And he flipped his notebook with a sound like a whipcrack.

After three weeks of reading magazines in his mental hospital, I looked at myself in the glass and thought, for God's sake get up and fight. School's not out yet.

But I couldn't. The drugs checkered my thinking and lost me my balance. To try and expunge the effect of my ill treatment, we moved house four times. And each time I carried its fear with me, and the outcome of the Enquiry was predictable – there were no witnesses. The classic physical signs of shock had long ago become apparent in me – loss of body hair and cessation of menstruation. Subsequent appointments with Dr Y. elicited trumpery enquiries about mood and appetite, and the insistence on more drugs with the attendant side effects of vertigo, incontinence, and blurred vision. Any reference to the nightmare that still hung over me was treated with studied disregard. I was still having bad dreams, and was still afraid of every corner I turned. The people who should have been easing my distress were keeping my mouth shut with sophism and chicanery. Unsurprisingly, breakdown followed breakdown.

ESTHER BENABU
The Chosen

Randall came in from the small, enclosed garden and sat with me in the pool room. No one played pool; blank sheets of art paper lay on the table. 'I think the radio is speaking to me,' he said. At that moment I knew he was mad. His skin was pale and coarse, fleshless, but his eyes glistened huge and alive, shimmering aspic on the dry plate of his face.

A few days earlier, in the thrall of the most passionate love affair of my life, I'd turned on the radio and heard an obscure symphony in which a violin climbed, hovered, strained against its base. This was how I felt. This violin soaring above choppy waves was our love affair. I stood over the radio until the music stopped. The announcer told me the composer was from the country which I had just visited with my new lover. The radio was speaking to me.

Here are some glimpses of three men I have loved: Randall, Edward, and John, who have occupied my inner life. My attempts to hold them there, or throw them out, have taken me into extreme states. These are states which no one would ever choose but where you have to go if you hold to your love, or are possessed by it. Often words failed me. If I am lucky, there is music to form the feeling, if not, grunts and howls.

A few years earlier: Randall crawls down a corridor on all fours towards me, wearing his shirt back to front. We are in Lewes gaol. We sit in a small barred room. 'What's your favourite song?' he asks. '"Just a Closer Walk with Thee",' I suggest, a track by Sonny Terry and Brownie McGhee on a 78 my then-lover John has given me. I love its haunting intimacy with a place of peace that can never be reached. 'Sing it,' Randall commands, and in a quavering voice in a prison cell I sing four verses. Randall listens in rapt attention. Tears run down my face and my voice breaks.

This time, sitting with Randall in that stuffy leisure room, I felt his madness spoke for me. He has a freedom to say things because he is 'mad', things which I would feel foolish saying. He speaks for us all, when in the grip of passion or despair: 'Oh darling, they're playing our tune.' A freedom; no choice. This time, Randall is locked in the secure unit of his local hospital. In a place that smells of stale defeat, only his eyes glow with life. I was not locked up for being in love any more than later, in the thrall of grief and despair, my desire for death was seen as unreasonable. It was a proper response. The line dividing the mad from the sane never ceases to move, shifted by changes in institutional practice, by public mood, by obscure leapings and plummetings in the hearts of each of us. When reason escapes the sane, our 'madness' is temporary, proper, not certifiable. Our madnesses confirm the definition of sanity.

I don't think it wrong that from time to time Randall is put in a secure unit against his will. I wish, I ache with the wish, that this did not have to happen. The rationale is that at such moments he is a danger to himself or to others. Sometimes, at these moments, he has been; sometimes he hasn't. He seems in the grip of a fever which keeps him endlessly awake for days and wastes his flesh, drives him to tangle with and flee from authorities, to search out the generosity of prostitutes and be fleeced by them, to stand in the bright-lit roar and acclaim of any theatre – a parade of Guards, a pub-fight, a swirl of fast-moving traffic which he imperiously holds up his hand to command to a stop – it as at these moments when he feels most alive, most himself. He feels he can do anything, be anything. There is a swelling strain of fear in him at such times, which so moves me with pity that I want to shrink, lick his hand like a small and harmless puppy. When he's depressed, he thinks I have a malign and awesome power.

The idea that hospital provides an asylum, a place of safety, is seductive; it soothes us in our reason, glosses our baser motives for wanting the mad locked up: look, we care, we make provision for the protection of the mad. The old common parlance of a loony bin is closer to the truth. 'They said I was mad; and I said they were mad; damn them, they outvoted me': Nathaniel Lee, seventeenth-century poet, confined to Bedlam.

From the enclosure of hospital Randall says, 'Get me out of here. I'm surrounded by mad people.' Which he is. The walls of this hospital are papered with notices announcing classes in keep fit, yoga, art. None of these ever takes place. Patients and staff, inmates all, know that these words on paper signify nothing. The same goes for the sheets of paper allocating each patient his named, personal nurse.

Same hospital, different admission, a couple of years later. I ring to confirm what I have already checked with a nameless nurse on a visit, that I am coming to take him out for a break the following day. Nurse no. 2 knows nothing of this. The next day, I ring again to say I'll be there at midday. Nurse no. 3 knows nothing of my impending visit and anyway says Randall is not there. They don't know where he is. During a day shaped by my hysteria I discover that he is alone at home, that his hospital bed has been given to someone else, he had nowhere to sleep, and spent the night sitting up talking to an unnamed nurse. I wonder if this is nurse no. 4 whom I watched a few days before, averting her face from an ebullient patient who wanted to talk. What does nursing mean in such hospitals? Counting the pills, checking the locks, putting in the time? Where is the row about nursing standards in psychiatric wards? About standards anywhere in this gulag of institutions we call public care?

Randall decided to leave the hospital to avoid another night sitting up without a bed, uncared for. I make a formal complaint. I am told, less than twenty-four hours later, that my complaint has been 'thoroughly' investigated, it has all been put right, nothing anyway was wrong, etc., etc. One doesn't have to be mad to believe this; simply more desperately in need of reassurance that someone else is taking some responsibility than powered by a rage to expose, denounce, to make it better.

Another episode, some years earlier. I have spent two days phoning friends, hospitals, police trying to find out where he is. He had been driven up to London by his sister and went voluntarily to the casualty department of a large hospital. In his manic state, he waits for three hours. Told he must wait yet more hours, he flicks some spray from his cola can over a security officer, who tries to arrest him. He runs away. I have learnt

this from John who cycled to the hospital, arriving a minute
after Randall has fled. At 10 p.m. Randall rings me. His voice
is blurred. He has, he says, taken the whole bottle of pills he
was prescribed the day before. I ring a mini-cab and go to his
flat. I phone the nearest hospital to ask if they will admit him.
No, not the right catchment area, they say. A friend arrives and
drives us to St Thomas's. We wait in casualty for two hours.
Randall has the elaborate calm and courtesy that only the mad
can assume when waiting for hours in casualty. I keep telling
them he has taken a whole bottle of pills. At 1 a.m. a psychiatric
consultant arrives. He wants a complete case history, every hospital, consultant, dates over ten years. His English is very poor.
'Whittington, what is Whittington?' he says. 'It's a large hospital in North London,' I say, with elaborately calm courtesy.
How can he not know? He checks the pill bottle which I have
retrieved and decides the dose is not fatal – evidently, as Randall
is lying on a bed looking highly alert. At 3 a.m. the consultant
decides; he cannot admit Randall. He will prescribe more pills.
I am so exhausted my legs are trembling. 'What happens,' I ask,
'if he just swallows all this bottleful as well?' 'What happens,'
replies the consultant, 'if he walks out of here and gets run over
by a bus?' A nurse raises her eyes behind his back as the consultant, literally, washes his hands of the problem.

I know, I *know*, Randall will not sleep tonight, tomorrow
night, until he is in hospital. He doesn't know what the hours
are which should intersperse the drug dosages. I don't know
what to do. It is 3 a.m. Sunday and I do not have a car. At that
moment, John walks in. He takes Randall to his home. And
finally, after a night during which Randall wanders out God
knows where, picks a fight, God knows with whom, and breaks
his hand, John gets him to a GP who gets him admitted to hospital. I tell this story to a friend, who says, 'God, you should
make a complaint.' But I don't.

I have, unintentionally, made a complaint, once. Another
episode: Randall rings me, in that barking voice that declares he
is high. He is at his local police station trying to make a complaint. He wants me to summon the best lawyers to support
him. His house has been burgled. In these times his house is

always burgled: he goes out, leaving the doors open; he comes back in with a revelrous crowd of local oddballs who cheerily pillage his flat as he dispenses largesse. Hugely expansive himself, he cannot believe there is any limit to his money or his goods. But at this moment, Randall is trying to make a complaint. My stomach clenches in apprehension; this is going to end in tears. He leaves me various phone numbers where I can reach him if he is not at the last number he has left. Soon, I begin ringing them. He is at none, though there are traces at several – a loud voice outside at 3 the previous morning, a broken window, a poem through a door. Someone says they think he's been arrested; the police were there. I ring the police station. I wait, listening to the phone ring for over twenty minutes. The station officer has no record of him. I insist. I am transferred to the detectives upstairs. 'What's his crime number?' I have no idea. I only know his name, his date and place of birth, the history of his mental disorder, his hospitalizations and imprisonments, his few friends and fewer moments of happiness. I do not know his number. Sorry, madam, can't help. I dial again, wait again, finally learn he has been arrested at the police station in the process of trying to make his complaint, and taken to the local hospital, from where he has been released as perfectly sane.

At 6 the following morning the phone rings and I hear a rasping croak. It is a very cheery Randall. He went to see his brother, was subsequently arrested, spent the night in a police cell singing throughout the dark hours to keep his fears at bay, lost his voice as a result. His brother takes him back to the hospital which less than twenty-four hours earlier refused to admit him. They now think him so dangerously mad they section him. I learn that his arrest the day before was carried out by eight police officers in riot gear. 'He was climbing the walls.' I learn from the hospital that, despite the section, they have no bed for him. They have phoned twenty-four hospitals in and around London and can find no bed. Shortly after midnight, they compulsorily sedate him, an injection in the buttocks, put him in an ambulance and drive him to a private hospital 150 miles away.

Two days later I go and visit him. The hospital, now owned

by an American insurance company but once a public hospital, has decked out its entrance hall like a gothic country-house hotel. All is muted. It does not smell fetid or sing with the sound of humans in distress. A receptionist with highlights, clacky heels, and eyes like blank shields asks me to wait. I sit on a tasteful chair and read the glossy brochures. Unlike public hospitals, this one is not designed to display Victorian philanthropy, or scientific modernity, or the disciplined uniformity of its nursing army, or even a hotchpotch of attempts to carve some private space for patients out of these previous eras. Smells and yells removed, it is designed to soothe the visitors, the paying customers.

A guard with a walkie-talkie takes me through the locked doors. It is very quiet. The lights are very bright. There are thick carpets. The guards/nurses have bright white shirts and all have walkie-talkies. Young persons sprawl in drugged somnolence on the floor. Randall's manic brightness glimmers through his drugs. He shows me round. I pick up a booklet for patients detailing how they will be un-waged and un-rewarded if they un-cooperate (words like punish are un-used here). Control of their behaviour (nursing) is conducted via the giving and withholding of cigarettes, the giving of drugs. Nothing to be afraid of.

Randall has a friend here. A young woman who has been touched by God. We talk religion. It is much easier to talk about religion, evil, the apocalypse, with mad people than it is to talk about income support or the weather. It is much more interesting. I am struck, again, by how elevated the discourse of mad people is; those who don't grunt and mumble wrestle with the languages of religion, mysticism, high politics to order their unusual experience, to capture its intensity. The only subject I get squeamish about is sex; the naked, poetic imagination of the mad is too frightening; it does not excise smells, violence, race, the texture of sexual desire.

I return home. Two days later I find he is being sent back to London. I talk to the consultant at the private hospital and extract the information that this decision has not been made on clinical grounds. It's a budgetary decision. I am quivering with outrage. I organize a joint letter from Randall's family and send it to the government minister responsible. We do not get a reply. I send it again. It is intercepted by a bright young thing from the National Health Service Management Executive (Complaints Division) who purrs she is glad everything has turned out all right, and advises Randall to drop in on his GP for further advice. Outrage unabated, I send this to Labour's spokesman, who is keen to take it up. When I tell him that Randall's mother has written to complain to her MP, a shire Tory, the Opposition man loses interest and I do not hear from him again. We had wanted his energy and skills to help us fight our battle. He had wanted our experience as material to fight his. The shire Tory has written an emollient letter saying he is sorry to hear about her little boy. Randall is, at the time, almost forty years old. My ambushed letter to Mr Bowis has, for some reason, now been forwarded to the local Community Care complaints officer; for months afterwards I get questionnaires asking me to tick, cross, fill in here as to how adequately my complaint has been treated. I didn't want to make a complaint. I wanted to fling the wretched human chaos of political (un)decisions in the face of those who (un)make them. But he, unlike us, is well guarded against such chaos.

I fell in love with Edward at half past two on a Friday. He said, 'I have read eight articles on multiple sclerosis. I want to know what it means for us.' The multiple sclerosis in my body, more specifically in the nerves of my brain, had been diagnosed some years earlier. There are many immediate reactions to being told you harbour, you have, you are, a chronic, incurable illness. One of mine was relief. Relief that I now had a badge of exemption; with my new label, I could somehow escape the pressure of life. (I didn't.) The other relief was – I'm not mad. For several years I had been haunted by Freud's descriptions of hysteria. Here was the explanation of the sensation of being on a heavily rolling ship, the sudden staggering and bouts of vertigo, the pricking and tingling that would encompass random sections of my body and disappear, leaving me (fairly) sure that I must have imagined it, and the irregular numb patches which John would light upon. Sex became a matter of avoiding the numb patches, and desire dwindled.

Diagnosis of a physical illness pronounces that you are neither mad – the histories of both epilepsy and multiple sclerosis have to be excavated from the story of hysteria – nor bad – except for zealot practitioners of alternative health who regard your refusal to take up their advice as wilful wallowing in the dirt of un-health. They think it's a matter of will and of choice; as did those who treated hysteria up to this century, and as do many who treat mental illness today. For some, the unconscious, an amorphous zone without form or time, is merely another manifestation of the individual's will.

When I had told John that I had MS he had said, gravely, that if the time came he would have me put down. This was his act of love. I thanked him. When Edward said, some five years later, he wanted to know 'what it would mean for us' I took this to mean that he would share my future, which meant sharing my illness. How can we say our lives are our own property when the desire for another to share possession, to walk with us, to enter us, is so profound? I felt as though I was flying, exploding in joy. All my walls and enclosures dissolved. I became as the air. I became a wind, powering through the sky. My self had been let fly from any physical form. The affair was a balloon of extreme tautness, a just-tolerable tension between the desires to be possessed and to be utterly myself, to lavish tenderness and acute attention on the other, and to leave him be. I cleared out my flat, throwing out sacks of old papers which I had stored for years, just in case. He gave me the gift of hope, a future.

I had not understood till then how much our idea of illness, mental or physical, is locked round the idea of dirt, of contamination. Pasteur, of pasteurization, was obsessed with the hordes of invisible dirt specks all round him; this was science, in contrast to centuries of purging. As though we are forever a few steps removed from a pristine, sterile state which we struggle to reach. Just a Closer Walk with Thee. The tension is because we *cannot* reach that pristine state, which would be death.

'Perfection is terrible, it cannot have children,' wrote Sylvia Plath.

There is a romantic fantasy that chronic illness, mental or physical, allows you to walk closer to a state of perfect peace. And also to experience life-expanding extreme states, available to ordinary mortals only through drugs. Perhaps this is why saints set about wrecking their health. The ill are the chosen. Perhaps the diagnosis gave me a brief asylum of the spirit. Not until Edward did I understand that a degenerative illness is a closure, not so much the dying in parts which Brigid Brophy spoke of, but an alien force appropriating your future. Do I 'own' this illness, or repel it as an assault? Some take it in; the naturalist W. N. P. Barbellion, who died of multiple sclerosis, had the Pasteur-ish belief that 'millions of bacteria are gnawing away at my precious spinal cord and if you put your ear to my back the sound of the gnawing I daresay could be heard'. I am unnerved by the knowledge it is an auto-immune disease, that my immune system attacks me instead of protecting me from invasive harms. It is an alien intrusion. I do not want it. I had not understood before how powerful a delusion I had that somehow death was just one more life-choice, no more than the time when one says, OK, I've had enough now, I'll let my life go.

If it hadn't been for John's death-wish for me I would not have fallen into the madness of love with Edward. If it hadn't been for Randall's inescapable reminders that unreason, wretchedness, danger are inescapable, I would not have soared into a realm of light and freedom, purged of illness. Edward gave me life because he gave me hope when I didn't know I had lost it. Paradoxically, he offered me the peace of ordinariness. During the innumerable summertime, early-dawn nights when I waited for him to arrive, I held him in an immeasurable tender-ness, weaving his out-of-this-world impact into a tapestry of humdrum daily life.

Edward and I had driven home from holiday playing *Rigoletto* all the way. Waiting for me on my answering machine were a series of messages from Randall, escalating from the loud monotone of the first to staccato bravura threaded with fear, then a message from his sister saying it was OK, he was in hospital. I drove Edward to the railway station; he would be back in two months. On my way home I saw a notice announcing that two months from that day an opera company was performing *Rigoletto*. 'Darling, they're playing our tune.' I went to book our tickets, Edward and mine. I have never seen him again.

When I knew he was not coming back, that the new life I had not realized I wanted was over before it began, I went into a wilderness. I had been shipped onto an Arctic plain, a place of desolation, a howling wilderness, a white blizzard. I raised my head and howled like a dog. I felt that a snakelike creature sat heavily coiled on my diaphragm and was winding up my throat choking me. I scrabbled at my throat and couldn't breathe. The new life that had been created in me had been killed, against my will. I wanted to die too.

At the same time, John went off on a tour. Before he left, he took me out for a last meal. He, whom I had ditched, was now happily, successfully, in a loving relationship with another. From the depths of my envy and despair, I spent our last evening shifting from snarl to silent tears. I hated him.

Five months later, his son rang to tell me he was comatose following a road accident. In an infinitesimal moment, my anger and hatred evaporated. In its place flowed, unbidden, the most pure love, a love purged of self, anger, reproach, disappointment. In the days that followed, as John lay unconscious in an intensive care unit, I chanted to myself, 'Be well, be happy,' and chanted this from when I first woke throughout the day. I wanted nothing more for him, nothing for myself. I don't know where this feeling came from. Had it always been there, and would it now be too late? Through the agency of his children, I got admission to the intensive care unit. I would drive listening to *The Archers;* Ruth was having a baby and the sounds of her labour pains accompanied my journeys. Was this creation of a new life a good or a bad omen? I talked to John and stroked him. Once, he suddenly opened his eyes, small, murky brown, and stared at me. Held me in his gaze. I stared back as though I could pull him back to life through the tiny pupils of his eyes. I called the nurse, who came and looked. 'Let him go back,' she commanded me. Go back where? I obeyed. I think now she did not know what to do and could not stand the tension.

I guessed he would die. He was dying from contamination, dirt in his lungs and blood. His body, once so powerfully muscled, was becoming emaciated by the hour. A nurse said it was the fever; he was consuming himself. I could hardly bear to look at the piteous, massive black bruising on his leg, his poor body that now twitched convulsively from the drugs. They performed a tracheotomy and he looked as though someone had driven a stake through his throat. When the nurse siphoned his breathing tube he would jerk up in a spasm of terror as his air was stopped. Throughout these days, the monitor bleeped with electronic precision, an artificial reassurance of actual life.

He died when they cut off the adrenalin that was keeping him alive.

I cannot now describe the depths of grief into which I fell. It began the night of his death when I got home and thought, 'I could search the whole world over and I wouldn't find him anywhere. He isn't anywhere.' For a long time I imagined, in unguarded moments, that if I concentrated with absolute, unbroken intensity, I could keep open a line to him in his other world, keep him alive as Orpheus was able, almost, to draw Eurydice back to his world.

The account does not fit here anyway. This is not an account of my life but rather a version of how the familiar themes – the difference between madness and sanity, the notion of self-possession, of will and of choice – play out in real persons. It is a statement that ill health is not invited but thrust upon you, and that in most cases it is not cured but managed. It is a rage against the psychiatric establishment, medical and political, which has simply given up trying, wrapping its inertia in colourful Charters, Rights to Complain, un-words of concern, quashing the tentative questions of desperate and fearful friends and relatives with complacent lies about wonder drugs and modern cures. If they believe the people they treat are 'cured', they have an abysmally low opinion of human beings. All they want is a peaceful life. And the gulag of the incurable will grow.

A. ALVAREZ
Back

The night I came back from the hospital, scarcely
Knowing what had happened or when,
I went through the whole performance again in my dreams.
Three times – in a dance, in a chase and in something
Now lost – my body was seized and shaken
Till my jaw swung loose, my eyes were almost out
And my trunk was stunned and stretched with a vibration
Sharper than fear, closer than pain. It was death.
So I sweated under the sheets, afraid to sleep,
Though you breathed all night quietly enough by my side.

Was it the *tremor mortis*, the last dissolution
Known now in dreams, unknown in the pit itself
When I was gripped by the neck till my life shook
Like loosening teeth in my head? Yet I recall
Nothing of death but the puzzled look on your face,
Swimming towards me, weeping, clouded, uncertain,
As they took the tube from my arm
And plugged the strange world back in place.

1961

MAUREEN FREELY
Still Life

1 The box room

I had worried about the lack of direct natural light when I first suggested it to him, but it turned out to be just what he wanted. He took the paints and brushes I had bought for him and assembled them at the far end of what was really not much better than a closet. He piled all the cushions I had found for him and propped them up against the wall with the small, high window that looked out on to the bedroom that would have been dark even if he had not insisted on keeping the curtains drawn at all times. He propped his huge sketchpad against the opposite wall, planted his bare feet to either side of it, and stared into the blank paper.

His wrists still had bandages on them. His arms and his thighs and his feet were covered with scratches. His hair and his clothes were clean only because I had made him take a bath and had washed his clothes while he was sitting in it, but his fingernails were black and his clothes looked as if he had slept in them and he had not brushed his hair in days.

'What do you think you'll do first?' I asked.

I tried to ask this question with just the right balance of interest and disinterest, but now he looked up from the pad with just the disdainful disbelief you'd expect if I were a chauffeur who didn't know my station and he were the ambassador to France.

'I'm going to do another tree.'

2 The other trees

They were already framed and proudly displayed all around the flat. Black trees, brown trees, some with leaves and berries and blossoms, each individually drawn, some with a tangle of bare branches, sometimes thick and sometimes thin, standing in front of skies that could be blue or black or red but were always devoid of detail. Despite their size they had (as dinner guests were always remarking) something in common with the Oriental miniatures. They were beautiful and unusual. They captured a mood. It was always the same mood but it was not a mood anyone could remember seeing in captivity before. Although it was a mood too dark for me to ever know how to name, I felt happy whenever I looked at them, especially if I was looking at them with people who had never seen them before. They were, or had been, proof that my baby brother had gone through a rough patch and survived it. Was to be admired at last for being different instead of pitied. Was not disturbed now but just artistic. Was not my fault.

3 Where this fear came from

At the time it was still not clear to me. My brother had always been different. Even when he was five, people used to remark that it was amazing how long he could keep himself amused without playmates, how many games he could invent with just a handful of pebbles and a stick. Most of these people were, like my parents, Americans who had come to teach in Istanbul in order to escape the fifties. My brother's ability to play without the aid of mass-produced toys was proof that they had been right to take their children away from the evils of conformity and consumerism. This is one of the stories my mother and father loved to tell about him: when he was eight we went back to New Jersey to visit my mother's family. He came across a baseball bat and, to my all-American grandparents' horror, asked, 'What's that?'

Another thing that horrified them: by the time he was eight he was already drinking wine at meals. This did not seem strange to us: I had always known I could have as much wine as I wanted and so had my sister. Wine was something that you learned to drink gradually in a civilized way at meals with your parents. Anyone who suggested otherwise was a puritan with a crewcut. But by the time my brother was nine we were finding him passed out next to empty raki and ouzo bottles. When he was ten he stole my father's sleeping pills and took them into school and offered to get his whole class high. Only the boys accepted. My brother got found out and suspended because instead of getting high in class that afternoon, all the boys fell asleep.

A few months later, my family went to New York for a year, and my brother discovered ice-cream. It was my mother who turned him on to it. She had long been in the habit of buying secret treats for herself. My brother was the only child with whom she shared them. He never blabbed about her hiding places. But there are not very many places where you can hide a gallon of ice cream. It got so he was getting up several times a night to feed his habit, and going through two to three gallons at a time. In two months he almost doubled in weight. My father accused my mother, not for the first time, of ruining his only son. To appease him, she put my brother on a diet. Two days later, he was arrested for shoplifting in a candy store.

Not long after they had returned to Istanbul, he was arrested for trying to blow up the Bosphorus Bridge. What he really had been doing was smoking hash with his best friend, the other school truant. They had thought that the base of the bridge would give them the privacy they could not get at home. They had not bargained on undercover policemen looking for terrorists. Although they escaped prison, he and his friend were suspended from school again. My father put my brother under what amounted to house arrest. My brother fought back by confining himself to his room and refusing to get out of bed. My mother tried to cheer him up by giving him oregano to smoke in his pipe. But no matter what she did, she couldn't get him out of bed.

I was the one who got him out of bed. By now I was nineteen years old and in my second year of university. I had just enough psychology to have a pat explanation for everything. When I woke up one morning to hear my mother try and coax little B. out of bed, and my father try and drag him out of it, and my father accuse my mother of ruining his only son by standing between them, I knew that I could not let them put him in a double bind, so I got up, walked into my brother's bedroom, told my parents they had gone too far this time, and asked them to leave. They did so at once and without protest. I shut the door behind them and it was as if I had locked myself in a closet. When I looked across the room, I could only just make out the bed.

There was only a single jagged line of light coming into the room through the curtains. I made my way towards it, stumbling over a book here and a shoe there. Even when I had drawn the curtains, there was still not much natural light to be had because of the tree pressing up against the windowpane. But now, at least, when I turned around, I could see my brother's trembling hand holding his blanket over his head.

'B.,' I said. 'B., can you hear me?'

He lowered the blanket and looked at me as if he were a man who had been mistaken for a corpse and I were the sceptical gravedigger who had decided to open up the coffin one last time before covering it with earth.

'Time to get up,' I said.

And without pausing to think, he got up.

4 The understanding we had

It had been a constant. Here is my earliest memory of my brother: an infant lying in a basket in our sitting-room. This was before we went to Turkey, when we were still in New Jersey. He must have been two or three months old. I must have been seven. I was watching *Lassie* or *I Love Lucy* or *The Last Days of Pompeii*. My mother was on her way out to the store on the corner, but halfway through the door she turned around and said, 'Now I want you to promise to stay in this room until I get back, and whatever you do, you are not to pick up the baby.' But as soon as she was gone, that's just what I did. He wasn't crying, not audibly, but I picked him up and rocked him in my arms until he went back to sleep, and then put him back into the basket, and everything was as peaceful when she got back as it had been when she left.

I had spent all my jealousy on my sister. I had none left over for my brother. All I wanted to do was help him grow up, and I knew there were times when I could help him a lot more than my mother. My mother knew nothing about drugs, less about sex. She really did think that my brother would learn to love oregano. She really didn't know what the word homosexual meant until she was thirty. My father did know, but he couldn't believe that any friend of the family might ever have untoward thoughts towards his children. Even when the evidence was there, he couldn't see what was going on. There was no way I could contrive not to see, but I had no way of knowing then that this type of attention was cruel or unusual and it never occurred to me that there might be more to some stories than others. All I knew was that it wasn't right, for example, for a married man to drop by at nine in the evening for a wrestling match with my ten-year-old brother and his two best friends. Here's another family legend: the time I stood at the top of the stairs, staring disapprovingly at my former music teacher, a terrifying seven-foot-tall man with a flat, broad, pasty white face that would make Boris Karloff scream, and just folded my arms and waited for him to let go of my brother and his two best friends, and then, when he had scrambled to his feet, refused to engage in a conversation. All I said was, 'Goodnight, Mr Klingman.' And without pausing to think, he left.

5 The catch

The catch was that I couldn't risk pausing to think any more than they did. Here are some of the things he told me about during his teenage years that I didn't pause to think about: the place under the Galata Bridge where he went to drink opium-laced wine, the men he met there who bought him his drinks, the bad acid trips he had while at boarding school in Ireland, including the one while in Dublin for a weekend during which he witnessed a murder that never really happened, the first suicide attempt after he broke up with his first girlfriend.

Here's what I thought about instead: how well he kept doing in his exams, what interesting poetry he wrote, how amazing these trees were that he had started painting, what courses he should take when he got to Yale.

6 At Yale he got two chances

The first time he slit his wrists – this must have been about three months after he started – they put him into an institution and because he was on a scholarship, the bill was on them. It was only after a second, more spectacular attempt involving more than one drug and a bloody scene at a second-storey window that they decided to send him home. Home was Athens by now, and I knew it would be the death of him. My father was drinking heavily. My mother was barely coping. There was no medical help for him there, and because he would not be allowed to work, there would be no way for him to build an independent life. And anyway, as I told my husband, I was the only one who could ever get through to him. I insisted on taking him in without pausing to think.

Also without pausing to think I told him I would take care of him until he got better. I repeated my promise to him every day. Every day I would go into my box room in Belsize Park to find him on a pile of paint-stained pillows, shivering under the blanket that he had draped over his shoulders, his wrists bandaged, his thighs and his forearms covered with scratches, his nails black crescents, and his eyes black holes. I would sit down across from him and I would ask him how he felt, and when he didn't answer I would tell him not to worry, that I would look after him anyway. I would tell him how important it was for me that he get better. I would tell him that I wasn't going to give up on him. I would ask to look at his tree-in-progress.

But every day it was harder to look at them, because I hated these trees he had lavished so much work on. I hated their thin and fat, black and brown trunks, and their thousand and one spider-web branches, and the way their million and one uniform oval leaves blocked out all but the tiniest dot of sky. It was the trees that stood between me and him. It was the trees he hid behind. It was the trees that kept me from getting through to him, the trees that kept him shivering underneath his own thoughts, the trees that kept me from finding the answers I needed: why he kept razor blades under his mattress, why he was insulted when I took them away from him, how he could spend whole days staring at the wall, what it was that made him shiver, what he thought about when he went to the psychiatrist I couldn't afford and refused to say anything, why he went straight to the medicine cabinet and swallowed everything in it if I left him just to go to the store on the corner, why, even after he had accepted that he was not to leave his cereal bowl in the middle of the sitting-room floor, he couldn't understand how the same rule applied to all the other rooms and floors in the house. Why, every time I was sure the medication he was now on had taken effect, he went backwards again, and returned to his blanket and the box room. Why, every time he did that, the box room looked longer and he farther away. Why kindness wasn't enough any more and reason couldn't reach him. Why his eyes were black holes. What he saw when he looked at me. And most of all, why, when he couldn't care less about his hair or his nails or his clothes or when the last time was he ate or took a bath, why he could spend an entire day going over and over the same dot of sky struggling to get past two uniform oval leaves making sure there was not a speck left of the paper's natural white.

I hated the trees, but because the trees were the only things that had shown any sign of progress, I felt compelled to keep telling him how much I admired them. And the more I lied, the larger they grew.

The break came with a conversation I had with him about two weeks after I found out I was pregnant. My husband and I were supposed to have gone to France for a week, but we cancelled the trip, partly because we couldn't see leaving my brother alone, and partly because I was suffering from morning sickness. A few days later, my brother told me that in staying home we had ruined his plans. He had wanted to kill himself. He told me how. Now that we weren't going away, he couldn't go through with it.

'Why were you waiting for us to go away?' I asked. He said,

'Because I didn't want to hurt you.' I asked, 'Don't you understand how that would have hurt us even more?' He didn't
understand at all. I took my question to the psychiatrist. He told
me that schizophrenics were incapable of understanding anything from any point of view other than their own. My brother
didn't want to hurt me. If I was not present when he did something, I couldn't get hurt because I didn't really exist.

But I couldn't understand how he could think that way, why
it had come to this, what I had done, what I could have done
but had not done, couldn't bear the way these questions dissolved all the things I had been surest about. He grew up on
shifting sands, the psychiatrist told me. That's one of the many
reasons why it's come to this. But if he had grown up on shifting sands, then so had I. Then everything I thought of as normal
was anything but. I could grasp the idea that there was more to
my childhood than I was willing to think about, but I was incapable, and for many years would continue to be incapable, of
understanding my childhood from any point of view other than
the one my mother and my father and my sister and I had conspired to share.

7 Still life

And so one day, I looked into the box room at the head of
unwashed hair and the blanket, and the scratched arms and the
mess of paints around the precisely gnarled branches of his latest tree, and I thought no, I don't want him here any more. I
don't want to think these thoughts. I don't want to feel this
way. I'm having my first baby now. I'm starting a new life. I
don't want to smell death. Let someone else take care of him.
Let someone else draw the inevitable conclusions. I picked up
the phone and got through to my mother and asked her to come
up to London to collect him. And she did come to the rescue, as
she would continue to do, as she does still, as she probably
always did even though I didn't see it that way. I was right
about one thing, though. Greece was almost but not quite the
death of my brother.

When things went wrong, did he blame me? Did he care that I didn't want to care for him any more? Did he even care where he was by then so long as people let him hide behind his trees? When I told him I was giving up on him, all he did was shrug his shoulders. He could have been Thomas Mann writing *Doctor Faustus*. I could have been a toddler breaking his concentration. Every appointment with reality was an exasperating interruption for him: breakfast, lunch, dinner, tea, medication, the psychiatrist, and most particularly the art therapist.

The art therapist was more of an annoyance to him, not just because he was unnecessary but because it was an hour's bus ride to his flat in Chelsea. On my brother's last visit – this was just before he went back to Greece, and weeks after I had stopped trying to get through to him – the art therapist set him up at an easel in his ornate sitting-room, apparently, put out a vase of daffodils on a small table, and told him he had half an hour to do a still life.

The painting he brought home was a storm of reds and yellows and greens. The daffodils looked as if they had been blown on to the paper. You could almost feel the cold spring wind pushing against the leaves and the petals. There were rough patches of white between the vase and the table, the table and the wall. The table was lopsided, as if flagging under the weight of the feelings it had to carry, and the vase was off-centre, as if too exposed, too battered, too weakened by torment to lend itself to symmetry.

'This is beautiful,' I said. 'This is really beautiful.' I said it without thinking: for once I wasn't lying to him. But for once he actually looked at me as if he was wondering if I was lying to him. As if there couldn't possibly be any value in something he had just dashed off.

But because I liked it, he gave it to me as his parting gift. I framed it and gave it pride of place over the mantelpiece, even though it answered every question I had ever wanted to ask him, every thought I had never paused to think. Even though every time I looked at it I saw all the wounds he had tried to hide from me, heard all the words that no other words can ever cancel out, and tasted the pain.

TED HUGHES
The God

You were like a religious fanatic
Without a god – unable to pray.
You wanted to be a writer.
Wanted to write? What was it within you
Had to tell its tale?
The story that has to be told
Is the writer's God, who calls
Out of sleep, inaudibly: 'Write'.
Write what?
Your heart, mid-Sahara, raged
In its emptiness.
Your dreams were empty.
You bowed at your desk and you wept
Over the story that refused to exist,
As over a prayer
That could not be prayed
To a non-existent God. A dead God
With a terrible voice.
You were like those desert ascetics
Who fascinated you,
Parching in such a torturing
Vacuum of God
It sucked goblins out of their finger-ends,
Out of the soft motes of the sun-shaft,
Out of the blank rock face.
The gagged prayer of their sterility
Was a God.
So was your panic of emptiness – a God.

You offered him verses. First
Little phials of the emptiness
Into which your panic dropped its tears

That dried and left crystalline spectra.
Crystals of salt from your sleep.
Like the dewy sweat
On some desert stones, after dawn.
Oblations to an absence.
Little sacrifices. Soon

Your silent howl through the night
Had made itself a moon, a fiery idol
Of your God
Your crying carried its moon
Like a woman a dead child. Like a woman
Nursing a dead child, bending to cool
Its lips with tear-drops on her finger-tip.
So I nursed you, who nursed a moon
That was human but dead, withered and
Burned you like a lump of phosphorus.

Till the child stirred. Its mouth-hole stirred.
Blood oozed at your nipple,
A drip feed of blood. Our happy moment!

The little god flew up into the Elm Tree.
In your sleep, glassy eyed,
You heard its instructions. When you woke
Your hands moved. You watched them in dismay
As they made a new sacrifice.
Two handfuls of blood, your own blood,
And in that blood gobbets of me,
Wrapped in a tissue of story that had somehow
Slipped from you. An embryo story.
You could not explain it or who
Ate at your hands.
The little god roared at night in the orchard,
His roar half a laugh.

You fed him by day, under your hair-tent,
Over your desk, in your secret
Spirit-house, you whispered,
You drummed on your thumb with your fingers,

Shook Winthrop shells for their sea-voices,
And gave me an effigy – a Salvia
Pressed in a Lutheran Bible.
You could not explain it. Sleep had opened.
Darkness poured from it, like perfume.
Your dreams had burst their coffin.
Blinded I struck a light

And woke upside down in your spirit-house
Moving limbs that were not my limbs,
And telling, in a voice not my voice,
A story of which I knew nothing
Giddy
With the smoke of the fire you tended
Flames I had lit unwitting
That whitened in the oxygen jet
Of your incantatory whisper.

You fed the flames with the myrrh of your mother
The frankincense of your father
And your own amber and the tongues
Of fire told their tale. And suddenly
Everybody knew everything.
Your God snuffed up the fatty reek.
His roar was like a basement furnace
In your ears, thunder in the foundations.

Then you wrote in a fury, weeping,
Your joy a trance-dancer
In the smoke in the flames
'God is speaking through me,' you told me.
'Don't say that,' I cried. 'Don't say that.
That is horribly unlucky!'
As I sat there with blistering eyes
Watching everything go up
In the flames of your sacrifice
That finally caught you too and you
Vanished, exploding
Into the flames

Of the story of your God
Who embraced you
And your mummy and your daddy,
Your Aztec, Black Forest
God of the euphemism grief.

JUDITH KAZANTZIS
Eye

Every bird sang,
only in her eye
every bird dressed
in a pinafore of ice.
Their feathers danced
like ice floes.
Their eyes hip-hopped
like fish roe.
It seemed in her eye only,
not the general view,
some tuck
to the cornea
that puckered the lens,
some tic of birth
for which her mother screamed
and had her skew-eyed.
No, not a squint,
she didn't wander,
she kept intact
as a winter hawk.
Its talons glued to the bark,
all winter
it trained its frozen eye
on a frozen fountain
of dancing balls of feathers:
for one day
there would come
from under the raised stare,
deeper down,

a translation,
a wave of voices crying
in her own tongue.

LAWRENCE SAIL
Asterisks

If words could have done, he would have used them. But what
was there to say? That he had come downstairs one morning to
find the clock in the hall at a standstill, and had been afraid of
the silence?

*

It was like coming back from a journey, when it is impossible
(you know as soon as you begin) to tell what it was really like.
What it was like at all.

*

Years ago, there had been an eclipse of the sun: and he had
ignored the teacher's command to look at it only through a
piece of smoked glass. As a result, he had burned an image on
his retina – a kind of empty, translucent triangle with a blob at
one of its lower corners. It bobbed into sight when his eyes
unfocused or grew tired. If he focused on it, it moved right to
left and went away, off the screen of his vision. It was the same
now: something and nothing, in the corner of his eye.

*

*Let no one talk of neglect, or even of self-indulgence. These
words which I utter on to the page will never be spoken by me.
They will remain true to the silence in which they were conceived.*

*

He knew what it wasn't. Not dread (as of a maths lesson at
school); not fear; not hunger; not greed; not desire; not the
giddiness of a childhood moment of truth, being caught stealing
or lying. Without smell, without any relation to touch or texture. But how could something that seemed ethereal be so
smothering, so materially lethal? How could it remove every-

thing into a foreign distance?

*

He was aware of relations and friends somewhere on the horizon. At another point, his place of work and his colleagues; the files; the system which raised them, circulated them, added to them, returned them to their cabinets, prepared a five-year plan for their replacement by computer. Somewhere else again, the dispensers of pills, herbs, dietary advice, gentle or tough enquiries about his past, his outlook, his soul.

*

When he was small, he would lie in bed concentrating on the colours and patterns which he could create by screwing his eyes tight shut. Always yellow, and a greyish green – some of it background, some of it a honeycomb of whirling blobs and spots. Sometimes there were brownish rods that drifted about. He had expected the colour of blood, or the rosy colour you got by shining a torch through your cheeks or your fingers. Instead, it was something paler altogether, closer to the greenish pallor given off by the glow of the plastic cherub his mother had fixed on the wall at the head of his bed.

*

Who spoke of 'a green and yellow melancholy'?

*

'I've got something in my eye. In the corner of my eye.'
'Where? Hold still. Let me see.'
'It's in the corner. Right in the corner.'
'I can't see. Keep still!'
His brother's large shadow blocking everything else out.
'It's making my eye water.'
'I know. But I don't think it's anything.'
'I can feel it.'
'There's nothing there. Or if there was, it's gone.'
As simple as that. Robbie, whom he loved.

*

It was all scumbled together in his head. Pills, capsules, waiting in small rooms with viciously uncomfortable chairs, walls flowering with notices about diseases, symptoms, social services, the effects of smoking, the consequences of breathing. Corridors. Files. Figures holding files, seen behind frosted glass. Voices just out of earshot. Changes of direction. Bright smiles.

*

Often, living in the material world, we desire and fear the shadow world of the possible. But when you live in the world of spoiled possibilities, of might-have-been, what happens to the actual? It passes somewhere in the distance, visible but out of reach; perhaps only audible, like the sighing hiatus of a train passing at night, somewhere between you and the horizon. A train closed in upon the purposes of its passengers, intent on a journey and a destination from which you are excluded.

*

He wrote as he had always written – furtively, with his arm and hand cupped round the top edge of the paper, like a schoolboy not wanting his work to be cribbed; with concentration, his tongue flicking in and out and curling round his lips. He recalled a street drifted with assorted clothes, trailing; and seemed to overhear someone saying, 'It's a well-known sign, you know. Box after box of things – all down the road.' He could feel the wanton brightness and high colour of his cheeks as he thought of it.

*

He read about a satellite that had spun out of control and broken free from its tethering spacecraft. It sparked huge voltages as it swung through space, trailing a twelve-mile-long broken umbilical cord. He saw it as a miracle of streaming lights, a great arc of crackling stars surrounded by darkness.

*

What can cure – can time, as people say? Affection? Patience?

Or even words? The words that lie beside one another, here on the page, as inert as toes tagged in the morgue. The supposed pattern. Beginning – narrative, quest, or problem – ending. Illness – cure. Love – death. Sleight of hand: necessary fictions of closure. The successful ending of the story: the reader's or the writer's cure.

*

Dispensers of prescriptions, dancers and singers round candles, counsellors with their heads at the angle of sympathy. What they all had in common, apart from the charismatics with their helpless God-given laughter, the element in which all of them floated, was words. Sometimes singly; sometimes straightforward dialogue (or, since he was so often silent, monologue); sometimes great looping structures of the things which developed their own bizarre rhythms and lost sight entirely of their point of departure, so that he had only to admire the rhythms as they went by. Sometimes, the scrambled hyperventilation of glossolalia seemed preferable.

*

Robbie, winner of book prizes, successful graduate and solicitor, husband of the beautiful Jilly, father of the beautiful pigeon-pair, Dominic and Nell. Robbie, whom he loved and could hardly talk to.

*

Hooking on. Falling between slats. To wake up under a great lid. The lid being lifted off. A stone lifted off. Or not. 'Asylum'. 'Asile'. A sigh, something Egyptian, a hinterland of rhyme with 'heal' showing through. The lightest of summer breezes.

*

He seemed to have been staring for a long time at one peepshow after another: the curtain was always rising and falling in the theatre of his mind. Or wherever it was. And he could not believe any of these representations. Not one. Not even the ill-looking woman with a long, curved face who told him to have faith and pray to Saint Dympna. Behind her head, the room in which she spoke was suffused with an unhealthy yellow light, which had perhaps infected her features with the colour of old tallow. He waited for her to finish, for the already distant words to tail off altogether. When she took his hands, he knew it would not be long: he sensed the awkwardness, really the absurdity of it, knew that the fervent lack of response from him would find its echo, the sense of an ending in her voice. Standing to go. An expression of thanks. Saying goodbye. The invitation, the injunction to come back again. Payment? Retrieval of his coat. A further goodbye. The opening and pulling to of the door. The cutting air outside, blissful despite the acrid traffic fumes.

*

Here. Now. This is a place to which no known route leads, and to which I cannot imagine looking back from some vantage point ahead. This is a story so simple as to be hardly worth the telling.

*

Sometimes he looked really intently at whoever was speaking to him: the lips, the teeth, the tongue coming and going, and the little fountains of saliva projected by certain sounds and combinations of sounds.

*

He could offer, in the face of all this, only passivity: the kind instinctively adopted by someone kicked to the ground and hoping to absorb further punishment with the least possible pain; or by the wounded pretending to be dead, praying to be ignored and passed by rather than bayoneted. But in doing so, he had no choice about what was visited upon him. Perhaps not even about what was thought into him.

*

Distant for a time, the letters regrouped into ugly bunches, came at him again in bizarre kaleidoscopic patterns. Tricyclics.

Monoamine oxidase. Seratonin re-uptake. Inhibitors. Chlor-
promazine? Largactil? Meaningless bunches. Crossword words.
Pretend threats. Play words. Pretend OK. Nonsense words.
*Trick cyclists. Monotone oxeyedaisy. Seraphim gee-up stakes.
Inner biters. Claw-paw magic. Lager kills.*

*

There came the memories with their images: altogether more
vivid, sometimes terrifying. He had to watch them pass. At first
he tried to find reasons – why these? Why not those? No
answers.

*

Two machines; either could have taken your fingers off. The
mangle with its big sloping tray of pale wood and a drainage
hole beneath the double rollers; the red wheel of the Berkel
bacon slicer in the grocer's that hummed with a hiss of pure
menace as it whirled its cutting edge, laying into the rind of
skin. Standing at his mother's side, barely coming up to her
waist, he desperately wanted to reach up, to stretch out his
hand.

*

*There is a green hill far away
Without a city wall,
Where the dear Lord was crucified
Who died to save us all.*
And there they were already, guilt and terror, the red blood of
Jesus shining and shining on the green grass: a horror bright
enough for him to wake, shrieking and howling, on the dark
landing outside his room. Enough for him to be sent away to a
home, even then, at the age of five or so. Far away. For how
long?

*

If he turned right from his poky flat, past the shops and over the
canal, he soon reached the bypass, where the traffic rushed past
overhead; and beyond it, the fields of pasture running up to a

small wood. Sometimes he would pause to look into the dark, still water of the canal.

*

When he and Robbie shared a room. Winter nights: the glow of the wick through the red celluloid window in the side of the oil stove: the petals of light thrown up on to the ceiling. There, the lights of the bus crossing too, intermittently, a shifting diagonal splay that moved in time with the changing of the gears as it went by far below.

*

A sudden flash of happiness. An old wall of red sandstone, hot to lean against, with stonecrop growing brightly out of it above my head. Does this fit?

*

The hand of the policeman, heavy on his shoulder. His heart flying into his mouth, because he had been into Woolworths and had thought of stealing a water pistol. Only this time, he hadn't. 'Don't do it, Sonny.' How could he know? A terrible giddiness came over him. But it was about the old beggar he had just passed, to whom he had given a penny in return for a box of matches, because he looked so sad and needy. 'Don't encourage them. Run along home now: go on.' He ran; and fast, the guilt rapidly giving way to relief, then anger.

*

He saw Robbie and himself lying together in the womb. He imagined it as something like two eggs cracked into a pan, not yet cooked, gelatinous, their edges not yet distinct from one another. But already, he knew, Robbie was taking the better things for himself – the better teeth, the better coordination, the better brain: the better luck. And later, when grown-ups insisted how alike they were to look at, how handsome, he knew that it was Robbie they really admired. Robbie was the one that came sunny side up.

*

Whichever memories he found himself facing, the message they transmitted was almost constant: another failure, another wrong turning. Why had he not been able to see how it was all building into such a doleful and, for God's sake, obvious progression? And if he did happen upon a good memory, more often than not it was tinged with the sepia sadness of the long gone.

*

At some point, the words have shifted, and I didn't see it. Alone became lonely; relaxed, relapse; truth, rue.

*

He was inconsolable, overcome by grief, as if stricken by the death of someone he loved. But who? He was present at a funeral where there was no body, foolishly holding on to a bunch of flowers. He had no right to be there. His tears were shameless.

*

He remembered taking his clothes off and lying down in the wood, where no one could see him. The acoustic was that of indoors: a secret room. The twigs and nubbles and needles of the spongy floor prickled and scratched his skin, sometimes digging into him. The danger of it made his heart race. So did the thought of the spiders and insects that might crawl upon him. To be alone in the wood when the moonlight shone in from the edge of the dewy field: to be safe there when the wind cut loose in the threshing treetops. Finally to be absorbed into the warm, soft ground where he lay: to melt into it and leave not a trace. To escape all the words. Only disconnect!

*

And somewhere, somehow, amid all this, there must have been continuing the daily business. Food of a kind, sleep of a kind. The opening and shutting of doors, windows, valves, sphincters. Systole and diastole. Now and then, a vacant smile. And, until he went on sick leave, the routines of work.

*

Sick leave: absent without leave. That road ended with his
father, who had made a career of absence. How long ago was
it, that rainy January day when the undertaker's burly men
tripped and almost dropped his coffin on the flagstones of the
nave? How had the flowers stayed on the lid of the coffin?

*

The bed itself repressed him. Among its increasingly rumpled
wastes, he had been robbed of the power to escape. He tried to
imagine what it would be like to throw back the counterpane,
kick upwards with his feet and swing them over the edge to the
floor.

*

*What had I been waiting for when I decided not even to try to
find a wife, to keep myself to myself? Something, I am sure.*

*

There was a sweet, consoling smell which had lived in his
mother's handbag, where there was always a tablet of rouge in
a tortoiseshell case, two lumps of sugar, a white hanky, and a
small round bottle of Eau de Cologne.

*

Perhaps Robbie found him an embarrassment. In fact, how
could it be otherwise?
'Oh, really? A twin too? And what does your brother do?'
'Lives alone. Is a clerk. We hardly ever see one another.'
'Really? That's interesting!'

*

His mother he saw perhaps three times a year. He had only ever
been able to recall her face by concentrating hard. When he was
younger that had made him feel bad enough. Now he knew
what would come tearing and shrieking at him when she died –
the questions not asked, the love not given, the gratitude

demanded and so withheld, the forgiveness neither sought nor granted. There was no one else.

*

And presently, without warning, he finds himself feeling immeasurably lighter, as if he could float lazily up into the air if he chose to do so. It is not just that the sky is clear and the sun streaming in through the small high window of his bedroom. It is something else. And though he realizes that this alleviation is as arbitrary as the onset had been, for the moment it is enough to know that now, out of the corner of his eye, he can see only the silvery morning light on the white wall.

*

I have counted the asterisks. Forty-two, so far. ('42, the year of my birth.) I begin to see them not just as dividing marks, but a star-burst of essential omissions.

*

Then, from somewhere below, faintly, for no particular reason, the sound of the clock. The words reassembling in a different order. *If* finding *then*. However provisionally, the story finding its cure.

JANE RULE
If There Is No Gate

Once before, when I was twenty, I thought I was losing my mind. Then, too, I'd been working hard, and I suppose I'd caught a touch of paranoia as one does a cold in the early spring, when there's a sudden thaw and a temporary aggression of crocuses. One feels unprepared, put upon. I don't remember just what it was, an excess of defensive energy, ill temper, loneliness. I only remember the fear, like a blown fuse in the nervous system, a darkness in the heart. I was driving out to the mental hospital to deliver a load of clothes and books my mother had collected from the neighbourhood. She spent all her time, and a good deal of mine, collecting comfort for distant, public catastrophes. It was her way of protecting herself and her family from the fraud of any private terror. We had no time for such nonsense. It was a compliment that she had allowed me to go, the first of her children to reach the age of immunity. She was a marvellously insensitive woman.

My old school uniform, neatly folded just as it had been in the bottom drawer of my dresser, was at the top of the box, an afterthought smelling faintly of camphor. I lifted the carton out of the trunk of the car and, following the signs marked OFFICE, carried it through the archway into the inner court. I had not intended to look around. I had intended to keep my eyes fixed on that shroud of my innocence, my anonymity, like a charmed relic of another life, but all about and above me the racket of cries startled me into the world. There behind great expanses of steel mesh, level upon level storeying up against the light, were trapped coveys of women, shrieking and calling like surprised birds. It was a gigantic aviary of madness. Some wailed, high and fierce, unmated in that limited and crowded sky. Others chattered and scolded to guard some memory of a shabby nest, of frail and greedy young. A few hopped mournfully, silently about, picking at scraps. There were pairs, too, bold and impersonal as doves under the eaves. One woman, holding another, rocked and sang a vacant lullaby, as pure as any bird song, as inhuman. I walked across the court, went into the office, and delivered the box. I was glad to walk back through that court, empty-handed.

Sometimes since then, when I have been disturbed at dawn by the distant, violent wings of geese or at dusk by the pedestrian entrance of a robin, I have used that human aviary as a touchstone of sanity. It has been for me one of the unnatural wonders of the world, like a great cathedral, a sanctuary where one can take all the fears of one's inhumanity, leave them at the feet of saints, and come away at peace.

But that day seems a long way back in my memory, in feeling vaguer than more recent prayers. It is hard to recall not the scene so much as the sense of it: the exact, unspectacular relief of being an intentional, inhibited, insensitive human being. Perhaps the experience no longer becomes me, fits too smugly over my middle-aged humility, like a confirmation dress or a wedding gown. But, if that is so, then sanity itself must be a convention one can outgrow. One can, but one mustn't. Surely recovery, not discovery, is the way back to health.

Here they do not want me to recall the particulars of my life, to retrace my steps until I find the place, the precise moment of error. I am to ignore my conscious memory and the ordering power of my brain, as if moral interpretation of experience were a disease to be cured of. Instead, I am to enter the world of dreams and visions, abandon myself to the freakish chaos of a night's sleep, awake clinging to the absurdities and obscenities out of Spiritus Mundi and talk or dance or paint them all the unordinary day long.

If I were in a cage, dressed in someone else's clothes, absent-minded, it would be so much simpler to be mad, but this is not a mental hospital. It is a kind of rest home, settled against the gentle Devon hills within taste of the sea. I have my own small room under the eaves, sunny, vines friendly at the window, like a picture in a children's book of poetry. I am free to do what I like, to go where I please, even out into the little village to buy fruit or a bottle of sherry. I wash out my own underthings, sew on buttons, send my clothes to the cleaner. And my mind, untouched by the sudden will-less attacks of fear that my body suffers, is more decorous and lucid than ever. I make polite, intelligent conversation with the doctors at afternoon tea in the garden. My own doctor, a woman of huge frame with a face warm and remote as the sun, was once a 'guest' here. She had gone from psychiatry to a silent order only to find, after five years, that it was not her vocation. It is peculiarly easy to talk to one in whom silence has lived so deeply. But it is peculiarly easy to talk to everyone here, guests and doctors. One simply learns to be mannerly in the presence of visions. If I come upon a girl dancing naked by the little stream that crosses the south-west corner of the property, I simply turn my eyes away to watch the gardener clipping the hedge or the swans copulating fiercely, awkwardly in the late afternoon sun. If I sit on a bench next to a boy who is sticking pins into the clay image of his father, I go on with my mending. But I am still, after all these weeks, appalled. I cannot and do not wish to dance naked in the sun. I loathe fine bits of clay which circle my nails and mute the lines in my palms. I haven't the skill to paint what I have seen awake or dreaming, and, if I can be taught to value nightmares, I cannot be taught to value my own crude approximations of them. I am still trapped in the hope of real articularity.

When I first came here, in a daze of sedatives, I could not dream at all. I fell into sleep like a stone into water, settling deep and undisturbed in the darkness. Only when I was awake was I victim to sudden, unreasoning fears, fits of trembling exhaustion. I was willing then to talk, afraid as I was to make the journey back through the years alone, no longer trusting my own memory. But I agreed that it could not be grief or shame that had driven me here. The first I suffered when the only child I could have was born dead. I was so brave, so dull, that my husband finally took his weight of sympathy and tenderness to someone else, someone who needed him. The shame I found bearable, too, first in anger, then in resignation. My husband is a nervous, high-spirited, good-looking man with a flare for misery. I have none. I agreed, too, that it is something vaguer, deeper than these very personal, very limited experiences that challenges stability – or maintains it. And so I went where the doctor took me, gradually allowing myself to be taught to dream, then more slowly to admit the dream into the waking world.

I did not find the new habit hard to form, and for a while dreams did seem to replace memory. The first were not difficult to understand, perhaps because I could relate them to what had actually happened. I stood on a great raft in a violent sea. All around me friends drank cocktails and chatted, unaware of danger for themselves or of the desperate struggle I was involved in. I saw my dying child in the sea, in its face my own, as if I looked from its eyes and yet felt my fear. I threw a rope, but suddenly my husband was drowning, and, each time I tried to pull him aboard the raft, I found myself dragged nearer the edge. That loved face, out of whose eyes I could now see my own life threatened. I was lying on an operating table, asking for a doctor. The psychiatrist, in the habit of a nun, looked down at me and said, 'You know your child is dead.' Yes, I know. I have always known that. Then I was much younger, pleading with my mother. I did not want to walk up to a strange house, ring the doorbell, and ask for donations of eyes, arms, teeth, genitals. Mother opened a suitcase to show me what she had already collected. The eyes were only painted eggs, the arms and legs the broken pieces of my own china dolls. Then I saw a row of decaying teeth, hooked loosely into bone. Rain fell, peacefully, peacefully, on shells, on sand, and my child slept among starfish and seaweed, rocking in the receding tide.

I did not mind recording those dreams; I had some conscious knowledge of each image, and gradually I recovered that old skill of sifting the simple facts from the irrelevant desires. The unconscious once recognized, however, will not continue to accommodate the moral intellect with fables.

What was I to do with the dream of myself soaking my husband's raincoat in the car radiator, then cutting it into strips and frying it for his breakfast? What was I to do with rules like 'Change I to you and add e-s' which I seemed to be teaching to strange natives? One night I dreamt of a gangster standing in the road, having his portrait painted by a dozen middle-aged

women while he made a speech about the evils of suicide. He
carried and waved two old frontier pistols to illustrate his talk,
then suddenly dropped dead, his hair changing from black to
red as he lay in the dust.

What shape could I make, standing in the studio before the
canvas? The woman next to me was painting a series of pictures
in which a crab slowly crawls from the surface of the earth to
the centre, curls and flowers into a mating couple. What power
she was in touch with I do not know as the mindless accuracy
of her hand traced each new meaning. No power prompted me
to paint strips of frying raincoat, a comic gangster.

I left the studio this morning for an appointment with my
doctor. As I turned into the walk, my way was blocked by a
young boy. He stood, exposing himself to a bird, a flower, or
me. I could not tell. As the bird rose up, I felt one violent
shudder of wings in my own passive womb, then the familiar,
terrible vacancy. I did not hurry past him. There was no need. I
walked as quietly as I have always walked down the path to the
house.

'I did not dream it,' I said to the doctor. 'I saw it. If only they
were my own dreams: I have seen spastic children cover their
distorted faces with Hallowe'en masks in order to frighten their
mothers. I have seen African tribal dancers chase imaginary
lions through Windsor Great Park. I have seen two women,
dressed for a party, wrestling in a row boat in the middle of the
Serpentine.'

She did not answer.

'I wish you could understand me.'

I waited in her silence, thinking in her silence. It is not the
unconscious world of my own nightmares where I find visions.
I have never neglected the beached treasures and horrors of my
own life. I know they are there, not to be collected and studied
and saved, but to be left where they are as part of the natural
landscape of the soul. It is not the child washing in the tide, the
husband gone, the hopes cut adrift that have wrecked me on my
own shore.

'It's the world outside myself and my control, the public
catastrophes I cannot be held responsible for. It's other people's

nightmares that live in my back garden.'

Still she did not speak.

'I can't go mad. I've tried. I have no vocation.'

'Nothing keeps you here,' she finally answered. 'There are no walls. There is no gate.'

My suitcase is open on the bed, my clothes neatly packed. As I stand here, waiting for the taxi to come, I can look down, through any one of the dozen small panes of the window, into the garden. There they all are in the ritual of afternoon tea. In the coming and going from the table, in the passing of cups, in the gathering and separating, it is rather like a dance, patterned and yet casual. There is the boy I encountered this morning, sitting quietly in the sun over by the stream. There is my painting companion, talking with the doctor. Now people begin to drift away, free in the garden, free in the world, a huge sky overhead, disturbed only occasionally by a cloud or a line of jet vapour droppings. It is I who am closed away in this small room under the eaves. If there are no walls, if there is no gate, I should like to have asked that huge-framed silent woman not what kept me in but what kept me out; but I should think, like me, she does not know.

VI

Griefs

RUTH FAINLIGHT
A Memoir of my Brother

I was in the kitchen, drinking a cup of tea and wondering what to cook for dinner, when the phone rang. An official voice with a Welsh accent identified itself as calling from Newtown police station, then asked if I was the sister of Harry Fainlight. That was how I learned my brother was dead. I had been abroad and we had not met all summer. We'd exchanged a few letters, spoken once or twice by phone – nothing special. Things were as easy between us as they'd been for a long time.

His body had been found outside his remote cottage by a local farmer. The date on his death certificate is given as between 28 August and 11 September 1982, the cause bronchial pneumonia. Because of the circumstances, an inquest was ordered, but it did not provide an unequivocal explanation. He had not killed himself or been killed by another person. He did not die from an overdose of any drug. He had not suffered a coronary. Over the years, I have come to believe that he must have perished from a combination of self-neglect and despair.

Harry was almost four years the younger. The troubled state of the world during the thirties affected our childhoods. He was less than five when our mother took us to a coalmining village in South Wales to avoid the London bombings. (Unlike me, he must have had good memories of that time, I'd thought, when he went back to Wales in the mid-seventies.) But within a year we set out for New York on a liner that was part of the last convoy from Northern Ireland to include civilian passengers. I remember my excitement and fear, the sight of warships on the horizon, the torpedo alerts, and even perhaps – for I am not sure if this is a real memory or a later embellishment – the news if not the actual sight of a sinking ship.

Although our mother had friends and relatives in New York, where she had grown up and where Harry and I had been born, and although all three of us were American citizens (in spite of

this, our current identity was 'British refugees' – the first of
many such anomalies), it was hard for her to manage with two
small children. I am sure Harry sensed her unhappiness and
loneliness as much as I did. Soon after arrival, on the recom-
mendation of the British War Relief Society, where she found a
job as a secretary, we were put into a boarding school on Long
Island.

About ten years ago, while in the States, I spent an afternoon
trying to find that school, but the large house (which I remember as resembling the louring American-Gothic family
home behind the motel in *Psycho*) had been demolished, and
the site and its neglected garden unrecognizably incorporated
into a swish residential development. When we had been there,
the school was a small establishment run by two women: the
large, white-haired, lame, and bookish headmistress whose ami-
able, scholarly manner impressed parents relieved to find somewhere to leave their problem children (and who let me sit in her
room for hours and read whatever I chose from her well-
stocked library), and her tough crop-headed partner, who
looked like my idea of a jailer and terrorized the little boys,
including Harry.

This experience was crucial for us both. There had already
been too many changes in our lives. By now our father was in
India with the RAF, and within a few months our mother had
been knocked down by a bus and seriously injured. We did not
see her for what seemed a very long time, and as far as I remember, no one else came to visit us. Whenever possible, we
would creep away to meet at a particular tree on the edge of the
playing field which we named 'the crying tree'. The obligation
to be the strong supportive one hardened and matured me.

We were rescued by our American aunt, Mother's elder sister,
who arrived from Washington, DC (where her husband was
working at the Pentagon), and after one shocked look, swept up
the unhappy convalescent and her two by now quite badly
undernourished and demoralized children, and took us to live in
her house 'for the duration'. We did not return to England or
see our own father again until Harry was eleven and I was
fifteen years old.

*

Harry was a handsome clever schoolboy whose parents doted on him. I was a difficult teenager in almost permanent conflict with my father, and had left home by the time Harry was fourteen. News of his career as prefect and member of the cricket team, highly praised chess and clarinet player, was relayed in letters which pointedly compared his triumphs to my unsatisfactory behaviour.

A few years later I crept back home for a while. Harry had started writing poetry, and I had written it since I could remember. The upheavals of childhood had made us allies; art was an even deeper bond. Writing this, I am listening to a broadcast of the Mozart Clarinet Concerto. I learned it from his practising. We spent evenings sitting on the floor in my room, reading aloud: T. S. Eliot, Dylan Thomas, Shelley, Keats. I had left again before he won a county scholarship to Cambridge.

For the next few years I was in Majorca, and apart from one Easter vacation when he came with a group of friends, we did not see each other again until after he had left Cambridge with only a second-class degree, disappointing many expectations. It was years before our mother referred, but only in the most circumlocutory, embarrassed phrases, to a nervous crisis during his first year as an undergraduate, and the fact that he had refused any professional help or counselling. He seemed very smooth and confident to me when we met one day at the end of the fifties at a coffee house in the middle of London: a young executive in a business suit, come from his advertising agency to take his bohemian sister and her lover out to lunch. This memory, so wrong in its perception of him (who must already have felt the impossibility of conforming to the demands and limitations of that self-protective, self-concealing image he was still trying to present to the world at large and to me in particular), is evidence of how difficult it was at such crucial times in both our lives to extend the necessary sympathy and understanding. In fact, Harry did not make the effort much longer. There was a period of tutoring – that last resort of the well-educated but maladjusted – then he went to the States.

*

The years of the sixties. When Harry returned from New York I was living outside Tangiers with husband and infant son. I also had fled – from mothers, mother-and-baby groups, the game of 'Happy Families', and everything they implied. Despite the distant location, Harry came for a visit. The only spare room was my husband's study; he kindly moved his papers out and joined us downstairs. Harry spent most of the day asleep, but I was very conscious of his presence as I tried to keep the baby from disturbing him. The maid told me that he had taken the rugs off the floor and draped them across the windows to block out any light. He would join us in the late afternoon, then usually go down the hill into town. When he stayed home, I could hear him moving restlessly around all through the night.

It was obvious that a lot had happened in New York. He looked worn and thin and seemed much more jumpy. His poetry of that period shows the influence of the Beats and the post-war French avant-garde. He became a well-known figure of the 'poetry scene' in the Village. I know that he was involved in film-making both as an actor and director, but never saw any of his work. The June 1965 poetry reading at the Albert Hall in London, when he participated with Allen Ginsberg, Gregory Corso, and others, was probably the moment of his greatest public success in England. Ginsberg later described how 'he sat head bent over his notebook before 7000 people hesitating agonizingly minute after minute unable to begin reading a long poem on the nature of consciousness inspired by New York Methamphetamine [note: it was an LSD experience, not an amphetamine one], the central image of which was a cosmic spider. The scene is vividly recorded in the film *Wholly Communion*, me shouting desperately offstage to him, "Read poem! Read poem!" '

During those years I was often abroad and we did not see much of each other. Somehow I heard that a collection of his poems had been accepted for publication at about the same time my first book was taken – but it was not he who told me. And the story of how he had raged into the publisher's offices, terrorized editors and secretaries and threatened to burn down the building if his manuscript was not returned at once – how he had, as it were, torn it out of the presses – remained a lurid rumour. Without saying a word, Harry made me uncomfortably conscious of the fact that my activity and identity as a poet was a problem for him. The relationship between us had become extremely complicated. He was not well and he was short of money. Whenever we met, I would give him some cash, but not until later was it put on to any sort of regular basis. Although, as far as I knew, Harry never managed to develop or sustain a long-term intimate relationship with another person, male or female, he inspired much affection, and there were always those who believed in him and helped him.

In the last fifteen years or so of his life there were several episodes of remand and hospitalization, from a few weeks to more than a year. Attacks of paranoia triggered bizarre behaviour which would involve him with the police. I quote again from Ginsberg, describing a visit when he was in London some years after the Albert Hall reading: 'His temperament seemed to be permanently altered ... he still worked his lips back and forth, protruding then drawing them in, halting of speech, silent long seconds at a time on the verge of pronouncing a phrase, suspicious of me and the electric surveillance of the British establishment over his consciousness.'

Harry's state of mind and being was heartbreaking; altogether too much for our parents. A further sadness was to observe how their old age was dominated and spoiled by the grief and rage and helplessness that ravaged them, and which I seemed unable to alleviate in any way. When the situation demanded, I had to become the family representative. I visited Harry in detention, talked to lawyers, social workers, psychiatrists, and doctors (even, finally, after our parents' deaths, the Official Solicitor), and when he seemed most in need of protection, tried to arrange places of refuge. Unrealistically, in spite of every past experience, I could not stop myself from trying to look after him, believing that this time it must be possible for him to live with us, then feeling guiltily insufficient after each failure. I could not have even considered this without the emotional and financial support of my husband. But it never lasted for more than a week or two. The psychic disturbance was intolerable to us all.

There were periods of weeks, seasons, when if the phone rang after midnight it would surely be Harry. If the doorbell shrilled in a certain insistent way, it must be Harry. He would look haggard, neglected, alarming – but would eat and drink whatever I gave him, have a bath and put on the clothes I had washed since his last visit, and then talk to us, harangue us, separately or together, for hours. He only wanted us to listen. Months would pass when I did not hear from him or know where he was. But always there was poetry, the final point of reference, the clear centre. Through whatever happened, he kept writing. His comments about other people's work, including mine, were perceptive and valuable. He was entering his forties, and there were times when I could let myself hope that he was beginning to achieve a state of comparative equilibrium. Then another crisis would arise.

In 1976 Harry was given the use of a cottage in Wales and our parents died. Soon after, he moved into their house in Hove, but the atmosphere of his boyhood home was so disturbing that once again he ended up in hospital.

We went twice to visit Harry in Wales. He lived about a mile and a half up an unpaved track off a 'B' road – such a rough way that on one of these occasions the car got mired in, and we had to find a farmer with a tractor to pull us out. The cottage was hidden in a sudden small valley with a stream at the bottom, concealed until the last moment by the lie of the land and by bushes and trees. The stream's opposite bank was so steep and so close that in winter there could have been only a few hours of daylight. Peering out through the small windows at vegetation burgeoning in every direction, I felt almost choked. But as soon as one walked a hundred feet up the track there were vistas of rolling hills, clouds, and sheep. Unfortunately, in spite of its isolation, that part of central Wales lies beneath flight paths used by the RAF for training. In this case, Harry's convictions of persecution – whether by the dogs of war, the spirit of his dead father, or whatever other name he gave to the malevolent force tormenting him – could be said to have an objective correlative.

Water came from the stream, light from candles and lamps, heat from a fire in the soot-blackened chimney and a paraffin stove we bought him. Everything he needed he had to carry from the village a few miles away. It was an existence of peasant starkness. But this hermit-life seemed to suit him. The very paucity of stimulation must have had a calming effect on his abraded spirit. He looked healthier, I thought, as he trudged through the spring mud up the path towards us, dressed in wellingtons and an old coat of our father's. We had arrived with a couple of cardboard boxes of provisions, but Harry had gone to a great deal of trouble to prepare for our visit. It was decades since I'd seen Mother's silver tea service in use.

Sardine sandwiches and Battenberg slices. The soft flickering of many candles, the glinting titles along the spines of many books, made the room look quite comfortable. But I had been there before, in full sunlight. I wished I could do something to change his life absolutely. That was the last time I saw him.

The Storm

Harry, I know how much you would have enjoyed it.
I can see your mouth's ironic curve as the heavens
opened. The umbrella over my head was almost
useless – rain and hail at the same slant
as your amused imagined gaze darkened
the side of my coat and trousers. Hard to resist
the thought that while we hurried back to the car
as soon as we could to wait it out, cold
and distracted, someone up there was paying attention,
taking notice. The sky had been clear

enough as we drove through the cemetery
gates into those horizontal acres
ignored behind the bonfire sites and toolsheds
of suburban gardens, then parked and walked
between memorial stones to our appointment.
A spare man in a mac held the casket
chest-high as he approached. I stretched
a finger to touch a corner. The brass plate,
engraved with your full name, flashed paler
in the altering light as cloud thickened.

Cut into the piece of ground that was
the grave of both our parents – a square hole,
its soil piled nearby. A superstitious
qualm made me look down: too shallow
to disturb them. It must have been the very
moment the sexton stooped to put your ashes
there – where I hoped you'd want to be:
with them – that the storm broke. Instead of a struggle
with grief, we were fighting the weather, reduced
to the ludicrous; instead of prayer, a dry
shelter was what seemed most important. Water
running across my hands, inside my sleeves,
I took the spade and, being chief mourner,
made the first movement to bury you. Harry,
I think you would have found the symbolism
too facile and pompous, and your sense
of humour stopped you taking it seriously –
though certainly delighted by the conceit
of Nature aghast and weeping at your interment,
my poor brother, her true and faithful poet.

In Memoriam H.P.F.

God, the dead, and Donna Elvira
all inhabit the same realm:
the great democracy of Imagination.

Every paradise and underworld
beyond a blue horizon –
Sheol or Elysium –
is a beautiful product of mental function:
conjuration, prayer, and purpose.

I shall not meet my dead again
as I remember them
alive, except in dreams or poems.
Your death was the final proof
I needed to confirm that knowledge.

MARGARET ATWOOD
King Lear in Respite Care

The daughters have their parties.
Who can cope?
He's left here in a chair
he can't get out of
in all this snow, or possibly
wallpaper. Wheeled somewhere.
He will have to be sly and stubborn
and not let on.

Another man's hand
coming out of a tweed sleeve that isn't
his, curls on his knee. He can move it with the other
hand. Howling would be uncalled for.

Who knows what he knows?
Many things, but where he is
isn't among them. How did it happen,
this cave, this hovel?
It may or may not be noon.

Time is another element
you never think about
until it's gone.
Things like ceilings, or air.

Someone comes to brush
his hair, wheel him to tea-time.
Old women gather around
in pearls and florals. They want to flirt.
An old man is so rare.
He's a hero just by being here.

They giggle. They disappear
behind the hawthorn bushes
in bloom, or possibly sofas.
Now he's been left alone
with the television turned on
to the weather program, the sound down.

The cold blast sweeps across
the waste field of the afternoon.
Rage occurs,
followed by supper:
something he can't taste,
a brownish texture.

The sun goes down. The trees bend,
they straighten up. They bend.
At eight the youngest daughter comes.
She holds his hand.
She says, *Did they feed you?*
He says no.
He says, *Get me out of here.*
He wants so much to say *please*,
but won't.

After a pause, she says –
he hears her say –
I love you like salt.

Two Dreams, 2

Sitting at noon over the carrot salad
my sister and I compare dreams.

She says, Father was there
in some kind of very strange nightgown
covered with bristles, like a hair shirt.

He was blind, he was stumbling around
bumping into things, and I couldn't stop crying.

I say, Mine was close.
He was still alive, and all of it
was a mistake, but it was our fault.
He couldn't talk, but it was clear
he wanted everything back, the shoes, the binoculars
we'd given away or thrown out.
He was wearing stripes, like a prisoner.
We were trying to be cheerful,
but I wasn't happy to see him:
now we would have to do the whole thing over again.

Who sends us these messages,
oblique and muffled?
What good can they do?
In the daylight we know
what's gone is gone,
but at night it's different.
Nothing gets finished,
not dying, not mourning;
the dead repeat themselves, like clumsy drunks
lurching sideways through the doors
we open to them in sleep;
these slurred guests, never entirely welcome,
even those we have loved the most,
especially those we have loved the most,
returning from where we shoved them
away too quickly:
from under the ground, from under the water,
they clutch at us, they clutch at us,
we won't let go.

MAUREEN DUFFY
Nightingales

For Dulan

Poking the papery bulbs into thin London grit
that sandpapers skin like the bottom
of a galvanized bath, an earth we used to share
(you by adoption, me by descent) just as we had
our October birthday in common, so hated
the drawing in of autumn, the first fist of frost
as much as you loved light over a lagoon, parrot
tulips jutting green beaks into Spring, Mozart, ebony notes
things it's hard now to enjoy without your indelible voice
chiding and praising by turns, I thrust each memory
deep down with a corm barky as liquorish root
or the mandrake tubers of dahlias you used to conjure
into Chinese lanterns to blaze against
the black scurf that clogs this time of year.

The heart constricts with pain and its palliatives
since we stood upright and saw on bowed and trembling legs
these farther shores, and plucked a leaf to ruminate on
blur our new awareness of gone or to come
barring the night with song to keep the dark away
as we two did across two decades, setting disc or tape
unreeling our loves, griefs, hopes into the night.
Returning again three years on I find
your absence as presence still inhabits the house.
We speak of you often those who love you, carefully
as if we might wound ourselves. Oh our dear
as long as we live there will always be
music and flowers that bloom you against Fall, our dank
    October:
Heraclitus' nightingales awake and singing.

NICOLE WARD JOUVE
Frou-Frou

'More coffee?' Frou-Frou asked.

We were sitting in her kitchen, as so many times. I had known them, Jacques and her, in so many houses. They'd bought cheap – grotty flats in unfashionable areas – done them up. He, breaking down walls, putting in the electricity, more of his labyrinthine piping, plastering walls – she, fixing Moroccan tiles in the kitchen, painting, nailing, sewing curtains, cushions, swaddling the floors with the rugs she'd brought back from adventurous expeditions to Turkey in the heroic days between the first husband and Jacques. Seven children between her sister and herself: in a mini-bus. They had escaped marauders, themselves and their teenage sons being raped by Tukish visa officers ... Now ... Never mind now. This was house number ?, and it was bigger and better than any of the previous houses. Each time Jacques and herself had gone up on the ladder of housing. Sold for more than they had paid, started again with some ruinous-looking place, but with potential, bigger, in a more pleasant part of town; which graft and their extraordinary creativeness had magicked into stylish ochre cocoons, Middle Eastern dreams. Now she had a garden sandwiched between two miniature houses just out in the suburbs of Paris. With climbing roses and a blue mosaic fountain spurting a timid jet, powered by a diminutive motor that lurked next to a bright green ceramic frog in the rosemary.

Now? Never mind now. Never mind those that were gone, the disasters, the deaths. We'd take each day as it came.

She was pouring fairly bitter, overstewed coffee into large Chinese bowls on the Moroccan-tiled table. Adding a lot of UHT milk and sugar, to drown the bitterness. Jacques would have said that she was a phenomenally bad cook. He always did the cooking, leaving heaps of dirty pots and the kitchen dotted with garlic and onion peel, mustard seeds, spilled cloves, bloody wooden blocks strewn with pepper and flecks of wood-ash from some exquisite *grillade* he had just carved. Now – well – now, Frou-Frou did the cooking. Bountifully. She was always throwing dinner parties, keeping as ever a gypsy hospitable house. Her friends braced themselves, brought patisseries for dessert – loved her – the company – the picking up the pieces – the open table.

There she stood now by the cooker, the briefest of all possible times ('cooking's not my thing'), making a *tagine* for the evening when 'everyone' would 'drop in', in a funnel-capped earthenware dish she'd brought back from Marrakesh, with the weirdest, most heretic ingredients. Jacques would have turned in his grave – never mind Jacques. For there she was, Frou-Frou, my Frou-Frou, pushing in plastic-bagfuls of frozen chicken pieces and frozen artichoke hearts from the corner *supérette*, mixing in jarred lemon slices ('saves on slicing up fresh ones'), pouring in pine kernels and fistfuls of spices bought fresh from a specialist Arab shop from the *beaux-quartiers* ('Half a packet? Will that be enough? Oh well, I'll put the whole lot in.'). She lowered the gas as the juices overflowed, adding to the brown pool already bathing the rings. 'My cooker's a disgrace – well, I can't be bothered. When my daughter comes she takes over. She scolds me. First thing she does when she arrives is make a bee-line for the fridge – cleans it up. Can you believe that?' (I can.) 'Makes me laugh. Gérard and I aren't suffering from food poisoning, are we? Bit of dirt never hurt anyone.' I think of Jacques' ineffable toenails – so long, curving downwards, like claws; and black. He was always going about barefoot, sensuous soles arching, feeling the cool of the tiles, the tepid floorboards – calloused enough not to be bothered by the odd sticking nail, upstairs in his studio . . . where now no one treads . . . Frou-Frou uses it sometimes to paint Florentine landscapes and Roman *trompe-l'oeil* still lifes on eccentric pieces of furniture. I often thought I couldn't have put up with Jacques' greasy hair, the toenails – despite the charm – oh, the charm!

I sermonize: about how now I've learnt the value of ordinariness. How I value people for simply being decent. My lifelong taste for the marginals, the eccentrics, my fascination for the stormy and for the passionate, artists and all: a big mistake. Now I value kindness, I say. Normality. No more storms for me, I say. In teacups or. on heaths. I've had my fill.

'Get on with you,' she says. '*I'm* still a sucker for a bit of flame. Anyone with a – personality, yes. Jacques and I – he was always inventing something – meeting somebody exciting. Artists, philosophers, craftsmen, politicians, businessmen . . .'

'About to go bankrupt,' I say.

'Yes, yes, but don't you see? That's what made them fun. Every day I had with Jacques was fun.'

'And misery,' I say. 'Don't you remember your time in the Faubourg St Antoine, when the two of you were going in for craftsmanship – painted furniture? In this weird windy court-yard with the Chinese cabinet-makers and the ivory- or brass-carvers, everyone going out of business apart from the Chinese – this huge studio the two of you had, the cobbled courtyard still just the same as in the days of *Les Misérables*, you could just imagine riots in the streets outside, and barricades – but Jacques – his black moods – talk about *les misérables* – he was gloom incarnate. That was when he sliced off the top of his thumb with the woodsaw, wasn't it?'

'Such fun days we had,' she says. 'We were out every night. One little *resto* after another. And the oldest *patisserie* in Paris, opposite the Rocher de Cancale, in the Marais, with its front all painted with grotesques, where Jacques used to store up on chocolate cakes. "Now I no longer take my sugar in my alco-hol," he'd say, "I need it from other sources." But you – you're just the same as ever. Think of that Louise Bourgeois exhibition we've just seen. She did have personality, that one. Where does she get her ideas from? *Où est-ce qu'elle va chercher tout ça?*'

'In her childhood,' I say.

'That room full of giant metal spiders . . .'

'Walking under their legs,' I say. 'Standing there, among their hard scrawny legs. Looking up at their bellies. You'd think it would be terrifying, but you feel safe like a baby.'

'Just like ants,' Frou-Frou says. 'A colony of gigantic, beauti-ful ants.'

She looks dreamy.

'Ants,' she says. 'That was it. Like coming home. You're safe with ants. I belong in there. I too know I'm only a little ant.'

And she tells me. I've vaguely known about it before. But never in such detail.

'Gérard's first few years did it,' Frou-Frou says. 'More coffee?'

I decline.

'Go on,' she says, pouring me another Chinese bowlful. 'Put plenty of milk and sugar in. You need fattening, as usual. Gone ever so scrawny. And have another *tartine*.'

'I never understood how you managed to survive,' I say. 'I never could have done.'

I'd known Gérard when he was fourteen – the youngest of four. Beginning puberty. Mental age of six. He'd been quite a handful those weekends we'd spent together, my three little ones, Jacques' two from his marriage to Annette – aged four and seven – and Gérard. Gérard had the self-righteous single-mindedness of a very young child about his share of treats – but also wanted to be recognized as *the* adolescent there: he was the eldest of the lot, he was almost grown-up. One of Jacques' kids was fiercely, cunningly jealous of him. Some combination of fighting was always in progress. I found it hell. Miraculously though, he got on with my six-year-old, deeply perturbed by the move from an English country school to a suburban French one. Gérard and he were deep into Martians. ETs were the only worlds they felt at home in.

Gérard. Frou-Frou's youngest. Her baby.

He'd looked all right when he had been born. A bit small, while the elder three had been hefty babies. But normal. The trouble however had started from day one.

He couldn't keep anything down. After each feed he threw up.

Eventually they did a diagnostic. Gérard had a high rate of uraemia – whatever you call it. The toxins from his kidneys and urinary tract were so potent they permanently poisoned his whole system. Every part of it. Not treatable. He couldn't keep anything down. He was sick six, seven, fourteen times a day, a night – for they'd told Frou-Frou to breastfeed a little at a time, every two hours, every hour. For months she never had more than two hours' sleep at nights. Gérard cried and cried. How could there be so much crying power in such a scrawny body . . . ? The disgusted husband, who had to 'earn the family living', now in Paris, having moved from Algeria in the nick of time, and who was in the process of developing a lucrative clientele as a real estate barrister – moved out of the bedroom. Then for weeks, months, out of the house. Frou-Frou suspected – discovered – a mistress. Not just flings. A steady one, to and from whom her husband returned periodically.

'You'd better look the truth in the face,' the consultant said. 'That baby won't see his third month. Just as well. The uraemia levels are damaging everything – brain, eyesight, digestive system . . .'

Frou-Frou ground her teeth and persisted. Breastfeeding. Then bottle-feeding, relayed by a nurse. Everything was tried in those bottles – fruit juice, carrot juice, gruel. All that changed was the colour of the vomit. What energy in the black-haired, vague-eyed baby – his irises covered with a veil. Whenever he got too ill, the hospital would put him on a drip.

'You might as well accept reality,' the consultant said. 'Let him go. Don't you see?'

'He's lived past three months,' Frou-Frou said. 'He's six months old.'

'Look at yourself,' the consultant said. 'Think of your other children. Only your obstinacy is keeping him alive. Let him go. You're neglecting your family, your husband . . .'

'Has he been to see you?' Frou-Frou snapped.

'We've talked on the telephone,' the consultant said warily. 'He *has* told me how obsessive you are, how . . .'

'The cheek,' she said. 'The infernal cheek. He doesn't even live at home! He comes in for his laundry!'

'The laundry!' Frou-Frou shook her head. 'Change of baby-clothes fourteen times a day. We had plastic all over Gérard, all over his cot – but he was an ingenious little monkey. He always managed to vomit somewhere that needed washing.' (Obstinate little monkey, I could guess her proudly thinking, this *Auvergnate* with her strong nape, her strong shoulders – skier,

rambler, rider – she'd hunted in Poland as a young woman, gal-
loping after a wild couple that ran ahead of the pack, spraying
the ground with a scent – flying over hedges.)

(Chip off the old block, I could hear her thinking. Hang on in
there.)

'You seem to be proud of his vomiting,' the consultant said.
'What sort of a life is it for a baby, for anyone? What sort of a
life is it for you? For be forewarned – however long you manage
to prolong the agony, he won't live past two. His system simply
can't survive. The longer you put off his death, the worse it will
be for you.'

At two he barely weighed more than at birth. He looked like
an imp from a drought-stricken area. Belly bloated, bones sticking out. Diminutive. Veiled vague eyes that didn't seem to see.
He could sit – just – propped on pillows. He had no words. But
he knew his mother.

Frou-Frou's husband had moved out for good, it seemed.
Been gone three months. The older children, bewildered,
hushed, went about their business, supervised by a kindly maid
who – her mistress evidently not caring about such things as
dust or ironing – concentrated on keeping things going. She
took relays to feed Gérard, so that Frou-Frou could sleep. Pap.
Gruel. Finely mashed soups. The baby's teeth distended the raw
gums, but still hadn't come through.

The maid went on her holidays. The Auvergnat grandparents
took the older children for theirs. No relief was to come from
Frou-Frou's parents: her mother had died of cancer just before
Frou-Frou's wedding: Frou-Frou had been four months pregnant. She had looked after her brothers and sisters, nursed her
ailing mother – who had died while in Germany, at a spa. Frou-
Frou had had to tell her father about the pregnancy. The colonel
had made her, all of seventeen, get married in a grey suit, to
advertise her un-virginal state to the world. Neater than a
scarlet letter.

But this was some years back. Now here she was, alone – her
husband still missing, Gérard acutely ill for the umpteenth time,
in hospital – the children and the maid away. She sat and sat. In
the kitchen mostly.

'I couldn't have cared less that it was so filthy. I could have asked the maid to clean it up before she left – I could have cleaned it – cleaning's not my thing, but every so often I have a go and I do a good job – blitz it – I don't like it too *bordélique* either. But by that stage I positively loved the dirt. Grease and blackness. You know, how spilt fat congeals and dust and bits of peel get caught in it, how it builds up and spreads, in the corners – especially under the sink. The dustbin was full, it had that sweet smell, you know – I didn't care. I liked it. The dustbin and I had much in common. Day in, day out, month in, month out, I'd been mopping, throwing away plastic bagfuls of vomit, bile, carrot juice, curdled milk. Been showered in it. It had flown all over me – my skirts. Gérard couldn't talk, he couldn't walk, he maybe couldn't see – but boy could he throw up!

'A colony of ants was thriving in there. Hundreds of them, under the dustbin, under the sink. A perfect place for them. A dustbin full of goodies. They hurried – have you noticed how they're always in a hurry? From under the skirting-board, to and fro, up the sides of the dustbin – busily ferrying a bit of gruel, a speck of carrot – loads as big as themselves. And they weren't going to let go, oh no, not they. Hurrying to and fro. I sat and watched. Entire days. I'd go to bed, nothing to do, what bliss, nobody there, no need to bestir myself. The soured milk cartons I didn't pour down the sink, I'd add half-full to the overflowing bin to see whether the ants would find a way in and yes sir they did. They're so clever. If they didn't I'd prize the top open a bit more. It stank – of vomit of course – the whole world did. That was the smell of life for me in those days. So I sat back and watched how the ants coped. Would they drown in the milk? Not they, oh no. They coped.

'One day I heard a voice. My sister Cocotte's. She was on a visit to Paris. She'd rung the bell, she'd tried several times, but as I hadn't answered, she'd got the *concierge* to open the door with her *passe*.

'"What on earth are you doing?" Cocotte asked. She sounded disturbed.

'"Can't you see?" I said. "Watching the ants."

'"What's so great about ants?"

'"They're just like me. I like them. I'm only a little ant. I've understood everything now, and I feel at peace. If only I can hang on to that. We're all of us ants. I'm a little – a very little – ant. *Je suis une toute petite fourmi.*"

'Cocotte screamed at me and went and bought some Ajax and Javel and DDT and emptied the dustbin and scalded it and scrubbed and God knows what. I sat on my chair, watching. Laughing to myself. "*Mais regardez-moi cette idiote.*" She had screamed – thought I was mad because I said I was just a little ant and there she went, behaving just like a little ant. Well groomed, well trained, the species programming her to clean, scrub, wash. She was doing her brave little ant's stint, but because she hadn't understood yet that she was only a little ant, she hadn't found peace. I had. Having finally understood I was only a little ant made me tolerant, gentle. I was full of compassion for her, what she was, how she hadn't understood. So I let her run the bath for me, undress me into it, wash me, shampoo my hair as if I were a child. I'd washed them all, ant-like, my little brothers and sisters, in my own time, when we had been children. All programmed. Everything was all right. If I could hold on to the peace of being a little ant, keep that ever in my mind, I'd be all right.

'We went together to see Gérard. He was wizened, the drip bloating the tiny vein in his stick of an arm, a huge bruise in it. I think she had a word with the consultant. She's always denied it, but she must have done. Because the next time I called, and Gérard was out of immediate danger and could come home, the consultant said that we needed to see a therapist for Gérard, what with his pushing three now and still not able to walk and speak, if he was going to live even a little longer we had to help him along.

'It took me a long time to twig it. There we were, Gérard, the therapist, and me. The therapist did play a bit with Gérard, trying to get him to grab toys he held out, to find out what he could follow with his eyes, what he took in with his ears – whether he could play. But most of the time he asked me questions. About Gérard to start with. Then about myself.

'I talked and talked and talked.

'I didn't understand what he was doing. He was treating me, of course. If they'd offered I'd have sent them packing, holding on to my vision of ants (what was the point now I'd found peace? I wasn't mad anyway). They were very canny about it – which is why I think that Cocotte must have put in a word. We children had always had to stick together, stand up for each other. We'd had to survive that way, what with Father as he was, and Mother so ill.

'I came out with the weirdest things. It took two years.

'All sorts of crazy things. It seems there were all sorts of crazy things. How when I was fourteen and Cocotte eleven we'd tried to find out what happened between men and women and questioned Aicha who'd talked about cocks and hens and we asked our mother saying, "Is it like cocks and hens?" and both been slapped hard in the face and told never to speak of such things again. How at my first teenage party having decided something must happen through the navel I'd jumped on the table and started a belly-dance and shouted, "Who wants me?" I've always been wild – and if nobody will tell you, nothing like finding out through experience, is there? How about a year before Gérard, when my "ex-"' (that's what she always called her ex-husband) 'had already begun to flirt, we'd gone mountaineering. At the refuge overnight the whole party had lain first-come first-served on the wall-to-wall sleeping bunk, and I'd been flattered because the two guides had crashed on either side of me. Then I'd woken and found one on top of me, unzipping my duvet. I *had* liked the look of him so I let him, and enjoyed it too. He had no sooner slipped off to his side than the other guide began to wriggle into position in his turn. I laughed so much I almost gave the game away – but he put his hand on my mouth and – I enjoyed that one too. The rest of the night was spent one on, one off. The difficult thing was to keep quiet. The next day we were all rather bleary-eyed. I've never seen guides struggle so wearily up a mountain. They looked so – deliberate. Inwardly I was splitting my sides . . .

'And other things. Not funny. Not funny at all. I was head over heels in love with him, of course. The therapist. I know it's par for the course but that was the truth of it and being so infat-

uated kept me going. I'd bundle up my Gérard and off we went
– something to look forward to, something cheerful even
though each time I cried my eyes out. I never thought there
could be so many tears in a human being. There hadn't been
room to cry when we were children. Got slapped if we did –
lack of character. I cried because I had so wanted my mother –
never available – I'd had to double up for her – and when it had
come to the crunch, my marriage, my babies, she was dead. The
only place I'd felt safe was with my grandparents, that year
Cocotte and I had spent with them in the Auvergne – but I
hadn't dared tell them anything, never dared ask if we could
stay longer. You didn't let the side down – and I'd felt sorry for
Mother – didn't want to betray her. And I told of my baby sister
who had died. Of my little brother who had killed himself on a
motorbike. His wife and he had had a moron for a baby because
of some infection caught at the clinic but they had not dared
complain because they were first cousins – maybe that was *why*
the baby was abnormal. They'd been childhood sweethearts, the
cousins. The baby had died – not long before my brother's
crash. His wife, who had been riding pinion on the motorbike,
had had both legs broken. She'd come to me to recover. But she
had not been able to stand it all. So under some pretext she
moved to her sister's. Took advantage of her sister's weekend
absence to swallow stuff on top of all the drugs she was on. She
died *standing*. There she was – standing in the kitchen –
propped up by a cupboard – when her sister and I found her
two days later.

'I was pouring it all out. Week after week, month after
month. I told how my "ex-" came and went – how I hated the
woman he left us for. I told how I couldn't let Gérard die: his
coming had broken the back of my marriage, for good. And
there had been too many deaths. Both my brothers-in-law . . .
But not Gérard. I couldn't let him go. Not Gérard.

'And I told him about Algeria. What as children we'd seen, we'd
known. Playing in the streets. Outside the barracks. Hearing
things from Aicha. The attraction to Arab children. The taboos.
The mystery of privilege. The guilt. The distance. The hatred.

'I told him of Ari-Ouzoum.

'We hadn't been married long. Philippe, our eldest, a thriving baby, was with us. My ex-'s career was beginning to take off. We'd been invited to a smart hotel in a resort in the mountains. You had to cross picturesque *gorges* to get there. It was good that this rich client was treating us. It meant acceptance into the right circles, it meant getting known by future potential clients: all a matter of whom you knew, what circles you moved in. We didn't own a car, so we'd hired a taxi for the weekend. Out on the Friday, back on the Sunday. Luxury while we were there. A perfect jaunt.

'We had some lovely times. We swam in the pool, drank cocktails, chatted on the terrace, with ochre cliffs in the distance turning orange and red in the setting sun. There were a few couples we already knew, and liked. Some had young children with them. Little boys and girls crowded round Philippe, fascinated by the baby, fighting to feed him, play with him.

'Everybody prepared to leave on the Sunday. It was a good three to four hours' drive back. We told our taxi driver to get ready too – he had stayed in the *personnel* quarters – but first he kept not appearing, wasting time – then he said he'd heard that the weather was about to turn. There was a sandstorm in the offing, he said. And anyhow, there was something wrong with the car, which he could only get fixed by the morrow. We'd just have to get back on the Monday. Spend another night at the hotel.

'My ex- argued with him. Pleaded: he would get into trouble at the office if he didn't turn up on the Monday. Had an urgent case to plead. There we were, in turns urgent, pathetic, menacing, in the courtyard, an impassive *maître d'hotel* on the threshold, frowning upon our noisiness: were we being vulgar? We were impostors, not really rich, powerless to sway our chauffeur. That's what he thought, we felt. We offered more money. And even more. By then most of the cars were gone, others were full, with young children at the back (we had a lot of gear with the baby) – no room for a lift for us. Others yet looked down their nose at us: undignified for Europeans not to carry the day. My ex- was fuming – called the taxi driver names. But in the end, we were forced to spend another night at the hotel.

'We wondered the next day, *en route* at last, if the taxi driver had been feeling unwell – if that was why he had been so stubborn. He was grey. As he drove, he kept looking right and left. We cracked a few jokes, which he brushed aside. We began to sing, and he turned upon us furiously. So we too fell silent. He was even worse through the *gorges*, which were breathtaking – his breath had certainly been taken away – he shushed us – drove so fast in the bends it almost made my ex- sick. Did he know for good that there was something seriously wrong with the car, that we might break down in the middle of nowhere, that he so anxiously urged each kilometre on?

'We got back. Paid him. Sulkily, what we had agreed. He did not bargain. Fled, without so much as a goodbye. "We know who never to use again," my ex- said. Who flew to the office, to make a late diplomatic appearance. Face the music.

'So it was him. Who heard first.

'Every single car of our party had been ambushed in the *gorges*. Every man, woman and child had been killed by bullets, or had their throats slit. Not one had survived.

'The little boys and girls who had leaned over Philippe's cot, called him *bébé*, shaken his rattle to make him laugh and kick. The tanned, bare-shouldered women who'd glided on the dance floor. Betty and Joseph, who had such contagious laughter, had made us sing *"Gentil coquelicot mesdames"* and "Le temps des cerises". Every one of them.

It was the first killing of the Algerian war. It signalled the beginning of the uprising. Ushered it in. Our taxi driver must have known about it. Where he'd heard, I don't know. Probably at the hotel: would he have agreed to the trip if he'd known earlier? So perhaps the impassive *maître d'hotel*, whom we thought had been contemptuous . . . and who had let the rest of the party go . . . Or the driver had heard from other sources, a waiter, a cook, a passing goatherd? He'd wanted to save his skin. Had he wanted to save ours too? We were only young, with a baby . . . Or was his only means to save his skin and not give the plan away to save ours too? He'd let everyone else leave. Couldn't he have given a warning? Would that have been more than his skin was worth? Just a guy who like thousands and thousands later no doubt just wanted to survive, to squeeze through somehow ... Or did he want the others – the Europeans – dead too? Was he in cahoots with the FLN, and he'd just saved us not to blow his cover?

'So much hatred.

'At the time I'd put a brave face upon it. Almost cracked jokes: how lucky we'd been! As I began to tell the therapist, I sobbed and sobbed – so violently it took me several sessions to come out with it. Bit by bit. The silence of the *gorges*. The beauty of the orange twilight on the distant *gorges*, and cliffs. I carried such a sense of menace – such guilt. All the others ambushed: ourselves alone, alive. All the other children, dead. Philippe only, alive. I couldn't bear it. I couldn't bear it.

'And my father, to become a general through that war.

'Three days after I had finished telling about Ari-Ouzoum, there was a new check-up for Gérard. I was all bedraggled – had done nothing but sob since the last session, and Gérard still couldn't sit up properly – not without being propped on cushions. He was beginning to look – you know – a bit like a moron. Overlarge head. Scrawny body. Orangy from the carrot juice that kept him alive.

'The consultant took me aside. Said they'd tried everything. All the drugs they knew. Nothing had worked. He had given me all the support he could, and more. I just had to gird my loins, accept the inevitable. Gérard might drag on in his present miserable state – how could any mother wish to prolong such an existence? The older he'd get, the worse he'd look. In any case he'd die before he'd reach seven. That was medically certain. Did I want to destroy myself over this – destroy my family? I wondered if he'd had another call from my husband. He went on and on. Give up, he was saying. Stop feeding this kid against all odds. Let him die. I kept thinking how Gérard's system kept producing poison instead of eliminating it. Turned against itself. That was why he had to be sick all the time. To try and throw the poison out.

'The consultant went on and on. He'd called in another expert. They both sat over me with a nurse, who nodded at every word they said, stroked my arm. Which I withdrew.

'The more they talked, the angrier I got.

'I didn't argue.

'I stood up. "Right then," I said. "I've heard you." I grabbed my Gérard, and out I stomped.

'I was in such a rage. Such a fury. If wishes could kill, the three of them would have been dead on the spot.

'"*Ah, c'est comme ça, mes petits cocos,*" I thought. "So that's your tune. Well, I am going to show you. I am going to show you all. Right, Gérard? You just wait. We are going to show them all."

'I rang the therapist. It was so unfair, I knew. He *had* helped. So much. But I had to. I had to.

'"I won't be back," I said. "We won't be back." And hung up.

'One of my great-aunts – who'd several times wanted to give me a break – lived in the mountains, in Switzerland. "Send me Gérard," she'd said. "The mountain air will do him good." Perhaps she planned for him to die at peace, and me away from him so that I didn't feel too bad, so I could accept it. I got into the car with my Gérard, anyway – and drove. Only stopping for the carrot juice. Then I left him. Went back to the others. I had neglected them dreadfully. It showed.

'Three months later Gérard had put four kilos on. Soon he was taking his first steps. Six months later he spoke his first word. "*Foumi*," he said. "*F'mi.*" "*Fourmi.*" Ant.

'"Takes after his mum," my aunt said. Cocotte must have told her a story or two about my own ants fad. "Loves watching insects. Delights in sitting in the grass, watching them crawl, fly. Proudly brought me a snail the other day. ' 'Cargo'? ' 'Scargot'?"

'So his eyesight was fine too.

'I was in such a rage. All that time it was as if I was walking on air, I was so angry. Later, rage took me to the hundreds of visits to the speech therapist, the orthophonist, the physiotherapist, the swimming lessons, the guitar lessons ... I was going to show them: all. I confronted my husband. Told him he had to choose: her, or me. Typical: first he chose us. Then, her. She was expecting his second child, canny bitch. He was a stud, my ex-. Couldn't resist more offspring in the offing. Especially given the last number I had presented him with.

'So we started divorce proceedings. But not until I had a job under my belt. No qualifications, see? Not even *le Bac*. I had had to get married instead. So that was when I challenged my husband's boss to give me a job. Gradually I earned my keep, and the children's.

'What rage can do for you. It was all done on rage. Rage was my adrenalin. "I'm going to show you." I soon enough got rid of the flat where we had lived as a family. Too expensive. Got a smaller place, thirteenth floor, in the *Treizième*. Hundred per cent credit. Before we moved, got cash selling the family furniture. Philippe helped me carry some of it down into the street. I stuck labels on: cheap. Cash and you collect. More upstairs, third floor left. Everything went. In two days I was rid of the lot. Enough cash for the removal, and a bit over.'

A few years, and plenty of living on (*'Ah, je te jure que les hommes ils ont défilé à cette époque'*) she'd met Jacques.

The back door opens. It is Gérard. He's left his guitar, crossed the garden. In search of food?

'What are you two up to?' he asks. 'Do you know what time it is? It's almost one and you're still having breakfast!'

'It will save us having lunch,' I say.

'But what about the *Libanais* restaurant?' Frou-Frou complains. 'I want to take you. And then we're going to the *Maison Arabe*. You've never seen such beautiful white light.'

'What were you talking about all this time?' Gérard insists.

Gérard is thirty-five. Couldn't live to seven, to ten, to puberty, the specialists had kept saying. *'Il ne pourra jamais faire sa puberté.'* He had done it.

He is not tall, but a good size. He has to watch his weight. He likes food: too much. Raves over gruyère, cornflakes, chocolate, meat. He reads, mostly comics; writes a large, slow, careful hand – enjoys calligraphy. He plays the guitar. Has a job in a state-sponsored supervised workshop, earns his pocket money. Travels to work, to the pictures, on buses, on the tube. Has friends. Some nice, some not so nice: like everybody. Has joy, has sadness: like everybody else. He confides in me sometimes –

because I have known him so long, but above all because I
appear to him bathed in the glory of coming from the land of
the Beatles, who are his gods. Even now, the world of the sixties, of sixties pop groups, of psychedelic images, is the world in
which he likes to take refuge. His hair is white. He is terrified
of storms. Still loves watching insects. Has a memory like an
elephant. The need to be reassured. And a sixth sense.

'What were you talking about?' he insists.

'Ants,' I stupidly joke.

'Don't pull my leg,' he frowns. 'What ants?'

Frou-Frou has a moment of inspiration.

'You know that film when the ants invade? That old film?
Quand la Marajunta gronde.'

A large smile spreads. Gérard raises his face to the ceiling and
laughs in clear remembrance.

'But of course. Colonies of giant ants. Of course I remember.
Well, if that's what you're talking about, run along. You'd
better go to the *Libanais*. Any gruyère left in the fridge?'

ALAN JENKINS
Chopsticks

She struggles with her chopsticks, and I watch her slyly
as she mounts a two-pronged attack on a mound
of noodles, or pincer-prods a shrivelled prawn around
its dish of gloop. I watch her as she shyly
sets down the chopsticks and picks up a spoon.
Chicken and cashews, sweet and sour pork; no shredded
    beef –
It's too difficult, what with my teeth –
and special fried rice. Dinner will be over soon,

ten years to the night since he died, and I concentrate
on fashioning from my chopsticks a mast
like the masts on the model clipper ships he built
and re-built and re-built and re-built
hour after hour, night after night, working late
threading cotton through the tiny balsa blocks – a stickler
    for detail –
to make the rigging shipshape on the imagined past
in which, every evening, he'd set sail . . .

Someone's singing *So merry Christmas, and a happy New*
    Year
and I pick up the chopsticks, tap out a beat
on her wineglass; *You're very quiet. Is everything all right?*
Everything's fine, mother, let me drink up my beer
and remember how we sat with him – ten years to the night –
and watched him try to breathe,
the white bed between us, and him on it, and grief
no easier now there's a tablecloth, a plate with one sad
    prawn, some meat;

remember how I sat at the piano with my sister
to play our duet – 'Chopsticks' – over and over, ad nauseam,
killing time until he came in to pour himself a Scotch
and start Christmas Day . . . The clipper ships
still have pride of place in the sitting room, the museum
where I'll sit for a nightcap, among his prints and pipes,
and pour myself another Scotch from his decanter, and watch
the late film while my mother dozes and my sister,

miles away, plays 'Chopsticks', for all I know;
where I'll sit and think of ten years gone and her two
    cats gone,
gone with the Christmas dinners, my grandmother and
    great-aunt,
with the endless Sunday mornings of Billy Cotton on
    the radio
and the endless Sunday lunches of roast beef,
gone with half her mind and all her teeth;
and she watches me as I place my chopsticks together, *Go
on.*
Finish up that last prawn. But I can't.

SARAH MAGUIRE
The Hearing Cure

I dunk my head
     under water
and come up
     deaf. My left ear

solid, as though
     half the world
is moored in perspex.
     My life

bifurcates. I turn
     around
and a jellied stillness
     drags behind me,

an abeyance of rustling,
     mortality hushed.
The rope of blood
     twists

in my ear, plaiting
     and unplaiting,
the world gone
     bone.

Each night
     the slow wax silts
into place
     coagulating sibilance,

muffling susurration,
     the soft moraine
lagging the tympanum,
     secluding

stirrup, hammer, anvil
      in a distant room.
The plug is full.
      When I was three

sound turned to stone,
      then festered;
my skull became
      a labyrinth of pain,

my taut throat
      stuffed
with liquid needles.
      That winter afternoon

you pushed my cot
      into the warm front room
and soothed me on your lap.
      There was the red wool

of your jumper
      unravelling
at one wrist,
      your kind heart

marking time. By tea
      it was dark outside;
the football results
      came on the radio;

Scottish League Division Two –
      Stirling Albion,
Cowdenbeath,
      Montrose, Arbroath,

Dunfermline,
      Heart of Midlothian,
Queen of the South –
      a litany

that lulled me
      into sleep.

I left you
        twenty years ago.

Since then
        we've hardly talked –
until I found you
        shrunken, frightened,

speechless
        on a geriatric ward,
your legs gone dead
        from grief.

You couldn't stand it
        when your brother died.
And now you cling to me
        for dear life,

your wasted,
        beautiful hands
messengers of fear.
        Weeks on,

you start to tell me things
        I've never heard before,
all that silence
        frozen in your limbs.

But when we got you home
        we found
they hadn't bathed you
        for a month

because you'd not complain,
        not ask, not bother anyone.
It made me sick.
        And now I'm ill, bewildered,

lonely – and I know
        you'll never make me better
any more. I feed
        the warmed sweet almond oil

with a dropper
          into my dead ear
and feel the good oil
          opening the wax.

In four days' time
          I'll hold
the white enamel kidney bowl
          against my neck

while the huge syringe
          shoots water
down the auditory canal.
          At first it thrums

like a far-off city
          and then the whole live ocean
rushes in.
          Afterwards,

one warm November dusk,
          I sat in the park
and watched two bats
          suturing

the darkening air,
          their zigzag flight
latticing the stark
          and emptying trees

with a fragile network,
          an impossible filigree
that fails
          as it describes

their hunger close to night.
          Their sight is sound –
those high-pitched cries
          light up the chestnut trees

with call and echo,
          making feeling

from reflection.
      And I can hear them!

There, right at the edge
      of sound,
like a quill on glass,
      an exquisite engraving

that I thought
      I'd lost for ever.
I raise my fingers
      and I rub them

near my mended ear
      to hear that precious music,
the pitch of flesh
      on flesh.

MICHÈLE ROBERTS
God's House

Inside the priest's house it was very dark. I flattened my palms against the invisible air then advanced step by tiptoeing step. I smelt dust and the dregs of wine. I'd left the heat outside. The curved edge of a stone doorway was cold, grazed my cheek. Groping forwards, I encountered glass, a metal catch. With a rattle and squeak of iron bars I undid the shutters, pushed them open. Light drowned me. I saw that I was in a kitchen, bare except for a cooker and oilcloth-covered table. Sunlight fell across glistening brown paint on to my hands. I turned around and leant back against the windowsill.

I was a burglar. My first break and entry. I wasn't sure what I wanted to steal.

I was back with you, in our old house where I'd been born twelve years before. Now a veranda had been added on at the front, bellying forwards into the garden, and your bed had been put there under the dome of glass. Half in and half out. You sat up when you saw me come in, and held out your arms.

– You haven't left yet then, I said.

The room behind us was full of relatives, a sort of party going on. You gestured towards me to come closer. You held all my attention: your lashless monkey eyes that were very bright, your translucent skin, your full, blistered lips, the outline of your head under its fuzz of curls. Everything that there was between us concentrated into that look we exchanged. Above the glass roof was the red sky, the break of dawn.

For a while the road ran through the plain, along the poplar-lined Canal du Midi, and then it rose, as the land lifted itself and became hillier. A straight road, running between golden-green plane trees, towards Spain. The rounded hills, brown and dark yellow, took us up, and up. We swung off the main road on to a smaller one, and one yet smaller.

Our village was called Beauregard-du-Perdu. We turned, as instructed, by the wash-house and fountain, and drove up the main street lined with plane trees. A green tunnel pierced with bits of dancing light. At its top I saw the stone bulk of the church, a rounded doorway decorated with zigzags. To the right, behind low gates of grey metal, was the house my aunt and uncle were renting from some French friends. We recognized it straight away from the photographs. I got out of the car and saw the other house, opposite. No. What I saw was the high wall enclosing it, the steps up to the padlocked wooden door in the wall, worn steps that curved sideways then went up to the church behind. A notice tacked to the door, just above the padlock, said A VENDRE. As I stared, the church bells began to clang out the hour and I started back from their dull, flat noise.

My aunt bent towards me.

– Lily. Would you like to be the one to knock on the neighbour's door and ask for the keys? Show us how well you speak French.

I inspected the gravel under my new shoes that I'd bought for the funeral. The gravel was grey like the metal gates, loose chips under my stiff toes. I lifted a foot and scraped it along the ground.

– No point, my uncle said: here she is anyway.

Our letter of introduction named her as Madame Cabazou, a widow. She came out of the alleyway opposite our house, below the wall with its wooden door and its FOR SALE notice. A blue enamel sign proclaimed that the alley was called Impasse des Saints. Madame Cabazou was as quick as one of the lizards on the hot wall nearby. Small and skinny, eyes black as olives in her brown face, grey hair cut short. Gold daisies in her pierced ears. Her marriage earrings, she told me later on: that she wore every day. Flick flick went her tongue in her mouth as she exclaimed and shook hands and pulled the key from her housecoat pocket and ushered us in. She darted off again with a wave of her hand, a promise to bring us a bowl of plums picked that morning from the trees in her field.

Our holiday home was a little house on three floors, its walls painted a cool blue-grey. Red speckled tiles underfoot down-stairs, unpolished wooden floorboards in the two bedrooms. Up here the windows had white shutters that creased up like con-certinas and let in long arms of brambles laden with roses, and tiny balconies, no bigger than windowsills, in white-painted wrought iron. The bed in my room was narrow and high, with a white cover. The chairs were old-fashioned, with curvy backs. They broke when you sat on them; they were just for show.

The garden was large considering it was in the middle of a village, my aunt said. It was mainly grass, with flowerbeds and tangly shrubs dotted about in it. The solid privet hedge sur-rounding it was such a dark green it was almost black. Over it reared the plane trees that lined the village street outside. Sage green, almond green, sea green, bottle green, those were the colours of the bushes and plants. The flowers were so bright with the light in them, mauve and pink. The sun dazzling down on the garden at midday made it white. Too hot to sit in with-out a hat. I felt scorched. I preferred the coolness of the broken-down barn with its earth floor, where swallows flashed in and out, quick blue streaks. On the first morning the swallows flew into my room when I was still in bed and I felt welcomed.

I was puzzled when the telephone rang. I hadn't seen one the night before. There it was, by the bed. I lifted the receiver and said hello.

Your voice sounded exactly as it always did.

– Hello, you said back to me: how are you getting on?

– D'you mean to say, I asked: that they've got telephones up there?

You laughed.

– Of course we have. How else could we get in touch? Now come on, I haven't much time, how's your father managing, and how are you?

– Oh he's doing fine, I said: more or less. You know. He's being extra careful when he drives the car.

Why did I say that? I don't know. Just then the church bells began to ring, battering the windowpanes, and your voice faded away under their onslaught.

*

My aunt and uncle were welded to their white plastic lounging chairs. Turned towards each other, they held hands and chatted. They were pink-faced, melting in the heat. I strolled past them with a wave, went out to explore the village.

The church door seemed locked. I shoved it with my shoulder but its resistance didn't yield. I wandered on past it, paused at an open pair of tall wrought-iron gates, went in.

I was in the cemetery. The village within the village. The houses of the dead neatly arranged side by side. The path ran all the way round, tombs on both sides. Some of the graves were just mounds of earth, with fragile, blackened crosses in crumbling iron at their heads. Others were doors laid down on the ground, thick polished stone bearing pots of pink and red porcelain roses, open porcelain books with gilt letters spelling out the names of the dead. Whole families seemed to be crammed into small tight plots. Some of the graves had photographs in black metal frames. Some had stone angels. One had a crucifix made of tiny black beads.

Madame Cabazou knelt by a shiny slab of white granite. She inserted mauve flowers, like the ones in our garden, into a black vase on top of it. I looked over her shoulder to read her husband's name carved into the stone. Emile.

– He died three months ago, Madame Cabazou said: I'm not used to it yet.

She stood up and clasped my arm. Then she held my hand in hers. Water shone in her eyes, tipped over, flowed down her cheeks.

Just behind the graves the hills began, high and round, crusted with yellow sunflowers. The landscape crackled with their dark gold and black. The earth was a rich brown. We were high up in a wild and lonely place. From here you could see the Pyrenees, misty blue shapes against the blue sky.

Madame Cabazou wore a black housecoat printed with pink roses. She let go of me and fished a handkerchief out of her pocket. She mopped her eyes.

– The village is dying, she said: we used to have vineyards up there but not any more. Only sunflowers now round here. So all

the young ones have gone. Just us old people left. It's good your
family has come to stay. You'll liven us up.

– They're not my parents, I told· her: they're my uncle and
aunt.

Madame Cabazou whistled. An ancient beagle bitch trundled
out of the bushes, panting, and followed us down the path. I
winced away from her in case she snapped or bit.

– Betty, Betty, good dog, said Madame Cabazou: oh she's a
good dog my Betty, all the dogs in the village are good, none of
them will harm you, they don't bite.

– My mother's just died, I said in the loudest voice I could
manage: so they've brought me away on holiday to be nice to
me.

Madame Cabazou stood stock still in the centre of the path
and cried some more.

– Oh poor child poor child poor little one.

She hung on to my hand again as she wept. Then she blew her
nose and shut the tall gates behind us. The church bells began
to clamour out the Angelus. Bash, bash, bash.

– Electronic, said Madame Cabazou: the old lady who used
to ring the Angelus, because her father did before her, she died
this spring. No village priest any longer, either. Just one who
serves all the villages in turn. The presbytery's been empty for a
long time.

She fingered the little silver crucifix slung round her neck on
a silver chain and sighed.

– The presbytery? I asked.

– The priest's house, she said: there.

We were going down the stone steps from the side of the
church, down into the well of green light under the plane trees.
She waved her hand at the high wall beside us, the wooden door
let into it. We paused there, on the corner of the alleyway, to
say goodbye.

– Oh this heat, she said: I do love it. And it's so good for my
arthritis.

She tapped me on the cheek.

– You must have faith. Your mother is with God. We must
believe that. She's up there in heaven. She's alive for all eternity.

She hurried off. The old dog lurched along after her, slack-bellied, velvety nose in the dust.

You grasped my hand. We took off together with a swift kick, we whirred into the night sky. Holding on to you I was drawn along, buoyant, an effortless progress under the stars above the wheeling earth.

We flew into the mouth of a dark tunnel. I could see nothing, I gripped your hand, felt cold air stream over my eyelids. You knew your way. You carried us both along, our arms were wings.

– I wanted to show you what dying was like, you said: I wanted you to know. Open your eyes. Look.

Below us, in the tunnel, were hospital beds crowded with sick people. They lay still and silent, faces upturned as we flew past. Then they dwindled behind us, and we burst out of the tunnel back into the soft blackness of the night.

– That was dying, you said: we've gone past death now.

Our curving flight traced the shape of the earth below. We swooped sideways, down. Another opening loomed. Another tunnel? I wasn't sure. The silvery stars rolled past. We were carried on the shoulders of the wind.

– There's a lot more I've got to find out about, you explained: I've got a lot more to explore. Come on, let's go in here next.

A mosquito whined in my ear. I cursed and sat up. You were no longer there.

We ate lunch in the garden, beside the hedge, under the shade of a big white umbrella. Onion tart and tomato salad, bread and cheese, a plate of dark blue figs. My aunt and uncle drank a lot of wine. They went indoors for a siesta.

I sat on, idly looking at the bushes, the flowerbeds. All sun-drenched, glittering. The shutters of the rooms upstairs were only half closed. I heard my aunt call out and laugh. Her noise rattled against my skin.

The dog Betty appeared in the farthest corner of the garden. She emerged from under the fig tree which grew there, began to toddle across the grass. She pursued her sedate, determined way

as though it were marked out for her, pushing aside tall clumps
of weeds that blocked her path, stepping delicately over the
empty wine bottle my uncle had let fall. She didn't bother looking at me. I decided she must be on some private dog-road,
some sort of dogs' short-cut via holes in our hedge we hadn't
seen.

She flattened herself by the gate and tried to wriggle under.
She was too fat to manage it. She whined and thumped her tail.
I got up and opened the gate. She trotted through, then paused.
She was waiting for me. I thought I would follow her to find out
where she'd go.

She crossed the road and turned into the alley. Madame
Cabazou's house, I knew, was the first one along. On the opposite side, on the corner with the street, was the priest's house
behind its high wall. Betty didn't go home to her mistress. She
nosed at a low wicker gate set into the wall near the end of the
alley.

I tore aside the rusty wire netting stretched across the top of
the gate and peered over it. A short path, overhung with
creepers, led steeply upwards to a stone façade half obscured by
leaves. I understood. This was a back way into the priest's
house, one not protected by padlocks and keys. In a moment I'd
climbed through the netting and over the gate and dropped
down on the other side. The branches of trees brushed my face
and arms. Soft debris of dead leaves under my feet. I stood still
and listened. The entire village seemed to be asleep. No sharp
voice, no tap on my shoulder, pulled me back. I crept up the
path. I forgot Betty: she'd gone.

The house rose up before me, wide, three solid storeys of
cream-coloured stone under a red-tiled roof. Blank-faced, its
brown shutters closed. Three steps led up to its double wooden
door. On either side of this were stone benches with claw feet,
and tall bushes of oleander spilling worn pink flowers along the
ground. I didn't hurry working out how to enter the house
because the garden laid insistent hands on me and made me
want to stay in it for ever.

From the outside you couldn't see that there was a ga
all. It was hidden. A secret place. It was small and s

overgrown, completely enclosed by the towering walls that
surrounded it: the house on one side, the neighbour's barn on a
second, and the walls of the street and the alleyway on the other
two.

Inside these walls the garden was further enclosed by a
luxuriant green vine trained on to wires. What must once have
been a tidy green plot edged by the vine, by bushes and trees,
was now a thicket you had to push your way into. I crept into
a little sweet-smelling box of wilderness. Just big enough to
hold me. Just the right size. In its green heart I stood upright in
the long grass and counted two cherry trees, an apple tree laden
with fruit, more oleanders, a lofty bush of bamboo plumes, and
several of blackcurrant. I picked a leaf and rubbed it to release
the harsh scent. There was an ancient well in one corner, fenced
about with cobwebs and black iron spikes. I lifted its wooden
lid, peered down at its black mirror, threw a pebble in, and
heard the far splash.

I was frightened of going into the house all by myself, so I
dared myself to do it as soon as the church bells began to strike
the hour. The doors were clasped together merely by a loop of
thin wire. I twisted a stick in it, broke it. Then I pushed the
doors open and entered the house.

Once I'd wrestled with the shutters in the kitchen and flung
them wide, screeching on their unoiled hinges, I could see. The
red-tiled floor, the white fireplace with columns on either side
and a white carving of scrolls and flowers above, the stone arch
I'd come through from the hall, the cooker black with grease,
the yellow oilcloth on the table.

A corridor wound around the ground floor. I passed a store-
room full of old furniture and carpentry things, a wine cellar
lined with empty metal racks, a poky lavatory with decorated
blue tiles going up the wall. I picked my way up an open
wooden staircase, like a ladder, to the salon and the bedrooms
above. The salon was empty, grand as a ballroom but desolate.
Striped blue and gold wallpaper hung down in curly strips,
exposing the plaster and laths behind. The floor was bendy
when I walked on it. The bedrooms were dusty and dark, falls
of soot piled in their fireplaces. Old stained mattresses rested on

broken-down springs, old books, parched covers stiff with dirt,
sprawled face down on the lino, old chairs with cracked backs
and seats were mixed up anyhow with rolls of lino, split satin
cushions.

I put out my hands and touched these things in the half-dark.
I draped my shoulders with a torn bedspread of scarlet chenille,
then passed my hands over the wounded furniture. I blessed it,
I told it to be healed now, and that it was forgiven. Then I
departed from those sad rooms, closing their doors behind me
one by one.

I crawled up a second wooden stair, to the attic. Bright spears
of light tore gaps in the walls and roof, pointed at a floor
littered with feathers and droppings. A headless plaster statue
leaned in the far corner. His hands clasped a missal. He wore a
surplice and cassock. I recognized him, even without his head,
as St John Vianney, the curé of Ars. We'd done him at school. I
looked for his head among the dusty junk surrounding him but
couldn't find it. So I went back downstairs, into the garden
again.

My bed in our old house was in the corner of the room.
Shadows fingered the wall next to me and lay down on me like
blankets. You'd draped a shadow over your face like a mantilla.
You advanced, carrying a night-light. I was afraid of the dark
but not of you, even though a grey cobwebby mask clung to
your eyes and mouth and hid them.

You bent over me and spoke.

– What a mess you've left everything in. Bits and pieces all
over the place. Silly girl.

You whispered in my ear.

– One day I'll tell you all the secrets I've ever known.

My aunt ladled cold cucumber soup from the white china
tureen into white soup plates. We pushed our spoons across the
pale green ponds, to and fro like swimmers. My spoon was big,
silver-plated; I liked its heaviness in my hand. My uncle drank
his soup heartily, stuffed in mouthfuls of bread, called for a
second helping. My aunt waved the ladle at the moths butting

the glass dome of the lamp she'd set on the table. It threw just enough light for us to eat by. The rest of the garden was swallowed by black night. From Madame Cabazou's house across the street came the sound of a man's voice reading the news on TV.

My aunt and uncle spoke to each other and left me in peace. I could lean against their chat like a pillow while I searched my memory.

– No, my father said on the morning of the funeral: I don't believe in the afterlife. Though your mother tried to. Bound to, wasn't she, being a Catholic. We just conk out, I think. That's the end of it. The end of consciousness.

My uncle's red cheeks bulged with bread. He caught my eye and lifted his glass to me. My aunt collected our empty soup plates and stacked them on one side of the table. My uncle swallowed his faceful of bread and fetched the next course. Stuffed red peppers. I lifted mine out of the dish on to my plate, inserted my knife, slit the red skin. The pepper fell apart easily, like a bag of thin red silk. Rice and mushrooms tumbled out, a strip of anchovy.

– Overcooked, frowned my aunt: your fault, Lily, for coming back so late. Whatever were you up to?

I shrugged and smiled.

– Oh we understand, she said: you're young, you don't want to hang around all the time with us middle-aged folks! And we trust you to be sensible. Not to do anything silly.

She began to toss green salad in a clear plastic bowl, moving the wooden spoons delicately between the oily leaves that gave off the fragrance of tarragon.

– Of course you need some time by yourself, she said: especially just now. You want to amuse yourself, spend time by yourself, that's fine. Of course we understand.

It was early evening when I arrived at the house. Climbing the hill had taken me several hours. Now the sky at the horizon was green, as sharp as apples. The moon rose. A single silver star burned high above the lavender-blue sea.

The house was built into the cliff, at the very top, where the chalky ground levelled out, became turf dotted with gorse, sea-pinks, scabious. The front door stood open so I went in.

The whole place smelt of freshly sawn wood. Fragrance of resin, of cedar. Large rooms, airy and light. The walls and ceilings were painted a clear glowing blue. Beds were dotted about, manuscripts spilled across them. I wondered who they were, the people who lived here and strewed their papers over their beds. Then I saw the figure of a woman in the far doorway, leaning against the frame of the door, with her back to me. The owner of the house. Would she mind my presence? I was uninvited. A trespasser.

She turned round.

I'd forgotten that you'd ever looked like this. Young, with thick curly brown hair, amused hazel eyes, fresh unlined skin. Not a trace of sorrow or of pain. You were healthy. You were fully alive.

– I'm living here now, you explained with a smile and a wave of the hand: in Brahma's house.

You walked me about the spacious blue rooms, up and down the wide, ladder-like staircases of golden wood.

– Tell your father, you said: the cure for grief is, you have to sit by an open window and look out of it.

Your face was calm. No fear in it. You weren't suffering any more.

– You look so well, I blurted out: and all your hair's grown back!

– It's time for you to go, you told me.

You stood on the front steps and waved me off. My eyes measured the width of the doorway. I thought I'd slip through, stay with you. You shook your head, slammed the door shut on my efforts to break back in.

At eight o'clock prompt each day a siren wailed along the main road. That second morning, Madame Cabazou leaned over our gates and called.

– The bread van. Hurry up, girl. It doesn't wait long.

I stumbled after her, half-asleep. She dashed along on nimble slippered feet, a thick cardigan thrust on over her white nightdress. The dog Betty trailed us, folds of fat swaying.

Down by the fountain we joined a queue of old people who all smiled and exclaimed. Madame Cabazou introduced me, made me shake hands all round. Once I was part of them they went on swapping bits of news. Madame Cabazou was the lively one. Her chatter was staccato, her hands flew about like the swallows that zigzagged between our house and barn.

– My wretched grandchildren, she cried: they hardly ever come and see me. Children these days. Oh they don't care.

I bought a bag of croissants and a thick loaf, one up from a baguette, that was called simply a *pain*. I walked slowly back up the street to the house. The voices of the old people rose and fell behind me, bubbles of sound, like the splash of water in the fountain. They were recalling the funeral they'd been to the week before. A young girl, from a farm over by the lake, had been trapped by her hair in her father's baling machine and strangled. The voices grew high and excited, like the worrying of dogs.

After breakfast my aunt and uncle drove off in the car to visit the castle at Montségur. I waved them goodbye, then prowled about the kitchen, collecting the things I needed and packing them into a basket. I shut the grey metal gates behind me and crossed the road into the alleyway.

Madame Cabazou was working in the little vegetable patch in front of her house. Her thin body was bent double as she tugged weeds from the earth. Today she had on a blue house-coat, and she'd tied her straw hat on like a bonnet, the strings knotted under her chin. I slunk past while her stooped back was turned and hoisted myself over the wicker gate.

Once inside the priest's kitchen I opened the shutters and the windows to let in light and air. I swept the floor with the dust-pan and brush I'd brought, dusted the table and the fireplace and the window-sills. I laid a fire, with sticks and bits of wood from the store-room. I'd brought a small saucepan to cook in. I had a metal fish-slice and one wooden spoon. For lunch I might have stewed apples, using the fruit from the tree outside. I might try mixing up some grape juice. I had three plastic bottles of mineral water in my basket, a croissant saved from breakfast, a blue and white checked teacloth, and a couple of books. I left all this equipment on the table in the kitchen, and went outside.

I dropped into the garden like a stone or a plant, taking up my place. The garden had been waiting for me. I belonged in it. I had discovered it and in that act had been accepted by it. Now I was part of it. Hidden, invisible. The long grass closed over my head, green water. The bushes stretched wide their flowering branches around me. The bright green vine walled me in with its jagged leaves, curling tendrils, heavy bunches of grapes. Around the edges of the garden rustled the tops of the trees.

I had plenty of time to get to know the garden. I had seven whole days in which to stare at the ants and beetles balanced on the blades of grass next to my face, to finger the different textures of stems, to listen to the crickets and birds. I rolled over on to my back, put my hands under my head, and stared at the sky through branches and leaves. My hammock. I swung in it upside down. It dandled me. I fell asleep and didn't wake for hours.

Over supper my aunt and uncle told me about the castle of Montségur, perched on top of a steep mountain. They'd climbed up the slippery rocks. They'd eaten their picnic in the lofty stronghold where the Cathars had held out against St Dominic's armies come to smash them and drag them down to the waiting pyre.

– God how I loathe the Catholic Church, cried my aunt: God how I loathe all priests!

My uncle poured red wine into tumblers.

– Nice day, Lily? He asked.

I nodded. My mouth was full of cream-laden spaghetti scented with rosemary and sage. I had the idea that if I kept on eating the memory of my mother wouldn't be able to climb out of my silence, out of the long gaps between my words, and disturb me. So I held out my plate for a second helping and bent my head over it. I concentrated on the pleasures of biting, of chewing and swallowing, the pleasure of feeling full.

I was in bed but I wasn't asleep. The room was dark, and very warm. Gold glow of a lamp in one corner. Rain beat against the window, I heard it shush-shush through the curtains. Around me was folded the softest and lightest of quilts. Like being tucked up in a cloud. Or held in your arms. For you were there, a dim presence by the lamp, humming to yourself while you read a book about gardening. Peace was the physical knowledge of warmth, of your familiar profile, your sleeve of dark pink silk resting on the plump arm of your chair, the dim blue and gold pattern of the wallpaper.

You repeated to me: you're safe now. Safe now. Safe now.

– Our last day, Lily, smiled my aunt: are you sure you don't want to come out with us for a drive? I can't think what you find to do on your own here day after day.

I shook my head.

– Well, she said: if you don't, you don't, I suppose. You could make a start on your packing, in that case.

Her words jolted me. For seven days I'd been in retreat, in my private green world. I'd ceased to hear the church bells banging out the hours overhead. Hunger was my only clock. A week, in which I'd lain on the grass reading or daydreaming, had flowed past without my knowing or caring what day it was. Back home my schoolbooks waited, and a timetable ruled into squares.

I had an ache inside me. A sort of yawn that hurt. A voice in my stomach that wanted to scream. I felt stretched, and that I might topple over and break in two.

Back home I'd enter an empty house. My mother was dead. If only that could be a fact that was well past, something I'd dealt with and got over. Recovered from. I didn't want to embark on a life in which she'd go on and on being dead, on and on not being there. I didn't want to let it catch up with me. I shut the grey metal gates and hurried across the road.

Madame Cabazou was sitting on her front step, picking fleas out of Betty's coat. She nipped them between her fingernails until their little black backs cracked. Crack! Crack! She brushed the fleas from her fingertips like grains of black sand.

– Do you want some melons? she asked: I've got far too many. Even with this tiny patch I've grown more, this year, than I can use.

She waved her hand at the tidy rows of tomatoes, melons,

and courgettes. The earth between them was spotless, fine as sieved flour. She scowled at it.

– We used to have proper fields of crops, and the vineyard. Not like this. This pocket handkerchief of a garden. Oh I do miss all that, I can't tell you how much.

– Perhaps one melon? I suggested: we're leaving tomorrow morning early. We could have melon tonight.

– Come and fetch it later on, she sang out: I'll pick you one that's really ripe.

She shoved Betty's nose off her lap, and got up. She put her hands in her pockets and gazed at me.

She jerked her head towards the wicker gate in the wall.

– Some German people coming to view the house this afternoon, she remarked: with a lady from the agency.

I tried to sound indifferent.

– Oh really?

– The man who drives the bread-van told me, she said: this morning. His brother-in-law works in the café next door to the agency in Carcassonne, he heard them talking about it when they came in for a beer. Didn't you hear him say so down at the van this morning? You were off in some dream.

Coldness clutched me inside. I stared at Madame Cabazou.

– If I were you, she said: I'd come and fetch that melon this afternoon. You dream too much, it's not good. Better wake up. Otherwise you can be sure you'll be in trouble. Too much time by yourself, that's your problem.

Her words hurt me like slaps on the face. I swung away without saying anything. Tears burned my eyes but I wouldn't cry while she was watching me. I heard her front door close, then her voice drifted through the window, scolding Betty, breaking into song. She was cold-hearted. She didn't care how much she'd upset me. She didn't know how it felt to be told I'd got to leave this house and this garden for good.

I'd believed for a whole week that it was my house, my garden. I'd hardly believed it even. I just knew it. I'd just been part of it. The garden had seemed to know me, had taken me in without fuss. Leaving it, going outside and not coming back, would be like having my skin peeled off. I might die. Something was tearing me apart inside. It frightened me. I was a piece of paper being slowly ripped in two. I staggered, and fell on to the little patch of tangled grass under the vine. I started crying and could not stop. The crying went on and on and the pain. It twisted me up, it sawed me, it squeezed my heart so I could hardly breathe. The worst thing was feeling so lonely, and knowing I always would.

Just before my mother died, the night before, I was with her. It wasn't her any more, this tiny person so thin under her nightie I couldn't bear to look at her, with clawlike hands and a head that was a skull. Her eyes were the same, that was the only part of her left that I knew. She looked out of the darkness she was in and recognized me. For a couple of minutes she fought her way up from the morphine and tried to speak. She looked at me so trustfully. My father had said I should say goodbye to her but I couldn't.

— You're not going to die just yet, are you? I said loudly: you're not going to die just yet.

Her cracked lips tried to smile.

— Oh yes, I am, she whispered: oh yes, I think I am.

That night I dreamed of her bed in the glass conservatory, half in and half out of the house. I woke up at dawn and saw the sky like red glass. My father came in and said my mother had just died.

I could think of her being alive. I could think of her being dead. What I could not bear to think of was that moment when she died, was dying, died. When she crossed over from being alive to being dead. I couldn't join the two things up, I couldn't connect them, because at the point where they met and changed into each other was pain, my body caught in a vice, my bones twisted and wrenched, my guts torn apart. I gave birth to her dying. Violently she was pulled out of me. I felt I was dying too. I could hear an animal howling. It was me.

I lay on the grass exhausted. I felt empty. Nothing left in me. I was an old sack used then thrown away. Now I was low as the grass, low as the ground. Flattened. I was worn out. As though a mountain had stamped on me.

A yawn possessed me and I looked up. My eyelids felt swollen

like car tyres, and my nose too, and my mouth. I licked the salt
tears off the corners of my lips, blew my nose.

I lay staring at the gnarled trunk of the vine, the weeds and
grasses stirring about its root, the yellow flowers mixed in with
them whose name I didn't know.

Then it stopped being me looking at the vine, because I dissolved into it, became it. I left me behind. Human was the same
as plant. This corner of the garden, the earth: one great warm
breathing body that was all of us, that lived strongly, whose life
I felt coursing inside me, sap blood juices of grass. Love was the
force that made things grow. Love grew the vine, the weeds, me.
I started crying again because of the joy. It swept through me.
The knowledge of love. Such sweetness and warmth inside me
and the vine and the grass under the light of the sun.

Madame Cabazou whistled for me as though I were Betty.
We both came running. I carried a melon home under each arm.
She kissed me on both cheeks to say goodbye, instructed me, if
I wished to be well thought of, to write to her. She snatched me
out of my garden, shook me, set me upright, told me to go home
now. She pushed me off.

Next morning I slumped in the back seat of the car as we
drove out of the village and headed for the motorway. I wanted
to take the road back, to go the other way, to stay. I cried as we
left the high golden hills and descended on to the plain. The
wind from the sea, that Madame Cabazou called the *marin*,
blew strongly. It meant the end of summer. It sang an elegy for
my mother. She was dead she was gone I had lost her she would
never come back and live with us again.

Every cell in every leaf had had a voice, which spoke to me.

– *Of course I am here. Where else should I be but here.
Where else could I possibly be.*

Douglas Dunn
Arrangements

'Is this the door?' This must be it. No, no.
We come across crowds and confetti, weddings
With well-wishers, relatives, whimsical bridesmaids.
Some have happened. Others are waiting their turn.
One is taking place before the Registrar.
A young groom is unsteady in his new shoes.
His bride is nervous on the edge of the future.
I walk through them with the father of my dead wife.
I redefine the meaning of 'strangers'.
Death, too, must have looked in on our wedding.
The building stinks of municipal function.
'Go through with it. You have to. It's the law.'
So I say to a clerk, 'I have come about a death.'
'In there,' she says. 'You came in by the wrong door.'

A woman with teenaged children sits at a table.
She hands to the clerk the paper her doctor gave her.
'Does that mean "heart attack"?' she asks.
How little she knows, this widow. Or any of us.
From one look she can tell I have not come
With my uncle, on the business of my aunt.
A flake of confetti falls from her fur shoulder.
There is a bond between us, a terrible bond
In the comfortless words, 'waste', 'untimely', 'tragic',
Already gossiped in the obit. conversations.
Good wishes grieve together in the space between us.
It is as if we shall be friends for ever
On the promenades of mourning and insurance,
In whatever sanatoria there are for the spirit,
Sharing the same birthday, the same predestinations.
Fictitious clinics stand by to welcome us,
Prefab'd and windswept on the edge of town

Or bijou in the antiseptic Alps,
In my case the distilled clinic of drink,
The clinic of 'sympathy' and dinners.

We enter a small office. 'What relation?' he asks.
So I tell him. Now come the details he asks for.
A tidy man, with small, hideaway handwriting,
He writes things down. He does not ask,
'Was she good?' Everyone receives this Certificate.
You do not need even to deserve it.
I want to ask why he doesn't look like a saint,
When, across his desk, through his tabulations,
His bureaucracy, his morbid particulars,
The local dead walk into genealogy.
He is no cipher of history, this one,
This recording angel in a green pullover
Administering names and dates and causes.
He has seen all the words that end in -oma.
'You give this to your undertaker.'

When we leave, this time it is by the right door,
A small door, taboo and second-rate.
It is raining. Anonymous brollies go by
In the ubiquitous urban drizzle.
Wedding parties roll up with white ribbons.
Small pools are gathering in the loving bouquets.
They must not see me. I bear a tell-tale scar.
They must not know what I am, or why I am here.
I feel myself digested in statistics of love.
Hundreds of times I must have passed this undertaker's
Sub-Gothic premises with leaded windows,
By bus, on foot, by car, paying no attention.
We went past it on our first day in Hull.
Not once did I see someone leave or enter,
And here I am, closing the door behind me,
Turning the corner on a wet day in March.

VII

Memories

J. BERNLEF
Out of Mind

I undress and crawl between the cold sheets. I lie absolutely still with my knees drawn up until I am completely warm. Only then do I turn over on my side. Just when I am lying comfortably Vera comes to wake me. Is it morning? Why all this hurry? And since when don't I put my clothes on by myself? She kneels in front of me and ties my shoelaces.

'Get up.'

'You're just like my mother when we used to go into town once a year to buy clothes.'

'I'm not your mother.'

As if I didn't know. What's the matter with her this morning?

Roast beef for breakfast? And who is that girl at the table? From her conduct I gather she knows who I am. Better wait and see. Maybe Vera will mention her name or she might make some remark that gives me a clue as to her identity. The Simic method makes no provision for this. It serves only to make you invisible. I have to yawn heartily a couple of times. I apologize but they pretend they haven't noticed. (That is very kind of those two women.)

I am not very hungry, but then, who would ever think of serving roast beef for breakfast? There, they are talking now, a conversation has started up between those two!

'Would you like some salad with it, Phil?'

Good, so that young one is called Phil. Join in straight away now.

'Don't you feel rather hot in that woollen sweater, Phil?' I say to the blonde girl.

She shakes her head, she has her pretty mouth full just now. Pity, I wouldn't have minded seeing her breasts. Vera used to have such beautiful ones, too, when she was young. And even now I still love to put my face between them.

They carry on eating and say nothing more. Every now and again they look at me as if expecting something of me. Vera gives the blonde girl another slice of roast beef. Well prepared, blood-red in the middle, that's how it should be. You can leave that to Vera.

'I've made a room ready for you upstairs,' she says to the girl, so I gather she is staying the night. Maybe she is a friend of Kitty's who has called in unexpectedly, thinking Kitty would be in. She is attractive. Full lips, the upper lip with a classical curve, and a high, slightly bulbous forehead. She reminds me of someone. Blue eyes, bright blue. Usually blue eyes are pale, mixed with a little grey, like mine, but not these ones. They look and they see. I would dare to speak to her, but as I don't know her name I say nothing.

She knows me, though. I can tell from her whole behaviour. Stalemate. I wait for a breakthrough. That is what is so annoying. More and more often I have to wait, be on the alert. What used to be self-evident (at least I have to assume it was) has now become enigmatic. And I don't want to keep asking questions all the time. So I wait, meanwhile slowly and painstakingly chewing a piece of meat.

Suddenly they have finished eating and immediately afterwards (the ladies seem to be quickening their tempo) there is coffee. I am given something with my coffee, a green capsule, or is it candy?

'Swallow it in one go, Maarten, don't bite on it.'

If Vera says so it must be all right.

'I thought it was candy,' I say by way of excuse.

The girl examines her nails. She seems to be bored. Whatever is she doing here, having coffee with two old people?

'You can turn the television on if you like,' I say to her.

She does so at once, and this makes me feel content. I have been able to please her in a small way. She sits down on the settee, arms spread out wide along the back, her legs crossed. She is wearing green knitted slippers on her feet. That surprises me, at this time of year.

'How are you feeling now, Maarten?'

'I couldn't tell you. Honestly, I'm sorry. I really don't know.'

'Try to say what you are thinking.'

'Everything happens in jolts and jerks. There is no flowing movement any longer, as there used to be. Nowhere. The day is full of cracks and holes. So to speak. No, really, honestly. It's no good any longer.' (Who or what forms these creaking sentences, which I try to utter – by means of interjections and insertions – more or less casually?)

'Who's that strange girl there?'

'But Phil isn't a stranger. You went for a walk with her this afternoon.'

'Oh yes, of course. So it is evening now. That's a stroke of luck, isn't it!' (Perhaps I pat her on the shoulder a bit too hard, sometimes I am not in full control of that either, dividing my strength among various activities; taking hold of a glass much too gently so it smashes to pieces, grabbing a towel as though it weighed twenty kilos.)

'Tomorrow is another day!' (This kind of sentence presents the least difficulty; proverbs, set phrases pop out all by themselves, with them my speech comes closest to normal talking.)

I get up and wave to a blonde girl who cheerfully waves back from the settee without moving her wrist.

Suddenly my body reels with sleep. I don't even bother to clean my teeth.

I wake up with a feeling as though I had drunk large quantities of beer. I go to the toilet but only a hesitant, thin hot trickle comes out. I shuffle back on bare feet through the dark passage. At the top of the stairs I see light burning under Kitty's door. Softly I climb the stairs, seeking support from the banisters.

Father and daughter, that is a very different bond from the one you have with a son. With Fred my contact is more choppy, but I like talking to Kitty.

When I enter her room she slaps her hands on her bare breasts in alarm. I smile and sit down on the edge of her bed. 'It's only your father,' I say.

She slides out of the bed on the other side, in her slip, snatches a blue T-shirt from the chair on which she has hung her clothes and quickly puts it on. (And suddenly, in a flash; this is the last time you will see this – how Kitty with her breasts jutting out and a hollow back pulls down a T-shirt tightly to below her darkly caving navel.)

'Yes,' I say resignedly, 'there comes a time when daughters don't want to be bare any more in front of their own father.'

From the corner of the room, beside the chair, she looks at me thoughtfully, holding her head at a slant. A strand of her blonde hair falls past her left shoulder across the T-shirt. On the pillow lies an open book which she has been reading. *The Heart of the Matter* by Graham Greene.

She walks around the bed and pulls me up with gentle force. 'Come,' she says in English. 'It's the middle of the night. You must go to sleep.'

'Oh, is it as late as that?'

Arm in arm we walk down the stairs. There is something stately, something solemn about it, as if I am going to give this girl, whom I do not know, in marriage to an as yet unknown bridegroom. Vera wakes up when the girl switches on the light in the bedroom. She talks to Vera as if I were a stranger.

'He was wandering around,' she says, again in English. The way your parents used to speak when they didn't want you to know about something.

Together they tuck me up in bed. I am not sick, but I let them do as they please. Behind my closed eyelids I see the light go out again. I am lying on my back. Beside me Vera turns over on to her side. At first I don't hear her breathing, but then she suddenly sighs profoundly a couple of times and I hear the deep, regular breathing of a sleeping person.

Nearly fifty years we have been lying side by side like this. It is almost impossible to comprehend what that means. The feeling of being two communicating vessels. Her moods, her thoughts; I can almost read them in her face, like Pop read the temperature of his thermometer. A graph of my love for Vera? An idea that Pop would not have understood. Once he spoke of his love for Mama, whom he always called 'wife'. That was when they had been married for forty years and he gave an after-dinner speech, a glass of red wine in his hand. He compared Mama to a piece of music, to the adagio from Mozart's

fourteenth piano sonata. 'Just as clear, bright, and unfathomable.' That was what he said. And after that I played the
adagio on our out-of-tune black piano and the tears came to
Mama's eyes, Pop told me, for I couldn't see it myself. I can't
sleep because I need to pee. Then it's no use remaining in bed, I
know that from experience.

Someone has left the light on in the hall. Clear, bright, and
unfathomable. Without women the world would be drab and
violent, says Pop. 'Maarten, will you play what I mean but for
which my words are inadequate?'

This sentence is the signal for me to walk to the piano. We
have agreed on this in advance, Pop and I.

I sit down at the piano, raise my hands above the keys, and
search. I can't find the beginning. Always I see it before me but
not now. Perhaps I ought to make light first. I switch on the
wall lamp and stand looking at the keys for a while. Then I sit
down again. I close my eyes, hoping that the distances between
the keys will return, that I will feel the first notes in my fingers
again, but nothing happens. I get up and look for the sonata
among the pile of sheet music on the piano. I put the album on
the stand and leaf through it until I have found the adagio.
There they are, the notes. But they won't come off the page and
into my fingers. It would be terrible to disappoint them all.
Perhaps I ought to limber up first, just a few notes, so the beginning will suddenly slip back into my fingers. As long as I have
the beginning, the rest will come all by itself. Harder and harder
I press the black and white keys, more and more keys I press in
order to find that one damned beginning. But there are thousands of possibilities. Yet I must find the beginning, I must!

'Maarten, what's the matter? Why are you crying?'

Vera in her dark dressing gown, her brown hair in a wild mop
around her head.

'The beginning, I can't find the beginning.'

I hear footsteps overhead, look up at the ceiling.

'That's Phil,' she says, looking up with me. 'You've woken
her up with your playing.'

I don't know who she is talking about, but of course I am
sorry. 'I was practising for the wedding and I can't find the

beginning any more.'

Someone enters the room. A young girl in jeans and a blue T-shirt. She is barefoot, which is odd for this time of year.

'Maarten always plays the adagio from Mozart's fourteenth piano sonata from memory. He's known it by heart for years. And now he suddenly can't find the beginning any more.'

The girl nods sleepily. I can see it doesn't interest her in the least (and rightly, for what a ridiculous situation this is, an old man playing the piano in the middle of the night in his pyjamas).

'I'll get something for him,' she says and leaves the room. Vera goes to the record player beside the television. She crouches by the record shelf. I feel cold, and I want some beer. I go to the kitchen.

Standing in the middle of the kitchen, with the handle of the refrigerator door in my hand, I suddenly hear the adagio coming from the living room. Clear, bright, and unfathomable. Slowly, almost solemnly, I enter the room to the rhythm of the music.

In the centre of the room stands Vera, amid the furniture. I have never seen her like this, so forlorn and so small as she stands there barefoot on the wooden floor in her dark shiny dressing-gown among the gleaming furniture. Her hands seem to be groping for a hold in the air.

I know I must have done something wrong. I want to go up to her and ask her, in order to bridge the distance between her and me. But then I am seized from behind and feel, right through my pyjama sleeve, a dull stab of pain shooting up in my left upper arm.

Vera is sitting on the settee. She is listening to Mozart's adagio. She has tears in her eyes. Like this she looks exactly like Mama.

I am led away by a stranger but I suppose it must be all right if Vera is suddenly so happy again. Therefore I smile and nod to the young woman beside me. I behave as though this were the way life is supposed to be.

A huge bed. Lying utterly hopelessly the wrong way round in it.

Terrible stink here. My ass smarts, icy cold buttocks I have. I try to raise myself but my ankles are tied down. What has happened to me? Where have I been moved to? Where is this bed? Now?

I recognize all those things around me, sure I do. Behind a closed door sounds an unfamiliar female American voice: 'Fill the bath up.'

Jesus, have I befouled the matrimonial bed? How do you like that! It's not my fault. If you tie a man to his bed! Strapped to the bars, I ask you. Who has done that to me? And where is Vera? I call out but you can bet nobody will come. I can't reach the straps that are cutting into my ankles. I wish I could bear the smell of my own shit as well as Robert.

'Robert! Robert!'

No one. Perhaps they've all gone. Leaving me to rot here in this bed. I hear water running. In a minute the place will be flooded and I can't get out of my bed. I kick about. The bed creaks but the straps don't give a millimetre.

Somewhere a door opens. I daren't look because I have no idea who's coming. And because I am ashamed to be lying here like a beast in my own muck. I keep my eyes tightly shut. I hear someone retching. Feel how hands strip the pyjamas from my body. They want me to move forward. Must open my eyes now and see an old man in the mirror, an old man with a slack wrinkly belly streaked with shit. I smile with relief. At least that isn't me!

Two women lift me into a bathtub, an old one and a young one.

I lie in this water as if I no longer had a body. Only where they touch me, wash me, does it briefly exist again.

Careful, I say to the younger one who dares not look at me because she is embarrassed by a male organ that floats in the soapy water and now rises, purple and gently quivering.

'Don't mind about it,' I say. 'The regime under the belt, Chauvas used to call it. Why do we cover it up so anxiously, why is there such a taboo on it? Do you know what Chauvas thought? Chauvas said the following: May I have your attention, please, because this cannot be put in the minutes, as you

will understand, certainly not by lady secretaries. We are afraid
of sexuality because it undermines the basis of our whole
society: the idea that every person is a unique individual with an
organized life. But if every man can, in principle, go to bed with
every woman and vice versa then all those stories about pre-
destination, preordination, destiny, and eternal love are so
much poppycock. We are floating through space like particles,
plus ones and minus ones. And where these meet, a fusion may
occur. Everybody knows this, but suppresses it. Man is not
capable of philanthropic sex because in that case there would be
no point in doing anything except this.'

I grab hold of the stiff prick in the water and feel it is my own.
From fright and shame I let go.

They pull me upright. They make no reply to my words as the
younger one dries me and the other one tries to pull a pair of
underpants over my rough damp buttocks, in order to with-
draw the subject of the conversation – which fortunately
becomes limp again – as quickly as possible from sight. Then
they bundle me into a dressing-gown.

'I don't have to go to bed, do I? Did you understand me,
madam?' I say to the older one, who looks rather dishevelled
with her damply drooping brown curls and her wrinkled neck.

'We've read Freud, too,' says the younger one sharply.

The arrogance of youth. Think they know something about
life when they've read a few books.

'Look around you,' I say. 'Not that I approve of Chauvas's
conduct. On the contrary. But no one can accept that what he
calls his life has been the only possible life for him. It could have
been different. If you had chanced to put your prick in a totally
different cunt, for instance. Or even stronger; if your father had
screwed someone other than your mother or your mother a different man, you wouldn't even have been here in the same
form.'

'Go and rinse your mouth out.' It is Vera who says this.

'All right,' I say. 'I will. Right away.'

They let go of me so I can reach the washstand. I pick up the
toothbrush and look in the mirror. There isn't anyone there.
Everything is white. I throw the toothbrush away. They take

hold of me. I let myself be led away, away from the white of that mirror.

Want to eat more. They won't let me. Simply take my plate away. How do you like that? They are strangers here so they give no answer when I ask a question. The simplest things: time, season, what are the plans for the day.

The fingers of my left hand are numb. Put the hand on the table, palm upward. Move my fingers. Clench, relax; clench, relax. Compared with the right hand: as if there's no current going through it any longer. Rub . . . rub . . . rub.

Thumping footsteps, suddenly very close by. Hurts my ears. Parts of the body are oversensitive, others totally insensitive.

Jump out of my skin with fright when suddenly someone is standing by the sink. A small woman in a lemon-coloured apron. She lets water run from a tap on to white plates. I ask her where Vera is but I get no answer. Her neck is wrinkled and brown from the open air. I don't know where I am.

Grab hold of the edge of the table and let go. And again. There is activity in the space around me that is totally detached from me. Sound of water gurgling away through a wastepipe. Very successful. Pity it stops – maybe we can imitate it.

Want to be near water, very near to water, hold this numb left hand in a fast running shallow brook. Sit motionless on the bank and then, suddenly see, caught in a quivering patch of sun on the silver-white sandy river bed, the slim shadow of a fish (where does this image come from, from what depths, it is as clear as if I could touch it; it is sad but true: you, Maarten, were once that little boy sitting by the side of that stream!).

A young woman with long straight blonde hair is sitting opposite me at the table. I nod to her, although I do not understand her presence. She asks me why I am rubbing the table with my hand.

I look and feel only now that the hand is rubbing across the red dotted oilcloth (how long has this been going on?).

When I have raised my head again I must quickly force a smile. 'I have become an old man. Quite suddenly, it seems,' I say. She shakes her head, but I know better.

She gets up and the red of her sweater becomes even redder than the dots on the oilcloth. She pulls me to my feet. How annoying to have to let go of the table. I grab her hand and she leads me away through an open door into a different space. There stands Pop's desk! I remember being allowed to draw at it on Sundays. A white paper on a baize-green blotter covered in the inkstains and scribbles of Pop's blotted letters. When you looked for a long time you saw all kinds of things in them: animals, faces. I used to copy them.

'As a boy I liked to crawl under that desk with a book. *The Travels and Adventures of Captain Hatteras. Captain Hatteras in Search of the North Pole.* They all dreamt of that in the days of Jules Verne. I used to like reading about it as a boy. Amundsen, Nansen, Captain Hatteras. Did you know he went mad in the end, and was locked up in an institution? I have never forgotten the ending of *The Ice Desert.* He is walking in the garden of the institution, which is surrounded by a high brick wall, always in the same direction, northward. Until he bumps into the wall. There, his arms stretched out against the bricks, he remains motionless for hours. And then I put my hands on the wood of Pop's desk and close my eyes and try to imagine what it is like to be Captain Hatteras, alone in a desert on ice floes.'

'Your father is dead.'

'Yes, well, stands to reason, doesn't it, if you're as old as I am.'

Again the edge of a table. And a chair. (Was it already there or has it just been pushed forward?) I sit down. Notice that the rubbing has resumed. Not unpleasant, actually.

'My favourite place to sit was under the desk. I'd push the chair back and crawl underneath the desk with a book. *The Travels and Adventures of Captain Hatteras.* In the end he went mad from all that whiteness around him. He ended up in an institution. While he was there he used to walk all the time in a northerly direction. Until he couldn't go any further. Until he ran into a wall. Then he would stand still for hours.'

Outside, a woman walks down a snowy garden to a blue car. She waves, I wave back. People are friendly here, that cannot be denied. She starts the car and reverses out of a drive (the view would be less empty, easier to cope with, if trees, like people, all had a name of their own).

A girl opposite me asks why I am rubbing the wood with my left hand.

'Otherwise I can't see the hand any longer.'

'See?'

'Yes.'

'Otherwise you can't feel your left hand any longer?'

'More or less. Yes, exactly. As I said.'

She has picked up an oblong book and opens it. Black pages. She turns the book over and pushes it towards me.

'No pictures, please.'

'But it's your own photo album.'

In order to please her I leaf through it. Wedding photos. Photos of children. I turn the album round and point at one of them.

'I never see them any more. Kitty was supposed to come over. Have you met her?'

'I'm sure she'll come.'

'And Fred even less. You never see them any more. They're no longer your children.' (Try not to cry now.)

'What's this?' She puts her finger on a photograph of a man walking beside a wide river. Across the water there is a row of big houses, strung along the bank which lies in the shade. The man is walking in the sun along a quay wall. He looks sideways into the camera.

'A river,' I say. 'The Rhine, maybe?'

'But who is that man?'

'Could it be me?'

'Of course. You haven't changed that much.'

'Yes, now that you say so, it is me. But I'm not so sure about the river. The Rhine?'

'And who is that?'

A woman in a little black hat with fluttering veil, pushing a baby carriage. Old-fashioned, tailored, two-piece suit.

'Mama I suppose. My mother, I mean, I beg your pardon. With me.' I look from the photograph to her face. 'Or am I wrong?'

'Have another look.'

'I honestly don't know just now.'

'It's your wife. It's Vera.'

'Please put the book away.'

'You must go on looking. If you go on looking and you think of her very hard, you're sure to recognize her again.'

'She has changed. Or maybe I am the one who has changed. She is a beautiful woman.'

'She is still beautiful now.'

I nod. Yes, she will remain beautiful for ever, with those green eyes behind that veil pleated for ever by the wind.

'The waters broke,' I say. 'All of a sudden. As if it was raining. She clutched at my shoulders. I got drenched.'

Again I look at the photograph of the woman with the baby carriage, at the veil that seems to want to fly away, at her narrow, hopeful face. Slowly and cautiously I nod. Then I start to talk. A story. A story about the woman with the hat and the veil. Vera. I place her with the baby carriage on the edge of Amsterdam. That is where she lives. I talk about the child in the carriage, who cannot be seen in the photograph but who is my son Fred in the story. I talk about the fields, the glasshouses, the ditches and the footbridges, which lie outside the rectangle of the photograph. I talk about the time in which the photograph was taken, the last year of the war. This does not altogether tally with the tailored suit, but this girl sitting here won't know that, she belongs to a generation born long after the war and in another continent. She nods and she listens. I talk. About the blocked sewers (because the Germans had turned off the electricity in the pumping stations) so that everywhere in the streets deep shit holes were being dug that stank horribly and created a real risk of infectious diseases like cholera and typhoid. I talk about old, stooping Mr Mastenbroek on the third floor who died of starvation two days before the liberation. You can't imagine that now, I say. What hunger is like. That dull, gnawing feeling, which resided not only in your stomach but everywhere. All your thoughts were governed by it. I talk of the arrival of the Canadians and Americans. Eisenhower's and Churchill's triumphal tour of the city in an open limousine.

How I stood among the crowds with Fred on my shoulders and tears running down my cheeks. About the freedom celebrations, the first bar of chocolate, the biscuit porridge (thick and nourishing and at first too rich for my stomach, which for months had feasted only on sugarbeet and fried slices of tulip bulb). How everyone fell in love with life again, with one another, how many children were born in the Netherlands roughly a year after that 5 May. I talk and talk and it is as if I am talking myself out of history, as if this were a book from which I am reading, or a text I know by heart; one thing is clear: what you tell you lose. For ever. Abruptly I fall silent and look around in alarm.

ANDREW MOTION
A Blow to the Head

On the metro,
two stops in from Charles de Gaulle,
somebody slapped my wife.

Just like that –
a gang of kids –
for moving her bag
from the seat to her lap:
a thunderclap
behind my back.

Very next thing
was reeling dark
and the kids outside
beside themselves:
You didn't see! You didn't see!
It might be him! It wasn't me!

For the rest,
she wept through every station into Paris,
her head on my shoulder like love at the start of its life.

*

By the merest chance
I had in mind
J. K. Stephen,
who damaged his head
on a visit to Felix-
stowe (Suffolk) in '86.

The nature of the accident is not certainly known;
in the Stephen family it was said he was struck
by some projection from a moving train.

Not a serious blow,
but it drove him mad
(molesting bread
with the point of a sword;
seized with genius –
painting all night),

and finally killed him
as well as his father,
who two years later
surrendered his heart
with a definite crack
like a sla . . .

*

. . . which reminds me.
When I was a kid
a man called Morris
slapped my face
so crazily hard
it opened a room
inside my head
where plates of light
skittered and slid
and wouldn't quite
fit, as they were
meant to, together.

It felt like the way,
when you stand between mirrors,
the slab of your face
shoots backwards and forwards
for ever and ever
with tiny delays,
so if you could only
keep everything still
and look to the end
of the sad succession,
time would run out

and you'd see yourself dead.

*

There is an attic flat
with views of lead
where moonlight rubs
its greasy cream,

and a serious bed
where my darling wife
lies down at last
and curls asleep.

I fit myself
along her spine
but dare not touch
her breaking skull,

and find my mother
returns to me
as if she was climbing
out of a well:

ginger with bruises,
hair shaved off,
her spongy crown
is ripe with blood.

I cover my face
and remember a dog
in a reeking yard
when the kid I was

came up to talk.
I was holding a choc
in a folded fist,
but the dog couldn't tell

and twitched away —
its snivelling whine
like human fear,
its threadbare head

too crankily sunk
to meet my eye
or see what I meant
by my opening hand.

MARTIN AMIS
Special Damage

Her first feeling, as she smelled the air, was one of intense and
helpless gratitude. I'm all right, she thought with a gasp. Time
– it's starting again. She tried to blink away all the water in her
eyes, but there was too much to deal with and she soon shut
them tight.

Someone leant over her and said with a voice so close that it
might have come from within her own head, 'Are you all right
now?'

She nodded. 'Yes,' she said.

'I'll leave you then. You're on your own now. Take care. Be
good.'

'Thank you,' she said. 'I'm sorry.'

She opened her eyes and sat up. Whoever had spoken was no
longer there, but other people were moving about near by,
people who for some reason were all there just to help her
through. How kind they must be, she thought, how kind they
are, to do all this for me.

She was in a white room, lying on a spindly white trolley. She
thought about this for a while. It seemed quite an appropriate
place to be. She would be all right here, she thought.

Outside, a man in white walked quickly past. He hesitated,
then poked his head round the door. His posture suddenly
relaxed. 'Come on, get up,' he said wearily, his eyes closed.

'What?'

'*Get up*. It's time. You're all right, come on.' He walked forward, glancing sideways at a low table on which various items
were scattered. 'These all your things?' he said.

She looked: a black bag, some scraps of green paper, a small
golden cylinder. 'Yes,' she said secretively, 'these all my things.'

'You better be off then.'

'Yes all right,' she said. She swung herself over the trolley's side. She stared down at her legs and moaned. The poor flesh was all churned and torn. Reflexively she reached down to touch. Her flesh was whole. The shreds were part of some wispy material laid over her skin. She was all right.

The man snorted. 'Where *you* been,' he said, his voice moistening.

'Can't tell,' she muttered.

He came closer. 'The toilet?' he said loudly. 'You want to go to the *toilet*?'

'Yes please,' she said, without much hope.

He turned, walked towards the door, and turned again. She stood up and tried to follow him. She found that heavy curved extensions had been attached to her feet. The idea was obviously to make movement very difficult, if not actually impossible. With one leg wobbling she came towards him at an angle along the slipped floor.

'Get your *things* then.' He shook his head several times. 'You people . . .'

He led her into the passage. Walking ahead of him now, and feeling his eyes on her back, she looked hastily this way and that. There seemed to be two kinds of people out there. Most of them were the ones in white. The other kind were smaller and bound in variegated robes; they were being carried or led about with expressions of defencelessness and apology. I must be one of them, she thought, as the man urged her down the passage and pointed to a door.

The first hours were the strangest. Where was her sense of things?

In the trickling narrow room, whose porcelain statuary she could not connect with herself, she placed her cheek against the cold wall and looked for clues inside her head. What was in there? Her mind went on for ever but contained nothing, like a dead sky. She was pretty sure this wasn't the case with other people – a thought that produced a sudden spurt of foul-tasting liquid in the back of her throat. She steadied herself and turned to face the room, catching the eye of a shiny square of steel on the wall; through this bright window she briefly glimpsed a startled figure with thick black hair who looked at her and ducked quickly away. Is everyone frightened, she wondered, or is it just me?

She didn't know how long she was expected to stay where she was. Any minute now the man would come and get her again; alternatively, she might be allowed to hang around in here for as long as she liked, perhaps indefinitely. Then it occurred to her that the world was her idea. But in that case it couldn't be a very good idea, could it, if she sensed such unanimity of threat, such immanence of harm?

The door was a puzzle she speedily solved. The man had gone when the narrow room let her out. Without pausing she moved in the general direction of the white-clad keepers and their slower charges, towards the light which raced in playful eddies along the colourless walls. Abruptly the passage widened into a place where movement ceased and new kinds of people stood about in furtiveness and grief, or lay sweating warily on white-decked tables, or yelled out as the trotting keepers smuggled them away. Someone covered in blood stood hollering spectacularly in the centre of the floor, his hands raised to his eyes. Beyond him open double-doors admitted a cool wash of air and light. She moved forward, careful to skirt the thrashing pockets of confusion and distress. No one had time to prevent her.

She hurried from the indoors. When she tried to accelerate down the glass passage the devices on her feet abruptly checked her with their pain. She bent down to examine them and found, to her pleased surprise, that she could remove them without much difficulty. Two passing men carrying an empty hammock shouted at her and frowned meaningly at the discarded machines on the floor. But she could smell the living air now, and she hurried from the indoors.

At first, outside seemed no more than a change of scale. Everyone was still required to keep on the move, loose herds in the tall spanned passages. Quite a few seemed damaged, but there weren't many to guide or carry them. Those in pressing need of velocity and noise used the trolleys, numberless and variegated, queuing and charging along the wide central lanes in vaporous, indocile packs. The streets were full of display, of symbols whose meaning was coolly denied to her. Through an absence of power or will – or perhaps simply of time – no one bothered to stop her joining the edgy human traffic, though many looked as though they would like to. They stared; they stared at her feet; they had all grown used to their own devices – and where were hers supposed to be? It was her first mistake, she knew: no one was intended to be without them, and she was sorry. But she moved, and kept on moving, because that's what everyone else was required to do.

There were six kinds of people outside. People of the first kind were men. Of all the six kinds they were the most fully represented and also the most varied within their kind. Some went where they had to go in an effaced and gingery shuffle, hoping no one would pick them out: not many of them looked at her, and then only with diffidence and haste. But others moved with a rangy challenge, an almost criminal freedom, their jaws held up to front the air: they certainly looked her way, and with enmity, several of them making sounds of cawing censure with their mouths. People of the second kind were less worrying; they were shrunken, compacted – mysteriously lessened in some vital respect. They limped in pairs, with such awkward caution that they hardly made any progress at all, or else whirled about with a fluttery, burst, directionless verve. Some were so bad now that they had to be wheeled round in covered boxes, protesting piteously to their guides, who were people of the third kind. The third kind resembled the first kind quite closely except at the top and the bottom; their legs were often unprotected, and they skilfully tiptoed on the arched curves of their elaborate devices (I must be one of them, she thought, remembering the narrow room and lifting a hand to her hair). They looked at her for just a moment, then at her numb feet, then turned away in pain. People of the fourth kind were men who couldn't get their hair right, some using hardly any at all, others smothering themselves with the stuff, and still others who actually wore theirs upside down – the matted face climbing towards a great globed chin of naked scalp. *They* seemed to think that this was all right. People of the fifth kind stood apart on corners or edged their way sideways through the guiltily parting crowds; they didn't talk like other people talked; they either muttered darkly to themselves or span away at an angle to wring their hands and admonish the air. She thought they must be mad. The people of the fifth kind included people of most other kinds. And they were never seen in pairs. People of the sixth kind, of course, were sorrily shod with tangled stockings, and weren't sure who they were supposed to be or where they were going. She thought she saw one or two of these, but on closer inspection they always turned out to be people of some other kind.

No one out there reminded her of anything much. She sensed that she was on the brink of the inscrutable, ecstatic human action, that all she saw was ulterior, having a great and desperate purpose which firmly excluded her. And she still couldn't tell to what extent things were alive.

No change yet, she thought.

Then something terrible started happening slowly.

Not too far above the steep canyons there had hung an imperial backdrop of calm blue distance, in which extravagantly lovely white creatures – fat, sleepy things – hovered, cruised and basked. Carelessly and painlessly lanced by the slow-moving crucifixes of the sky, they moreover owed allegiance to a stormy yellow core of energy, so irresistible that it had the power to hurt your eyes if you dared to look its way. But then this changed. The tufted creatures lost their outlines, drifting upwards at first to form a white shawl over the dome of the air, before melting back into a slope of unbroken grey beneath their master, which lost its power and boiled red with rage – or was it just dying, she thought, as she started to see the terrible changes below. With humiliation, candour, and relief, people of all kinds duly began to hasten in hardened fear. Variety grew weary, and its pigments gave up their spirits without struggle, some with stealth, others with hurtful suddenness. Soon the passages and their high glass walls appeared to be changing places – or at least they agreed to share what activity remained: the daredevil roadsters broke in two and raced their ghosts away. Above, the bruised distance seeped ever nearer. Baying in panic with their wheels out, showing their true colours now, the trolleys of the sky warped downwards towards the earth, as further below the people made haste to escape from beneath the falling air.

Where were they all going to hide? Soon there would be no people left and she would be here alone. Someone of the second kind hobbled past, paused and turned, and said shyly,

'You'll catch your death.'

'Will I?' she asked.

She moved on. People lingered in the well-lit places. Sometimes you walked in glazed bleak silence, measuring yourself to the yellow relays of light; then you turned into a buzzing gallery of action and purpose. Alone or in small groups they eventually ducked into the darkness, determined to get somewhere while they still could. They went on staring at her, some of them, but perfunctorily now – at her feet, at her face, and perhaps at her feet again, depending on the kind of people they were.

For a time breakdown arrived on the streets. They teemed with a last, released, galvanic hate. People experimented with their voices, counting the harsh sounds they could make; others dashed headlong into the deepest shadows, as if only they knew a good secret place to hide. It was then that her sense of danger started climbing sharply, in steep swerves. Each turning seemed more likely to deliver its possibilities of hurt and risk; soon, someone or something would feel the need to do her special damage.

Enough of this, she thought, deciding to get these things over with and out of the way.

Not until the world was moving past her at quite a speed did it occur to her that she was running . . . Running pleased her, she realized. It was the first clear and urgent prompting that had come her way. The bricked passages reeled by. Such people that remained turned after her; a few shouted out. For a while one of them lolloped clumsily along in her wake, but she moved clear ahead. She seemed to be able to go just as fast as she liked.

She thought that running would save time, that by speeding things up it would inevitably make the next thing happen sooner.

At last she made it to a place where there were no people left. The concrete floor spanned out into another kind of life. This was the end of whatever she was in. Beyond spiked rods green land rose in a calm swell. Overhead, she noticed, the fat creatures had crept back beneath their spangled roof – all heavy and red now, and their deity a sombre silver in the lake of darkness. Suddenly she saw a gap in the cage: a lane fed straight into the green land, with only a horizontal white bar to mark the point. She moved forward, bent herself beneath the bar, then ran as fast as she could up across the soft ground.

She soon found a good place to hide. There was a moist hollow at the foot of a leaning tree. With her breath lurching she lay down and folded herself up. Her body began to quiver: this is it, she thought, this is my death. The pain that she had harboured all day burst from the tight crux of her body. Her face leaked too, and some convulsion within her was squeezing unwanted sounds through her lips. She told herself to be quiet. What was the point of hiding if you made all this noise? The shadows put on weight. The ground gave way to receive her. At the last moment the air seemed to hum with iron and flame as one by one, above the vampiric sky, the points of life went out.

TONY HARRISON
The Mother of the Muses

In memoriam Emmanuel Stratas,
born Crete 1903, died Toronto 1987

After I've lit the fire and looked outside
and found us snowbound and the roads all blocked,
anxious to prove my memory's not ossified
and the way into that storehouse still unlocked,
as it's easier to remember poetry,
I try to remember, but soon find it hard,
a speech from *Prometheus* a boy from Greece BC
scratched, to help him learn it, on a shard.

I remember the museum, and I could eke
his scratch marks out, and could complete
the . . . however many lines there were of Greek
and didn't think it then much of a feat.
But now, not that much later, when I find
the verses I once knew beyond recall
I resolve to bring all yesterday to mind,
our visit to your father, each fact, *all*.

Seeing the Home he's in 's made me obsessed
with remembering those verses I once knew
and setting myself this little memory test
I don't think, at the moment, I'll come through.
It's the Memory, Mother of the Muses, bit.
Prometheus, in words I do recall reciting
but can't quote now, and they're so apposite,
claiming he gave Mankind the gift of writing,

along with fire the Gods withheld from men
who'd lived like ants in caves deprived of light
they could well end up living in again
if we let what flesh first roasted on ignite
a Burning of the Books far more extreme
than any screeching Führer could inspire,
the dark side of the proud Promethean dream
our globe enveloped in his gift of fire.

He bequeathed to baker and to bombardier,
to help benighted men develop faster,
two forms of fire, the gentle one in here,
and what the *Luftwaffe* unleashed, *and* the Lancaster.
One beneficial and one baleful form,
the fire I lit a while since in the grate
that's keeping me, as I sit writing, warm
and what gutted Goethestrasse on this date,

beginning yesterday to be precise
and shown on film from forty years ago
in a Home for the Aged almost glazed with ice
and surrounded by obliterating snow.
We had the choice of watching on TV
Dresden destroyed, then watching its rebirth,
or, with the world outside too blizzardful to see,
live, the senile not long for this earth.

Piles of cracked ice tiles where ploughs try to push
the muddied new falls onto shattered slates,
the glittering shrapnel of grey frozen slush,
a blitz debris fresh snow obliterates
along with what was cleared the day before
bringing even the snowploughs to a halt.
And their lives are frozen solid and won't thaw
with no memory to fling its sparks of salt.

The outer world of blur reflects their inner,
these Rest Home denizens who don't quite know
whether they've just had breakfast, lunch, or dinner,
or stare, between three lunches, at the snow.
Long icicles from the low roof meet
the frozen drifts below and block their view
of flurry and blizzard in the snowed-up street
and of a sky that for a month has shown no blue.

Elsie's been her own optometrist,
measuring the daily way her sight declines
into a growing ball of flashing mist.
She trains her failing sight on outside signs:
the church's COME ALIVE IN '85!
the small hand on the *Export A* ad clock,
the flashing neon on the truck-stop dive
pulsing with strobe lights and jukebox rock,

the little red Scottie on the STOOP & SCOOP
but not the cute eye cast towards its rear,
the little rounded pile of heaped red poop
the owners are required to bend and clear.
To imagine herself so stooping is a feat
as hard as that of gymnasts she has seen
lissom in white leotards complete
in trampolining on the TV screen.

There's one with mashed dinner who can't summon
yet again the appetite to smear
the food about the shrunk face of a woman
weeping for death in her 92nd year.
And of the life she lived remembers little
and stares, like someone playing Kim's Game
at the tray beneath her nose that fills with spittle
whose bubbles fill with faces with no name.

Lilian, whose love made her decide
to check in with her mate who'd had a stroke,
lost all her spryness once her husband died . . .
He had a beautiful . . . all made of oak . . .
silk inside . . . brass handles . . . tries to find
alternatives . . . *that long thing where you lie*
for words like coffin that have slipped her mind
and forgetting, not the funeral, makes her cry.

And Anne, who treats her roommates to her 'news'
though every day her news is just the same
how she'd just come back from *such a lovely cruise*
to that famous island . . . I forget its name . . .
Born before the Boer War, me, and so
I'm too old to remember I suppose . . .
then tries again . . . *the island's called . . . you know . . .*
that place, you know . . . where everybody goes . . .

First Gene had one and then a second cane
and then, in weeks, a walker of cold chrome,
now in a wheelchair wails for the Ukraine,
sobbing in soiled pants for what was home.
Is that horror at what's on the TV screen
or just the way the stroke makes Jock's jaw hang?
Though nobody quite knows what his words mean
they hear Scots diphthongs in the New World twang.

And like the Irish Sea on Blackpool Beach,
where Joan was once the pick of bathing belles,
the Lancashire she once had in her speech
seeps into Canadian as she retells
whose legs now ooze out water, who can't walk,
how she was 'champion at tap', 'the flower'
(she poises the petals on the now frail stalk)
'of the ballet troupe at Blackpool Tower'.

You won't hear Gene, Eugene, Yevgeny speak
to nurses now, or God, in any other tongue
but his Ukrainian, nor your dad Greek,
all that's left to them of being young.
Life comes full circle when we die.
The circumference is finally complete,
so we shouldn't wonder too much why
his speech went back, a stowaway, to Crete.

Dispersal and displacement, willed or not,
from homeland to the room the three share here,
one Ukrainian, one Cretan, and one Scot
grow less Canadian as death draws near.
Jock sees a boozer in a Glasgow street,
and Eugene glittering icons, candles, prayer,
and for your dad a thorn-thick crag in Crete
with oregano and goat smells in the air.

And home? Where is it now? The olive grove
may well be levelled under folds of tar.
The wooden house made joyful with a stove
has gone the way of Tsar and samovar.
The small house with eight people to a room
with no privacy for quiet thought or sex
bulldozed in the island's tourist boom
to make way for Big Macs and discotheques.

Beribboned hats and bold embroidered sashes
once helped another émigré forget
that Canada was going to get his ashes
and that Estonia's still Soviet.
But now the last of those old-timers
couldn't tell one folk dance from another
and mistakes in the mists of his Alzheimer's
the nurse who wipes his bottom for his mother.

Some hoard memories as some hoard gold
against that rapidly approaching day
that's all they have to live on, being old,
but find their savings spirited away.
What's the point of having lived at all
in the much-snapped duplex in Etobicoke
if it gets swept away beyond recall,
in spite of all the snapshots, at one stroke?

If we *are* what we remember, what are they
who don't have memories as we have ours,
who, when evening falls, have no recall of day,
or who those people were who'd brought them flowers?
The troubled conscience, though, 's glad to forget.
Oblivion for some's an inner balm.
They've found some peace of mind, not total yet,
as only death itself brings that much calm.

And those white flashes on the TV screen,
as a child, whose dad plunged into genocide,
remembers Dresden and describes the scene,
are they from the firestorm then, or storm outside?
Crouching in clown's costume (it was *Fasching*)
aged, forty years ago, as I was, nine
Eva remembers cellar ceiling crashing
and her mother screaming shrilly: *Swine! Swine! Swine!*

The Tiergarten chief with level voice remembered
a hippo disembowelled on its back,
a mother chimp, her charges all dismembered,
and trees bedaubed with zebra flesh and yak.
Flamingos, flocking from burst cages, fly
in a frenzy with their feathers all alight
from fire on the ground to bomb-crammed sky,
their flames fanned that much fiercer by their flight;

the gibbon with no hands he'd had to shoot
as it came towards him with appealing stumps,
the gutless gorilla still clutching fruit
mashed with its bowels into bloody lumps . . .
I was glad as on and on the keeper went
to the last flayed elephant's fire-frantic screech
that the old folk hadn't followed what was meant
by official footage or survivors' speech.

But then they missed the Semper's restoration,
Dresden's lauded effort to restore
one of the treasures of the now halved nation
exactly as it was before the War.
Billions of marks and years of labour
to reproduce the Semper and they play
what they'd played before the bombs fell, Weber,
Der Freischütz, for their reopening today.

Each bleb of blistered paintwork, every flake
of blast-flayed pigment in that dereliction
they analysed in lab flasks to remake
the colours needed for the redepiction
of Poetic Justice on her cloud surmounting
mortal suffering from opera and play,
repainted tales that seem to bear recounting
more often than the facts that mark today:

the dead Cordelia in the lap of Lear,
Lohengrin who pilots his white swan
at cascading lustres of bright chandelier
above the plush this pantheon shattered on,
with Titania's leashed pards in pastiche Titian,
Faust with Mephisto, Joan, Nathan the Wise,
all were blown, on that allied bombing mission,
out of their painted clouds into the skies.

Repainted, reupholstered, all in place
just as it had been before that fatal night,
but however devilish the leading bass
his demons are outshadowed on this site.
But that's what Dresden wants and so they play
the same score sung by new uplifting voices
and, as opera synopses often say,
'The curtain falls as everyone rejoices.'

Next more TV, devoted to the trial
of Ernst Zundel, who denies the Jews were gassed,
and academics are supporting his denial,
restoring pride by doctoring the past,
and not just Germans but those people who
can't bear to think such things could ever be,
and by disbelieving horrors to be true
hope to put back hope in history.

A nurse comes in to offer us a cot
considering how bad the blizzard's grown
but you kissed your dad, who, as we left, forgot
he'd been anything all day but on his own.
We needed to escape, weep, laugh, and lie
in each other's arms more privately than there,
weigh in the balance all we're heartened by,
so braved the blizzard back, deep in despair.

Feet of snow went sliding off the bonnet
as we pulled onto the road from where we'd parked.
A snowplough tried to help us to stay on it
but localities nearby, once clearly marked,
those named for northern hometowns close to mine,
the Yorks, the Whitbys, and the Scarboroughs,
all seemed one whited-out recurring sign
that could well be 'Where everybody goes . . .'

His goggles bug-eyed from the driven snow
the balaclavaed salter goes ahead
with half the sower's, half the sandman's throw,
and follows the groaning plough with wary tread.
We keep on losing the blue revolving light
and the sliding salter, and try to keep on track
by making sure we always have in sight
the yellow Day-glo X marked on his back.

The blizzard made our neighbourhood unknown.
We could neither see behind us nor before.
We felt in that white-out world we were alone
looking for landmarks, lost, until we saw
the unmistakable McDonald's M
with its '60 billion served' hamburger count.
Living, we were numbered among them,
and dead, among an incomputable amount . . .

I woke long after noon with you still sleeping
and the windows blocked where all the snow had blown.
Your pillow was still damp from last night's weeping.
In that silent dark I swore I'd make it known,
while the oil of memory feeds the wick of life
and the flame from it's still constant and still bright,
that, come oblivion or not, I loved my wife
in that long thing where we lay with day like night.

Toronto's at a standstill under snow.
Outside there's not much light and not a sound.
Those lines from Aeschylus! How do they go?
It's almost halfway through *Prometheus Bound*.
I think they're coming back. I'm concentrating . . .
μουσομητορ 'ἔργανην . . . Damn! I forget,
but remembering your dad, I'm celebrating
being in love, not too forgetful, yet.

Country people used to say today's
the day the birds sense spring and choose their mates,
and trapped exotics in the Dresden blaze
were flung together in their flame-fledged fates.
The snow in the street outside 's at least 6ft.
I look for life, and find the only sign 's,
like words left for, or *by*, someone from Crete,
a bird's tracks, like blurred Greek, for Valentine's.

Toronto
St Valentine's Day

MICHAEL IGNATIEFF
Scar Tissue

I once saw a television documentary about the neurologist and surgeon Wilder Penfield, in which he opened the top of a woman's skull under local anaesthetic, exposing the glistening surfaces of her brain. He applied an electrical stimulus to a portion of her hippocampus, and the patient began talking in a low, faraway voice about an afternoon when she and her sister were on a garden swing and one of their feet caught their mother's tea set and sent it flying through the air onto the grass. It seemed wonderful that in the palpitating square of a woman's flesh was memory, the thing itself, the source of that disembodied whisper.

Penfield's experiments, conducted in the forties and fifties, appeared to prove that memory functions were localized in different segments of the brain. Procedural memory – the combination of skills necessary for riding a bicycle, for example – was held to be stored in one place; perceptual memory – what home looks like – was stored in another fold of tissue. How did neurologists know this? Because there were people who could still ride a bike, but couldn't remember the way home.

Localization of function also implied that the memory images stored in different parts of the brain were activated every time recollection occurred. This theory, which Penfield's experiments appeared to confirm, was surely the origin of my belief that my mother's memories were still intact, like a butterfly collection left behind in the attic of an abandoned house.

I began to think that there was something wrong with the idea that her memories were localized and that illness was obliterating them one by one. It was not that she was forgetting discrete events; she was unable to place herself in a meaningful sequence of those events. She knew who she once had been, but not who she had become. Her memories of childhood were intact, but her short-term recollection had collapsed, so that past and present were marooned far from each other.

I suspected that the breakdown in her memory was a symptom of a larger disruption in her ability to create and sustain a coherent image of herself over time. It dawned on me that her condition offered me an unrepeatable opportunity to observe the relation between selfhood and memory. I began to think of my mother as a philosophical problem.

My mistake had been to suppose that a memory image could subsist apart from an image of the self, that memories could persist apart from the act of speaking or thinking about them from a given standpoint. It was this junction between past and present that she was losing. She was wondering who the 'I' was in her own sentences. She was wondering whether these memories of a blue beer mug in a warm suburban garden were really her own. Because they no longer seemed to be her own, she began to throw them away.

In spite of this, her gestures, her smile, her voice remained unchanged. A blurred vision of her charm survived, together with hints of her sense of humour. She was suffering a disturbance of her soul, not just a loss of memory, yet *she* was still intact. I was back where I started.

My difficulties in understanding her were not made any easier by the jargon doctors used to describe her condition. What in my childhood had been called 'hardening of the arteries of the brain' was now called 'premature senile dementia'. The one was as absurd as the other. My mother was disturbed but she was anything but senile. Then the doctors took to calling her condition a disease. This, at least, had the merit of conferring clinical interest upon what, until then, had simply been regarded as the demented confusions of the elderly. When post-mortem examinations of these patients revealed a characteristic pattern of scar tissues in the neural fibres, doctors suddenly believed they had a clinical mystery to unravel.

However, the more that doctors discovered, the more puzzling the disease became. While the tangles and plaques – the scar tissue – did obstruct the neurochemical transmission of electrical messages in the brain, they also showed up in alert people whose symptoms were confined to the mild memory loss associated with normal ageing. Some experts weren't even sure whether the scars were a cause or consequence of the forgetting.

'I told you,' my brother, a doctor, said. 'There's a lot we don't know.'

'You don't tell the patients that.'

'I'm telling you. We're not there yet.'

And what about the interaction of heredity and environment? Some authorities maintained that clear evidence of genetic transmission was evident only in early onset cases. Others insisted that genetics was also the dominant factor in late onset cases like my mother's.

My brother must have got tired of fielding my questions and so he arranged for us to meet the big specialist in the city. I couldn't see why we were bothering, and I told him so.

'Don't you want to know?' he said.

'Know what?'

'Where we are. How much time there is.'

'Do you?'

'Besides,' I said, 'neurological investigations are humiliating. Urine samples, blood samples, X-rays, CAT scans, PET scans. Christ, what do we need this for?'

And so it proved. Mother was led, naked and uncomprehending, into a tiled room and sealed inside a machine that resembled one of those iron lungs in a B-movie. I stood in the control room, on the other side of the glass, watching her terrified glances as her head was placed inside an instrument to measure cerebral activity. Like a fool, I began to wave, though she couldn't see me. Her legs made small, struggling gestures of fear and a technician flicked on the intercom and told her not to. I stood there, beyond the glass, wanting to kill my brother for putting her through this. Then the sedation took hold and she lay awake but motionless, while a stream of images of the neurochemical activity within her brain flowed across the monitors in the control room. The technicians were talkative. They told me what to look for: bright blue for the skull casing, red for the cerebral lobes, purple for the tracer. I stood there watching brightly coloured neural images of Mother's fear and dread.

*

Three weeks later, we are all sitting in the neurologist's office getting the results, my father, my brother, my mother, and I. The doctor is a fashionable middle-aged woman who happens to be a paraplegic in a wheelchair. Beneath her desk I can see her withered legs in a pair of smart black stockings and buckled shoes. With guilty goodwill, I think here at last is someone who will understand.

Looking over the top of her bifocals, she says with a warm smile,

'How are we today?'

Mother says, 'We are fine today.'

'Good, good,' replies the doctor.

'So what's the situation?' my father asks, looking up from his hands.

The doctor smooths open the clinical file. 'Mother,' she says, 'is performing pretty well on some tests, not quite so well on others.'

It doesn't seem right to be talking about her in the third person when she is in the room. I glare at my brother, who rises and escorts Mother out. My brother and the doctor exchange a nod as Mother makes her laboured transit to the door.

When the door shuts behind her, the doctor resumes. 'The scans are confirming what you already know,' and here she gestures at the reports. 'Discernible shrinkage of the cerebellum, reduction in size and volume of hippocampus, possible evidence of cerebral trauma.'

At the word trauma, my father raises his eyes. 'Must be the car accident.'

'Tell me about that,' she says, taking up a pen. In the shattered silence after impact, I see my father's bloody face lying against the steering wheel and my mother's broken body slumped beside him. Words are resounding in my head, my brother is looking at me, his hands at his temples, blood streaming through his fingers.

The doctor says head trauma, in road accident victims and in boxers, can produce amnesias of Mother's sort. So head trauma is pencilled into her list of causative factors, beside heredity, environment, exposure to neuro-toxins. She says the more causes that can be enumerated, the more we are likely to understand. Actually, it seems to me, the more causes you can identify, the more mysterious her condition becomes; but I decide not to argue the point. 'Of course,' she goes on, 'the gold standard for all diagnosis in these cases is . . .'

'Autopsy,' I butt in.

A thought crosses her mind.

'So you know about these things?' she says, brightly. I nod and I don't know whether she is marking me down as one of those tedious neurological autodidacts or as a mature professional she can take into her confidence. Whatever she thinks, she knows I will be doing the talking. My father has withdrawn into a cave of silence.

I ask her the prognosis. She looks at my father's bent head and says, in a softer voice than before, 'Your wife will be dead in three years.'

My father sits with his hands on his knees as if steadying himself.

'I'm sorry,' she says.

She takes my father through the entire *via dolorosa* ahead: which function will break down when, how soon she will cease to recognize us, how soon epilepsy is likely to set in. There is no doubt that she believes such candour is a way of treating us with respect, and I feel grateful for it, but I keep thinking there must be some mistake. 'But each case is different.'

'There are recurrent features,' she begins.

'I mean, in some early onset cases, you do die in three years, but in late onset cases, the process can take longer, surely . . .'

She looks down at the papers on her desk. 'I'm looking at these scans.'

I shift tack. 'I used to think she was just falling apart. Now I think she has developed strategies of her own for dealing with this.'

The doctor nods. I see her place her hand on her knee and shift her inert leg and its fashionable shoe.

'Take the business about her language,' I say. 'She can't maintain a conversation, but the way she listens, and laughs when you say something that amuses her, nods to let you know she's following what you say.'

The doctor seems interested. 'Her semantic and syntactic memory functions have collapsed, but prosodic variation is still intact.'

'Prosodic variation?'

She means tone of voice, facial expression, gestures. Some patients begin to drawl or stutter in a voice they have never used before. 'They hear themselves speak,' she says, 'and they think who is this?'

'That's not Mother. She still knows who she is. She may not talk correctly, but she's still able to take part in a conversation. She still has her social skills.'

The doctor is good-naturedly persistent. 'Her prosodic variation is still intact.'

It is the word 'still' that bothers me.

'You keep telling me what has been lost, and I keep telling you something remains.'

'I just see what I see. From the clinical point of view,' the doctor says, looking at me over the tops of her bifocals. There is something admirable about this candour, about this refusal to indulge my hopes. Much against my will, I can't help but like her, though I can tell we see my mother so differently that there is no middle ground between us.

I want to say that my mother's true self remains intact, there at the surface of her being, like a feather resting on the surface tension of a glass of water, in the way she listens, nods, rests her hand on her cheek, when we are together. But I stumble along and just stop.

The doctor tries to help me out. 'This seems to matter to you.'

'Because,' I say, 'a lot depends on whether people like you treat her as a human being or not.'

She is too clever to rise to this. She deals with beleaguered and hostile relatives all the time. 'This is difficult for you. I know that. My job is to give you the facts.'

I wonder what my brother has told her about me, and why they both feel certain I need such an astringent dose of reality therapy. I change tack again. 'It's important not to humour her.'

'I never humour anyone.'

'She has to believe we understand her. Otherwise she'll just give up.'

'*Do* you understand?'

'Sometimes, sometimes not.'

'Well, isn't that humouring her?' she parries.

'So I pretend,' I reply. 'She needs respect,' I say, unsure why I am saying it.

'Of course.' And then she says, reflectively, 'Though who knows what respect means.'

'Just giving her the benefit of the doubt. Just assuming there might be some method in the madness.'

The doctor smiles. 'So act "as if" she is rational. Behave "as if" she knows what she is saying.'

'Exactly.'

I tell her how Mother goes in and out of the bathroom five times an hour. Because she does not want to wet herself but can't tell when she last went to the bathroom. So her strategy is to behave 'as if' she needs to go to the bathroom, whenever the thought occurs to her. There is a method here. This is not just random, panic-stricken behaviour. Self-respect is in play here. This is how she manages to avoid making a mess of herself. My voice rises at this point and both of us go silent.

'From a clinical point of view,' she says, taking up the thread, 'disinhibition begins with disintegration in the frontal lobes. Your mother's frontal lobes are not yet affected,' the neurologist goes on, 'which would help to explain why she is continent and why she is gentle.'

'She's gentle,' I say, 'because that's the kind of person she is.'

'I know how you must feel.'

'Besides,' I say, 'disinhibition is an ugly word.'

'I know,' she said, with a nod in the direction of the hospital wards somewhere down the corridor. Those wards are brimful of disinhibition. It is this doctor's life.

'Disinhibition suggests everything is just beyond her. Actually, she is struggling.'

The neurologist looks at me evenly, as if debating whether to despatch this illusion as well. She must have heard it from relatives a thousand times before. She decides to say nothing. It doesn't matter. I change tack once more.

'You sound like my brother.'

'I'll take that as a compliment,' she says.

'I mean it.' Our smiles declare a truce.

It is pointless to go on and we both know it. The doctor looks at Mother's PET scans and sees a disease of memory function, with a stable name and a clear prognosis. I see an illness of self-hood, without a name or even a clear cause.

My father is becoming restive, as if wishing to remind us that we are arguing about his wife.

The doctor reaches into a drawer in her desk and takes out a form. She fills in something at the top and then passes it across the desk to my father.

'I would like to include your wife in our study. The clinical picture she presents will be of great interest to us.' She touches the form with a red fingernail. 'I'll need your consent on her behalf.'

'Consent for what?'

'To allow us to remove her brain following autopsy for special study here at the clinic.'

My father looks down at his hands for a moment and then, drawing in his breath like someone about to lift a heavy load, raises himself to his full height. He picks the paper off the desk and flicks it back at her with a brisk gesture of contempt. Then he strides out of the room.

VIII

Lives

ALAN BENNETT
The Lady in the Van

'I ran into a snake this afternoon,' Miss Shepherd said. 'It was coming up Parkway. It was a long, grey snake – a boa constrictor possibly. It looked poisonous. It was keeping close to the wall and seemed to know its way. I've a feeling it may have been heading for the van.' I was relieved that on this occasion she didn't demand that I ring the police, as she regularly did if anything out of the ordinary occurred. Perhaps this was too out of the ordinary (though it turned out the pet shop in Parkway had been broken into the previous night, so she may have seen a snake). She brought her mug over and I made her a drink, which she took back to the van. 'I thought I'd better tell you,' she said, 'just to be on the safe side. I've had some close shaves with snakes.'

This encounter with the putative boa constrictor was in the summer of 1971, when Miss Shepherd and her van had for some months been at a permanent halt opposite my house in Camden Town. I had first come across her a few years previously, stood by her van, stalled as usual, near the convent at the top of the street. The convent (which was to have a subsequent career as the Japanese School) was a gaunt reformatory-like building that housed a dwindling garrison of aged nuns and was notable for a striking crucifix attached to the wall overlooking the traffic lights. There was something about the position of Christ, pressing himself against the grim pebbledash beneath the barred windows of the convent, that called up visions of the Stalag and the searchlight and which had caused us to dub him 'The Christ of Colditz'. Miss Shepherd, not looking un-crucified herself, was standing by her vehicle in an attitude with which I was to become very familiar, left arm extended with the palm flat against the side of the van indicating ownership, the right arm summoning anyone who was fool enough to take notice of her, on this occasion me. Nearly six foot, she was a commanding figure, and would have been more so had she not been kitted out in a greasy raincoat, orange skirt, Ben Hogan golfing cap, and carpet slippers. She would be going on sixty at this time.

She must have prevailed on me to push the van as far as Albany Street, though I recall nothing of the exchange. What I do remember was being overtaken by two policemen in a panda car as I trundled the van across Gloucester Bridge; I thought that, as the van was certainly holding up the traffic, they might have lent a hand. They were wiser than I knew. The other feature of this first run-in with Miss Shepherd was her driving technique. Scarcely had I put my shoulder to the back of the van, an old Bedford, than a long arm was stretched elegantly out of the driver's window to indicate in textbook fashion that she (or rather I) was moving off. A few yards further on, as we were about to turn into Albany Street, the arm emerged again, twirling elaborately in the air to indicate that we were branching left, the movement done with such boneless grace that this section of the Highway Code might have been choreographed by Petipa with Ulanova at the wheel. Her 'I am coming to a halt' was less poised, as she had plainly not expected me to give up pushing and shouted angrily back that it was the other end of Albany Street she wanted, a mile further on. But I had had enough by this time and left her there, with no thanks for my trouble. Far from it. She even climbed out of the van and came running after me, shouting that I had no business abandoning her, so that passers-by looked at me as if I had done some injury to this pathetic scarecrow. 'Some people!' I suppose I thought, feeling foolish that I'd been taken for a ride (or taken her for one) and cross that I'd fared worse than if I'd never lifted a finger, these mixed feelings to be the invariable aftermath of any transaction involving Miss Shepherd. One seldom was able to do her a good turn without some thoughts of strangulation.

It must have been a year or so after this, and so some time in the late sixties, that the van first appeared in Gloucester Crescent. In those days the street was still a bit of a mixture. Its large semi-detached villas had originally been built to house the Victorian middle class, then it had gone down in the world, and, though it had never entirely decayed, many of the villas degenerated into rooming-houses and so were among the earliest candidates for what is now called 'gentrification' but which was then called 'knocking through'. Young professional couples, many of them in journalism or television, bought up the houses, converted them and (an invariable feature of such conversions) knocked the basement rooms together to form a large kitchen/dining room. In the mid-sixties I wrote a BBC TV series, *Life in NW1*, based on one such family, the Stringalongs, whom Mark Boxer then took over to people a cartoon strip in the *Listener*, and who kept cropping up in his drawings for the rest of his life. What made the social set-up funny was the disparity between the style in which the new arrivals found themselves able to live and their progressive opinions: guilt, put simply, which today's gentrifiers are said famously not to feel (or 'not to have a problem about'). We did have a problem, though I'm not sure we were any better for it. There was a gap between our social position and our social obligations. It was in this gap that Miss Shepherd (in her van) was able to live.

October 1969. When she is not in the van Miss S. spends much of her day sitting on the pavement in Parkway, where she has a pitch outside Williams & Glyn's Bank. She sells tracts, entitled 'True View: Mattering Things', which she writes herself, though this isn't something she will admit. 'I sell them, but so far as the authorship is concerned I'll say they are anonymous and that's as far as I'm prepared to go.' She generally chalks the gist of the current pamphlet on the pavement, though with no attempt at artistry. 'St Francis FLUNG money from him' is today's message, and prospective customers have to step over it to get into the bank. She also makes a few coppers selling pencils. 'A gentleman came the other day and said that the pencil he had bought from me was the best pencil on the market at the present time. It lasted him three months. He'll be back for another one shortly.' D., one of the more conventional neighbours (and not a knocker-through), stops me and says, 'Tell me, is she a *genuine* eccentric?'

April 1970. Today we moved the old lady's van. An obstruction order has been put under the windscreen wiper, stating that it was stationed outside number 63 and is a danger to public health. This order, Miss S. insists, is a statutory order: 'And statutory means standing – in this case standing outside number 63 – so, if the van is moved on, the order will be invalid.' Nobody ventures to argue with this, but she can't decide whether her next pitch should be outside number 61 or further on. Eventually she decides there is 'a nice space' outside 62 and plumps for that. Nick Tomalin and I heave away at the back of the van, but while she is gracefully indicating that she is moving off (for all of the fifteen feet) the van doesn't budge. 'Have you let the handbrake off?' Nick Tomalin asks. There is a pause. 'I'm just in the process of taking it off.' As we are poised for the move, another Camden Town eccentric materializes, a tall, elderly figure in long overcoat and Homburg hat, with a distinguished grey moustache and in his buttonhole a flag for the Primrose League. He takes off a grubby canary glove and leans a shaking hand against the rear of the van (OLU246), and when we have moved it forward the few statutory feet he puts on his glove again, saying, 'If you should need me I'm just round the corner' (i.e. in Arlington House, the working men's hostel).

I ask Miss S. how long she has had the van. 'Since 1956,' she says, 'though don't spread that around. I got it to put my things in. I came down from St Albans in it, and plan to go back there eventually. I'm just pedalling water at the moment. I've always been in the transport line. Chiefly delivery and chauffeuring. You know,' she says mysteriously – 'renovated army vehicles. And I've got good topography. I always have had. I knew Kensington in the blackout.'

June 1971. Scarcely a day passes now without some sort of incident involving the old lady. Yesterday evening around ten a sports car swerves over to her side of the road so that the driver, rich, smart, and in his twenties, can lean over and bang on the side of the van, presumably to flush out for his grinning girlfriend the old witch who lives there. I shout at him and he sounds his horn and roars off. Miss S. of course wants the police called, but I can't see the point, and indeed around five this morning I wake to find two policemen at much the same game, idly shining their torches in the windows in the hope that she'll wake up and enliven a dull hour of their beat. Tonight a white car reverses dramatically up the street, screeches to a halt beside the van, and a burly young man jumps out and gives the van a terrific shaking. Assuming (hoping, probably) he would have driven off by the time I get outside, I find he's still there, and ask him what the fuck he thinks he's doing. His response is quite mild. 'What's up with you then?' he asks. 'You still on the telly? You nervous? You're trembling all over.' He then calls me a fucking cunt and drives off. After all that, of course, Miss S. isn't in the van at all, so I end up as usual more furious with her than I am with the lout.

These attacks, I'm sure, disturbed my peace of mind more than they did hers. Living in the way she did, every day must have brought such cruelties. Some of the stallholders in the Inverness Street market used to persecute her with medieval relish – and children too, who both inflict and suffer such casual cruelties themselves. One night two drunks systematically smashed all the windows of the van, the flying glass cutting her face. Furious over any small liberty, she was only mildly disturbed by this. 'They may have had too much to drink by mistake,' she said. 'That does occur through not having eaten, possibly. I don't want a case.' She was far more interested in 'a ginger feller I saw in Parkway in company with Mr Khrushchev. Has he disappeared recently?'

But to find such sadism and intolerance so close at hand began actively to depress me, and having to be on the alert for every senseless attack made it impossible to work. There came a day when, after a long succession of such incidents, I suggested that she spend at least the nights in a lean-to at the side of my house. Initially reluctant, as with any change, over the next two years she gradually abandoned the van for the hut.

In giving her sanctuary in my garden and landing myself with a tenancy that went on eventually for fifteen years, I was never under any illusion that the impulse was purely charitable. And, of course, it made me furious that I had been driven to such a pass. But I wanted a quiet life as much as, and possibly more than, she did. In the garden she was at least out of harm's way.

The old van was towed away in April 1974 and another one provided by Lady W. ('a titled Catholic lady', as Miss S. always referred to her). Happy to run to a new (albeit old) van, Lady W. was understandably not anxious to have it parked outside her front door and eventually, and perhaps by now inevitably, the van and Miss S. ended up in my garden. This van was road-worthy, and Miss S. insisted on being the one to drive it through the gate into the garden, a manoeuvre which once again enabled her to go through her full repertoire of hand signals. Once the van was on site Miss S. applied the handbrake with such deter-mination that, like Excalibur, it could never therefore be released, rusting so firmly into place that when the van came to be moved ten years later it had to be hoisted over the wall by the council crane.

This van (and its successor, bought in 1983) now occupied a paved area between my front door and the garden gate, the bon-net of the van hard by my front step, its rear door, which Miss S. always used to get in and out of, a few feet from the gate. Callers at the house had to squeeze past the back of the van and come down the side, and while they waited for my door to be opened they would be scrutinized from behind the murky wind-screen by Miss Shepherd. If they were unlucky, they would find the rear door open with Miss S. dangling her large white legs over the back. The interior of the van, a midden of old clothes, plastic bags, and half-eaten food, was not easy to ignore, but should anyone Miss S. did not know venture to speak to her she would promptly tuck her legs back and wordlessly shut the door. For the first few years of her sojourn in the garden I would try and explain to mystified callers how this situation had arisen, but after a while I ceased to care and when I didn't mention it nor did anyone else.

December 1974. Miss S. had been explaining to me why the old Bedford (the van not the music hall) ceased to go, 'possibly'. She had put in some of her home-made petrol, based on a recipe for

petrol substitute she read about several years ago in a newspaper. 'It was a spoonful of petrol, a gallon of water, and a
pinch of something you could get in every High Street. Well, I
got it into my head, I don't know why, that it was bicarbonate
of soda, only I think I was mistaken. It must be either sodium
chloride or sodium nitrate, only I've since been told sodium
chloride is salt and the man in Boots wouldn't sell me the other,
saying it might cause explosions. Though I think me being an
older person he knew I would be more responsible. Though not
all old ladies perhaps.'

June 1977. On this the day of the Jubilee, Miss S. has stuck a
paper Union Jack in the cracked back window of the van. It is
the only one in the Crescent. Yesterday she was wearing a head-
scarf and pinned across the front of it a blue Spontex sponge
fastened at each side with a large safety pin, the sponge meant
to form some kind of peak against the (very watery) sun. It
looked like a favour worn by a medieval knight, or a fillet to
ward off evil spirits. Still, it was better than last week's effort,
an Afrika Korps cap from Lawrence Corner: Miss Shepherd –
Desert Fox.

June 1980. Miss S. has gone into her summer rig: a raincoat
turned inside out, with brown canvas panels and a large label
declaring it the Emerald Weatherproof. This is topped off with
a lavender chiffon scarf tied round a sun visor made from an old
cornflakes packet. She asks me to do her some shopping. 'I want
a small packet of Eno's, some milk, and some jelly babies. The
jelly babies aren't urgent. Oh and, Mr Bennett, could you get
me one of those little bottles of whisky? I believe Bell's is very
good. I don't drink it – I just use it to rub on.'

February 1981. Miss S. has flu, so I am doing her shopping. I
wait every morning by the side window of the van and, with the
dark interior and her grimy hand holding back the tattered
purple curtain, it is as if I am at the confessional. The chief
items this morning are ginger nuts ('very warming') and grape
juice. 'I think this is what they must have been drinking at

Cana,' she says as I hand her the bottle. 'Jesus wouldn't have wanted them rolling about drunk, and this is non-alcoholic. It wouldn't do for everyone, but in my opinion it's better than champagne.'

February 1983. A. telephones me in Yorkshire to say that the basement is under three inches of water, the boiler having burst. When told that the basement has been flooded, Miss S.'s only comment is, 'What a waste of water.'

April 1983. 'I've been having bad nights,' says Miss S., 'but if I were elected I might have better nights.' She wants me to gather nomination papers so that she can stand for Parliament in the coming election. She would be the Fidelis Party candidate. The party, never very numerous, is now considerably reduced. Once she could count on five votes but now there are only two, one of whom is me, and I don't like to tell her I'm in the SDP. Still, I promise to write to the town hall for nomination papers. 'There's no kitty as yet,' she says, 'and I wouldn't want to do any of the meeting people. I'd be no good at that. The secretaries can do that (you get expenses). But I'd be very good at voting – better than they are, probably.'

October 1984. Some new stair carpet fitted today. Spotting the old carpet being thrown out, Miss S. says it would be just the thing to put on the roof of the van to deaden the sound of rain. This exchange comes just as I am leaving for work, but I say that I do not want the van festooned with bits of old carpet – it looks bad enough as it is. When I come back in the evening I find half the carpet remnants slung over the roof. I ask Miss S. who has put them there, as she can't have done it herself. 'A friend,' she says mysteriously. 'A well-wisher.' Enraged, I pull down a token piece but the majority of it stays put.

March 1987. The nuns up the road – or, as Miss S. always refers to them, 'the sisters' – have taken to doing some of her shopping. One of them leaves a bag on the back step of the van this morning. There are the inevitable ginger nuts and several packets of sanitary towels. I can see these would be difficult articles for her to ask me to get, though to ask a nun to get them would seem quite hard for her too. They form some part of her elaborate toilet arrangements, and are occasionally to be seen laid drying across the soup-encrusted electric ring. As the postman says this morning, 'The smell sometimes knocks you back a bit.'

May 1987. Miss S. wants to spread a blanket over the roof (in addition to the bit of carpet) in order to deaden the sound of the rain. I point out that within a few weeks it will be dank and disgusting. 'No,' she says, 'weather-beaten.'

She has put a Conservative poster in the side window of the van. The only person who can see it is me.

This morning she was sitting at the open door of the van and as I edge by she chucks out an empty packet of Ariel. The blanket hanging over the pushchair is covered in washing powder. 'Have you spilt it?' I enquire. 'No,' she says crossly, irritated at having to explain the obvious. 'That's washing powder. When it rains, the blanket will get washed.' As I work at my table now I can see her bending over the pushchair, picking at bits of soap flakes and redistributing them over the blanket. No rain is at the moment forecast.

July 1987. Miss S. (bright green visor, purple skirt, brown cardigan, turquoise fluorescent ankle socks) punts her way out through the gate in the wheelchair in a complicated manoeuvre which would be much simplified did she just push the chair out, as well she can. A passer-by takes pity on her, and she is whisked down to the market. Except not quite whisked, because the journey is made more difficult than need be by Miss S.'s refusal to take her feet off the ground, so the Good Samaritan finds himself pushing a wheelchair continually slurred and braked by these large, trailing, carpet-slippered feet. Her legs are so thin now the feet are as slack and flat as those of a camel.

Still, there will be one moment to relish on this, as on all these journeys. When she has been pushed back from the market, she will tell (and it is tell: there is never any thanks) whoever is pushing the chair to leave her opposite the gate but on the crown of the road. Then, when she thinks no one is looking, she lifts her feet, pushes herself off, and freewheels the few yards down to the gate. The look on her face is one of pure pleasure.

January 1988. I ask Miss S. if it was her birthday yesterday. She agrees guardedly. 'So you're seventy-seven.' 'Yes. How did you know?' 'I saw it once when you filled out the census form.' I give her a bottle of whisky, explaining that it's just to rub on. 'Oh. Thank you.' Pause. 'Mr Bennett. Don't tell anybody.' 'About the whisky?' 'No. About my birthday.' Pause. 'Mr Bennett.' 'Yes?' 'About the whisky either.'

March 1988. 'I've been doing a bit of spring cleaning,' says Miss S., kneeling in front of a Kienholz-like tableau of filth and decay. She says she has been discussing the possibility of a bungalow with the social worker, to which she would be prepared to contribute 'a few hundred or so'. It's possible that the bungalow might be made of asbestos, 'but I could wear a mask. I wouldn't mind that, and of course it would be much better from the fire point of view.' Hands in mittens made from old socks, a sanitary towel drying over the ring, and a glossy leaflet from the Halifax offering 'fabulous investment opportunities'.

March 1989. There is a thin layer of talcum powder around the back door of the van and odd bits of screwed-up tissues smeared with what may or may not be shit, though there is no doubt about the main item of litter, which is a stained incontinence pad. My method of retrieving these items would not be unfamiliar at Sellafield. I don rubber gloves, put each hand inside a plastic bag as an additional protection, then, having swept the faecal artefacts together, gingerly pick them up and put them in the bin. 'Those aren't all my rubbish,' comes a voice from the van. 'Some of them blow in under the gate.'

April 1989. Miss S. has asked me to telephone the social services, and I tell her that a social worker will be calling. 'What time?' 'I don't know. But you're not going to be out. You haven't been out for a week.' 'I might be. Miracles do happen. Besides, she may not be able to talk to me. I may not be at the door end of the van. I might be at the other end.' 'So she can talk to you there.' 'And what if I'm in the middle?'

Miss C. thinks Miss S.'s heart is failing. She calls her Mary. I find this strange, though it is of course her name.

April 1989. A staple of Miss S.'s shopping list these days is sherbet lemons. I have a stock of them in the house, but she insists I invest in yet more so that a perpetual supply of sherbet lemons may never be in doubt. 'I'm on them now. I don't want to have to go off them.'

I ask her if she would like a cup of coffee. 'Well, I wouldn't want you to go to all that trouble. I'll just have half a cup.'

27 April 1989. A red ambulance calls to take Miss S. to the day centre. Miss B. talks to her for a while in the van, gradually coaxing her out and into the wheelchair, shit streaks over her swollen feet, a piece of toilet roll clinging to one scaly ankle. 'And if I don't like it,' she keeps asking, 'can I come back?' I reassure her, but, looking at the inside of the van and trying to cope with the stench, I find it hard to see how she can go on living here much longer. Once she sees the room they are offering her, the bath, the clean sheets, I can't imagine her wanting to come back. And indeed she makes more fuss than usual about locking the van door, which suggests she accepts that she may not be returning. I note how, with none of my distaste, the ambulance driver bends over her as he puts her on the hoist, his careful rearrangement of her greasy clothing, pulling her skirt down over her knees in the interest of modesty. The chair goes on the hoist, and slowly she rises and comes into view above the level of the garden wall and is wheeled into the ambulance. There is a certain distinction about her as she leaves, a Dorothy Hodgkin of vagabonds, a derelict Nobel Prize-winner, the heavy folds of her grimy face set in a kind of resigned satisfaction. She may even be enjoying herself.

When she has gone I walk round the van noting the occasions of our battle: the carpet tiles she managed to smuggle on to the roof, the blanket strapped on to muffle the sound of the rain, the black bags under the van stuffed with her old clothes – sites of skirmishes all of which I'd lost. Now I imagine her bathed and bandaged and cleanly clothed and starting a new life. I even see myself visiting and taking flowers.

This fantasy rapidly fades when around 2.30 Miss S. reappears, washed and in clean clothes, it's true, and with a long pair of white hospital socks over her shrunken legs, but obviously very pleased to be back. She has a telephone number where her new friends can be contacted, and she gives it to me. 'They can be reached,' she says, 'any time – even over the holiday. They're on a long-distance bleep.'

As I am leaving for the theatre, she bangs on the door of the van with her stick. I open the door. She is lying wrapped in clean white sheets on a quilt laid over all the accumulated filth and rubbish of the van. She is still worrying that I will have her taken to hospital. I tell her there's no question of it and that she can stay as long as she wants. I close the door, but there is another bang and I reassure her again. Once more I close the door, but she bangs again. 'Mr Bennett.' I have to strain to hear. 'I'm sorry the van's in such a state. I haven't been able to do any spring cleaning.'

28 April. I am working at my table when I see Miss B. arrive with a pile of clean clothes for Miss S., which must have been washed for her at the day centre yesterday. Miss B. knocks at the door of the van, then opens it, looks inside and – something nobody has ever done before – gets in. It's only a moment before she comes out, and I know what has happened before she rings the bell. We go back to the van where Miss S. is dead, lying on her left side, flesh cold, face gaunt, the neck stretched out as if for the block, and a bee buzzing round her body.

It is a beautiful day, with the garden glittering in the sunshine, strong shadows by the nettles, and bluebells out under the wall, and I remember how in her occasional moments of contemplation she would sit in the wheelchair and gaze at the garden. I am filled with remorse for my harsh conduct towards her, though I know at the same time that it was not harsh. But still I never quite believed or chose to believe she was as ill as she was, and I regret too all the questions I never asked her. Not that she would have answered them. I have a strong impulse to stand at the gate and tell anyone who passes.

Miss B. meanwhile goes off and returns with a nice doctor from St Pancras who seems scarcely out of her teens. She gets into the van, takes the pulse in Miss S.'s outstretched neck, checks her with a stethoscope and, to save an autopsy, certifies death as from heart failure. Then comes the priest to bless her before she is taken to the funeral parlour, and he, too, gets into the van – the third person to do so this morning, and all of them without distaste or ado in what to me seem three small acts of heroism. Stooping over the body, his bright white hair brushing the top of the van, the priest murmurs an inaudible prayer and makes a cross on Miss S.'s hands and head. Then they all go off and I come inside to wait for the undertakers.

I have been sitting at my table for ten minutes before I realize that the undertakers have been here all the time, and that death nowadays comes (or goes) in a grey Ford transit van that is standing outside the gate. There are three undertakers, two young and burly, the third older and more experienced – a sergeant, as it were, and two corporals. They bring out a rough grey-painted coffin, like a prop a conjuror might use, and, making no comment on the surely extraordinary circumstances in which they find it, put a sheet of white plastic bin-liner over the body and manhandle it into their magic box, where it falls with a bit of a thud. Across the road, office workers stroll down from the Piano Factory for their lunch, but nobody stops or even looks much, and the Asian woman who has to wait while the box is carried over the pavement and put in the (other) van doesn't give it a backward glance.

Later I go round to the undertakers to arrange the funeral, and the manager apologizes for their response when I had originally phoned. A woman had answered, saying, 'What exactly is it you want?' Not thinking callers rang undertakers with a great variety of requests, I was nonplussed. Then she said briskly, 'Do you want someone taking away?' The undertaker explains that her seemingly unhelpful manner was because she thought my call wasn't genuine. 'We get so many hoaxes these days. I've often gone to collect a corpse only to have it open the door.'

In the interval between Miss Shepherd's death and her funeral ten days later I found out more about her life than I had in twenty years. She had indeed driven ambulances during the war, and was either blown up or narrowly escaped death when a bomb exploded nearby. I'm not sure that her eccentricity can be put down to this any more than to the legend, mentioned by one of the nuns, that it was the death of her fiancé in this incident that 'tipped her over'. It would be comforting to think that it is love, or the death of it, that unbalances the mind, but I think her early attempts to become a nun and her repeated failures ('too argumentative', one of the sisters said) point to a personality that must already have been quite awkward when she was a girl. After the war she spent some time in mental hospitals, but regularly absconded, finally remaining at large long enough to establish her competence to live unsupervised.

The turning-point in her life came when, through no fault of hers, a motorcyclist crashed into the side of her van. If her other vans were any guide, this one too would only have been insured in heaven, so it's not surprising she left the scene of the accident ('skedaddled', she would have said) without giving her name or address. The motorcyclist subsequently died, so that, while blameless in the accident, by leaving the scene of it she had committed a criminal offence. The police mounted a search for her. Having already changed her first name when she became a novice, now under very different circumstances she changed her second and, calling herself Shepherd, made her way back to Camden Town and the vicinity of the convent where she had taken her vows. And though in the years to come she had little to do with the nuns, or they with her, she was never to stray far from the convent for the rest of her life.

All this I learned in those last few days. It was as if she had been a character in Dickens whose history has to be revealed and her secrets told in the general setting-to-rights before the happy-ever-after, though all that this amounted to was that at long last I could bring my car into the garden to stand now where the van stood all those years.

SIMON ARMITAGE
A Painted Bird for Thomas Szasz

It was his anorak that first attracted me.
The foam lining was hanging from a split seam
and a tear that ran the length of his back was patched
with sellotape and sticking plaster. So I watched
as he flitted between the front seats of the bus
and fingered the synthetic fur around his hood.

The next time I noticed was at the terminus
where he was pretending to direct the buses.
From then there was a catalogue of incidents,
moments and locations where we coincided,
and each time I watched him talking to the drivers
who ignored him, and jotting down the route numbers.

One particular time he was in the arcade
eyeing the intricacy of a timetable.
He caught me watching the reflection of his face
so he exhaled onto the surface of the glass
and wrote his name on it. Billy. I passed by him,
breathing in, and he smelt like a wet dog, drying.

Another time I noticed more than I meant to
was a lunchtime at the Probation Day Centre
where I squinted through the gap in the serving hatch
to see him watching the traffic on the bypass.
His focus settled on a simple bicycle
which he followed till it slipped below the skyline.

I also saw him, once, in the covered precinct
pissing himself through his pants onto the concrete
and fumbling with the zip on his anorak.
He bothered me, and later I had to walk back
across where the dark circle of his stain had grown
and was still growing, slowly, outward, like a town.

Candia McWilliam
You Can't Be Too Clean

I'm the woman who lives on the step of the bank and eats soap. That's my name and how they speak of me when they fold away their eyes and move a wee bit aways off their track even though it's the bank they've come to see and they'll have to pass me. Often I see them holding their noses without even lifting their hands, which is odd, because I think you can't be too clean.

I've other names but they're put away and I can't see when they'll come out again, for they're locked up in the other bodies I was. For the moment I live on the step of the bank, unless it's winter when I get a bit closer and move in between the portals. Dogs'll not pee there, it's too skeetery. It's mosaic on the floor between the portals, very smooth till you lie on it and then it's all small corners and you lose the picture in close-up like that. If you stand away from it you can see that there's a picture of a woman all made of squares pocketing her wages with the help of a lion and an owl also made from these small hard tiles, each with the four corners when you lie on it. I settle down after the bank's stopped getting visits. Then God's in his small corner and I in mine. I can take the mosaic if I put my blanket down on it. This blanket is the main thing. The blanket and the soap.

This blanket I brought with me out of the first life and right through the other ones up till now. It has covered the many forms of nakedness I have lived inside as the time and the place changed. The blanket had its moment of glory in the shop, where it was part of the list of things I thought came with being married and the one I was about to marry agreed and marked the box next to 'pure wool Witney blanket, 72″ × 84″, cream, satin bound' with a '6'. We'd a house with three double beds that soon. Maybe it was then I should have heard a red light. All the beds got used, so the wastage didn't seem like it might to me now I've been poured through the many lives. We'd people in to lie under those blankets several times a year, and we

kept the beds ready to be made up, covered with white coun-
terpanes over the mattress protectors, the folded blankets, and
the sleeping naked pillows.

The quantities of unused linen, clean and folded, that lay
ready for use then makes me feel weak like remembering kisses
used to. It all comes up into my chest and heart and I raise up
my head and smile right deep into the eyes of what's in my mind
– and it's clean sheets in there, clean sheets radiating whiteness,
and the smell of soap you'd so much of you kept it folded in its
paper between the heavy cold sheets, the scented soap just lying
there ready among the sheets that were ready too, waiting to be
extracted, flung and soothed over beds that were aired three
times a week and mattresses that were turned each month.

I think of the stuff I've used up without thinking as I've gone
through and I wonder how the world can take it, the weight of
materials needed for a person to live a modern life.

The other moments of glory belonging to the blanket are
various and include some happiness. Its label is soft now and it's
only got threads going across the way. The sheeny blue and
yellow words about Made in England have all unwound from
the sturdy threads. It's a blanket from the time of market towns
and church attendance.

For sleeping in the threshold of a bank, though, a city like this
is by some way superior to a market town, where there's not
enough to do so then they turn to those of us who repose out-
doors in most weather conditions.

The blanket came in a lorry from a shop to the first house,
boxed up with five others and paid for by a guest at the
wedding who had hopes of some business arrangement with my
intended loosely to do with an implement for crushing used
cans. Later he went away for a while and while he was away
doing that his wife took the first quite big overdose but he got
out with a discreet companion from the right side of the law for
a couple of days of compassion during which she achieved a
more efficient job of counting and succeeded in her ambition so
then he received a little more leave during which arrangements
were made for the children who became swiftly used to the
habits of their grandparents and learned how to turn off lights

and keep their voices down.

So in the end they got a good education though I was worried lately when I saw in one of those catalogues that people don't notice falling out of their magazines as they walk along looking at the shiny pages for what to buy next that someone else has brought out a contraption for crushing used cans, not the man who introduced the blankets into my life, or I should say, the blanket. *Empty* used cans, these machines can compress, though few householders understand empty in its full form, meaning containing nothing, not a scrape, not a lick, not a wipe or a dribble of food.

I cut out food practically when I achieved my present way of life, though I keep up my fat intake with the soap and have managed to rectify my dreams at one and the same time, the soap giving a safe taste to dreaming. It's probably not an indigestible food and of course you sleep all clean inside. I'll take you through that when I've set it all straight about the blanket. Soap leaves nothing lying around inside you, that much I'll say. Inside me it's calm and empty as a basin.

At the time of receiving my blanket I did not pay it sufficient attention. I slept under it, certainly, or under what may have been only one of its fellow blankets, that were so like it, but at that time I slept under my blanket, or even, in winter, blankets, with the intervention of a sheet. On top of it all, like cream over a sweet and rich pudding, lay a sack of feathers sewn into furrows and trapped in there with flowers printed onto cloth.

The depicted flowers that were so plentiful in that first married house didn't do more than give it pattern and colour at first. There was no scent of course. A shocking absence of decay soon gave a hint of the truth about these blooms. They turned their heads at me, the roses, the lilies, the auriculas, and gillyflowers, and watched and turned again to each other to pass remarks on the state of my appearance and see how I compared with them in being pressed into flatness and colour and odourlessness.

They talked at first only when I was out of the room. The harebells on the cushions confided in the curtain hydrangeas, the ivy on the trellis silk-screened on the paper throughout the hall began to close over the areas of white; so I grew short of light and air while the leaves approached one another to exchange the words the flowers and leaves all spoke from the walls and windows and beds of the house where I had been taken to live. The flowers despised my changeability, my moods, my unreliable way of being alive. They were unchanging, open always even in the absence of sun, firmly forward-looking.

I had worked out the way out of the bower by then. I lit it up to shut it up. The fire was stubby and noisy and I was right – it did talk louder than the flowers. Soon after it had started to win, though, he arrived home from where he went in the day and duffed it up with a blanket. But it left a good gasp of smoke choking each flower in the room where I was meant to sleep, so at least that kept them quiet overnight while I pruned all the chintz curtains downstairs and took the throats out of the floral cushions, which got me peace of a kind when he drove me in the car at night against all these lights coming at you with the promise of colour over your face coming in stripes till you felt it must lie over you in ribbons and I parted the ribbons of light I'd collected in the back of the car and walked out into the place where they sorted the first body I'd had and ushered in the next one which began after the doctor lay me down and helped me to sleep without talking or behaving at all like a flower and even replaced the blanket after. My own blanket.

The place had a room for sitting and a chair for sitting too in that room for sitting, also a television and a notebook for writing what you wanted to watch in. There were people staying there wanted to watch things I can't stop seeing now right inside my head even if it's so cold in the portals of the bank you'd cut your side open just to get your hands on the warmth inside. Not all of the people at the place wanted to watch things you'd get on actual television I didn't think but he said, the doctor said, that we keep these ideas inside us at our peril. So that is how I got some of the ideas someone had put outside of themselves inside me and it is why I wail from time to time in the doorway of the bank, not able to sleep the idea out of my head or wash it out no matter how much soap I use in and out.

They were logical things and all very practical and written in the slow helpful way a recipe is made out: Take a woman and bend her double till you see right up through her so you're looking out of her mouth at the stars and then you take the one and then the other and fold her up small and put her in the pan and boil her up three times bearing in mind that the cheeks and forearms yield up the best and finest fats. To keep the next one young-skinned use this rich substance made from the previous one's smoother parts.

Leaving the place was sad enough though because of the doctor and the way he listened to the flowers too when I had explained, coming close on the pillow to hear when the embroidered buds chattered among themselves on the hem of the linen sent from home to this place where they provided me with a bare room that was the least talkative as to the walls I've slept in ever. I have more faculties than those who do not hear the flowers speak and the leaves spread their rumours, but others can't take the news I have for them – that we should ward off decay by sitting motionless and keeping clean and remaining in the proximity of money.

The last luxury, my blanket. And the other that is an essential, the soap. I eat it without water, in the slice, but for washing I do use some water from the Ladies round the way. I never wash with the eating brand, or vice versa.

From the bank in the morning come noises like the sounds in a deserted zoo. The sleeping money is unbarred, its movements and territory marked for the day. It breathes and its breath is not warm, though that of its suitors may be.

After that time at the place with the doctor the old body got lost and the new body grew big at home and unloosed its little prisoner. I felt the blanket cover him and me and the new one and wished the world away. The walls and windows no longer commented. In my absence they had been frozen white and iced cream. Only in the room of the new one were there flowers, metal, in a bunch, and they blared pleasure out of all their bulbs of light over the bed where new small blankets covered the third one of us.

Not knowing where we began and ended was what I called

love but they went off into their own bodies more than I could allow so I bound us together while they slept and he sat up and that was how their selves got caught and fell and the rope pulled tight although it was not thick, indeed thin being made of the strings that feed electricity to light bulbs and help them keep up their shouting till you turn them off by rocking their tonsils or flicking their tongues.

So the smaller one was pulled up by him as he sat up. The smaller one hung there from the vein that fed the light and twisted round and round at the neck till the light was very uncomfortable, it was pulled so tight by the heavy baby hanging there.

All the strength from the poor lights failed. The little one rocked there for a moment between us and we were all held close in the dark and I knew love bound us in this house where the flowers had stopped their talking.

The little one made a noise himself and then swung and the man started making a loud noise which I did not like since it interrupted the love. Even more so when he was pushing the little one hard all around the heart and eating its face. And I tried to take the little one away and make sure it stayed clean, with no dribble on it. But there was an ugly thing at the neck of the little one, so I said, 'I must go and get some soap to wash away the mark around its neck.'

Then he said much that another person might have regretted. He took the little one and folded it in the blanket that was off the bed where the three of us had been. He laid the little one down and begged it to move.

After I saw it stir, I told him, and he was jealous I had seen it first, I suppose, because he screamed at me and pushed me over and held me down and made me a nice necklace with his hands and I knew what he wanted and set about helping him and he screamed again and threw me like a bale of bitter weeds across the room. All along I was reading what was happening but could not translate it. It was certain that the little one had done something very wrong, or it would not have been so sad and still.

When it moved, and he saw it too, he fell on his knees and

called out to God. How I loved him then. He was forgiving our naughty little one, as a father should. The blanket began to fold and wrinkle as the small legs moved inside it. I saw that the blanket held everything we had.

Later in the next room that they found me for sitting in on my own with visits and gossiping trees outside all the windows, he brought me a blanket. I do not know if it is the same one that held the baby, but it is certainly similar. I fold it at night around the soaps and over my head and I lie in the portals of the bank. The soap hardly stirs or breathes but how it glows.

I am only a little disturbed by the tedious statements of the traffic lights as they mark the passing cars. The blanket and the soap never trouble me by talking. I see flowers carried sometimes by those who come to visit their money, but the flowers don't speak to me now that I have faded to a state where I am no longer their rival.

Selima Hill
Travels With My Tongue

The Member of My Own Family

I know I ought to love you
but it's hopeless.
Screaming is the best I can do.
I scream at you for such a long time
that even when I stop the scream goes on.
It screams between us like a frozen street
with stiff exhausted birds embedded in it.

The Addict

Although your girlfriends
have somehow got used to me
lying beside you stubbornly all the time –
skilfully topped up with sleeping pills
and turned with my face to the wall –
it isn't long before I'm back in hospital,
and you are walking home to sunny Ireland.
No amount of rain will put you off.
Your yellow hair, streaming down your back,
shivers in the wet
like well-brushed fish.

The Violinist

Pursued by men with razor blades for hands,
you stumble, blinded, out into the yard
and fall into a fluffy bed of rabbits
who've spent the day as usual doing nothing
but lying in soft heaps in the sun.

BLAKE MORRISON
The Woman on the Doorstep

A woman stands on the doorstep: tense, greying, fiftyish, tight lips, green coat. She understands I work for the *Independent* (the Sunday, used to, but never mind), looked me up this morning in the telephone book (I've been meaning to go ex-directory) and has come straight round. She has an article she wants to give me, for publication. What's it about? I ask. She doesn't want to go into detail, not out on the step, but she can assure me the article's good – more than good, sensational. I explain I'm not at the paper any more, have only ever worked on books pages, am probably the last person capable of judging what's sensational or not. No matter, she says, that's fine: if I could just read it, I'll see.

Nervous and resentful, conscious of some line being crossed, I ask the woman in. We stand just inside the hall, the door still ajar, and she hands me a plain brown envelope. Lines burned in her brow below the cropped grey hair, she watches as I take the article out. It's long: fifty closely typed pages or more. I say I'll need some time to get through it, that I can't read it now, in front of her. All right, she says, as long as I promise not to show it to anyone else, I can keep it overnight. Will I promise? Sure, I promise. Till tomorrow, then. There's her number and address at the bottom of the last page, if I finish it earlier and want to call. I hold the door open for her. She nods and walks briskly off, businesslike, turning right up the road, not a sign of author's nerves.

I've work to do. But I can't resist skimming through the piece. It's a long essay demonstrating that Iris Murdoch is a Soviet agent. The evidence for this is internal, based chiefly on a reading of the names of Murdoch's characters, which are, it seems, in code. The first clues can be found in *Under the Net*, and are planted in each subsequent novel, culminating in *The Sea, The Sea*. There are long quotes, and tortuous explanations of how the philosophy and necromancy in Murdoch's novels are actually elaborate instructions to Moscow paymasters. The author of the article seems to have read widely in espionage, Soviet history, and the occult. She writes with indignation not so much against Iris Murdoch as the British literary establishment, which is either stupid or, worse, in collusion with Moscow. She very badly wants something done about the scandal. As I read her closing peroration – 'a tissue of lies, conspiracy, and cover-up' – I try to think of her face, and to remember small giveaway details, like staring eyes or foam-flecked lips. I remember only grey hair and a small, tense mouth.

I go downstairs, to the basement, where the message light is blinking on the answering machine and sheaves have stacked up on the fax. I try to work, but all I can think of is the article in the envelope on the dining table and the woman standing on the step. The piece is mad. But is she? It's not the first time I've been handed a piece of writing that borders on the insane. I ran an evening class once: poetry for beginners. Most of the poetry brought for discussion had begun as therapy; most of it ended as therapy, too, not making it as art, or even sense. I was sniffy: I thought poetry should be shaped, structured, transcendent, should aspire to the impersonal. I banned all biographical preambles: the poems had to work as poems, I said, had to be read cold on the page, without us being told when, why, how, during which life crisis and on what medication they had come. In time, I became less sniffy. There was a man who read a poem with unusual passion. We sat round and discussed in neutral tones why his I-I-I cry of pain failed as rhetoric: how a change of adjective here, a less abstract image there, might have improved it. He fell silent and didn't seem to be paying much attention. I asked him, when we'd done dissecting, if he had anything to add. He said he'd written the poem on the brink of committing suicide: he had the razor out, and the bath running, but sat down and wrote the poem instead. No answer to that. Literary criticism seemed beside the point. Had the world ever known a more important poem? I looked back at my own slim output and saw that I too had written poems as therapy: private lyrics not intended for magazines or composed in the hope of getting on. Some people need to set words down to make life tolerable. There are a lot of us about.

Maybe the woman on the doorstep is like this. Maybe writing about Iris Murdoch has kept her sane, even if the article itself is mad. Maybe she needs me only in order to acknowledge or vindicate her, and reading her article, not publishing it, will be enough. Maybe it *is* publishable, and I've missed the point. I go back upstairs and sit down with it in the dining room, under the high candle-bulbs. It's clean and neatly typed – few typos or misspellings, and no dog-eared page corners to suggest it has done the rounds. It doesn't look mad. But it doesn't read any less madly. I flick on through Iris Murdoch's career as a spy in the hope of finding something I can be kind about. I check the tone of the last pages, in case there's something unexpected there, a *volte face* of some kind – sudden lightness – as the author admits the exercise has been a spoof, a satire on a school of literary criticism. Not a chink, not a glimmer. I haven't read all of them, it's true, but the woman seems to mean every word.

Should I have seen she was mad and just told her to fuck off? She could have written, rather than come to my house. I'm not obliged to help. But to refuse even to look at her article would have been churlish, rude, more unpleasant than she deserved. I look at her address, on the last page. It's local, a quiet residential street, not an institution. I look again: the woman's name isn't there, and this unnerves me. She's a stranger, perhaps unstable enough to do something dangerous. I've let her into my house, but don't even know her name. She made me promise not to show the piece to anyone else. Not show it to anyone else, even though she wants it published: what can that mean? How many layers of paranoia are here? Will she be telling me, next, that people are following her? At that poetry group there had been a man so fearful of showing his work that it was nearly the end of term before he found the nerve. Pale and shaking, he passed round carbon copies, counting them out as he did. The poem was as trite as a greetings card: an ode to spring, in nineteenth-century diction, which he read in a quaking voice. His hands quaked too, gripping the long table as he spoke of trilling redbreasts and Phoebus peeping twixt the boughs. Even down my end, the far end, remote from him, the table shook. We were kind to him, encouraging, feeling his nerves through the wood. I didn't lie that the poem was brilliant, nor resist suggesting he try to write more as he might speak. But I was conscious of his vulnerability, and held back criticisms I might have made to someone else. At the end, he demanded his poems back, and counted up twelve copies in case one had been stolen. The images he'd used were original, he said, he'd not had them patented yet, he didn't want people copying them and ruining his chances of publication. Afterwards, a couple of other students complained to me. It wasn't the man's vanity that offended them, but the affront to the gentle, cooperative spirit of the workshop. I worried how to explain to him he shouldn't be so distrustful of his fellow-writers. I shouldn't have. He didn't show up again.

I think of him now, stooping over his briefcase, stowing the precious copies away. Is the woman on the doorstep like him, at best deluded, at worst certifiable? But feeling protective of one's work, and worrying that others may steal from it, is natural enough in writers, even more so in freelance journalists trying to make a mark. Nor is holding conspiracy theories – even conspiracy theories about Iris Murdoch – a mark of madness. I've had conspiracy theories, too: about friends, enemies, the British government, about a world invented solely for me to be exposed as its dupe. Which of us can say we're not a bit mad in small ways? Or even in big ways? Angels have appeared to me in the small hours, though they looked like the bedroom's hanging lampshade. I've heard voices warning me, and seen foxes sitting at my typewriter. I've done crazy things, even without the excuse of drink.

Has this woman unnerved me because she's facing me with some madness of my own? As a child, I thought the madness was all out there, not within, or close to home. The other kids seemed to think the same. Bananas, barmy, bats, bonkers, crackers, crazy, cuckoo, daft, doolally, dotty, funny, gone, half-there, kooky, loco, loony, loopy, mental, nutty, potty, screwy, twisted, weird: we used the words unthinkingly; we used them about each other, with varying degrees of affection and derision. We knew there were others the words must be true of, but not who they were or how they looked. There were institutions for such people, and we had words for those, too: bin, booby hutch, bughouse, funny farm, loony bin, nuthouse. Suitable places for treatment. Or perhaps unsuitable: bugs are low on the evolutionary scale; farms and hutches are places for animals; bins are where rubbish is thrown away. Not human, then, by the sound of it, let alone humane: how, as kids, were we to know? Menston was our nearest: we'd pass it on the way to Leeds, a wall too high to see over. What lay behind it I'd no idea, and that was part of the fascination. A grinning mouth behind a grille. A solitary lightbulb dangling from a flex. Cutlery drumming on a mile-long refectory table. Straitjackets. Foaming mouths. Staring eyes. Gothic towers and turrets, like the rigging on medieval ships of fools. Though ours was a hamlet, too small to boast a village idiot, we didn't lack the imagery. The wings of the madhouse had passed over us, we'd been brushed by its shadow and were afraid. 'Menston, Menston, you'll end up in Menston' was the taunt for all silly, uncoordinated, or just spontaneous behaviour. I dreamt of being admitted, victim of a misdiagnosis, condemned never to re-emerge. School doctors and nurses frightened me: I was healthy, wasn't I, so what were they getting at, with their tests? Had I a squint? No. A stammer? Not that either. How long was my attention span? Hard to say. Was I insomniac? No. Was I a nail-biter? Yes, but not excessively so. Was I eneuretic, a bed-wetter? No. Encopretic, then, a pants-shitter? Please, do we have to go into this. Cause for concern, it seemed. They felt my scrotum and jotted surreptitious notes. My testicles ought to have descended by now. This way madness lay, and Menston.

That was the story of childhood, or my childhood, or the end of it: discovering madness wasn't a foreign country, that it might begin at home. Auntie Shirley, for instance, who'd stay with us each holiday, and take me to see the moo cows beyond the bottom of the garden, a teacher who lived alone, sweet natured and dependable, it seemed, but madder as the years passed (the first cracks showing in my teens), and ending up dead at sixty, after rumours of mayhem and disgrace. That woman on the doorstep looks a bit like Auntie Shirley. She certainly doesn't seem a stranger. I stay up late, under the candle-bulbs, not reading her article but imagining the life that brought her to the moment she wrote it from: a loner, and has been for years; went to small private girls' school (perhaps Catholic, certainly boarding) and did well at O and A level; worked for the Civil Service, as a glorified typist (the best a woman could hope for in those days); loved a man once, who betrayed her, with a so-called friend, since which she's never trusted men, and few women either; began to suffer from depression, off and on; left her full-time job for a less stressful one; left that too; more depression, various forms of treatment for it, but nothing serious, she's all right now, wants to give help rather than receive it; is into causes (anti-bloodsports, anti-EEC), writes letters (never published) to national newspapers; believes passionately what she thinks; has noticed some people are scared by her passion, and move away when they see her coming; has no time for such people; treats them with scorn.

Headlights cross the ceiling, and I lie there inventing her. A fantasy about a woman who has herself invented a fantasy. I know she's not a stranger now. But I'm too alarmed to think of her as a friend.

The doorbell goes at ten the next day. There she is, on the step, a little tenser perhaps, and shorter than I'd remembered, but otherwise as before. She walks through the hall to the dining room, where I've left the article on the table. I tell her as gently as I can that I don't think it's publishable – that it's much too long, needs cutting and reworking, even then probably wouldn't be accepted, because the evidence for its claims is too slight. I'm happy to pass it on to an editor at the *Independent*, if that's what she wants, but I'm sure he would say the same. There is a pause, and silence, and then she takes the article back from me, sharply, just short of a snatch. Unnerved by her silence, afraid I've been too harsh, I say I'm sorry I can't be more helpful, that I'd been interested by the thesis, if only the evidence for the Soviet agent theory were more solid . . . At which point she snaps, and makes a short speech, full of suppressed contempt, about how, of course, I'm in the same literary mafia as Iris Murdoch, the same lousy establishment, just as all newspapers are part of the same CIA world-conspiracy, and that's why I'm against the article, and of course it was naive to think I might be interested in the truth, no one in any position of influence is interested in the truth any more, she will have to go on fighting her battle alone, but one day she will win it, no doubt of it, and then I'll be sorry, then my time will be up, and everyone who failed to believe her will be full of shame. She doesn't shout. It's all said quickly, through tight lips, while she stands in the hall, under the brass lamp, with something important to say, quaking with anger but unshaken in her beliefs. I show her out, this woman whose name I still don't know. Closing the door, I lean with my back against it, palms and fingers spread on the wood, eyes shut, like someone in a film, the old movie-pose that says: Phew, lucky escape.

I see the woman in the street sometimes: same coat, same crop, same purposeful air, though she mumbles to herself as she walks. We look away when we pass each other, like strangers, but not before I register she's spotted me and, as she does, her look of deep contempt.

BIOGRAPHICAL NOTES

A. Alvarez is a poet, novelist, literary critic, and author of non-fiction books on topics ranging from suicide – *The Savage God, Life after Marriage* – to poker, North Sea oil, and mountaineering – *The Biggest Game in Town, Offshore, Feeding the Rat*. His most recent book is *Night: An Exploration of Night Life, Night Language, Sleep and Dreams*.

Martin Amis's novels include *The Rachel Papers, Money, London Fields, Time's Arrow* and *The Information*. He is also the author of two collections of essays, *The Moronic Inferno* and *Visiting Mrs Nabokov*. He lives in London.

Simon Armitage was born in 1963 and lives in Yorkshire. He has published five books of poetry, including *The Dead Sea Poems* (1995). His latest collection, *Moon Country*, is published in November 1996. He has written extensively for television and radio, and is also a playwright and prose writer.

Margaret Atwood is the author of more than twenty-five volumes of poetry, fiction, and non-fiction, and is perhaps best known for her novels, which include *The Edible Woman* (1970), *The Handmaid's Tale* (1983), and most recently *The Robber Bride* (1994). The poems included here appeared in her most recent volume of poetry, *Morning in the Burned House*, published by Virago in 1995.

Esther Benabu writes, teaches and lives in London.

Alan Bennett first appeared on the stage in the revue *Beyond the Fringe*. His plays include *Forty Years On, Habeas Corpus, The Old Country*, and *The Madness of George III*, and he also adapted Kenneth Grahame's *Wind in the Willows* for the National Theatre. His TV plays include *An Englishman Abroad*, the series of monologues *Talking Heads*, and *A Question of Attribution*. 'The Lady in the Van', which was shortlisted for the Mind Book of the Year/Allen Lane Award in 1990, was first published by the *London Review of Books*, and forms part of his collection of autobiographical pieces *Writing Home*.

J. Bernlef was born in 1937. He has worked as a bookseller and translator. Since 1962 he has been a freelance writer in Amsterdam. He has won many prizes for his fiction, most recently the AKO Literatuurprijs. *Out of Mind* was his first novel to be published in English, and won the Mind Book of the Year/Allen Lane Award 1988.

Rosie Boycott is a writer and journalist who co-founded *Spare Rib* and Virago in the 1970s. Her autobiography, *A Nice Girl Like Me*, from which this extract is taken, chronicled seventies life as well as alcoholism. In 1987 she published a novel, *All for Love*. Since 1992 she has been editor of *Esquire* magazine, and she also co-presents BBC Radio 4's *Start the Week*.

Melvyn Bragg is a novelist and broadcaster. Born in 1939, he was educated locally and at Oxford where he read Modern History. He joined the BBC as a general trainee in 1961 and then moved to London Weekend Television to start editing *The South Bank Show* in 1977. He is now Controller of Arts at LWT. He presents BBC Radio 4's *Start the Week* and is president of the UK National Campaign for the Arts. He is also president of Carlisle Mind. His latest novel, *Credo*, was published in 1996.

Marie Cardinal was born in Algeria in 1929. She studied philosophy in Paris and has taught at the universities of Salonika, Lisbon, and Montreal. Her first novel, *Ecoutez la mer* (1962), won the Prix International du Premier Roman. Since then she has written many other books, including *Devotion and Disorder* (1991). *The Words to Say It* (1975), was translated into English by Pat Goodheart. Marie Cardinal has three children and divides her time between France and Canada.

Wendy Cope read History at Oxford, and then taught in London primary schools for fifteen years. She entered analysis in 1972, began writing poems in 1973, and published her first book, *Making Cocoa for Kingsley Amis*, in

1986. This and her second collection of poems, *Serious Concerns* (1992), both reached the bestseller lists. She has won a Cholmondeley Award, and the American Academy of Arts and Letters Michael Braude Award, and is a Fellow of the Royal Society of Literature. She gave up teaching in 1986. She lives in Winchester.

Margaret Drabble was born in 1939 in Sheffield, and educated in York and Cambridge. She had three children with her first husband, Clive Swift, and is now married to the biographer, Michael Holroyd. She has published thirteen novels, the last of which, *The Witch of Exmoor*, appeared in October 1996. She also edited the fifth edition of the *Oxford Companion to English Literature*. She has a long-standing interest in psychotherapy and is a patron of the Child Psychotherapy Trust.

Maureen Duffy is a novelist, poet, and playwright. Her most recent publication was a biography, *Henry Purcell*. She is at present at work on a new novel.

Douglas Dunn was born in Renfrewshire in 1942. He has written seven collections of poetry, the most recent being *Dante's Drum Kit* (1993). Douglas Dunn's first wife died in 1981, a loss which inspired him to write the collection *Elegies* (1985), from which 'Arrangements' is taken. He is Professor and Head of the School of English at the University of St Andrews.

Ruth Fainlight has published ten collections of poems as well as short stories and translations; she has also written for the Royal Opera House and Channel 4 television. Born in New York City, she left the US at the age of fifteen, and now lives in London with her husband, the author Alan Sillitoe. In 1994 she received a Cholmondeley Award for Poetry and published a collection of poems, *This Time of Year*, and a volume of short stories, *Dr Clock's Last Case*. An updated, expanded edition of her *Selected Poems* appeared in 1995.

U. A. Fanthorpe was born in Kent and educated at Oxford. After teaching for sixteen years she became a middle-aged drop-out, and was lucky enough to get a job as clerk/receptionist at a neurological hospital in Bristol. She has published six collections of poetry (Peterloo Poets), and her *Selected Poems* was published as a King Penguin in 1986. She has been a writer-in-residence at various places, and is a Fellow of the Royal Society of Literature. She lives in Gloucestershire.

Vicki Feaver was born in Nottingham in 1943. She has published two collections of poetry, *Close Relatives* (1981) and *The Handless Maiden* (1994). A selection of her work is also included in volume two of the Penguin Modern Poets. She teaches at the Chichester Institute, where she leads an MA in Creative Writing.

Alison Fell is a Scottish poet and novelist who lives in London. Her novels include *Mer de Glace*, which won the Boardman/Tasker Award for mountain literature, and *The Pillow Boy of the Lady Onogoro*, which has been translated into many languages. She has published two poetry collections, many short stories, and edited and contributed to the experimental anthologies *Seven Deadly Sins*, *Seven Cardinal Virtues*, and *Serious Hysterics*.

Maureen Freely was born in Neptune, New Jersey, in 1952, grew up in Istanbul, Turkey, and has lived in Britain since the early 1980s. She has a degree from Harvard University, four children, and two stepchildren. She has published five novels (*Mother's Helper*, *The Life of the Party*, *The Stork Club*, *Under the Vulcania*, and *The Other Rebecca*), as well as two works of non-fiction (*Pandora's Clock* and *What About Us?*). She writes regularly for the *Guardian* and the *Observer*.

Esther Freud was born in London in 1963. She has written two novels, *Hideous Kinky* and *Peerless Flats*, and her third novel will be published in 1997.

Janice Galloway's first novel, *The Trick Is to Keep Breathing*, won the Mind Book of the Year/Allen Lane Award in 1990 and was shortlisted for the Whitbread First Novel and Scottish Book of the Year awards. The stage version has been performed at the Tron Theatre in Glasgow, the Du Maurier Theatre in Toronto, and the Royal Court in London. Her second novel, *Foreign Parts*, won the 1994 McVitie's Prize for Scottish Writer of the Year and the E. M. Forster Award, presented by the American Academy of Arts and Letters. Her latest collection, *where you find it*, was published in May 1996.

Tony Harrison was born in Leeds in 1937. He has published numerous collections of poems, including *The Loiners*, *A Kumquat for John Keats*, *V and Other Poems* (1989), from which 'The Mother of the Muses' is taken, and *The Gaze of the Gorgon* (1992). He is also Britain's leading theatre and film poet, writing for the National Theatre, the New York Metropolitan Opera, BBC, and Channel 4 TV.

Zoë Heller is a freelance journalist. She has written for a range of publications including the *New Yorker*, *Vanity Fair*, the *London Review of Books*, the *Independent on Sunday*, and the *Sunday Times*. She is currently living in Los Angeles, California.

Selima Hill is a well-known poet and tutor, currently teaching at the Exeter and Devon Arts Centre and working on her seventh collection, *Violet*, to be published by Bloodaxe in 1997. Awards include an Arts Council Bursary, the Cholmondeley Award, the Arvon/*Observer* First Prize, and a UEA Writing Fellowship. She lives in a small seaside town with her three children and three grandchildren.

Ted Hughes was born in 1930 in Yorkshire. He went to school in Mexborough, South Yorkshire, where his parents ran a newsagent's shop. In 1948 he won an exhibition to Cambridge University. He was married to the American poet Sylvia Plath, who died in 1963. He remarried in 1970. He was awarded the OBE in 1977 and created Poet Laureate in 1984. His many collections of poetry include *The Hawk in the Rain* (1958), *Lupercal* (1960), *Wodwo* (1967), *Gaudete* (1977), *Flowers and Insects* (1986), and *New and Selected Poems 1957–94* (1995), from which 'The God' is taken.

Michael Ignatieff is a Canadian writer, historian, and journalist based in London. Born in Toronto in 1947, he was educated at the universities of Toronto, Harvard, and Cambridge. He is the author of *A Just Measure of Pain: Penitentiaries in the Industrial Revolution* and *Wealth and Virtue: The Shaping* *of Political Economy in the Scottish Enlightenment. Asya*, his first novel, was published in 1991. *Scar Tissue* was published in 1993, and was shortlisted for the Booker Prize. It won the Mind Book of the Year/Allen Lane Award 1993. He is a regular presenter of arts and cultural programmes on British TV.

Alan Jenkins was born in 1955 in London. From 1982 to 1990 he was poetry and fiction editor of the *Times Literary Supplement*, and since 1990 he has been deputy editor. His own volumes include *In the Hot-house* (1988), *Greenheart* (1990), and *Harm*, which won the Forward Prize for Best Collection in 1994. His new collection, *Dead White Male*, is due in 1997.

Nicole Ward Jouve was born and bred in Provence and has lived her adult life in Britain. She tends to write fiction/autobiography/family history in French, and essays in English, but this neat bilingual pattern is evidently changing. She has written books on Baudelaire, Colette, criticism as autobiography (*White Woman Speaks with Forked Tongue*, 1991), a study of the Yorkshire Ripper case (*The Streetcleaner*), thoughts on her own writing and gender (*The Semi-Transparent Envelope*, with S. Roe and S. Sellers), short stories (*Shades of Grey* and *The House Where Salmon Perched*), and one novel in French (*L'Entremise*).

Judith Kazantzis has published five collections of poetry. Her *Selected Poems 1977–92* came out in 1995. Her sixth collection, *Swimming through the Grand Hotel*, will be published by Enitharmon in 1997. She lives in London and spends much time in America. She started writing poetry in 1973, partly as a result of a fruitful, if interminable, analysis.

A. L. Kennedy has published two collections of short stories and two novels, all of them winning prizes including the Somerset Maugham Award, the Encore Award, and the Saltire Award. She is listed as one of the twenty *Sunday Times/Granta* Best of Young British Novelists. Her next book, *Original Bliss*, will be published by Jonathan Cape in 1997. A. L. Kennedy also writes for the stage, film, and television. Her play, *The Audition*, won a Fringe First at the Edinburgh Festival in

1993. Her first full-length film, *Stella Does Tricks*, went into production in 1996. She was born in Dundee and lives in Glasgow.

Sir Ludovic Kennedy, writer and broadcaster, was born in Edinburgh in 1919. His recent publications include *Euthanasia: The Good Death* (1990) and *Truth to Tell* (collected writings, 1991). His autobiography, *On My Way to the Club*, from which this extract was taken, was published in 1989.

Benedicta Leigh was born in Hampshire in 1922. After working as a VAD during the Second World War, she trained at the Royal Academy of Dramatic Art, and has since performed widely in the theatre. *The Catch of Hands* won the Mind Book of the Year/Allen Lane Award 1991.

Doris Lessing's first novel, *The Grass is Singing*, was published in 1950 with outstanding international success. Mrs Lessing has been honoured with, among others, the Prix Medici, the Austrian State Prize for European Literature (1981), and the German Federal Republic Shakespeare Prize (1982). She has twice been shortlisted for the Booker Prize. Most recently, *Under My Skin*, volume one of her autobiography, won the James Tait Black Memorial Prize (1994).

Mary Loudon was born in November 1966, and read Theatre Studies at Warwick University. Her first book, *Unveiled: Nuns Talking* (1992), won a *Cosmopolitan* Achievement Award. Her second book, *Revelations: The Clergy Questioned*, was published in 1994. Mary Loudon writes weekly for *The Times*, and occasionally for the *Independent*, *Guardian*, *Sunday Times*, and the *Mail on Sunday*.

Sheila MacLeod was born in 1939 in the Isle of Lewis, Scotland. After reading English Literature at Oxford she worked for a time at the Clarendon Press. Some of her short stories appeared in Faber's 1963 collection, *Introduction 2*. Since then, she has written six novels (*The Moving Accident, The Snow White Soliloquies, Letters from the Portugese, Xanthe and the Robots, Circuit-Breaker, Axioms*) and two nonfiction books: *The Art of Starvation* which won the Mind Book of the Year/Allen Lane Award 1981 and *Lawrence's*

Men and Women. She has also written two plays for BBC television and innumerable pieces of journalism for innumerable newspapers and magazines. In 1997 she should, with any luck, have a BA in French from London University.

Sarah Maguire was born in London in 1957. She left school early and trained as a gardener before reading English at the universities of East Anglia and Cambridge. Her first collection of poems, *Spilt Milk*, was published in 1991. In 1994 she was one of the Arts Council/Poetry Society 'New Generation Poets'. Her second collection, *The Invisible Mender*, will be published by Cape in 1997.

Candia McWilliam was born in Edinburgh in 1955. She has written three novels, *A Case of Knives*, *A Little Stranger*, and *A Debatable Land*, as well as many short stories. She has three children.

Blake Morrison was born in Skipton, Yorkshire, and attended Nottingham University. He is the author of two volumes of poetry, *Dark Glasses* (1984) and *The Ballad of the Yorkshire Ripper* (1987), a children's book, *The Yellow House*, critical studies of The Movement and Seamus Heaney, and the memoir *And When Did You Last See Your Father?*, which won the *Esquire*/Waterstones Prize for non-fiction (1993). Formerly the literary editor of the *Observer* and the *Independent on Sunday*, he now lives and works as a freelance writer in London. He has been one of the judges of the Mind Book of the Year/Allen Lane Award since 1991.

Andrew Motion was born in 1952, and read English at Oxford. From 1976 to 1980 he taught English at the University of Hull, before becoming editor of *Poetry Review* and poetry editor at Chatto and Windus. He is now Professor of Creative Writing at the University of East Anglia. His most recent collections of poems are *Love in a Life* (1991), from which 'A Blow to the Head' is taken, and *The Price of Everything* (1994).

Sharon Olds was born in San Francisco, California, and attended Stanford and Columbia Universities. Her latest collection, *The Wellspring*, was published in 1996. In the US she has also published *The Father*, *The Gold Cell*, *The Dead and* *the Living*, and *Satan Says*, and in the UK *The Father* (short-listed for the T. S. Eliot Prize), *The Sign of Saturn*, and *The Matter of This World*. Ms Olds teaches at New York University, and helps run a writing workshop for the severely physically disabled at a public city hospital.

Adam Phillips was formerly Principal Child Psychotherapist at Charing Cross Hospital in London, and is the author of *Winnicott*, *On Kissing, Tickling and Being Bored*, *On Flirtation*, and *Terrors and Experts*.

Dr Roy Porter is Professor in the Social History of Medicine at the Wellcome Institute for the History of Medicine. He is currently working on a general history of medicine, on the history of Bethlem Hospital and on the Enlightenment in Britain. Recent books include *Mind Forg'd Manacles: Madness in England from the Restoration to the Regency* (1987), *A Social History of Madness* (1987), *In Sickness and in Health: The British Experience, 1650–1850* (1988), and *Patient's Progress* (1989) – these last two co-authored with Dorothy Porter – and *London: A Social History* (1994).

Tom Pow was born in 1950 in Edinburgh. His first two collections of poetry, *Rough Seas* (1987) and *The Moth Trap* (1990), both won Scottish Arts Council Book Awards. *The Moth Trap* was also shortlisted for the Saltire/*Scotsman* Book of the Year. His third collection, *Red Letter Day*, was published by Bloodaxe in 1996. He teaches at Dumfries Academy.

Michèle Roberts is half English and half French and lives in both countries. She has published seven novels, three collections of poetry, and one collection of short stories. Her novel *Daughters of the House* was shortlisted for the Booker Prize in 1992 and won the W. H. Smith Literary Award in 1993. She has also written for TV and the theatre. She is a regular presenter of BBC Radio 3's *Nightwaves*. She has been one of the judges of the Mind Book of the Year/Allen Lane Award since 1991.

Jane Rule, born in 1931, lives on Galiano Island, British Columbia, Canada, and is the author of the novels *Desert of the Heart*, *This Is Not for You*, *Against the Season*, *The*

Young in One Another's Arms, Contract with the World, Memory Board, and *After the Fire*. Her short story and essay collections include *Outlander, Inland Passage, Lesbian Images, A Hot-Eyed Moderate,* and *Theme for Diverse Instruments,* which contains 'If There Is No Gate'.

Salman Rushdie's books include *Midnight's Children* (which won the Booker and the James Tait Black Memorial Prizes), *Shame,* and *East, West,* from which 'The Harmony of the Spheres' is taken. *Satanic Verses* won the Whitbread Prize for best novel, and *Haroun and the Sea of Stones* won a Writer's Guild Award. He is Honorary Professor of Humanities at the Massachusetts Institute of Technology, and a Fellow of the Royal Society of Literature.

Lawrence Sail has published seven collections of poems, most recently *Building into Air* (1995) and *Out of Land: New and Selected Poems* (1992). He has compiled and edited a number of anthologies, including *First and Always: Poems for Great Ormond Street Children's Hospital* (1988). He was editor of *South West Review* from 1981 to 1985, and chairman of the Arvon Foundation from 1990 until 1994. In 1992 he was awarded a Hawthornden Fellowship, and an Arts Council writer's bursary in 1993. In 1994 and 1995 he was on the jury of the European Literature Prize.

Will Self has published two collections of short stories, *The Quantity Theory of Insanity* (1991) and *Grey Area* (1994), two novellas, *Cock* and *Bull* (1992), a novel, *My Idea of Fun* (1993), and collected journalism, *Junk Mail* (1995).

William Styron is the Pulitzer Prize-winning author of *The Long March, Lie Down in Darkness, Set This House on Fire, The Confessions of Nat Turner, Sophie's Choice, This Quiet Dust and Other Writings,* and *Tidewater Morning*. He lives in Roxbury, Connecticut and Martha's Vineyard.

Fay Weldon was born in England and raised in a family of women in New Zealand. She took degrees in Economics and Psychology at the University of St Andrews in Scotland and then, after a decade of odd jobs and hard times, began writing fiction. She is now well known as a novelist, screenwriter and critic; her work is translated the world over. Her novels include, most famously, *The Life and Loves of a She-Devil* (a major movie starring Meryl Streep and Roseanne Barr), *Puffball*, *The Hearts and Lives of Men*, *The Cloning of Joanna May*, *Darcy's Utopia*, *Growing Rich*, and *Life Force*. She has been one of the judges of the Mind Book of the Year/Allen Lane Award since 1981.

Elizabeth Young was born in Lagos, Nigeria, and educated in London, Paris, and York. A literary journalist who also writes fiction, she is co-author of *Shopping in Space: Essays in American 'Blank Generation' Fiction* (1992). Her next book is *Pandora's Handbag: Selected Criticism*.

Benjamin Zephaniah was born in Birmingham in 1958, and spent some of his early years in Jamaica. He came to London aged twenty-two, and his first book, *Pen Rhythm*, was published soon after. Subsequent books include *The Dread Affair*, *In a Liverpool*, *Rasta Time in Palestine*, and *City Psalms*. His latest book, *Talking Turkeys*, is a poetry book for children.

ACKNOWLEDGEMENTS

Mind and the editors would like to thank all the authors, agents, and publishers who have generously contributed their work and time to this collection. We gratefully acknowledge the following permissions:

'Back' by A. Alvarez copyright © A. Alvarez 1961 by kind permission of the author; 'Special Damage' extracted from *Other People, A Mystery Story* by Martin Amis (Picador 1982) copyright © Martin Amis 1981 by kind permission of Peters Fraser and Dunlop; 'The Stuff' and 'A Painted Bird for Thomas Szasz' by Simon Armitage from *Zoom!* copyright © Simon Armitage 1989 (Bloodaxe 1989) by kind permission of Bloodaxe Books; 'King Lear in Respite Care' and 'Two Dreams, 2' by Margaret Atwood from *Morning in the Burned House* copyright © Margaret Attwood 1995 (Virago 1995) by kind permission of Little, Brown UK; 'Randall' by Esther Benabu copyright © Esther Benabu 1996 by kind permission of the author; extract from 'The Lady in the Van' by Alan Bennett copyright © Alan Bennett 1989 from *Writing Home* (Faber 1995) by kind permission of Peters Fraser and Dunlop, and Faber and Faber Ltd; extract from *Out of Mind* by J. Bernlef copyright © J. Bernlef 1984, 1988, this translation copyright © Adrienne Dixon 1988 (Faber 1988) by kind permission of Faber and Faber Ltd; extract from *A Nice Girl Like Me* by Rosie Boycott copyright © Rosie Boycott 1984 (Chatto and Windus 1984) by kind permission of the author; 'Out of my Mind with Terror' by Melvyn Bragg copyright © Melvyn Bragg 1996 by kind permission of Richard Scott Simon Ltd; extract from *The Words to Say It* by Marie Cardinal copyright © Marie Cardinal 1975, this translation copyright © Pat Goodheart 1983 (Women's Press 1984) by kind permission of The Women's Press; 'Learning to be Myself' by Wendy Cope copyright © Wendy Cope 1986 (first appeared in *The Listener* 1986) by kind permission of the author; 'Umbrella of Darkness' by Margaret Drabble copyright © The Child Psychotherapy Trust 1996 by kind permission of the author and The Child Psychotherapy Trust; 'Nightingales' by Maureen Duffy copyright © Maureen Duffy 1996 by kind permission of the author; 'Arrangements' by Douglas Dunn from *Elegies* copyright © Douglas Dunn 1985 (Faber 1985) by kind permission of Faber and Faber Ltd; 'A Memoir of my Brother' by Ruth Fainlight copyright © Ruth Fainlight 1996 by kind permission of the author and Turret Books 1986, 'In Memoriam' and 'Storm' from *Selected Poems* copyright © Ruth Fainlight 1995 (Sinclair-Stevenson 1995) by kind permission of Reed Books Ltd; 'Walking in Darkness' by U. A. Fanthorpe copyright © U. A. Fanthorpe 1996 by kind permission of the author; 'Pills' by Vicki Feaver copyright © Vicki Feaver 1996 by kind permission of the author; 'In the Event of Plane Crash Burn These Diaries' by Alison Fell copyright © Alison Fell 1996 by kind permission of the author; 'Still Life' by Maureen Freely copyright © Maureen Freely 1996 by kind permission of the author; 'For No Reason' by Esther Freud copyright © Esther Freud 1996 by kind permission of the author; extract from *The Trick is to Keep Breathing* by Janice Galloway copyright © Janice Galloway 1989 (Minerva 1991) by kind permission of A. P. Watt; 'The Mother of the Muses' by Tony Harrison from *V and other Poems* copyright © Tony Harrison 1984, 1985, 1986, 1987, 1988, 1989 (Farrar Strauss Giroux 1990) by kind permission of Bloodaxe Books; 'The Chemistry of Happiness' by Zoë Heller and Roy Porter copyright © *Prospect* 1996 by kind permission of the authors and *Prospect* magazine; 'Travels With My Tongue' by Selima Hill copyright © Selima Hill 1996 by kind permission of the author; 'The God' by Ted Hughes from *New and Selected Poems 1957–94* copyright © Ted Hughes 1995 (Faber and Faber 1995) by kind permission of Faber and Faber Ltd; extract from *Scar Tissue* by Michael Ignatieff copyright © Michael Ignatieff 1993 (Vintage 1994) by kind permission of Sheil Land Associates; 'Chopsticks' by Alan Jenkins copyright © Alan Jenkins 1996 by kind permission of the author; 'Frou-Frou' by Nicole Ward Jouve copyright ©

Nicole Ward Jouve 1996 by kind permission of the author; 'Eye' by Judith Kazantzis copyright © Judith Kazantzis 1996 by kind permission of the author; 'Avoid the Spinning Plates' by A. L. Kennedy copyright © A. L. Kennedy 1996 by kind permission of the author; extract from *On My Way To The Club* by Ludovic Kennedy 1988 (Harper Collins 1989) by kind permission of Harper Collins *Publishers* Ltd; extract from *The Catch of Hands* by Benedicta Leigh copyright © Benedicta Leigh 1991 (Virago 1991) by kind permission of Little, Brown UK; 'Dialogue' by Doris Lessing from *The Temptation of Jack Orkney* copyright © Doris Lessing 1963 by kind permission of Jonathan Clowes Ltd; 'Blocking the Writer' by Mary Loudon copyright © Mary Loudon 1996 by kind permission of the author; extract from *The Art of Starvation* by Sheila Macleod copyright © Sheila Macleod 1981 (Virago 1981) by kind permission of the author; 'The Hearing Cure' by Sarah Maguire copyright © Sarah Maguire 1996 by kind permission of the author; ' You Can't Be Too Clean' by Candia McWilliam copyright © Candia McWilliam 1996 by kind permission of the author; 'The Woman on the Doorstep' by Blake Morrison copyright © Blake Morrison 1996 by kind permission of the author; 'A Blow to the Head' by Andrew Motion from *Love in a Life* copyright © Andrew Motion 1991 (Faber 1991) by kind permission of Faber and Faber Ltd; '19' by Sharon Olds copyright © Sharon Olds 1984 (*TriQuarterly* magazine 1984) by kind permission of the author; 'The Disorder of Uses: a Case History of Clutter' by Adam Phillips copyright © Adam Phillips 1996 by kind permission of the author; 'Black Daffodils' by Tom Pow copyright © Tom Pow 1996 by kind permission of the author; 'God's House' by Michèle Roberts from *During Mother's Absence* copyright © Michèle Roberts 1993 (Virago 1993) by kind permission of Little, Brown UK; 'If There is No Gate' by Jane Rule from *Theme for Diverse Instruments* copyright © Jane Rule 1975 (Talon Books 1975) by kind permission of the author and Georges Borchardt Inc.; 'The Harmony of the Spheres' by Salman Rushdie from *East, West* copyright © Salman Rushdie 1994 (Vintage 1995) by kind permission of Aitken, Stone and Wylie Ltd; 'Asterisks' by Lawrence Sail copyright © Lawrence Sail 1996 by kind permission of the author; 'Dave Too' by Will Self copyright © Will Self 1996 by kind permission of the author; extract from *Darkness Visible* by William Styron 1990 copyright © William Styron 1990 (Cape 1991) by kind permission of Random House UK Ltd; 'A Gentle Tonic Effect' by Fay Weldon from *Moon Over Minneapolis* copyright © 1991 (Harper Collins 1991) by kind permission of Sheil Land Associates Ltd; 'Mother Can Take It' by Elizabeth Young copyright © Elizabeth Young 1996 by kind permission of Serpent's Tail; 'Family Values' by Benjamin Zephaniah copyright © Benjamin Zephaniah 1996 by kind permission of the author.